SS REF
CNVY
GAR

HOME INFORMATION PACKS

FOR REFERENCE ONLY

WITHDRAWN

Related titles by Law Society Publishing:

Conveyancing Handbook (13th edition)
Frances Silverman
1 85328 558 7

Conveyancing Checklists
Frances Silverman and Russell Hewitson
1 85328 983 3

Leasehold Enfranchisement and the Right to Manage: A Practical Guide
Christopher Sykes
1 85328 999 X

Commonhold: Law and Practice
Gary Cowen, James Driscoll, Laurence Target
1 85328 867 5

Understanding Stamp Duty Land Tax (8th edition)
Reg Nock
1 85328 982 5

Understanding VAT on Property (2nd edition)
David Jordan
1 85328 994 9

Renewal of Business Tenancies: A Practical Guide
Michael Haley
1 85328 993 0

Planning and Compulsory Purchase Act 2004: A Guide to the New Law
Stephen Tromans, Martin Edwards, Richard Harwood, Justine Thornton
1 85328 925 6

Profitable Conveyancing: A Practical Guide for Residential Conveyancers
Stephanie Dale
1 85328 862 4

A Guide to the National Conveyancing Protocol (5th edition)
The Law Society
1 85328 997 3

Licensing for Conveyancers: A Practical Guide
Tim Hayden and Jane Hanney
1 85328 966 3

Environmental Law Handbook (6th edition)
Trevor Hellawell
1 85328 978 7

Titles from Law Society Publishing can be ordered from all good legal bookshops or direct from our distributors. For further information or a catalogue, e-mail our editorial and marketing office at **publishing@lawsociety.org.uk**.

HOME INFORMATION PACKS

A Guide to the New Law

Michael Garson

The Law Society

ISBN 10: 1–85328–989–2

ISBN 13: 978–1–85328–989–7

Published in 2006 by the Law Society
113 Chancery Lane, London WC2A 1PL

Typeset by J&L Composition, Filey, North Yorkshire
Printed by MPG Books Ltd, Bodmin, Cornwall

CONTENTS

FOREWORD

The road towards the implementation of Home Information Packs has been a long and, at times, a tortuous one for the government. It all started shortly after the General Election of 1997 when the government announced proposals for the Sellers Pack. Those proposals contained in the Homes Bill perished at the time of the next General Election in 2001 but the government was undeterred and reintroduced them under the new name of the Home Information Pack (HIP). The Law Society has been heavily involved in the consultations and numerous working parties that have taken place over the years through the Conveyancing and Land Law Committee and Home Information Pack Working Group and in the last 15 months through the Home Information Pack Task Force. This is a controversial piece of legislation and its supporters and opponents have been equally vociferous in putting forward their conflicting views.

I have known the author of this most, if not uniquely, authoritative guide for some years. Michael Garson has, like me, been heavily involved in all the consultations and I know his contributions to the process have been invaluable. The relevant part of the Housing Act 2004 is short, but the Regulations, recently passed by parliament, are far from short and are very detailed. Michael takes the reader through this detail in his inimitable fashion by giving clarity to the often impenetrable.

The author is also uniquely placed to give consideration to the practical effects on the housing market of HIPs. He is a solicitor of more than 30 years standing with great experience of residential conveyancing but it goes further than that. Michael has run a very successful solicitors' property centre for more than 20 years and, to show even further multi-talent he is in training to become a Home Inspector.

I have great pleasure in recommending this guide to all who may wish to delve into it and inform themselves of the new world of HIPs. I am sure it will become the most invaluable source on this subject particularly for solicitors, estate agents and, of course, those Home Inspectors too!

DENIS CAMERON
Member of the Law Society Council and of the
Home Information Pack Task Force
1 October 2006

PREFACE

The rationale for reform is that the housing market has grown and averages around 1.2 million transactions a year. Although there are downturns in price and volumes (2004 reduction to around 1 million sales) and home buyers and sellers enjoy low transaction costs compared to other European neighbours, complaints have mounted for a generation that the system is slow. The former minister Keith Hill expressed it in these terms:

> The present home buying and selling process is deeply flawed: it is painfully slow by international standards, it is inefficient and wasteful, there is a high rate of failed transactions, it does not operate in the best interests of consumers, it causes buyers and sellers considerable frustration and stress, and there is wasted expenditure.
> Keith Hill (HC Standing Committee, February 2004)

The government embarked on reform in 1997 and the rest is history. This book is a guide to where the law stands now, but the law never stands still and in this instance it is moving apace. Readers should be aware of the need to check and challenge whether arrangements set out in the book have moved on.

Websites can change their addresses and those included are believed to be correct at the time of writing. Governments have been known to alter their stance – and the progress of HIPs can be said to be 'fluid'. This book relates the position which appertained at 31 July 2006 (unless otherwise stated) but with the cautionary observation that changes will undoubtedly continue to flow and impact the direction of future market changes. Hence the author's views are sensitive to their present day context.

As the policy at the heart of this book has passed through the legislative process the ministry with responsibility has metamorphosed from the Department of the Environment, Transport and the Regions (DETR) through the Office of the Deputy Prime Minister (ODPM) to the current Department for Communities and Local Government (DCLG) so there may be instances where nomenclature ignores historic accuracy.

I ask readers of this book to indulge my use of the masculine gender to include the feminine. This is simply to reduce the word count and similar considerations apply with the use of the term solicitor to include licensed conveyancers and legal executives and singular to include plural.

I express appreciation and thanks to my partners, family, friends and fellow colleagues on the Law Society Council and Property Section who have stayed the tortuous course and helped me along the way with encouragement and feedback. I must, however, take full credit for any mistakes – they are all my own.

MICHAEL GARSON
July 2006

ABOUT THE AUTHOR

Michael Garson has practiced as a solicitor since 1973 in a City and high street general practice carrying on residential and commercial property work of different types for a range of private and business clients. In 1986 he formed a solicitors' estate agency, which then operated a 'one-stop shop' offering conveyancing along with financial services and estate agency services.

Michael Garson is a council member of the Law Society and a member of the National Association of Estate Agents. He is a member of the Society for Trust and Estate Practitioners (STEP) and was a member of the Council of the Law Society with the seat for Residential Conveyancing (2001–2005). He now represents the constituency of Central and South Middlesex and is currently chair of the executive committee of the Law Society Property Section.

He has pursued an active interest in regulatory processes affecting the development of new governance structures for the legal and agency professions and has published a number of articles. Michael Garson remains firmly of the view that an independent self-regulated profession accountable to the public and government offers the healthiest environment for professionals and consumers. He believes a strong set of ethical values backed by high standards of conduct and work, rigorously enforced, is rightly recognised as the hallmark of the true professional.

TABLE OF CASES

TABLE OF STATUTES

TABLE OF STATUTORY INSTRUMENTS AND EUROPEAN LEGISLATION

Statutory instruments

European legislation

ABBREVIATIONS

the Act	Housing Act 2004
the Regulations	Home Information Pack Regulations 2006, SI 2006/1503
ABBE	Awarding Body for the Built Environment
AHIPP	Association of Home Information Pack Providers
AVM	automated valuation models
b2b	business to business
b2c	business to consumer
CCAS	OFT Consumer Codes Approval Scheme
CML	Council of Mortgage Lenders
CoPSO	Council of Personal Search Organisations
CPD	continuing professional development
CSG	Central Stakeholder Group
DCLG	Department for Communities and Local Government
DER	dwelling carbon dioxide emission rate
DETR	Department of the Environment, Transport and the Regions
EAA 1979	Estate Agents Act 1979
EPC	Energy Performance Certificate
FPM	first point of marketing
HCR	Home Condition Report
HI	Home Inspector
HIP	Home Information Pack
HSV	Home Buyers Survey and Valuation
LACORS	Local Authorities Coordinators of Regulatory Services
NAEA	National Association of Estate Agents
NALHI	National Association of Licensed Home Inspectors
NCIS	National Criminal Intelligence Service
NLIS	National Land Information Service
ODPM	Office of the Deputy Prime Minister
OEA	Estate Agents Ombudsman
OFT	Office of Fair Trading
PCN	penalty charge notice

PDA	personal digital assistant
PI insurance	professional indemnity insurance
PMA 1991	Property Misdescriptions Act 1991
RdSAP	reduced data standard assessment procedure
RICS	Royal Institution of Chartered Surveyors
SEAL	Solicitors Estate Agency Limited
TER	target carbon dioxide emission rate
TSO	Trading Standards Officer
URN	Unique reference number

INTRODUCTION: THE HISTORY AND PURPOSE OF HIPS

HISTORY OF THE LEGISLATION

When the Housing Act 2004 (the Act) received Royal Assent on 18 November 2004 it was intended that Part 5 should be brought into force in January 2007. These reforms have been 10 years in the making.

The starting point was a promise in the Labour Party manifesto of 1997 to look into the evils of gazumping. The consultation by the Department of the Environment, Transport and the Regions (DETR) in 1998 – *The Key to Easier House Selling* – was followed by studies of foreign jurisdictions, the Bristol pilot and draft legislation. The Homes Bill, which contained the first attempt to introduce a seller's pack, failed as it stalled in the House of Lords when the 2001 general election was called.

In March 2003 a draft of a second Homes Bill was published for pre-legislative scrutiny. This substituted civil offences for the criminal sanctions of the earlier bill but areas of discord remained with the estate agency industry holding dear the principle of 'first day marketing'. The requirement for a pack that must precede any marketing of a property is regarded as an inhibition to the property market and a deterrent to sellers, at least in the short term.

The commencement order for Part 5 of the Act will be made under s.270(6) and is expected to be 1 June 2007. The first set of regulations to be made under the Act were laid before Parliament on 14 June 2006 in SI 2006/1503 (the Regulations) and most provisions will come into force on 1 June 2007.

On 18 July 2006 it was announced that the implementation of the pack would be phased and that the Home Condition Report (HCR) would not, at the outset, be a mandatory requirement. This decision recognised a number of difficulties that surrounded this contentious element of the Pack. It is not clear whether this will be the precursor to a number of amendments. Government policy is amended so that the inclusion of an HCR will be voluntary in the hope that, by this method, it may gain broad market acceptance. At the time of writing the direction of policy remains unclear and the full results of the December 2005 consultation on the draft regulations issued in October 2005 have not been made public.

The government promised at the final stages of debate in 2004 not to launch the reforms until after a trial period:

> We have no intention of introducing the home information pack until we are satisfied that all the pieces of the jigsaw – and it is a jigsaw – are in place. We will not, for example, introduce the home condition report until we are satisfied that adequate numbers of appropriately qualified and insured inspectors are available.
>
> Lord Rooker – *Hansard* 13 September 2004 column 972

It did not then specify how or where this trial period would be set up. The 'Dry Run', as it is known, has been the subject of continuous discussion. It emerged in spring 2006 as a set of processes for obtaining assurance on key elements of the infrastructure for operating the HIP system and for giving feedback to government. It was hoped that service providers would voluntarily undertake the provision of a full or partial pack without the HCR and without cost to the consumer. As a result of the statement made on 18 July 2006 the government was forced to reassess proposals for the Dry Run.

This was in line with the acceptance by government that, unless they were satisfied that the system could operate effectively, the start would be delayed:

> I can give an absolute assurance that we will not bring this system in until we are absolutely clear that it is going to work. We envisage various kinds of dry run to ensure it is working properly.
>
> Keith Hill – *Hansard* 8 November 2004 column 632

PURPOSE OF THE LEGISLATION

It is inevitable that, in whatever form the scheme is introduced, the residential property market will continue along a path of irreversible change. The scheme was designed to impose a set of statutory requirements upon the workings of the market and much debate focused on the choice between compulsion and enablement. The government chose to mandate requirements for the reasons explained by Keith Hill as follows:

> The amendments would replace a compulsory home information pack scheme with a voluntary one. The notion of voluntarism is seductive and there was much talk in the other place of the reforms being an unjustified restriction on people's right to buy and sell homes as they please in a market that functions perfectly well as it is. However, those of us who inhabit the real world know that that is not the case. The home buying and selling process does not function properly. Hundreds of thousands of people every year are put through the wringer because of the inadequacies of the current system. Hundreds of millions of pounds are wasted on transactions that get nowhere. That is money that ordinary hard working families can ill afford to lose.
>
> Three out of 10 sales fall through between offer acceptance and exchange of contracts and more than half of all sales experience some sort of problem during that period. It is no wonder that, whenever they are asked, people say that they are hugely dissatisfied with the current system. Nine out of 10 people said that in one

independent survey last year. That is hardly a ringing endorsement for a system that is supposed to work well.

Hansard 8 November 2004 column 631

The retreat from this position came on 18 July 2006 with the announcement that the introduction of the HCR would be market led. As a consequence methods of marketing property may evolve differently across regions and types of property.

Parallel developments also make further market adjustment inevitable. Rolling changes to Land Registry practice and procedure in what is broadly termed 'e-conveyancing' are to be piloted in autumn 2006 along with further development of cross platform technologies. With this development traditional timescales for property transactions will shorten and, in some cases, may disappear.

Following the Office of Fair Trading (OFT) investigation into local searches and enquiries (*Property Searches: A Market Study*, September 2005 (OFT 810)) and the Regulations, new and revised procedures for local searches are prescribed. Structural shifts can be expected as the market adapts to the requirements of the legislation and meets continuing consumer demands for speed and competitive pricing. Increasing political sensitivity to concerns about the environment and energy conservation as well as new methodologies for valuations by lenders all form part of the backdrop against which the HIP is to be introduced.

Assuming the HIP makes its 'debut' in the residential market in 2007, the traditional procedures for selling a home will then be changed for all property owners. This will affect numerous connected trades and services and this is not restricted to the property practitioners who provide advice in the course of valuing, marketing, surveying, giving financial assistance and those who arrange and execute transactions. It also affects trades and suppliers that benefit from the housing market activity such as builders, decorators and suppliers of white goods and furniture.

The primary aim of the legislation is to make the market relating to the sale and purchase of residential property more transparent and this, it is reasoned, will result in fewer abortive transactions and a speedier conclusion to all 'live' ones. A further driver is compliance with EU directives relating to energy efficiency and the expectation that the introduction of the HCR will lead to a general improvement, over time, in the physical condition of the nation's housing stock.

The principle of 'caveat emptor' is not expressly reversed though this may arguably have been an underlying intention. Unless the buyer can rely upon the disclosures made by the seller, the steps necessary to protect the buyer's position remain relatively unchanged. This issue has not been addressed in the context of how it affects the timetable of transactions. However, the principle could be eroded were a buyer to negotiate a warranty about seller disclosures at the contract stage. The more limited the content of the pack the less likely this is to arise leaving current practice and procedure to continue unaltered.

PURPOSE OF THIS BOOK

This book is intended to offer, as a first step along the way to what remains at this stage an unclear destination, a commentary on the legislation and, through that, an insight into changes that must affect the way in which practitioners shape their service offerings. In the period following the primary legislation there has been a good deal of confusion and worry as to how existing market operators will be affected. Hopefully, readers other than solicitors and student lawyers will, through the pages of this book, find developable ideas and new scope for collaboration between property professionals. As the government sets about informing the public of the new way by which property is to be sold and bought, so professionals may gain fresh insights into the role that their expertise can play. It is clear that professional skills will still be vital for the residential market to operate in an orderly and efficient manner.

The new regime is no longer being introduced on a 'Big Bang' basis. This will extend the period for adjustment and encourage further amendments and a programme of rolling reform. It had been expected that there would be heightened market activity in the months preceding the commencement date as sellers rushed to 'beat' the obligation to have a pack and the transitional provisions were introduced in an attempt to offset this. Market impact will be reduced by the proposal for 'phasing in' of the pack and it is questionable at this point in time what demand there will be from buyers for the production of an HCR on a voluntary basis.

Ultimately, the success and shape of the scheme will always be influenced by political decisions and events, as well as economic factors and further legislative reforms. Price and market distortions may arise depending upon local geophysical factors or the blight caused to certain properties at the margin of rate changes for SDLT.

The shortage of trained Home Inspectors and the unwillingness of the lending industry to endorse the Home Condition Report were given as reasons for the change in government thinking. However, it seems likely that the report published by Oxford Economic Forecasting for GMAC-RFC in June 2006 (*The Impact of Home Information Packs*, accessible at **www.gmacrfc.co.uk**) may have influenced the government's revised thinking. It modeled the economic impact of the introduction of HIPs (as originally proposed) were it to cause a 10 per cent or 25 per cent reduction in property sales. The adverse impact that was forecast implied too great a risk for the Treasury to ignore.

This book will take the reader through the detail underpinning the core of Part 5 of the Act 2004 including:

- the requirement that residential property for sale in England and Wales must not be marketed unless and until the person responsible for the marketing has possession of a HIP;

- that a copy of the HIP must be made available to a potential buyer who meets qualifying conditions;
- that pack documents within the HIP comply with the regulations;
- that Trading Standards Officers are to enforce the legislation;
- that sellers, estate agents and persons committing a 'qualifying act' as defined in the legislation will be subject to enforcement procedures;
- the status of an HCR and Energy Performance Certificate;
- the report required for 'new homes';
- that certain 'non-residential' property is excluded;
- that Home Inspectors are to be trained, licensed and registered to carry out physical inspection of each property to be sold;
- that the HCR will be entered on a register;
- that consumers will have redress against Home Inspectors who must be insured and belong to an accredited scheme;
- that consumers will have redress against estate agents who will be required to belong to a redress and complaints scheme;
- that consumers may have redress against the providers of search reports.

Readers are reminded that the Guidance on the DCLG website is not statutory and is subject to alteration – there is a stated intention to produce further guidance at a later date. The Explanatory Notes published with the statutory instrument are not extensive. Readers should also note that information posted to and available on the website may change without warning.

1 NEW CONCEPTS AND DEFINITIONS

Part 5 of the Housing Act 2004 (the Act) introduces a number of new concepts and redefines some expressions already in common use. These will need to be understood by anyone embarking upon the sale of a residential home and it may be only at the end of the commentary, when viewing the whole picture 'in the round', that some features explained at the outset can be fully appreciated. This chapter sets out to familiarise readers with the definitions in Part 5 and to highlight some of the questions that practitioners will need to address in everyday situations.

1.1 HOME INFORMATION PACK

The Home Information Pack (HIP) as defined in s.148(2) of the Act is 'in relation to a residential property, a collection of documents relating to the property or the terms on which it is or may become available for sale'. The pack is a dossier of documents some of which are 'required' and therefore mandatory, whilst others are optional and designated as 'authorised'. As will become evident, the documents within the HIP can be prepared or obtained in more than one way and by or through more than a single source. The regulations made under s.163 of the Act, the Home Information Pack Regulations 2006, SI 2006/1503 (the Regulations), define the documents and information that form the content of a HIP. Prescribed forms contained in the draft regulations of 31 October 2005 do not appear in the Regulations. They are, however, recommended for use in the trial period referred to as the 'Dry Run' as part of an informal consultation on their efficacy and can be found at **Appendix G**. The Dry Run is discussed in **Chapter 11**.

1.2 RESIDENTIAL PROPERTY

Residential property is a concept recognised by property professionals, but in the context of the Act applies to a defined category of land and buildings. The definition in s.148(1) of the Act was limited to apply to the domestic market for residential homes.

The Regulations have clarified the meaning of residential property to exclude certain categories of property in identified situations (see **para.1.5** and **Chapter 2**).

The HIP will only be required for 'premises in England and Wales consisting of a single dwelling-house, including any ancillary land' and a 'dwelling-house' means 'a building or part of a building occupied or intended to be occupied as a separate dwelling'. This includes a building under construction or to be built in the future. So, both houses and separate flats forming part of a building are brought within the definition, but the definition does not include mobile homes. The building must actually be occupied or be intended to be occupied as a separate dwelling. This, in principle, excludes mixed-use buildings such as a flat above a shop marketed together as one unit of property rather than separately, and this exception is further detailed in **para.2.5.4**.

'Occupied or intended to be occupied' speaks for itself – sales in both the second-hand and new homes market are within the provisions of the Act and the wording 'and includes one that is being or is to be constructed' draws in houses and flats in the course of construction, whether sold by the builder against the sample of a show home or off-plan.

The use of the phrase 'single dwelling-house' reinforces the intention that the requirement for a HIP is to give consumer protection. The buyer of a portfolio of properties, be they a row of terraced houses or a block of flats, is unlikely to be an owner/occupier and so this will be treated as a business transaction rather than a consumer sale, provided that the marketing is consistent with the business objective (see reg.27).

'Ancillary land' means 'in relation to a dwelling-house or sub-divided building, any land intended to be occupied and enjoyed together with that dwelling-house or building' (s.177). This would include the garden and garage and any other out-buildings (such as sheds and greenhouses), forming part of the parcel to be sold. The Explanatory Notes to the Act state that this refers to land being sold with a house or flat such as a garden. This suggests that a sale of just the ancillary land would not require a pack, which is consistent with the definition of residential property in s.148(1). So, the sale of a detached garage or part of a garden for development or a barn for conversion would be excluded from Part 5. They would not, after the sale, 'be intended to be occupied and enjoyed together with' the original dwelling-house or building. This interpretation has been thrown into doubt by the wording of reg.22(2) which suggests that ancillary land is any land enjoyed with a dwelling-house and therefore requires a HIP, unless it falls within one of the conditions in reg.22(3). These are described more fully in **para.2.5.1**.

1.3   SUB-DIVIDED BUILDINGS

Section 171 is intended to bring within the Act a situation where there are two units for sale together within the same building. This would include a granny flat that is sold with the main residence, even if it is tenanted. It will have the effect of including part possession houses where there is a tenant or lodger in a flat within the building. This exception overrides the provisions of s.160 requiring a sale to be with vacant possession. The exception contained in reg.27(2) for portfolio sales does not apply where additional dwelling-houses being sold are ancillary to a principal dwelling-house.

A sub-divided building is 'a building or part of a building originally constructed or adapted for use as a single dwelling which has been divided (on one or more occasions) into separate dwelling-houses' (s.171(4)). Information in relation to amenity land for a block of flats or converted building will need to be included in the pack by the seller of a flat or maisonette as it is ancillary land.

1.4   NON-RESIDENTIAL PROPERTY

Regulations 22–29 clarify the types of property falling outside the definition of residential property, the sale of which does not trigger the duties under Part 5. These are discussed in detail in **para.2.5**.

1.5   VACANT POSSESSION

Generally, the duties under the Act will apply only when a residential property is sold with vacant possession. Property will be deemed to be marketed with vacant possession unless the contrary expressly appears (s.160). This means that an investment property marketed with a sitting tenant is outside the scope of Part 5. Sales of part-possession houses or where a lodger remains in occupation from one ownership to the next are subject to Part 5 (s.171(2)). The sale of council houses under a 'right to buy' scheme was considered in parliamentary debate to be outside the scope of the Act on the basis that the property would not be subjected to marketing. It is arguably the case that such transactions are excluded simply because they are not sales with vacant possession. A similar situation can arise where sales are arranged by landlords to tenants in occupation, which is a popular type of transaction for first-time buyers in the current market conditions.

1.6   MARKETING

The wording of s.149 envisages that a property 'is or may become available for sale' and thus introduces a statutory definition of marketing. This wording will challenge estate agents and sellers who might wish to circumvent the pack legislation. Section 149 goes on to express the related concepts that trigger the obligation to have a pack and it is important to fully consider the actions that can bring about the need for the HIP.

'A residential property is put on the market when the fact that it is or may become available for sale is, with the intention of marketing the property, first made public in England and Wales by or on behalf of the seller' (s.149(2)). This limits the definition of the 'market' to 'the residential property market in England and Wales' (s.149(1)).

It should be noted that this requires both an action making public the fact of the property's availability for sale and an intention to market the property for sale. The action and intention in question may be that of the seller or an estate agent on the seller's behalf. Individuals cannot avoid the pack requirements by advertising and marketing personally rather than through an estate agent and this marks a difference from the previous 'Sellers' Pack' proposals. The territorial limitation means that advertising abroad at foreign property exhibitions would not be affected, but the in-flight magazine of an international airline would be, at least when the aircraft entered territorial airspace.

What is meant by 'first made public'? Publication within England and Wales is relatively easy to understand but s.149(4) both assists and confuses when it states 'A fact is made public when it is first advertised or otherwise communicated (in whatever form and by whatever means) to the public or a section of the public'. So, an advertisement in a newspaper or property particulars displayed in an estate agent's window is unambiguous – unless, of course, the newspaper or agent's window advertising for sale a house in England or Wales is across the Scottish border. The Minister's response to questions on this point offered the following clarification:

> A seller in Scotland who is selling to a buyer in England would not be caught. Across the border between Jedburgh and Berwick, there might not be the same requirements. However, I feel that I can live with that.
> (Keith Hill, Standing Committee E, *Hansard*, 5 February 2004, col.445)

The widespread marketing of property on the Internet from sites at home and abroad raises other issues. Publication may occur when information is located before downloading, but the intention to market would be evidenced by the uploading of an advert to the web or by any direct marketing material distributed by e-mail or physical delivery.

It was not the primary intention of the legislation that intermediaries or publishing agents would be treated as 'Responsible Persons' (see **Chapter 5**) for the purposes of the legislation. The Office of Fair Trading (OFT) issued guidance on this question on 13 December 2005, and the press release drawing attention to this (no.228/05) can be accessed on the OFT website (see **www.oft.gov.uk**).

The intention behind the words 'to the public' seems clear, but is then extended to 'a section of the public'. This was the focus of discussion in Parliament on a number of occasions when various scenarios were discussed in an attempt to clarify the concept. Thus, a privately agreed sale between two individuals talking in a pub is not considered to be marketing. It was accepted that a seller telling work colleagues that he is selling his house is probably not communicating the fact 'to the public' or even to 'a section of the public'. Similarly, placing an advert on a notice board in the staff canteen probably does not equate to making the fact of the availability for sale known to the public or a section of the public. But the position could be otherwise if the seller is employed by a multi-national company with numerous branches countrywide or internationally and the advert is placed in the in-house corporate newspaper. The existence of the intention of marketing to a wide group of people may be casting such a wide net for a buyer as to constitute advertising or communicating to a 'section of the public'. In practice this wording is likely to be tested, as privately discussed arrangements may for some time be tried out as an alternative to complying with Part 5. However, unless a sale is arranged with a buyer who has neither a dependent transaction nor a need for mortgage finance, the private sale option is not an attractive one for a seller.

1.7 PUTTING A PROPERTY ON THE MARKET OR TAKING IT OFF

Once a property is on the market the ensuing obligations only cease with regard to the property when 'it is taken off the market or sold' (s.149(3)). 'Taken off the market' is not separately defined and should therefore have its everyday meaning. However, it seems clear that taking a property off the market will have to be properly documented to ensure compliance with the legislation, and to protect against unwanted responsibility under the Act. If the owner or seller wishes to withdraw from the marketing of the property, mere verbal instructions to an estate agent will probably not be sufficient, nor indeed sensible, in the context of the legislation.

But what is meant by 'sold'? Does this mean 'under offer' or 'sold subject to contract'? It arguably means exchange of contacts, whether conditional or uncondi tional, rather than legal completion and this is supported by the definition of 'sale' in s.177 as 'a disposal or agreement to dispose'.

The time at which the marketing commences is termed the 'first point of marketing' (FPM) and is defined in reg.3, which also contains provisions that recognise two different situations in which a property might be 'taken off' the market. Regulation 3 provides a specific protection for sellers who may wish to pause marketing for up to 28 days or withdraw a property from the market after an offer has been accepted 'subject to contract' (see **para.5.2.3**). The estate agent instructed by the seller will wish to ensure that there are clear instructions on these points and, to avoid complaints, may design a procedure for setting a timetable for bids from interested parties which has similarities with the system in Scotland.

1.8 ESTATE AGENTS

Section 150 of the Act has been drafted to ensure that Part 5 is not circumvented by sellers simply avoiding the use of estate agents for marketing. The seller's own actions bring the requirements of the legislation into play. The responsibility for compliance can be passed to anyone instructed to market the property but unless that person carrying out the marketing is an estate agent, as defined, the responsibility remains with the seller. For the purposes of Part 5 'a person acts as an estate agent for the seller of a residential property if he does anything, in the course of a business in England and Wales, in pursuance of marketing instructions from the seller'.

In some respects this definition of an estate agent is similar to that under the Estate Agents Act 1979 (EAA 1979). However, EAA 1979, s.2 excludes solicitors, whereas under Part 5 a solicitor might well market a property for sale 'in the course of a business' and be bound as an estate agent 'if he does anything . . . in pursuance of marketing instructions from the seller'. Section 150(3) emphasises that it is substance and not form that counts as 'it is immaterial for the purposes of this section whether or not a person describes himself as an estate agent'.

Section 150(2) stipulates that 'a business carried on (in whole or in part) from a place in England and Wales' is subject to Part 5 which means that off-shore operations with just a 'shop window' within the jurisdiction will still have to comply. An estate agent whose entire business was based outside England and Wales would not be within the jurisdiction. So, instructing such an agent would leave the responsibilities relating to the HIP with the seller, who is responsible if the property to be sold is within the jurisdiction.

> If a property is marketed in England and Wales, the estate agent will be responsible if he is in England and Wales. If a property is marketed in England and Wales and the estate agent is located abroad, the seller is responsible and must have a pack.
> (Keith Hill, Standing Committee E, *Hansard*, 5 February 2004, col.445)

If both the seller and the estate agent of a residential property in England or Wales were non-resident the requirements of the pack would apply but enforcement might pose difficulties. In such a case the seller's solicitor might be considered to be the agent of the seller and would need to take care not to take any steps that made him an estate agent for the purposes of the Act.

The 'place' from which the selling is carried out does not need to be an office, showroom or business premises so any persons acting for an owner will need to be mindful that under the Act they could fall within the definition of 'seller' or of an 'estate agent'. In this situation, much will depend upon whether there are 'marketing instructions'.

1.9   RESPONSIBLE PERSON

Any person coming within the wide definition of an estate agent is regarded as a 'Responsible Person' (s.151). The responsibilities considered later are not intended to include entities such as newspapers or Internet service providers who provide a medium through which the marketing is carried out. It is suggested in the Explanatory Notes to the Act that the person receiving the marketing instructions will be limited to those in a direct contractual relationship with the seller for providing the marketing services and introducing potential buyers.

In short, the Responsible Person will be the estate agent instructed to market the property or, where no such estate agent is instructed, the person responsible will be the seller.

1.10   QUALIFYING ACTION

Section 159 deals with the situation that may arise where an estate agent is trying to sell a property in such a way as to avoid the usual responsibilities under the Act. A 'qualifying action' is one:

> . . . taken with the intention of marketing the property which:
>
> (a)   communicates to any person in England and Wales the fact that the property is or may become available for sale; but
> (b)   does not put the property on the market or make public the fact that the property is on the market.

One example might be the situation where an estate agent telephones a list of potential buyers to advise them of the availability of a property, whilst not actually advertising or putting the property openly on the market. Another would be that of a sub-agent who may not be the Responsible Person under the Act but advertises a property that has been put on the market by another agent. The wording is not intended to include an estate agent telling a spouse or office colleague that a property is likely to come on the market, or truthfully answering a query from a neighbour or passer-by regarding a property which he is seen measuring, photographing or valuing. Certain identified duties apply where a qualifying action is taken (para.5.7).

1.11   MARKETING INSTRUCTIONS

These are defined as 'any activities with a view to effecting the introduction to the seller of a person wishing to buy the property; or selling the property by auction or tender' (s.150(2)).

This is not intended to have the effect of making newspapers and Internet portals become Responsible Persons where they act on the instructions of an estate agent rather than on the direct instructions of a seller. Could it be otherwise where a seller acts without an agent? It appears from the Explanatory Notes on the Act that unless the media agent is giving marketing advice it is not intended that they shall be deemed to be estate agents. The OFT Intermediaries Guidance clarified the activities that will bring Internet agents within the definition.

1.12   RELEVANT INFORMATION

Section 163 gives powers for the Secretary of State to prescribe documents or information required or authorised to be included in the HIP. Initially, the contents have been defined by the Regulations. Changes may be made later to include any 'information about any matter connected with the property (or the sale of the property) that would be of interest to potential buyers'. In addition, further changes will deal with the status of the Home Condition Report (HCR) and prescribed forms.

1.13   HOME CONDITION REPORT AND ENERGY PERFORMANCE CERTIFICATE

The most radical innovation of the HIP is the HCR; for many this is at the heart of the legislation, bearing in mind that it would apply to all second-hand homes whereas, previously, only about 20 per cent of properties underwent a formal survey. Both ss.163 and 164 explain the HCR and give the Secretary of State power to include a requirement for 'relevant information' about 'the physical condition of the property (including any particular characteristics or features of the property)' and 'the energy efficiency of the property'.

The energy assessment enables the government to implement the Energy Performance of Buildings Directive (EU Directive 2002/91/EC), adopted on 16 December 2002 and which came into force on 4 January 2003 and must be implemented by January 2009. It requires Member States 'to introduce requirements for energy performance certificates and to ensure that these are made available by the owner to prospective buyers when a property is sold'.

Section 164(1) states that the Secretary of State may make regulations that require documents dealing with the physical condition and the energy efficiency of the property to be included in the HIP. These will be the HCR and Energy Performance Certificate (EPC). **Chapter 4** discusses the HCR, the EPC and the content of Sched.5 to the Regulations. The government announced on 18 July 2006 that it intends to amend the status of the HCR so that it is an authorised, not required, component of the HIP at the commencement of the scheme in June 2007.

Substantial investment is needed to prepare for the introduction of suitably qualified and accredited Home Inspectors (HIs) to carry out the HCR. Certification schemes for regulating HIs must be established with approved terms and conditions for conduct of business as well as consumer redress procedures and suitable professional indemnity insurance arrangements (regs.33–35). In 2004 it was estimated that 7,500 HIs would be needed, and the latest estimate in spring 2006 was still in the range of 5,000 to 7,400 (see **para.4.4**).

1.14 REDRESS SCHEME

Under s.172 the Secretary of State may require every estate agent (or person so acting) to belong to an 'approved redress scheme'. This was a late amendment to the legislation in 2004 to introduce a further measure of consumer protection following criticism of the industry in March 2004 highlighted in an OFT investigation (*Estate Agency Market in England and Wales* (OFT 693)). This concluded that the estate agency market works well in many respects but that there was significant consumer dissatisfaction about estate agency services and that customers found it difficult to complain and obtain redress.

The government, through the Department of Trade and Industry (DTI), responded to the report on 22 July 2004 and proposed a package of measures building on and strengthening the OFT's proposals to give enforcers the regulatory tools needed to tackle rogue agents without unnecessarily driving up costs to house sellers. The key elements of the government response were to:

–   Consult on how the OFT's proposals could be brought into effect and what more could be done to strengthen the regulation of estate agents.
–   Take a power to require estate agents to belong to any industry redress scheme approved for the purpose by the Secretary of State.
–   Work with stakeholders to develop methods to evaluate trends in consumer detriment in the estate agency market and the case for an industry qualification and national quality standards for estate agents.

(DTI fact sheet URN No.05/1716)

Further steps are still awaited and would bring greater coherence to the concept of the HIP.

The Housing Bill was amended to require estate agents to belong to industry redress schemes, but only to deal with complaints about HIPs. To obtain approval a redress scheme must meet the requirements set out in s.173 (see **Chapter 10**).

A 'relevant complaint' is one made by the seller or a potential buyer of a residential property and the complaint must relate to an action or omission in relation to a HIP that is (or will be) required for that property. This will include the giving of advice as to whether such a pack is required (s.172(6)). No order has yet been made under s.172(1) to bring this provision into force, whilst wider scope reform remains under consideration at the DTI. At the time of writing it seems likely that further legislation may be announced in the Queen's Speech 2006.

1.15 DEFINITIONS IN SECTION 177

1.15.1 'Sale' and 'seller'

A 'sale' covers a disposal, or agreement to dispose, by way of sale, of a freehold or long leasehold interest and any option to acquire a freehold interest or a long leasehold interest. The definition of a long lease is a grant for more than 21 years.

It excludes a mortgage term and also the disposal of an interest less than the whole. Thus, the sale of an equitable interest in part or of part of an interest in a freehold or long leasehold reversion would be excluded along with the sale of a share in the equity under a home reversion scheme. Regulation 2(1) defines a 'property interest'. It remains to be seen whether corporate structures could be used as a means of avoidance.

A 'seller' is a person contemplating the sale of a property interest in a residential property. The definition of a 'seller' will not necessarily coincide with ownership of the property and so the obligations in the Act affect those who assume responsibility for the sale on behalf of the ultimate beneficial owners. Sales by mortgagees, receivers or administrators are covered as well as those by executors and trustees.

1.15.2   'Buyer'

A 'potential buyer' is 'a person who claims that he is or may become interested in buying a residential property'. This is an extremely wide category. However, it could be narrowed down by the exercise by estate agents of the discretion granted to them under s.156(4) (see **para.5.5.1**). Unless specifically so instructed by a seller client, it would not have been normal practice in the past for an estate agent to limit the group of applicants to whom details would be offered, and this is just one of a number of areas of practice where changes will occur.

1.15.3   Additional definitons

The Regulations contain additional definitions, but as these relate to specific regulations rather than the primary legislation generally they are discussed in later chapters as and where relevant.

Key points

■ Consider definitions which differ from everyday usage or other legislation.
■ Consider changes to standard agreements, manuals and procedures to accommodate new definitions.
■ Estate agents should:
  – apply to join redress scheme (consider voluntary scheme and code of practice);
  – prepare training requirements for staff;
  – create procedures to define commencement of 'marketing';
  – consider procedures for recording seller instructions and for termination of appointment as estate agent;
  – create procedures for taking property off the market.

2 TRANSITIONAL PERIOD, EXCLUDED PROPERTY AND NEW HOMES

2.1 TRANSITIONAL PROVISIONS (REGULATION 30)

The five-month period from 1 June 2007 to 31 October 2007 has been designated as a transitional period. Prior to the change of policy announced on 18 July 2006 there had been increasing speculation that the market would be flooded with property prior to June 2007 (avoiding the requirement for a HIP) but that supply would dry up after the commencement date. Transition arrangements were added to the draft regulations to meet this situation.

If a property is already on the market and is being actively marketed on 1 June 2007, a HIP is not required for the property and neither the seller nor the seller's estate agent is a Responsible Person for the purposes of Part 5. Further, if, during the transitional period, such a property is taken off the market as a result of an offer being accepted and that offer is withdrawn or the sale does not proceed for any reason, it will still be protected by the transitional provisions provided that the property goes back on the market within 28 days of the sale falling through.

If the property is still on the market at 31 October 2007, a HIP will be needed and the duties of Part 5 come into force. Since the HIP may take 5–15 days or longer to prepare, the progress of any imminent sale will need to be closely monitored as the end date approaches.

Whilst this transitional period may be an attempt to mitigate the impact of the new regime on the market, such a short period for the transitional arrangements may cause problems for sellers and their estate agents unless the property is competitively priced to achieve a sale.

During the transitional period some buyers may be attracted to a property that comes with a HIP. Other buyers may not be fully aware or understand why some properties do and some do not have a HIP. By late autumn 2007 buyers may be reluctant in any event to offer on a property that has been on the market since before 1 June 2007, especially if a sale has fallen through in the meantime.

It seems likely that Trading Standards Officers (TSOs) would adopt a relaxed approach during this period and simply monitor the market. (See **Chapter 8** for a discussion of the role of TSOs in ensuring compliance.)

2.2   MINISTERIAL POWERS

The overriding powers in ss.161 and 162 enable the Secretary of State to extend exceptions and exclusions. Section 161 states:

> The Secretary of State may by regulations provide for other exceptions from any duty under sections 155 to 159 in such cases and circumstances, and to such extent, as may be specified in the regulations.

There was consultation on the draft Housing Bill in 2003 as to whether properties in low value areas would be exempted from the duty to have a HIP when marketed, but no provision was made for this. It was considered that special designation given to properties in certain wards would cause more problems than it solved. It was widely believed that to mark out these properties in a special way would limit their potential to increase in value and also possibly adversely affect their saleability. The cost of a HIP may, however, be of acute relevance in such cases.

Section 162 has reserved power to the Secretary of State to bring the entire scheme or any part of the scheme to an end either permanently or for a temporary period of time:

(1) The Secretary of State may make an order suspending (or later reviving) the operation of any duty imposed by sections 155 to 159.

(2) An order under this section may provide for the suspension of a duty to take effect only for a period specified in the order.

(3) A duty which is (or is to any extent) revived after being suspended under this section is liable to be suspended again.

It is anticipated that these powers would only be used by the Secretary of State in exceptional circumstances. These provisions were introduced as a safeguard in case the scheme was not considered to be ready on time. An early example occurred on 18 July 2006, before the Regulations were in fact made, when the housing minister announced that the Dry Run and introduction of the HCR would be deferred, although implementation of the EPC would proceed as planned. It is anticipated that this change will be handled through amendment to the Regulations rather than ministerial order. If other parts of the scheme or all of it were to prove unpopular or unworkable the ministerial powers could be exercised at short notice. Whilst this allows for flexibility and speed of response, it may at the initial stages also add to uncertainty in a market that already lacks confidence.

2.3   EXCLUDED PROPERTY

The Regulations refine the definition of non-residential property and exclude certain types of residential property provided that the property is marketed in a way that meets the specified criteria.

The Act states that the only property affected by Part 5 is residential property situate in England and Wales when sold with vacant possession. By definition that excludes properties that are not in England or Wales, non-residential properties and properties that are and remain occupied from the commencement of marketing to completion of the sale (subject to the specific exception in s.171 (see **para.1.3**)).

The exemption for properties not in England and Wales is straightforward as, save for with Scotland, there are no land boundaries and there can be no mistake as to whether a property can be excluded because of its physical location.

2.4   VACANT POSSESSION

The duties under ss.155–159 do not apply 'in relation to a residential property at any time when it is not available for sale with vacant possession' (s.160(1)). Vacant possession is not defined by Part 5 and accordingly bears its usual meaning. The test is firstly whether the buyer will acquire possession free from any form of occupation or from any claim to a right to possession by the seller or by a third party and secondly whether what is left behind prevents or interferes with enjoyment of a substantial part of the property. Chattels and rubbish that may interfere with enjoyment of the property must therefore be removed. In *Cumberland Consolidated Holdings Ltd* v. *Ireland* [1946] 2 KB 264 it was held that a vendor who had left a considerable quantity of rubbish in the cellars of the premises sold had failed to give vacant possession. This decision was approved and followed in *Norwich Union Life Insurance Society* v. *Preston* [1957] 1 WLR 813 where it was held that failure to remove a substantial amount of furniture from the premises prevented the giving of vacant possession.

Thus, the sale of a freehold (or leasehold) property part vacant or subject to a tenancy, such as the freehold reversion of a leasehold flat or of a house occupied by tenants on tenancy agreements or even a lodger, will not require a HIP (subject to the exception in s.171). However, under s.160(2) a residential property is presumed to be available with vacant possession unless the contrary appears from the manner in which the property is being marketed. Therefore, to overcome the requirement to have a HIP, a tenanted property must be marketed with full detailed information of the tenancy, making clear that it is not a sale with vacant possession. A residential property investment sold as a 'buy to let' transaction with a sitting tenant is outside the scope of Part 5 (see also **para.1.6**).

2.5   NON-RESIDENTIAL PROPERTIES

This exemption should be straightforward as the Act only seeks to impose duties where the property being sold is residential. However, at the committee stage of the Bill in the House of Commons there was debate about a more limited definition that would have excluded properties that were not intended for immediate occupation or were unsuitable for occupation, being designated for redevelopment or refurbishment (Standing Committee E, *Hansard* 5 February 2004, col.401).

In such cases, it was argued that the buyer would be a commercial enterprise and not in need of consumer protection. A sophisticated buyer might decide to carry out certain searches but would not necessarily need an HCR. In that situation the requirements of the Act could only add unnecessarily to costs. The amendments then proposed were, at that time, rejected but regs.22, 28 and 29 now provide for properties defined in those regulations respectively as 'non-residential', 'unsafe' or 'suitable for demolition' to be excepted from the duties under Part 5, subject to safeguards to discourage avoidance.

Regulations 22–29 contain detailed provisions as to those and other properties that may fall outside the scope of the legislation.

2.5.1   Regulation 22 – non-residential

Premises are not residential where the current or most recent use was non-residential. This includes a dwelling-house that is being converted for primarily non-residential use at completion of the sale provided that all relevant planning permissions and consents have been obtained. The position must be made clear by the marketing and all advertising must be consistent with this intention.

Regulation 22(2) seeks to clarify whether ancillary land must be treated as part of a residential property. It can be classified as non-residential by reference to the conditions in reg.22(3). These are that the land covers an area in excess of 5 hectares (12.4 acres) and that its most recent use is or was primarily for horti-culture or cultivation, breeding or keeping of animals or livestock or as grazing land or woodland. Thus, even if the land is regarded as ancillary to a residential property, such as a farmhouse, it may be treated as outside the scope of Part 5 if it meets the above conditions.

2.5.2   Regulation 23 – specified non-residential premises (anti-avoidance provision)

This provision seeks to avoid misunderstandings by making it clear that a property will not be excluded if it is to be converted to a dwelling by the time the sale completes or if it is a dwelling-house or a property ancillary to a dwelling-house and used for home working or for letting. Therefore, a building on land adjoining a dwelling-house that may be separate but is let as a studio or which is used by the property owner as a home office will not be excepted from the duties relating to the pack if and when the dwelling-house is marketed for sale.

2.5.3   Regulation 24 – seasonal and holiday accommodation

If a property is subject to a planning condition that either inhibits occupation for more than 11 months in any 12-month period or restricts the use of the property to holiday accommodation then it is excepted from Part 5. The marketing of such a property must make clear that the planning restriction exists.

This excludes from Part 5 developments of cabin or lodge style homes that have been allowed in areas of natural beauty or interest on condition that they are not permanently occupied.

2.5.4   Regulation 25 – mixed sales

This Regulation provides exemption for property which is sold with or forms part of non-residential premises such as a shop with a flat/maisonette on the floor or floors above it.

To fall within the exemption, the residential property must be ancillary to the non-residential property and, at what would have been the FPM if a HIP was required, the seller must have no intention to sell the residential property separately from the non-residential property. The marketing of the properties must make this intention clear.

It is not clear what degree of risk there might be of enforcement if the seller sells the residential property separately. Trading Standards Officers can call for a HIP relating to a property for six months after its sale has completed. It is conceivable that a TSO, alerted by a complaint that the residential part of a mixed property sale had completed whilst the non-residential part remained on the market, may ask for a copy of the HIP for the residential property. If one does not exist, then the burden of proof would rest with the Responsible Person to show that the marketing of the property complied with this regulation and that the moment when the seller changed his intention came suitably late in the day.

2.5.5   Regulation 26 – dual use of a dwelling-house

If a property has dual use as both a dwelling and as non-residential (business) property then Part 5 duties do not apply, provided that this is the most recent use of the property and the marketing makes it clear that the property can be used either for a non-residential use or for dual use. Thus, if it is marketed as having potential as a residential property alone, a HIP will be needed. Care must be taken in the marketing of properties that seek exemption as even a verbal expression of possible residential use could give rise to the need to have a HIP.

Live work units that are popular in former commercial areas of inner cities would fall within this exception.

2.5.6   Regulation 27 – portfolio sales

Commercial agents frequently transact portfolio sales both 'off market' and at auction. This regulation exempts sales of a dwelling-house with other residential property from the need for a HIP on condition that:

- the sale is of more than one residential property;
- s.171(1) does not apply to the properties;
- there is no intention on the part of the seller, at the time when a HIP would have been required but for this exemption, to sell any of the properties in a single separate sale; and
- the marketing makes it clear that the seller will not sell the properties separately.

This exception does not apply to the sale of a dwelling-house or houses that are ancillary to a main house.

As with the exemption for mixed sales the seller's intention and the marketing are critical. The risk of enforcement of a penalty after the sale or sales is a possibility. It will be vital to ensure there is an audit trail particularly as portfolio sales often take place at auctions. What is the position if, as commonly happens, the properties are marketed as a portfolio but there are no successful auction bids and a later bid is made for lots separately? This seems likely to qualify for the exemption and contrasts with the position where a lot is sold separately prior to auction after receipt of a generous high bid. It may be more difficult here for the seller to prove his true state of mind at the relevant times.

2.5.7   Regulation 28 – unsafe properties

To come within this exception the property to be sold must not be occupied; its condition must pose a risk to occupants or visitors and, again, the marketing of the property must make clear that it is unsuitable for occupation in its current condition.

Regulation 28 does not state the time at which the property must be unoccupied but this presumably means at the time a HIP would have been required had the property not fallen into this exception.

2.5.8   Regulation 29 – demolition and redevelopment

This exemption is only available if the property is marketed as suitable for demolition and the resultant site as suitable for redevelopment.

All relevant permissions and consents for the demolition must exist and, with regard to the redevelopment of the site, outline or full planning permission must exist together with listed building consent if it is required.

Outline planning permission is defined as a permission for the erection of a building with elements such as site, design, external appearance, access and landscaping remaining outstanding for agreement with the planning authority.

As with other exemptions, the regulation does not make clear when these conditions have to be met but it is assumed to be when the property is first marketed and when, but for the exemption, it would need a HIP.

2.6 NEW HOMES

Where new houses or flats are to be built or are under construction then upon completion of a sale by the builder or developer a new property interest will be granted. Chapters 3 and 4 detail the contents of a HIP for all properties including new homes.

Some specific requirements of the pack in relation to new homes are governed by the state of the property at the FPM. A property is defined as a new home by reference to reg.2(3) and whether it is 'physically complete'. This will be the case if building work is complete and it is wind and weather proof, safe and sanitary for occupation, has facilities for supply of space heating, hot and cold water and electricity and has washing and drainage facilities.

The regulation does not say that the services have to be connected or that heating has to be commissioned and working. A building might therefore be deemed physically complete at a date earlier than that when a buyer would be prepared to complete a purchase. The guidance extrapolates the definition of physically complete to mean 'basic living amenities' and it could be deemed to have the basic amenities even if the utilities are not fully connected.

Where a property is marketed for sale and it is not physically complete, then in place of an HCR the HIP must contain a report that provides the information required by Sched.7 to the Regulations. This must contain details of the date when it is expected that the property will be physically complete and a statement of the type of property to be built whether a house, flat etc. and if a house whether it will be detached, semi-detached, terraced etc. If it is to be a flat, there must be a statement of the number of floors in the building, the number of flats in the building and whether there will be a lift to the floor on which the entrance to the property will be situated.

The report must contain a statement of the approximate useable floor area in square metres and the proposed method of building. This can include trade names for materials (an exception to the prohibition of marketing within a HIP) and a description of the materials for the exterior. There must be a description of the heating and hot water systems and a statement as to the finishes for gardens and landscaping.

There must be a statement as to whether a new homes warranty complying with Sched.6 to the Regulations will be offered at completion and whether the property will qualify for the warranty. If the property will not qualify for a warranty there must be a statement of the name and address of the professionally qualified person supervising the building. Any self-build project would need a suitably qualified professional to be engaged to ensure compliance with building regulations or to bring the development within the homes warranty scheme.

There must be a location plan showing boundaries, neighbouring property and roads serving the property and a layout plan giving the measurements for proposed rooms in the property attached to the report. There must also be a predicted Energy Performance Certificate (EPC) for the property.

Equipped with a Sched.7 report, units in a development can be sold off plan, but the position changes if the property becomes physically complete after the FPM and before the property has been sold. This situation brings the property within reg.19. The Responsible Person must then replace the report prepared under Sched.7 with either an HCR complying with Sched.5 or the terms of a new homes warranty to which the property is expected to be subject at completion of the sale together with a cover note.

Additionally, an EPC must be included where an HCR is not.

The changes to the Regulations that will follow the government announcement on 18 July 2006 could leave or remove the alternative requirement for an HCR when a property becomes 'physically complete'. An EPC will, however, be required and with it a Sched.6 new homes warranty.

2.7   NEW HOMES WARRANTY

A warranty dealing with any defects in the design or building of the property must contain the minimum terms which are described in Part 3 of Sched.6 to the Regulations. Any liability under a warranty must be backed by an approved insurance policy by an insurer authorised under the Financial Services and Markets Act 2000. The minimum warranty period for a new homes warranty is 10 years from its start date and this must be confirmed in a certificate provided to the first buyer of the property. The warranty must be transferable without charge to a subsequent owner. The scheme is similar to but not identical with the current NHBC Buildmark certification process.

The warranty provider must undertake under the warranty terms that it has conducted reasonable checks and inspections during the building or conversion of the property and has carried out a final inspection. The warranty provider must be satisfied that the property is physically completed and finished to a reasonable standard so that the structure will be fit to withstand normal wear and tear for 60 years if properly maintained. The warranty provider must also undertake that the building of the property meets all statutory requirements in relation to the building work carried out.

The warranty provider must undertake that either it or the developer will put right or give financial compensation for any damage to the property caused by defects to the structure or common parts if they occur during the first 10 years of the warranty period.

Any conditions caused by defects in the design, workmanship, materials or other components of the structure and common parts which become apparent during the first 10 years of the warranty period and which cause imminent danger of destruction or damage to the property are included in the cover.

In addition under para.12 the warranty provider must undertake that it or the developer will put right or give financial compensation for any defect and damage to the property occurring during the first two years of the warranty period in relation to such items as windows, doors, floor covering, electrical wiring, drains, tiling and finishes. A full list is in Sched.6, para.12.

The total financial compensation or cost of remedial work for new build property may be limited to either £500,000 plus an annual increment or the value of the property at the point of sale, also inflation proofed. Similar compensation is available for converted property save that the sum of £500,000 is halved to £250,000 (on the basis that new foundations have not been needed).

The warranty will also cover the reasonable cost of alternative accommodation and professional fees, subject to limits as to scope and amount.

Key points

- Transitional period 1 June 2007 to 31 October 2007.
- Ministerial powers to suspend whole or part.
- Excluded property – intention and mode of marketing.
- Vacant possession.
- Outside England and Wales.
- New homes:
    - definition of physically complete;
    - Sched.7 report;
    - Sched.6 warranty – terms and cover note;
    - predicted EPC.

3 CONTENTS OF THE HOME INFORMATION PACK

3.1 INTRODUCTION

The Regulations prescribe what is needed to form a complete HIP. Regulation 4 states that there are 'required' documents and information that must be included in the HIP and 'authorised' documents and information that may be included and that nothing else may be added to form part of the HIP. This regulation also stipulates that the pack documents must be separate and clearly distinguished from other documents that are not 'required' or 'authorised' and from any written materials provided 'in close proximity' to the HIP or any document in it. Close proximity, given its obvious meaning, would primarily mean physically close but a time dimension should also be taken into consideration. To assist in demarcation of the HIP, a logo had been devised to appear on the front page of each of the documents in the pack but has been abandoned because of practical difficulties it presented.

The HIP is intended to contain information that is or would be of concern to a prospective buyer of that property. The position is not frozen forever and new regulations are to be expected from time to time as desirable components become available. For example, the government has stated that the HCR will become a required component once the government is convinced it is workable and has gained some acceptance. More generally, it is known that the government would be keen to include a report on ground stability when this has been designed to meet government approved standards.

The suppliers of content for the HIP will have a contractual responsibility to the person commissioning them. In addition, in specified cases (searches, HCR and possibly, EPC) they will have a potential liability to others, including a buyer and any person who relies on the information. In respect of this content those publishing the HIP may wish to limit their exposure to claims and normally this could be achieved by way of disclaimers to the extent that this is permitted by the general law. Here any limitation is constrained by the requirement that packs must not contain anything other than prescribed content. It is therefore left to a Responsible Person (see **para.1.9** and **Chapter 5**) to seek alternative ways to reduce exposure, possibly by requiring a buyer to accept specific disclaimers under the terms of a separate agreement.

Generally, the principle of 'caveat emptor' still applies to any sale of property and the buyer must therefore satisfy himself concerning any information specific to the buyer's particular needs or necessary to make the property fit for his specific purposes. The buyer will take the risk of any hidden defect in the property. If the seller has knowledge about a latent defect and fails to disclose this or if information disclosed is untrue or misleading the buyer may have a remedy (see **Chapter 9**).

The common law position may be adjusted by the terms of the written sale and purchase contract agreed at a later date between buyer and seller.

3.2 REQUIRED DOCUMENTS – ALL PROPERTIES

3.2.1 The index (regulation 8(a))

Every pack must have an index that lists its contents and complies with Sched.1 to the Regulations.

The format of the index is not prescribed in or by the Regulations but a specimen form has been recommended for the purposes of the Dry Run and can be found in **Appendix G**. This may become a prescribed form at a later date and can also be accessed at the DCLG's website (**www.communities.gov.uk**). This form of index is in three parts: Part 1 must be completed for all properties, Part 2 is for commonhold and Part 3 is for leasehold properties. It can be completed by anyone, but is the responsibility of the seller and/or the estate agent. It must be completed accurately and updated to comply with regs.15–20.

3.2.2 Sale statement (regulation 8(b))

This document must contain the information set out in Sched.2 to the Regulations. It will include the address and postcode and details of the property interest being sold. The statement will indicate whether title is registered or not and whether it is a new title to be created out of an existing one.

The sale statement can be completed by 'someone on behalf of the seller' but must give the name of the 'seller' of the property and, unless he is the owner, the capacity in which the seller is acting. Oddly, this does not require the identity of the owner to be given or for the statement to be signed by its author.

The property will normally be sold with vacant possession but in a case within s.171(2) where there are one or more occupants within a sub-divided building the type of occupancy must be disclosed.

Although the price will be the term of most immediate interest for a buyer, this is not a term to be included in the sale statement and will appear separately from the pack, probably in the estate agent's particulars of sale.

Where the leasehold interest in a flat is sold together with a share in the free-hold then details of both interests will need to be included. Where a new lease or a property has not yet been completed or converted the statement must be completed as if the new property interest already existed.

An example of a sale statement which also provides for additional leasehold infor-mation can be viewed at the DCLG website (**www.communities.gov.uk** and in **Appendix G**). This form, like the index above, is for consultation and may be adopted as a prescribed form at a later date.

During the 1998 DETR Consultation *The Key to Easier Home Buying and Selling*, consideration was given to the inclusion of a draft sale agreement in the pack. It was decided that this was not appropriate and posed too many potential dangers in a situation where the opportunity to obtain independent and objective advice ought to be protected, if not actively encouraged.

3.2.3   Property interest being sold (regulation 8(c)–(g))

For registered land this is a straightforward requirement to include official copy entries of the land registers (proprietorship, property and charges) with an offi-cial copy of the title plan. These will contain the necessary title information and describe the extent of the property to be sold. Official copies of other filed documents may be included in the pack as authorised documents under reg.9(f).

Where the interest is commonhold, official copy entries relating to the unit must be included together with the entries for the common parts along with the additional documents listed in Sched.3 to the Regulations (discussed at **para.3.4.1**).

Where the interest is leasehold then the documents listed in Sched.4 to the Regulations must be included (discussed at **para.3.4.3**). Although reg.8(c) could have been worded to explicitly require inclusion of the freehold estate out of which a leasehold is derived, this does not appear to be the intention and the Guidance does not comment on this situation.

For unregistered land the HIP must contain an official search of the index map in form SIM and an epitome or abstract of title. This will involve copying the root of title document as well as all deeds and documents containing matters affecting the title or a full abstract of such information. Where this includes plans they must be accurately coloured (reg.5(2)). In the case of complicated titles the cost of preparing the HIP and that of subsequent copying for a potential buyer will be higher and separate charges are likely. Generally, it is noted that under the Land Registry Fees Order 2006, SI 2006/1332 the cost of obtaining official copies of entries and lease documents in particular have been increased to reflect current commercial cost.

Where the seller is not the owner, further documents will be needed to show that the seller has authority to sell. Such evidence would include grants of probate or letters of administration where the sale is by executors and court orders where a sale has been ordered by the court, for example, on divorce or in cases of administration or bankruptcy. Where these are not strictly documents of title and might not be included in the abstract or epitome of title, they can be included as required documents under reg.8(d)(ii) being documents on which the seller can reasonably be expected to rely in order to deduce title.

Before these marketing reforms it was common practice for title information to be produced when issuing a draft contract to the lawyer for the successful buyer. However, with the new timetable for disclosures at the pre-marketing stage, the disclosure becomes public rather than private. Where adjustments to any of the registers relating to the property held at the Land Registry need to be made in order to bring it up to date, ideally these should be made prior to compilation of the HIP but if made later the HIP must then be updated (see regs.15–20 and para.7.11).

Land Registry reforms are under development which will encourage the updating of the register prior to issue of the pack or any contract for a sale and these are expected to be piloted in late 2006.

Where part of the property is let or will become occupied on completion of the sale, it may fall within s.171(2) of Part 5 and any leases and licences to which the sale is subject must be included (reg.8(g)).

3.2.4   Search and enquiry reports (regulation 8(m), (n) and (o), Schedules 8, 9 and 10)

A great deal of consideration has been given to deciding what searches should be treated as necessary in every sale. A prodigious number of searches are available from a variety of sources and issues have arisen concerning the monopoly of suppliers of certain information and the different ways in which search reports may now be sold. Advisers currently choose a combination of search reports on a pragmatic basis depending upon what may be considered relevant to a particular case, taking into account the property location, a client buyer's specific needs and the requirements of a lender.

The OFT report published in September 2005 entitled *Property Searches: A Market Study* (OFT 810) recommended that the information held by local and other statutory authorities should be made more widely available electronically through a number of competing distribution channels. In December 2005 the DTI response (URN 05/1946) accepted the main OFT recommendations believing them necessary to avoid distortions in the market caused by the ownership by local authorities of the raw information needed by search companies. The Regulations have assumed that the necessary changes will take place and set new standards and terms for all search reports, including enquiries made of local authorities.

The searches that are compulsory for inclusion in the HIP are:

- a search of the appropriate local land charges register either in the form of an official search certificate or in any other form so long as it complies, if it is a personal search, with Parts 1 and 2 of Sched.8 to the Regulations: reg.8(m);
- a search report that complies with Parts 1 and 2 of Sched.8 and with Sched.9 (which deals with local enquiries): reg.8(n); and
- a search report that complies with Parts 1 and 2 of Sched.8 and with Sched.10 (which regulates drainage and water enquiries): reg.8(o).

Schedule 8

Schedule 8 to the Regulations is divided into three parts:

- Part 1 (paras.1–3) contains general provisions that relate to all searches and search reports, other than an official search certificate of the local land charges registry;
- Part 2 (paras.4–10) deals with specific required search reports; and
- Part 3 (para.11) deals with authorised search reports.

All search reports must contain the information set out in Part 1 of Sched.8 which requires the inclusion in the search report (but not in an official local land charges search certificate) such basic information as the address of the property, the enquiries raised and the results and the date of the search. It must also state who carried out the search, who prepared the search report and how to obtain copies of documents referred to in the search. The report must set out the terms of the contract for carrying out the search including the statutory terms found in paras.4, 5 and 6 of Sched.8. The names and addresses of the persons carrying out the search and preparing the resultant report must be included, as must the names of anyone responsible for any negligence or incorrect entry in the records searched or the interpretation or recording of such interpretation in the search report.

Details must also be given if there is a complaints or redress procedure. Details of the insurance cover available must be given in every case.

These provisions introduce greater transparency to the processing of information by requiring disclosure to be made of 'any personal or business relationship' between the person who conducts the search or prepares the report and 'any person involved in the sale of the property'. Under the definition section of the Regulations 'sale' includes a 'potential sale'. It is worth noting that a search company owned by a potential lender may not come within a narrow interpretation of these provisions. Paragraphs 1(i) and (j) are further examples of the transparency required of search contracts and reports and the liability of persons responsible for primary records as well as those who search, interpret and record information from them.

Additional information can be included of the type set out in para.2 – this could be an explanation of the search report. Whilst documents may be attached to the search report, advertising or marketing material is prohibited.

The search report is also required, under para.3, to include a statement identifying any information that was not available.

Part 2 imposes minimum standard terms in the contracts for search reports. These must provide that:

- reasonable skill and care will be used;
- a Responsible Person may copy and issue copies of any search report to comply with duties under Part 5 of the Act;
- the contract under which the report is prepared may be enforced by the seller, buyers or potential buyers and lenders without any need to rely upon the Contracts (Rights of Third Parties) Act 1999;
- there is insurance cover in place to meet any claims for financial loss if such claims are not met by the search provider or any other person involved in the sale of the property.

The insurance provision is a new and absolute obligation on search companies, unlike complaint and redress procedures that have to be disclosed only if they exist. It should also be noted that the wording in para.6 suggests that someone other than the search provider can take responsibility for claims in respect of the search report – the advisers to the seller, buyer or lender perhaps?

Paragraph 7 provides for the amount of compensation that would be payable for such claims to be limited to the value reasonably believed to be the residential use value of the property concerned at the date of the search report. Compensation for lost development value is therefore unlikely to be paid but disagreements over value can be envisaged since the claim can be the amount 'the potential or actual buyer reasonably believes . . .' which leaves the position uncertain.

The statutory contract terms cannot be excluded or limited although additional terms (such as for payment) may be included in the contract, particularly if they are more favourable to a seller, buyer or lender (para.8). Any attempt to include terms less favourable to these parties will result in the search being non-compliant (para.9).

Any document that fulfils the requirements of a search, as set out in para.1, must comply with the schedule even if described by another name or the information is given in another pack document (para.10).

Paragraph 11 provides that additional searches may be included in the pack as authorised documents under reg.9(k) and (l), but a contract to provide an authorised search can be made on any terms and those set out in paras.4, 5 and 6 do not have to be included. There is ambiguity in para.11 which states that an authorised search may comply with both Parts 1 and 2 of Sched.8 while reg.9(k) requires authorised searches to comply with Parts 1 and 3. The guidance confirms that compliance with Part 1 is necessary. Third party rights are therefore not automatically available as they are for required searches.

Schedule 9: Local authority enquiries

Schedule 9 regulates the enquiry reports to be obtained from local authorities and these must also comply with Parts 1 and 2 of Sched.8.

Paragraph 1 of Sched.9 contains definitions that relate specifically to the Schedule and para.2 stipulates that a search report must contain the enquiries set out in the following 16 paragraphs of Sched.9, Part 2. They must relate to the property in question.

These enquiries cover, in paras.3–18, matters such as planning and building decisions and applications, proposed use and development, conservation area information, local authority planning designation for the relevant area, highways information, land for public purposes, land required for road works, classification and creation of new roads, road improvements or alterations, road, traffic and railway schemes in the vicinity of the property, building regulation and planning notices and enforcement, compulsory purchase, contaminated land, drainage consents and agreements and radon gas.

This reflects the matters historically addressed by Part 1 of the form CON 29. If that form continues in use it will need to be adapted to give all the information that is required to comply with the requirements set out in Scheds.8 and 9.

Schedule 10: Drainage and water

Drainage and water enquiries are required documents under reg.8(o) and are regulated by the provisions in Scheds.8 and 10. The information required is that currently obtained in form CON 29 DW.

Part 1 of this Schedule contains definitions that relate to this Schedule and explains the format to be used.

The report on drainage and water enquiries must list the enquiries that are set out in subpara.(1) of each paragraph in Part 2. The response to each enquiry must be one of the responses given in subpara.(2) of each of the paragraphs. Thus, Part 2 sets out the enquiries and requires a response in one, and one only, of the provided answers. If a pre-printed form is used care must be taken to strike out inappropriate responses to ensure that there is only one response to each enquiry.

Some of the pro-forma responses contain words in italics (see enquiries 12, 15, 16, 17, 18, 19, 20, 23, 24 and 25) and where this is the case the specific information must be given and, if the response refers to a document, that document must be attached to the search report.

These enquiries cover matters such as sewer maps, public adoption of sewers, sewage treatment works, foul drainage and surface water, water and sewerage charges, mains supplies, drainage agreements, public water mains maps, water supply, water meters, overloaded public sewers, poor water pressure and water quality.

The search must set out the result of searching for the records dealing with these matters indicating the availability and cost of copies if copies are not attached to the search report. As with other searches and enquiries, a clear statement must be made in the report if any information or record is not available.

All 'required' searches must be completed no more than three months before the date when marketing of the property first commences (reg.14(2)).

It seems likely that the cost of search reports will reduce following the acceptance by the government of the OFT recommendations for reform. This can be achieved through complete electronic delivery of searches once the necessary investment has been made.

Property search services

MacDonald, Dettwiler and Associates Limited (MDA) is active in the supply of property search services in England and Wales and through subsidiaries holds a licence to run the National Land Information Service (NLIS) hub. The hub is an online means of obtaining local authority property searches. It transmits requests from NLIS channel operators to the local authorities and distributes their replies back. The intention is to increase the number of permitted channel operators, but of the three currently licensed, at present two (TransAction Online and, since 2006, Searchflow) are controlled by MDA.

Results from the service have been disappointing to users as the search and delivery processes involved can be slow and are still in many cases manual and rely upon the availability of local authority personnel. The market has produced an alternative solution in the form of personal search companies whose charges are comparatively low but they are constrained on speed of delivery by other obstacles.

So long as they retain a price advantage, private search companies are likely to grow in popularity and for the purposes of the HIP will be superficially attractive to sellers. For buyers, lenders and their advisers there are other concerns as to accuracy and reliability and this has led to efforts by some organisations to self-regulate through their membership of the Council of Property Search Organisations (CoPSO) (see **www.copso.org.uk**).

The reforms contained in Sched.8 suggest that pricing structures are likely to change as increased levels of transparency, insurance for consumer protection and liability for mistakes bring new costs. Balancing this is the likelihood of increased search volumes and more competition between public authorities and private search companies.

The inclusion of a non-compliant search would render the HIP non-compliant.

3.2.5   Home Condition Report and new homes warranty (regulation 8(h), (i) and (j), Schedules 5 and 6)

The HCR is a new concept and as such is discussed in detail in **Chapter 4.** Regulation 8(h) requires an HCR complying with the requirements in Sched.5 to be included where a property is 'physically complete' (a term explained in **Chapter 2**) at the FPM. It must be no older than three months at the FPM. Alternatively, no HCR is needed if a new homes warranty of the type described in Sched.6 is being offered and is available for completion at the time of the sale. The pack must contain the proposed terms of the warranty and the warranty cover note. The cover note will have been issued by the scheme provider as confirmation that a home is physically complete and meets the scheme's requirements. The warranty must commence after completion of the first sale of the property following physical completion. Once a warranty is in existence the Regulations require an HCR for any subsequent marketing for sale of the property.

If a property is marketed for sale within 12 months of the date when an HCR is completed that HCR must be included in the HIP (reg.8(j)) but only if produced for the current seller (reg.11). It is anticipated that the terms of indemnity cover available for an HI will only cover the sale by the seller for whom the report is produced.

Following the government statement of 18 July 2006, these provisions are subject to amendment to reflect the voluntary basis on which the HCR can now be included.

Energy performance certificate (EPC) – regulation 8(h)

The EPC is described in **para.4.8** and must be added to the HIP. It is a requirement for every property that is 'physically complete', even where that occurs after the property is put on the market (reg.19). New homes that are 'not physically complete' require a predicted EPC.

Warranty – regulation 8(i)

Any warranty in force of the type described in Sched.6 to the Regulations that has not expired or will not have expired by the time the sale is completed must be included in the HIP.

3.2.6   New homes 'off plan' and 'under construction' (regulation 8(l) and Schedule 7)

If the property is not 'physically complete' before the FPM a report must be included in the HIP containing the information set out in Sched.7 to the Regulations. This is discussed in **Chapter 2**.

3.3   AUTHORISED DOCUMENTS – ALL PROPERTIES

Regulation 9 sets out the documents authorised for inclusion in the HIP, which include the following:

- An accurate translation into any language of any of the documents in the HIP.
- An additional version of any document in the HIP in another format such as Braille or large print.
- A summary or explanation of any HIP document.*
- Information to identify the property such as a map, photo or drawing.*
- Information about the source or supply of the HIP or any document or information in it and any complaints and redress procedure available in relation to the supplier.*

* Note that these elements are additions to those in the draft Regulations. The summary or explanation will have to be carefully considered and prepared, as it is likely that a buyer might rely on it for comprehension of the HIP. It does, however, provide the opportunity to include guidance or a 'health warning' for any potential buyer to seek independent advice on the HIP.

- In the case of registered land, official copies of documents referred to on the register of the property to be sold. If the seller wishes he can include edited information documents. Application can be made to the Land Registry for the full version of a document to be exempted from appearing on the register on the ground that it contains confidential information of a commercial or personal nature. Any such application must attach an edited version for registration (the edited information document) and this can be produced either as an authorised enclosure or as a required element if it is the only version available.
- Where the property being sold is commonhold then any documents such as are specified in para.3 of Sched.3 to the Regulations may be included (these are discussed at **para.3.4.2**).
- If the property being sold is leasehold then any documents of the kind specified in para.3 of Sched.4 to the Regulations may be included (the detail of these is discussed at **para.3.4.4**).
- Documentary evidence of any works carried out on the property since the date of any HCR in the HIP.
- Any warranty, policy or guarantee relating to defects in the design, construction, completion or conversion of the property to residential use.
- Additional search reports may be included such as those relating to common land, ground stability and mining, environmental hazards or contamination, flooding. If such searches are included they must comply with the requirements set out in Sched.8. However, these authorised search reports do not have to include all the terms specified in Part 2 of the Schedule which must be included for a required search in the pack (Sched.8, para.11). The intention is that they must contain the information specified in Part 1, notwithstanding the inconsistency between reg.9(k) and para.11 of Sched.8.

- Search reports may be included that relate to land 'in the vicinity' if it is considered that the information contained in them would be of interest to a buyer.
- Any matters that may be of interest to a potential buyer that relate to the topics set out in Sched.11. This is a list of additional relevant information of the kind that was to be found within the draft Regulations in the Home Use Form and Home Contents Form. These forms can be accessed at the DCLG website (**www.communities.gov.uk**) and, like the other forms referred to, are recommended for use in any Dry Run as part of a further consultation (see also **Appendix G**).
- The Seller's Property Information Form (4th Edition) (part of the Law Society TransAction Scheme) may be suitable for use, subject to necessary adaptation.
- Any documents referred to in a search report.

3.4   COMMONHOLD AND LEASEHOLD PROPERTIES

For sales of leaseholds and commonholds there are additional 'required' and 'authorised' information and documents that must or may be included. Details are to be found in Sched.3 for commonholds and in Sched.4 for leaseholds. It is the policy of the legislation that, save for official copies, the documents required are those in the seller's possession or control or which he can access or obtain with reasonable effort.

3.4.1   Commonhold property: additional required documents and information (Schedule 3, paragraphs 1 and 2)

Documents

- Official copies of the title registers and title plan to the common parts together with an official copy of the commonhold community statement.
- A copy of any regulations made outside the commonhold statement.
- The most recent demand for payment of the commonhold assessment, reserve fund and insurance relating to the 12-month period preceding the FPM.

Information

- The name and address of any managing agent currently or proposed to be appointed by the commonhold association and anyone else who might be involved in the management.
- Any amendments proposed to the commonhold community statement or the rules and regulations.
- A summary of any works being undertaken or proposed that affect the property.

3.4.2 Commonhold property: additional 'authorised' documents and information (Schedule 3, paragraph 3)

Documents and information

- Commonhold community statement.
- The rights or obligations of the unit holder and the commonhold association under the commonhold community statement and whether each has complied with these.
- Information about the commonhold association including any that might affect the unit holder's relationship with it.
- Information about any agent of the commonhold association or other manager of it including any that might affect the unit holder's relationship with it.
- Information about membership of the commonhold association.
- The memorandum and articles of any company related to the management of the property or the commonhold association.
- Any commonhold assessment payable and whether payments are up to date.
- Any reserve fund levy relating to the property (the unit) or the commonhold (the common parts) and whether these are up to date.
- Any planned or recent works.
- Insurance information including who is responsible for insuring, the terms of insurance and whether payments are up to date.
- Any lease, tenancy or licence of the property.

3.4.3 Leasehold property: additional required documents and information (Schedule 4, paragraphs 1 and 2)

Documents

- A copy of the lease or leases together with, it is suggested, any deed of variation or other leases and/or licences that are relevant to or affect title to the property. This may take the form of any copy, not just an official copy of the lease(s) and licence(s) but an 'authentic' copy (see **para.5.6**) must be used which suggests that a 'made up' copy of a draft or final document may not be acceptable. A lease in the form of an edited information document may be used if that is the only available document.
- Any rules and regulations currently in force and made by the landlord or any managing agent.
- Statements or summaries of service charges relating to the 36 months preceding the FPM.
- The most recent request for payment of service charge, ground rent and insurance relating to the 12-month period preceding the FPM

Information

- The name and address of the current or proposed landlord, of the managing agents or proposed managing agents and of any other person(s) who might manage or be likely to manage the property.
- Any amendments proposed to the lease or regulations.
- A summary of any works being undertaken or proposed that affect the property.

3.4.4   Leasehold property: additional 'authorised' documents and information (Schedule 4, paragraph 3)

Documents and information

- The memorandum and articles of association of any company related to the management.
- Any lease relating to the property (headlease or underlease).
- Any licence or tenancy affecting the property.
- Any freehold interest linked to the property being sold including any proposals to buy such an interest.
- The rights and obligations of either the landlord or the leaseholder under the lease or otherwise including whether there has been compliance with these.
- Information about the landlord including any that might affect the leaseholder's relationship with the landlord.
- Information about any agent or manager of the landlord including any that might affect the leaseholder's relationship with the landlord, manager or agent.
- Membership or existence of any entity involved in managing the property.
- Rent payable including whether payments are up to date.
- Service charge payable including whether payments are up to date.
- Any reserve fund for works to the property or the building of which it forms part and whether payments to such fund are up to date.
- Any planned or recent works to the property or the building of which it forms part.
- Insurance information including who is responsible for insuring, the terms of insurance and whether payments are up to date.

3.5   NEW PROPERTY INTERESTS

3.5.1   New freehold homes

For new freehold homes involving a sale of part of a registered or unregistered title there are no separate provisions. They are treated as coming within the scope of reg.8(c) and (d) although there is a need to identify the property on a plan in the sale statement for a sale of part of a registered freehold title and also in the report under Sched.7 to the Regulations.

Schedule 7, para.2 also requires a location plan and layout drawings for homes not physically complete. Further photographs, maps and drawings could also be included under reg.9(d).

3.5.2 Commonholds or leaseholds created out of superior interest

Regulation 10, Schedule 3, para.4 and Schedule 4, para.4 set out additional documents to be included in the HIP in relation to the creation of 'new interests' where commonholds or leaseholds are created out of a superior interest.

Sale statement

Regulation 10 requires that the sale statement be completed as though the property interest has already been created and other documents and information must be produced as if the interest was already in existence. The test as to what should be included as required or authorised documents and information is, in each case, its relevance to the property interest to be created.

Where a new interest is a commonhold, the following must be included in the HIP:

- the proposed commonhold community statement; and
- an estimate of the anticipated financial contribution towards the commonhold assessment, reserve funds and insurance for the first 12 months after completion (Sched.3, para.4).

Where the new interest is leasehold, the following must be included in the HIP:

- the proposed lease; and
- an estimate of the anticipated financial contribution towards service charges, ground rent and insurance for the first 12 months after completion (Sched.4, para.4).

3.6 ADDITIONAL INFORMATION (REGULATION 9(N))

Buyers of leasehold or commonhold properties may well wish to see other documents such as insurance schedules and policies. Since the policy has been to designate only those documents that a seller should either have or be able to obtain without difficulty, documents that might need to be obtained from 'private' third party sources are not included in the mandatory category. If available they can be included in the HIP under reg.9(n). This allows a considerable amount of additional information to be included if the seller so wishes.

Sellers who have sold properties before or who have the benefit of professional advice may seek to pre-empt a buyer's adviser raising a substantial number of supplementary enquiries and will consider including under reg.9(n) information such as the following:

- a company search where the management company is either the freeholder or superior leaseholder to show that the company is properly constituted and still a going concern;
- planning applications or permissions current at the time of the FPM as buyers will want to know the current status on planning and any building works done or to be done;
- building control certificates since, at present, local authorities do not have a duty to retain these and, accordingly, this information will not be revealed by a search; however, once legislation is passed to require local authorities to do so, it is anticipated that building control certificates may become 'required' documents;
- certificates confirming that the electrical installation complies with Part P of the Building Regulations and that any replacement windows conform to the FENSA standard;
- notices under ss.20/20ZA of the Landlord and Tenant Act 1985 (which require landlords to consult with long leaseholders in connection with contracts in excess of 12 months' duration and for works in excess of a prescribed amount) where costs have not already been invoiced and paid and where full consultation has either not yet taken place or where the result of the consultation is not yet known;
- information on reserve funds that may be relevant to a prospective buyer, as it will indicate both the liquidity of the management company and the possibility of an unusually high service charge demand in the near future.

3.7   UNOBTAINABLE REQUIRED DOCUMENTS (REGULATION 17)

Regulation 17 recognises that there might be documents that through the passage of time are unobtainable. The Responsible Person must make reasonable efforts and enquiries to locate these documents. Provided he does so and believes on reasonable grounds that the document no longer exists or cannot be obtained or created by anyone it is accepted that the following may be omitted from the HIP:

- unregistered title documents;
- leases and licences relating to a sale referred to in s.171(2);
- any new homes warranty that has not expired;
- commonhold information; and
- leasehold information.

3.8   SUMMARY

The creation of the two classes of disclosure documents – mandatory and discretionary – could encourage a wide range of HIPs in the marketplace. Some packs will fulfill the bare minimum requirements whilst others may contain a full disclosure of documents with information that anticipates foreseeable queries by or for a potential buyer. The balance of the legislation has shifted during its progress (and the pendulum may swing in either direction) and, at the time of writing this guide, favours minimal disclosure. Practice will vary widely and fuller disclosure may be adopted for certain types of property and according to regional preferences.

Section 163(8) of the Act suggests that the contract under which any document in the pack is prepared might be enforceable by a potential or actual buyer or future lender in addition to the party commissioning it. This has been carried through only to a limited extent as the Regulations have extended third party rights only in relation to required search reports (Sched.8, para.5) and the HCR/EPC (Sched.5, para.3) and not other reports and statements in the HIP.

The detailed terms of the contract or contracts entered into by the seller (or some-one acting on the seller's behalf) with the provider of the HIP and its constituent parts including the HCR/EPC and searches will clearly be of vital importance. It should be noted that the Regulations require HIs and providers of search reports to hold indemnity insurance to meet claims.

Generally, the terms on which HCRs and search reports are to be produced opens up the potential for claims and this is discussed in **Chapter 9**.

The liabilities that could arise from the HIP or any of its contents may lead some estate agents to decide against taking any direct role in the production of the HIP. They may prefer so far as possible to pass responsibility to reputable HIP providers who, in turn, offer to insure the HIP and indemnify the Responsible Person against possible claims.

The legislation is intended to provide the buyer with sufficient information to enable negotiations and offers to proceed more easily and with greater transparency of information. The cost is placed on the seller who may not, after all, be successful in selling the property or who may, with or without any change in circumstances, decide not to sell.

Ultimately, caveat emptor has not been displaced and so at this early stage in the development of the new processes it is difficult to see why or how a buyer would rely upon the HIP rather than his own searches and investigations. In circumstances where the seller has provided information (either full or minimal) which is not relied upon by the buyer there will be a duplication of certain costs. Whether the HIP is a sale brochure or a due diligence document depends ultimately upon the terms of the written sale and purchase agreement negotiated between a willing seller and a willing buyer. Whether consumer pressures affect market practice to influence the outcome remains to be seen.

Key points

■ Pack:
  – documents which are required/authorised;
  – prohibited materials.

■ Required:
  – index, sale statement, title documents, EPC, search and enquiry reports, existing new homes warranty.

■ Authorised:
  – HCR and other optional elements.

■ Search and enquiry reports – prescribed terms.

■ Additional required and authorised components for commonhold and leasehold.

■ Additional requirements for new homes:
  – Sched.7 report and new homes warranty.

■ Unobtainable documents.

■ Caveat emptor survives.

4 HOME CONDITION REPORT AND ENERGY PERFORMANCE CERTIFICATE

4.1 GENERAL (REGULATIONS 33–35 AND SCHEDULE 5)

The requirement for a formal inspection of every home prior to marketing is a radical initiative. The development of a form of report and new infrastructure of inspectors and regulators has, however, proved complex and time consuming. As a result the government announced in July 2006 that the HCR will not form a compulsory element of the HIP from 1 June 2007. It is proposed that its introduction should proceed on a voluntary basis. This chapter considers the HCR from the position that it will become mandatory in the form described by the Regulations at some future point in time and discusses the issues then arising.

Government research in 1998 elicited that only 20 per cent of buyers commissioned a private survey. In addition, of the 28 per cent of all transactions that failed according to the research, half were said to become abortive because of something that was disclosed by the survey. Where a loan is being arranged for buyers then a lender's valuation is invariably required and in about 40 per cent of cases an RICS Homebuyer Survey and Valuation (HSV) is sold to buyers. This report on the condition of the property for the buyer highlights defects that are visible, and also provides a valuation. The alternative RICS Building Survey does not contain a valuation and reports in more detail on elements of the construction of the property and aspects that affect the particular buyer or that buyer's specific plans for the property.

Where an HSV or Building Survey is arranged it is normally subject to a number of limitations. It will contain disclaimers for covered and inaccessible spaces that cannot be inspected and this often gives rise to blanket recommendations for treatments for rot and infestation. Drainage and electrical tests are not included.

Problems may be identified as in need of further specialist investigation. The risk arising from any defect including latent defects lies entirely with the buyer.

Where a buyer discovers a defect or suffers damage from an unexpected event then a claim may be brought under his contract with the surveyor. Alternatively, a remedy may be considered for any misrepresentation made by the seller or the seller's agent.

Although the format of the HCR may improve the presentation of the report, many potential problem areas remain unresolved.

The Act proposed two components to the HCR, these being information about:

  (d) the physical condition of the property (including any particular characteristics or features of the property); and
  (e) the energy efficiency of the property.

(s.163(5))

Full details of the HCR are set out in Sched.5 to the Regulations. A sample of the HCR and the EPC taken from *Part 2: Technical Standards, The Home Information Pack; Certification Scheme Standards* appear in **Appendices E** and **F** respectively.

The HCR will be commissioned as part of the HIP by or on behalf of the seller. The document may replace the buyer's survey to the extent that it is satisfactory to buyers and, more importantly, acceptable to lenders. The buyer will, however, need to commission his own report for advice on any specific matter outside the scope of the HCR. It is therefore important for buyers to understand that the principle of caveat emptor has not been replaced.

In the early part of 2006 the Council of Mortgage Lenders (CML) made a number of announcements to signal that the lending industry was not committed to adopting the HCR or to abandoning the need for a mortgage valuation derived from a physical inspection of each property. In the case of loans for up to 70 per cent of the value of the security, some lenders are committing to desktop valuations using automated valuation models but a research paper published by the CML on 27 April 2006 (*UK Mortgage Underwriting Report* by Oxera Consulting Limited) indicates that progress across the industry will not be rapid enough to displace the need for the traditional type of valuation by mid-2007. This was reinforced by a further report on 11 July 2006 (*Mortgage Lenders, HIPs and the Future of Valuations* by Octavia Research and Consultancy). These reports can be accessed on the CML website (**www.cml.org.uk**).

The position and attitude of the lenders was cited by government as its reason for withdrawing the mandatory HCR.

4.2   CERTIFICATION SCHEMES – PART 7, REGULATIONS 33–35

Section 164 of the Act and regs.33–35 set the framework for certification schemes to regulate HIs.

The structure is controversial in that more than one body is being encouraged to obtain approval. Government believes this provides a robust model and avoids the risk of a monopoly situation that could result in high cost to the consumer. It does, however, open up the potential for differential regulation where the HI works to different rules depending upon who is commissioning a report. This is particularly the case where some industry HIP providers may become approved bodies and commission HCRs to be carried out under the regulation of their own captive scheme.

Before the Secretary of State will approve any scheme he must be satisfied that it contains provisions to ensure that:

- members of the scheme are fit and proper persons who are qualified (by their education, training and experience) to produce HCRs;
- members of the scheme have in force suitable indemnity insurance;
- there is a scheme for the resolution of complaints against members of the scheme;
- HCRs made by members of the scheme are entered on the register mentioned in s.165;
- a public register of the members of the scheme is kept; and
- a standard form of HCR is used for each type of property.

(s.164(5) and reg.33)

Regulation 34 requires that approved certification schemes promote the reliability of HIPs and make provisions for a code of conduct, guidelines for carrying out inspections and for ensuring that its members use a standard form of HCR.

Regulation 35 refers to the minister's power to withdraw approval of a scheme. Approval could be withdrawn with immediate effect or on notice and can be a permanent or temporary withdrawal.

Every approved scheme is required to keep a register of its members and will be required to set up a procedure to deal with customer complaints. The HCR itself must contain a statement setting out the HI's obligation to provide a copy of the scheme's complaints procedure upon request. It is anticipated that the complaint will be handled in the first instance by the organisation operating the scheme with provision for unresolved complaints to pass through a mediation or ombudsman scheme (see Chapter 10).

4.3   TERMS AND RULES

Any contract under which an HCR is prepared must include the terms set out in paras.2 and 3 of Sched.5 without any exclusion or limitation but can include additional terms so as to cover, for example, payment of fees and charges and any credit arrangements. These statutory terms require that the HCR is prepared with care and skill and gives an objective report on the property based upon a physical inspection.

The HI must identify defects which require repair or replacement work or which are serious and require immediate attention and also matters that need further investigation.

The Responsible Person and others (such as employees and advisers) must be permitted to copy and provide copies of the report for the purpose of complying with duties under Part 5, thereby limiting any copyright of the HI in the HCR.

Paragraph 3 stipulates that the HI's contract must contain terms enabling sellers, buyers or potential buyers and lenders to enforce the terms of the contract notwithstanding that they may not be a party to it. This will avoid any need to rely upon the provisions of the Contracts (Rights of Third Parties) Act 1999. It is the idea that the buyer must rely upon the 'seller's survey' that challenges the prevailing culture in the market.

Paragraph 1 requires the HCR to be entered upon the register to be established under s.165. This will be a central database that will give each report a unique reference number (URN) to be constituted under a government procurement contract. The rules for access to the central database are to be established by separate statutory instrument. The certifying bodies are expected to establish structures involving local registrars to supervise their own body's register and the relationship with the central register.

4.4   HOME INSPECTORS

The HI must be a 'fit and proper' person suitably qualified by education, training and experience to carry out an inspection and prepare the HCR. The HI will have to reach the qualifying standard set by the Awarding Body for the Built Environment (ABBE) and satisfy the scheme or schemes to which he applies for membership that he is suitably qualified and holds the necessary indemnity insurance. It was originally proposed that where a person had been convicted of certain serious criminal offences, including offences involving dishonesty, that person would automatically be disqualified from becoming an HI and the Rehabilitation of Offenders Act 1964 would not apply.

The DCLG standards for certification schemes can be accessed on its website (**www.communities.gov.uk**). Part 1 ('Business Standards') sets out guidelines for assessing the fitness of persons applying to be registered as HIs. The scheme must require full disclosure from the applicant and make enquiries of the Criminal Records Bureau. However, it seems possible that a person who has been convicted of a criminal offence involving theft or dishonesty could become an HI. The author believes this remains an oversight and needs to be remedied.

The HI is required to maintain indemnity insurance within the minimum terms set by the certification scheme. The insurers will be required to cover claims in excess of £2,500 irrespective of the policy excess of the HI and his ability to meet that part of the claim. The cover must offer six years run-off protection and the first two and a half years are costed within the annual premium. The indemnity cover is limited to claims within six years on the basis that liability for latent defects for up to 15 years would not arise under the HI contract.

As buyers and lenders are entitled to rely upon the HCR the duty of the HI is extended beyond a single responsibility to the seller. Therefore, in order to limit exposure to claims, reg.11 states that the HCR must not be included in the HIP unless completed on behalf of the current seller. The subject of claims and remedies is considered in more detail in **Chapter 9**.

One of the acknowledged difficulties attached to the mandatory inclusion of the HCR in the HIP from June 2007 was the anticipated shortage of qualified HIs. All property professionals understand how the need for a valuation inspection or survey on a property can cause delay in the offer of mortgage finance and subsequent exchange of contracts. Although technically a property might in the first instance be marketed without an HCR under reg.15 this omission could present difficulties at a later stage.

If the HCR becomes a requirement at the HIP, the HI will come under a great deal of pressure to make appointments to inspect and to report as quickly as possible. Delays are inevitable unless there is a sufficiently widespread pool of HIs. They will only be able to inspect a limited number of properties each day and much will depend upon the accessibility and size of the property involved. Delays would defeat one of the objectives of the legislation – that is, a speeding up of the process. To meet the increased need for persons qualified to carry out an HCR a range of courses are available for the training of HIs and assessment centres have been established. A list of ABBE accredited course providers is available from the ABBE's website (**www.abbeqa.co.uk**).

Following the change of policy announced on 18 July 2006 the future direction of training courses is uncertain.

The DCLG report published in May 2006 under the title *Report on the Number of Home Inspectors Required from Introduction of Home Information Packs* is accessible on its website (**www.communities.gov.uk**). This estimates that the number of HIs needed would be in the region of 5,000 to 7,400 with 6,000 as a mean average. These estimates are based on assumptions as to the size of the market (a 10 per cent reduction on 2005 levels), the location of full- and part-time inspectors and to take into account the number of working days a week and the number of likely inspections per day. Eventually, in July 2006 the government recognised the risk that there would not be a sufficient number of qualified HIs and became concerned that this would lead to delays and increased cost.

4.5   CODES OF CONDUCT

The HI faces a number of situations with the potential for conflicts of interest. These were considered by various stakeholder working parties. The certification schemes are required to publish codes for regulating the conduct of HIs and the way in which inspections are carried out. As for other professionals, the HI will have an overriding duty to act with integrity and identify actual or possible conflicts of interest before they arise. It is hoped that relationships between HIs inspectors and their employers that could give rise to the perception of biased advice will be prohibited. Undoubtedly, situations will arise in practice where conflicts that might be perceived as giving rise to biased advice will need to be managed in order to avoid claims and complaints. This is a topic of some uncertainty as some HI's will be connected to firms of sellers' estate agents or be employed directly or indirectly within a corporate or group structure. Many may be commissioned to act for lenders and provide the valuation that is not part of the HCR. The confidence of buyers is crucial in relation to the HCR and once shaken would not easily be restored.

Although it is now a matter for individual certifying bodies to determine, the working party convened by government identified situations where a conflict arises and where disclosures ought to be mandatory. These included situations where the HI:

- undertakes the preparation of an HCR on the HI's own property;
- undertakes the preparation of an HCR on a property from which the HI will benefit from the proceeds of sale;
- provides advice or other services to buyers or potential buyers of a property on which the HI has undertaken the HCR.

Other less obvious situations, which it was considered might give rise to perceptions of conflict and accusations of bias were:

- undertaking an HCR for a member of the HI's family – disclosure of the relationship to be mandatory but notwithstanding this it could give rise to allegations of bias;
- undertaking an HCR on a property which the HI's employer is marketing or offering other services to the seller – disclosure of the relationship is now a required element of the HCR (Sched.5, para.6(b));
- providing additional services to the seller such as supervising repair works – this might give rise to questions about the reliability of the HCR;
- where an associate or associate company of the HI is providing services to the seller any fee or commission arrangement that exists;
- where the HI is separately instructed by a lender to provide a valuation for mortgage purposes for a potential buyer; and
- where the HI, acting in a different capacity, is requested to provide services to the buyer who has completed the purchase of a property on which the HI undertook an HCR.

The view was expressed at one stage by the Royal Institution of Chartered Surveyors (RICS) that no conflict arises where the HI is employed within a group of companies where one member of the group acts for one client and another company acts for a different client so long as the companies are separate legal entities; there are no common directors, partners or employees; there is no direct or indirect fee-sharing between the firms; and there is no access to information or common internal data-sharing arrangements relating to the area of conflict.

Consideration has also been given to requiring all HIs to carry an approved form of identity card with their membership details to assure homeowners that the person inspecting their house is a member of an approved body.

4.6   THE INSPECTION AND REPORT

4.6.1   The remit of the Home Inspector

The inclusion in a HIP of an invalid HCR would render the HIP non compliant with Part 5, leaving the Responsible Person (the seller or the estate agent) exposed to enforcement proceedings and/or a civil claim. An approved certification scheme must require its member HIs to complete the HCR using a standard form of report that contains the terms set out in Sched.5, para.2 and also a numerical rating scale for recording the condition of the property (see below). The report must contain statements as to the procedure for resolving complaints and for dealing with any inaccuracies in a particular report and rectification of the register of HCRs. Although there is no standard form of HCR to be used by all HIs, Part 2 of the DCLG Certification Scheme Standards sets out in detail the way in which an HCR must be formulated, including the mandatory text required. This two-part document can be accessed on the DCLG's website (**www.communities.gov.uk**). The format of a sample HCR and EPC are shown at **Appendices** E and F respectively.

Paragraph 1 of Sched.5 provides that the HCR must be completed by an HI following a physical inspection carried out by him in accordance with the provisions for doing so set down by an approved certification scheme of which he is a member. The report must be in the form adopted by his certification scheme for the particular type of property being inspected. It is anticipated that each scheme will agree a number of standard types of report to be used by its members.

A document must not be described as an HCR unless it complies with Sched.5 (reg.11(2)).

It is intended that the HCR will set out information about the construction and condition of the property at a given date and indicate if there are any follow-up enquiries or inspections needed. It is intended that the HCR should highlight problems that are serious or require immediate attention to protect the fabric of the building or, in more serious cases, to prevent threats to personal safety. The report is to be formatted to give 'condition ratings' to the structure of the main building inspected and also to any outbuildings. It will not necessarily draw attention to or comment on what the HI, within his terms of reference, regards as minor defects and maintenance issues. There is obviously scope for a mismatch of expectation as between the HI and a prospective buyer. The HI/seller may see unreported matters as of no significance whereas a buyer who acquires the property and then has to deal with problems that are not within the scope of the HCR may consider that there should have been disclosure or warnings.

The HI's remit specifically excludes an open market valuation of the property and the HI does not need to consider information relevant to that assessment. So, location and amenities such as proximity to schools, transport links and shopping are not relevant to his remit. The report will, however, provide a valuation for building insurance purposes and the same HI could be separately instructed by a lender to report on value for mortgage purposes at a later date.

The HCR will not advise on other specific matters that might affect a buyer's decision to buy a particular house. It will not advise or specify the detail of any repairs or remedial work that should be carried out or estimate the cost of such work. These would all be matters on which a buyer may need to commission a separate report. Early drafts carried a *de minimis* qualification for defects valued at up to £1,000, but this has now been omitted.

A seller or buyer (or a lender) may need to arrange for additional inspections to meet any particular concerns. If the HI is asked by the buyer or lender to provide any additional services these must be the subject of a separate agreement with the HI. Before accepting that further instruction, the HI would need to consider the code of conduct of his certifying body and any possible conflicts of interest.

The HI is required to inspect the main building and any permanent outbuildings externally and internally and also to inspect the visible parts of the utility services. It is a non-invasive inspection. The HI will not take up carpets or floor coverings, move furniture, undo electrical fittings, remove the contents of cupboards or remove secured panels. It is expected that there will be a simple rating system for each element with prescribed responses as follows:

Condition rating	Definition
NI	Not inspected
1	No repair is currently needed. Normal maintenance must be carried out.
2	Repair or replacement are needed but the HI does not consider these to be serious or urgent.
3	There are defects which are either serious and/or require urgent repair or replacement.

Although the HI will not report on location generally, the report will disclose if the property is in a Conservation Area or if it is a listed property, the date of construction and the date of any additions or extensions.

4.6.2   The scope of the Home Condition Report

Paragraph 6 of Sched.5 lists the information that the HCR must contain and this includes information relating to the property being inspected (for details see Sched.5) and whether the HI has any business or personal relationship with 'any person involved in the sale of the property'. This could include the seller, estate agents for the seller, the company facilitating the preparation of the HCR and the

HIP or any other linked party such as the search report provider. Details must be included in the HCR of the approved certification scheme or schemes to which the HI belongs, the date of the inspection and date of completion of the report and whether any parts of the property to which access ought to have been available were inaccessible on the date of inspection. This list is not exhaustive as the approved certification schemes are at liberty to add further requirements.

Paragraph 8 of Sched.5 expressly prohibits the inclusion of any information in the HCR that would allow a living individual to be recognised, or that expresses an opinion about a living individual or provides security information about the property.

By using a rating system for all elements of the HCR it is hoped to make the inspection simple, relatively fast and cost effective. There will be a standard report form that will be completed by the HI while on site. This can be transformed into the required format by the use of specialist software loaded to a PDA (personal digital assistant). These systems are expected to be required by certifying bodies so as to simplify the processes of monitoring and registration that they must carry out at speed once the inspection is carried out.

The HCR contained within the HIP must be made no earlier than three months before the FPM (reg.14(2)) but all HCRs carried out in the 12–month period prior to the FPM must also be included (reg.8(j)). The exception to this is where such reports were produced for or on behalf of a previous seller (reg.11). This could cover a report commissioned by the estate agent of a previous seller although this is not clear from the wording.

While it had been considered useful to have all previous reports in the HIP, it has been decided that an HCR carried out for someone other than the current seller might present out-of-date information and give rise to unnecessary queries. There is also a difficulty in the HI obtaining indemnity insurance to extend cover beyond the period of a live sale instruction.

Unless it is discovered that an HCR has been included in contravention of reg.11 (because it is more than 12 months' old or has not been commissioned for the current sale) the HCR should not be removed from the HIP under the updating procedure in reg.18.

4.6.3   Carrying out the inspection

The HCR will note the type of accommodation and give the number of rooms and the gross external floor area in the case of a house and the gross internal floor area for a flat.

There will be an indication of reinstatement cost for insurance purposes for the property but excluding such leisure facilities as a swimming pool. This assessment of re-building costs will need to be reviewed by the buyer as building costs change over time. It is intended to give an indication of the amount of insurance cover required for fire and other risks, but this figure will exclude the cost of the

land on which the building stands. If the HI regards the property as having special features or being of unusual construction which might require specialist
assessment for building costs, this element of the report will be left blank and the
report will explain why. There is a risk for HIs if a fire or other insured event
occurs and it transpires that the buyer (or lender) has underinsured following the
advice of the HI.

The HCR will note the available utility services connected to the property. There
is no requirement to test the supply of services, electric wiring or heating. Where
accessible the HI will inspect the drainage to the property.

The HCR is expected to identify any areas that require investigation if there are
signs of structural damage or evidence of ground movement. The HI can assume
that the property does not contain hazardous materials and is not built on contaminated land. If hazardous material is found on site or if the HI finds evidence
of land contamination, this will be noted in the HCR with recommendation for
further enquiry. The HI may recommend that certain legal aspects be investigated
or draw matters to the attention of the conveyancer.

When carrying out the external inspection of the property the HI will not be
expected to stand on walls or go onto adjoining property or land. The HI will
inspect from vantage points on the property or from public land – he will not be
expected to examine roofs and chimneys from anywhere higher than a three
metre ladder and, due to the risk of damage, the HI will not walk on flat roofs. In
respect of flats the HI will not be responsible for inspecting the entire roof of the
building unless there is a roof immediately above the flat.

The HI should enter a roof space to inspect the roof structure, but this inspection
will not be carried out if there are obstructions – in this case there will be a cur-
sory inspection from the access point and the fact of this restricted inspection will
be noted in the HCR.

When inspecting the interior condition of a property, the HI is to carry out a
non-invasive inspection without causing damage. If the HI believes there may
be a defect in a particular area but cannot confirm this without the risk of
causing damage, the HCR will note this to be the case and recommend further
investigation.

Damp penetration checks will be carried out in suspect areas by using a moisture-
measuring meter and any evidence of dampness will be noted on the report.
Since it is unlikely that the HI will have the necessary specialist equipment, no
inspection of or comment will be made about sound insulation or chimney flues.

As services are usually hidden under floorboards the HI will inspect only the visible parts and no specialist tests will be carried out. This means that there will be
no assessment of the efficiency or effectiveness of the service or of its compliance
with modern standards. If any of these services such as the central heating boiler
and system are not in operation at the time of the inspection the HI will not turn
them on but merely state that they were not working at the time of inspection.

The HI is only required to check mains services so will not look at or comment on other installations such as security systems, cable or satellite communication systems or appliances such as cookers, washing machines and fridges even where these are built in, integral to the property and to be included in the sale.

The HI will carry out some simple checks such as opening and closing doors and windows and turning on taps.

Minor defects will be noted where there are so many as to undermine the overall assessment of the condition of the property and would 'normally' affect a buyer's decision to purchase the property.

Details of other facilities such as a garage (and whether integral, single or double, on or off site) or other parking spaces, gardens and other outbuildings are to be ⁧⁧⁧⁧⁧⁧⁧ There is a requirement to report whether footpaths and roads are made up and maintainable by the local authority.

The HI will walk the grounds, if any, to the property to inspect the condition of these grounds, any boundary fences or walls and outbuildings. For the purposes of the HCR outbuildings are features that are not part of the main structure and will include conservatories with either translucent or clear roofs attached to the main buildings, garages, permanent store sheds and a building containing a swimming pool or other sports facilities. The HI will only inspect and comment on the building containing the facilities not on the facilities themselves. Whilst the HI will comment on the general condition of any garden there will not be any report on the way it is stocked.

The HI will also note if part of the property is used commercially and, if so, the approximate percentage of such commercial use.

In the case of flats, the HI will be expected to note if the building is purpose built or a conversion, the number of floors, the floor on which the inspected flat is to be found, the number of flats in the block or building and whether there is a lift.

When inspecting the exterior of a flat, the HI will carry out a non-invasive inspection taking account of the fact that the maintenance of the fabric of the building will not be the sole responsibility of a single flat owner. The HI will therefore only give information to enable checks to be made as to the adequacy or otherwise of maintenance provisions in the lease or other title documents. Whilst the HI will inspect and comment on access to the particular flat and any garage or parking area relevant to that property, there will not be any inspection of other common areas such as separate stairs and access ways or the lift motor room or storage cupboards. Where a flat has a roof space this will only be inspected if access can be obtained safely from inside the flat in question.

4.7   THE REGISTER OF HOME CONDITION REPORTS

Section 165 requires a register of HCRs to be established. As the intention is ultimately to have a register of the state and condition of all residential property in England and Wales, the Act provides that this could be maintained centrally or by an appointed organisation on behalf of the Secretary of State. It was intended that, because of the timetable for the Dry Run and start date of 1 June 2007, there would be a tender process for the setting up and operation of the central register; however, the timetable for this has been altered by the government's statement on 18 July 2006. The approved certifying bodies will each administer their own local register of reports from their HIs and feed reports into the central register.

The register will be electronic and safeguards will be put in place to protect the security and confidentiality of the register(s) from unauthorised or malicious interference or access. All HCRs must be entered on the register and a URN issued by the Registrar and a fee will be payable for this. Likewise, a fee will be charged for any inspection of the register or for production of copies of an HCR or any document on it. Rules have yet to be made covering access for categories of persons other than the owner.

It is expected that access to the register will be restricted to those with a bona fide need to inspect, namely, sellers, buyers, lenders and their respective agents together with enforcement authorities such as TSOs.

The Secretary of State is aware of privacy concerns and accordingly no personal information will be registered and there will be a criminal offence for improper disclosure with a fine up to level 5 – currently £5,000 (s.165).

The fact that there will be an accessible register will make homeowners wary that an adverse HCR could have a detrimental effect on the sale price and saleability of a property.

Sellers will be anxious to avoid blight attaching to their property and the market response may be a pre-marketing inspection. Surveyors and builders are aware of the opportunity that the legislation presents. They are likely to be asked by potential sellers to make a preliminary appraisal of a property and to advise and give estimates for repair of defects that need attention prior to the formal instruction to an HI to prepare the HCR. This would give the homeowner the opportunity to put right any problems so as to ensure a 'clean' HCR.

Whilst the HCR may increase the cost of selling a home it should have the effect over time of improving the condition of the housing stock nationally. Sellers may have increased costs on a sale, but those buying another home will have the benefit of the availability of the HCR on that property.

The seller has no statutory right to compensation in relation to an erroneous report but approved schemes will need to state the procedures for rectifying errors in HCRs. It is not clear if this will extend to the removal of an erroneous report from the Register of Home Condition Reports (reg.33).

4.8   ENERGY PERFORMANCE CERTIFICATE (REGULATION 8(M))

Prior to the laying of the Regulations before Parliament in June 2006 the government stressed the importance of the EPC to homeowners and sellers. Much was also made in the debates that followed of the HIP being the best method of complying with the EU Directive on the Energy Performance of Buildings (Directive 2002/91/EC).

This Directive required, by Art.7, that:

> Member States shall ensure that, when buildings are constructed, sold or rented out, an energy performance certificate is made available to the owner or by the owner to the prospective buyer or tenant, as the case might be. The validity of the certificate shall not exceed 10 years.

The government has gone further than required by stipulating that the EPC must be renewed on each transfer of property. Although not pertinent to HIPs, concern has also been expressed with regard to the need for an EPC for each and every letting of a property where the 10-year period appears adequate.

The Directive requires the creation of a general methodology to calculate the energy performance of buildings and the introduction of a certificate to be made available when a building is constructed, rented or sold. The certificate will give home buyers and sellers A to G ratings for the property's energy efficiency and carbon emissions.

Currently, Elmhurst Energy Systems Ltd are developing the reduced data standard assessment procedure system (RdSAP) for the Department for the Environment, Food and Rural Affairs in conjunction with the other members of the Federation of Energy Rating Organisations and the Building Research Establishment. The certificate for housing will be based on RdSAP and for existing housing will include recommendations for improvements. The HIP requires an energy efficiency rating for each property, using RdSAP calculations.

To produce the rating an appropriately qualified person will need to be appointed. Relevant training standards are to be set and are expected by February 2007. To comply with the Building Regulations all new dwellings are required to have a SAP energy rating (Part L). Prior to 6 April 2006 this was usually produced at the completion of the project but with the new Regulations the SAP, target carbon dioxide emission rate (TER) and dwelling carbon dioxide emission rate (DER) have to be calculated before the project can be submitted to Building Control, with a further check on completion of the project. These are carried out by an SAP accredited surveyor from drawings.

It is clear from the Regulations that the EPC was intended to form part of the HCR and to be prepared by the HI. It remains a required element of the HIP. The government's stated intention is to proceed with energy efficiency at the forefront when implementing the reforms in June 2007. The requirement for this document at point of marketing contrasts with the position in Northern Ireland where there is no HIP legislation and where the Directive will be implemented at point of sale. Scotland is also planning to introduce the EPC at the point of sale

The rating depends on such matters as the thermal efficiency of the building fabric and the type of heating system and its controls. The report also provides information on measures that could reduce fuel costs, increase comfort and improve environmental protection. The certificate will be provided through authorised establishments such as Elmhurst Energy Systems Ltd (see **www.elmhurstenergy. co.uk**) using data supplied to them. It is not yet clear who will be authorised to supply property specific data if an HI has not been appointed. The role could fall to estate agents but they will no doubt need to obtain the requisite qualification or call upon accredited assessors. Amending legislation will be needed to clarify these aspects.

Where a property is not physically complete then the predicted EPC will be a stand-alone document included in the pack under para.2(c) of Sched.7 as part of the Sched.7 report. Where the property becomes physically complete after marketing has begun then an EPC will be needed and reg.19 may be amended to meet this situation.

Where the property is physically complete and an HCR or new homes warranty is required under the Regulations, a separate EPC will now be required if there is no HCR. If the report for the EPC is carried out separately and dated later than any HCR that includes an EPC, the later version must be included in the HIP as a separate document.

4.9   COST

The likely fees for the HCR were estimated by the government (2003 and 2006) to average £350 plus VAT but these are not fixed or certain. There is every likelihood that the market will offer a variety of differing charging structures regionally and according to property type. There could be a fixed fee or a graduated scale depending on the value or size of the property or the amount of time needed by the HI to carry out the inspection and the report. More sophisticated offers may be introduced where charges are packaged with additional services either pre-HCR or post HCR.

The costing models provided by the government are in disarray following the 18 July statement. There is no stated estimate of the cost of preparing a stand-alone EPC as this was not regarded as a likely scenario save for new homes where cost was not regarded as crucial. It is mooted that a stand-alone EPC could cost between £150 and £250. The housing minister has suggested that it will represent better value for a seller to pay for a full HCR that includes the EPC and hopes that this will encourage sellers to opt for the voluntary HCR.

There is another variable cost attached to HCRs, which will arise where expert reports are commissioned from a structural engineer or damp expert or arborologist. Additional disbursements may also be charged for registration on the central register and for carrying out searches to obtain copies of previously registered reports.

4.10   THE FUTURE

The shift in government policy has far reaching consequences for the future of the HCR. The removal of the HCR creates the need for a framework for the provision of the EPC. It is assumed that the requirement for all HCRs of less than 12 months of age to be disclosed will be relaxed if sellers are to be encouraged to try out the voluntary HCR.

> **Key points**
> - Home Condition Report is no longer mandatory.
> - Energy Performance Certificate is mandatory.
> - Who will provide the EPC?
> - Terms for provision of the EPC?
> - New Regulations awaited.
> - Home Inspector certification schemes.
> - Home Condition Report central register.

5 RESPONSIBLE PERSON

5.1 INTRODUCTION

Part 5 of the Act places statutory duties on the seller or the seller's estate agent and sometimes on both. Section 154 requires that, during the period when a property is on the market for sale, the person responsible for marketing must comply with ss.155–159. In short, the obligations of a Responsible Person and a person committing a qualifying action are:

- to have a HIP; and
- to provide a copy of the HIP on request.

The duty to provide a copy of the HIP (s.156(1)) may be limited by the conditions set out in ss.156 and 157, which are discussed later in this chapter.

Under s.151(3) 'only the seller or a person acting as estate agent for the seller may be responsible for marketing the property' although s.151(4) adds that 'a person may be responsible for marketing the property on more than one occasion'.

It is suggested by government that about 95 per cent of all properties are sold using estate agents so first we examine the responsibilities of an estate agent or as Part 5 puts it, 'a person acting as an estate agent'.

5.2 ESTATE AGENTS

5.2.1 Who is an estate agent?

It is important to revisit the definition of an estate agent for the purposes of Part 5:

> A person acts as an estate agent for the seller of a residential property if he does anything, in the course of a business in England and Wales, in pursuance of marketing instructions from the seller.
>
> (s.150)

This is similar to, but not the same as, the definition under EAA 1979 which applies to all types of property transaction and the estate agent's role of introducing buyers to sellers and vice versa. It should be noted that solicitors are excluded from the express obligations of EAA 1979.

For the purposes of Part 5, organisations and professionals, such as solicitors or surveyors, can come within the definition of 'estate agent', as could anyone who adopts the role of an estate agent irrespective of what they call themselves. Section 150(3) emphasises that it is substance, not form that matters: 'It is immaterial for the purposes of this section whether or not a person describes himself as an estate agent.'

This is illustrated by the case of a letting agent who would be acting as an estate agent under Part 5 by marketing an empty investment property for sale. This could easily happen on an occasional basis even if it is not the agent's mainstream business, particularly in the case of foreign investors or where the owner/landlord is abroad.

The territorial limitation in the Act enables overseas agents to avoid obligations under Part 5 if their trading operation is wholly outside England and Wales. In such a case the responsibilities relating to the HIP fall upon and remain with the seller. Thus a seller, marketing through an agent outside the jurisdiction, is required to comply with Part 5 and have a pack available for potential purchasers even if that seller is non-resident. In practice this is unlikely to arise save perhaps in the English/Scottish borders.

The 'place' where these activities are carried out does not have to be either exclusively or mainly business premises. Anyone running a business from home could be caught within the definition and such an introducer would be an estate agent for the purposes of Part 5 with all the attendant obligations and responsibilities.

Where residential property is sold by auction rather than private treaty it will require a HIP. The information presently offered in auction packs prepared by lawyers is not very different from that envisaged by the Regulations. The major difference would be the provision of an HCR, but this is not yet obligatory and so only an EPC is a new requirement. In terms of timing, however, auctioneers will need to exercise caution as marketing to databases of investors and other buyers often begins far ahead of the finalisation of the auction diligence pack. In future the preparation of the brochure and the HIP must progress side by side even though they remain separate publications.

5.2.2   Starting and ceasing to act

Section 152 describes when the responsibilities of a person acting as an estate agent arise and cease:

(1)   A person acting as an estate agent becomes responsible for marketing the property when action taken by him or on his behalf –

(a)   puts the property on the market; or

(b)   makes public the fact that the property is on the market.

(2)   That responsibility ceases when the following conditions are satisfied, namely –

(a)   his contract with the seller is terminated (whether by the withdrawal of his instructions or otherwise);

(b)   he has ceased to take any action which makes public the fact that the property is on the market; and

(c)   any such action being taken on his behalf has ceased.

(3)   Any responsibility arising under this section also ceases when the property is taken off the market or sold.

It is worth noting that the act of placing a property on the market or making that fact known (where the seller has put the property on the market) both trigger the duties of a Responsible Person. As soon as the estate agent (or someone on his behalf) on the seller's instructions takes action to put the property on the market or publicises the fact that the property is on the market, he becomes responsible for marketing and for complying with the duties in ss.155–159. Whilst a sub-agent might advertise that a property is on the market he is not deemed to be acting as the 'estate agent' because there is no direct instruction from the seller (but see s.159 and **para.5.7** concerning 'qualifying action').

The termination of responsibility comes about only when the estate agent is no longer instructed by the seller and he takes no further steps that make public the fact that the property is on the market. In addition, any action on his behalf, by employees or sub-agents, must also have ceased. These three tests are cumulative and so duties will continue until they have all been met.

The marketing agreement entered into by sellers for the appointment of estate agents should define the precise arrangements and timing for termination of instructions; dealing with both the responsibility for taking action to market a property and also, upon certain events, to remove it from the market.

Responsibilities come to an end when the property is 'taken off' the market, by being withdrawn from the market or when the property is sold. Withdrawal may be temporary and this is accommodated by the terms of reg.3 (discussed in **para.5.2.3**).

The 'first point of marketing' (FPM) is defined under reg.3(1) to mean the first time a duty arises under ss.155(1) or 159(2) for the Responsible Person, or a person committing a qualifying action, to have a HIP.

Different FPMs can arise for dealing with unavailable documents and updating of 'required' and 'authorised' documents. These provisions are contained in regs.15(2)(a), 18(3) and 20(3), discussed in **Chapter 7**.

5.2.3   Interruptions to marketing

Where a property is withdrawn from the market for more than 28 days and then put back on the market a new FPM arises when the property is placed back on the market.

This means that documents which must not be more than three months old at the FPM, such as Land Registry entries, search reports and the latest HCR, may become out of date as a result of temporary withdrawal from the market (reg.3(5)). These documents may need to be renewed and earlier HCRs will also have to be checked to see if they should no longer be included where they have become more than 12 months' old at the new FPM.

Where the property is withdrawn from the market but placed back on the market within 28 days then that does not constitute a fresh marketing. This means that documents which must be no more than three months old at the FPM will not be treated as out of date because of this temporary withdrawal from the market (reg.3(3)). In reality they will, however, be that much older and therefore less reliable for the purposes of a buyer.

It is not clear from the wording whether the period of '28 days' means a single continuous period (and whether only one such continuous period is allowed) or if it can be made up of a number of shorter periods totaling 28 days in all. Regulation 2(5) provides that a reference to a number of days (or months) is to a consecutive period. This supports the view that, in reg.3, the period or periods of withdrawal do not need to be aggregated but should be considered separately.

These Regulations could facilitate the situation where a seller wishes to remove instructions from one estate agent and appoint another in his place. Where this occurs there might be an immediate transfer of instructions or, as is more likely, there will be either an overlap or a gap.

If the property is withdrawn from the market by one estate agent it poses questions as to whether the original HIP will, at a later stage, be both compliant and reliable when a second estate agent remarkets the property. Regulation 3(3) allows for a pause in marketing of no more than 28 days, which might also allow time for remedial works to be carried out in response to an adverse HCR.

For this reason, whenever a second or new marketing agent is involved it is advisable for him to carry out his own due diligence in relation to the HIP for which he will be responsible.

Although estate agents have a general duty to a seller client to report all offers from potential buyers until contracts are exchanged, in practice active marketing often ceases when the property is 'under offer'. Estate agents will, after an offer has been made and accepted, generally try to keep in touch with other prospective buyers just in case a chain breaks down or other problem arises causing the prospective purchaser to withdraw before exchange.

Whilst the agent continues to market the property he remains responsible to provide a HIP, which means that, during the period a contract is under negotiation, gazumping may occur. This can give rise to complaints from disappointed applicants for the property where the position is not clearly and fully explained to them. The Regulations encourage the withdrawal of a property from the market once an offer is accepted and proceeding.

Regulation 3(5) gives a measure of protection for sellers against increased costs being incurred when a property is taken off the market as a result of an offer to buy. If the property is withdrawn from the market for this reason (and this can be for any period of time, not restricted to 28 days) and provided it is put back on the market within 28 days of the date the transaction fails, the FPM remains the original FPM. This means a seller is not prejudiced in relation to the cost of a HIP if a buyer insists upon a lock-out agreement whilst negotiations proceed towards an exchange of contracts. Again, this could have the effect that the HIP is of no value for a buyer – the documents could be over six months old.

5.2.4   Ending responsibility

The duties of the Responsible Person cease when the property is withdrawn from the market or 'sold'. The definition of a sale in s.177 of the Act refers to an agreement and thus indicates an exchange of contracts. There is no reference to conditional sales and so the inference is that a property may be regarded as sold even where a conditional contract is exchanged.

It is plain that an estate agent must take positive steps to ensure that, when his responsibility has come to an end, he makes that change as public as he did the marketing of the property. Property particulars will therefore need to be removed from any display in or on the agent's premises and website and any 'For Sale' board erected at or around the property taken down. Withdrawing the property from sub-agents will also be necessary. Special care will need to be taken regarding on-page advertising as this has a lead time for printing that could result in a property appearing in an estate agent's advertisement after the date his retainer has ended.

It should be remembered that, depending upon commission terms in the estate agent's marketing agreement, termination of instructions may not cancel the entitlement of the agent to commission if, some weeks or even months later, a buyer he introduced during the period of his retainer proceeds to buy the property.

Regulation 21 requires an estate agent, where he is the Responsible Person, to provide the seller on request with a copy of the HIP or any of the documents in it to enable the seller to check their accuracy. Although not expressly stated the implication seems to be that there can be no charge for this 'service'.

5.3   SELLER

The responsibility of the seller follows the same wording as for the responsibilities of an estate agent. Section 153 states:

(1)   The seller becomes responsible for marketing the property when action taken by him or on his behalf –
    (a)   puts the property on the market; or
    (b)   makes public the fact that the property is on the market.

In addition, the seller will be responsible along with his estate agent unless all conditions in s.153(2) are satisfied. These conditions are that:

(a)   there is at least one person acting as his estate agent who is responsible for marketing the property;
(b)   the seller has ceased to take any action which makes public the fact that the property is on the market; and
(c)   any such action being taken on the seller's behalf has ceased.

In the normal course the seller will not be responsible if his estate agent is, so long as the seller does not take any steps to market the property. If the seller or a person acting for him (who could then be regarded as an estate agent under Part 5) distributes property details or arranges viewings privately this could make him jointly responsible together with the agent.

Section 153(4) confirms that the responsibility ceases, as it does for estate agents, when the property is taken off the market or sold. Similarly, the provisions relating to temporary withdrawal from the market (reg.3) apply to sellers in the same way as they do for estate agents.

Thus, there will always be a Responsible Person where a residential property in England and Wales is being marketed – either the seller, where no estate agent is instructed (or the agent does not have a place of business in England and Wales) or his estate agent when there is. If the seller wishes to 'avoid' responsibility he will need to ensure that there is one or more estate agents who are the Responsible Persons. If the seller wishes to continue to actively seek interested buyers or promote his property for sale he will remain, together with the agent, a Responsible Person.

5.4   DUTIES

The duties of the Responsible Person are central to Part 5 and are set out in ss.155–158 of the Act. It is the duty of a Responsible Person to have control of a HIP and to provide an 'authentic' copy of the HIP upon request. The duty to provide a copy to a potential buyer can be limited by the qualifying conditions discussed below.

The duty to have a pack is set out in s.155:

(1) It is the duty of a responsible person to have in his possession or under his control a home information pack for the property which complies with the requirements of any regulations under section 163.

(2) That duty does not apply where the responsible person is the seller at any time when–

  (a) there is another person who is responsible for marketing the property under section 152; and

  (b) the seller believes on reasonable grounds that the other responsible person has a home information pack for the property in his possession or under his control which complies with the requirements of any regulations under section 163.

The seller also has a duty to have a HIP in his possession or under his control unless he has reasonable grounds to believe that his estate agent can discharge this duty. The additional words 'or under his control' refer to the likelihood that the HIP will be supplied and held by the Responsible Person in electronic form. The Responsible Person will be deemed to have an electronic version under his control if he can download and make it available upon request. The wording indicates possession or control rather than ownership and carries implications in relation to copyright and the freedom of a seller to change estate agent in the course of marketing a property. If the ownership of a HIP resides with an estate agent then the seller's ability to transfer his marketing instructions is restricted. Contracts with estate agents may be drafted to contain provisions that require the original HIP to be delivered to the seller upon request but in most cases agents will require any unpaid costs for preparing the HIP to have been paid. Questions relating to copyright and ownership are discussed in **para.7.13**.

The duty of providing a copy of the HIP on request is set out in s.156(1):

(1) Where a potential buyer makes request to a responsible person for a copy of the home information pack, or of a document (or part of a document) which is or ought to be included in that pack, it is the duty of the responsible person to comply with that request within the permitted period.

The 'permitted period' is, subject to a condition explained at **para.5.5.3**, 14 days beginning with the day on which the request is made (s.156(9)).

Section 156(2) clarifies the scope of the duty:

(2) The responsible person does not comply with that duty unless–

  (a) he provides the potential buyer with a document which is–

    (i) a copy of the home information pack for the property as it stands at the time when the document is provided, or

    (ii) a copy of a document (or part of a document) which is included in that pack,

  as the case may be; and

  (b) that pack or document complies with the requirements of any regulations under section 163 at that time.

To be compliant the HIP must contain the mandatory documents described in **Chapters** 3 and 4. The Responsible Person will not be able to avoid direct responsibility for the Index to the pack or the Sale Statement (reg.32(a)). This contrasts with the position concerning the other components where the Responsible Person needs to believe on reasonable grounds that the pack is compliant. 'Reasonable belief' provides a possible defence for the Responsible Person against enforcement by way of a penalty charge notice under s.168. The relieving provision does not extend to any other type of complaint or claim (see **Chapters** 9 and 10).

The wording 'as it stands at the time when the document is provided' ensures that the potential buyer receives the most up-to-date version of the HIP, being one which includes documents that may have been added after it was first issued. The HIP must, of course, comply at all times with the Regulations as to content.

The ability/obligation to add documents is clarified by regs.15, 16, 18, 19 and 20, which are discussed in **Chapter** 7. A revised or new version of a document can be inserted in the pack and an older version removed should the Responsible Person wish to do so in the case of 'authorised' content – whereas he must do so where a new document replaces an existing document in the 'required' content. There is no obligation to provide revised or updated versions to potential buyers who received a copy of the HIP before the later version was added.

It should be noted that offering the buyer an electronic version of the HIP discharges the duties of the Responsible Person only if the buyer is prepared to accept it in that form (s.156(10)).

5.5   REFUSAL OF A HOME INFORMATION PACK

5.5.1   Discretion over supply of Home Information Pack

This legislation does not entitle anyone and everyone to require that an estate agent (or other Responsible Person) provide a copy of the HIP on demand. Section 156(4) contains important qualifications. That duty does not apply:

> . . . if, before the end of the permitted period, the responsible person believes on reasonable grounds that the person making the request –
>
> (a)   is unlikely to have sufficient funds to buy the property in question;
> (b)   is not genuinely interested in buying a property of a general description which applies to the property; or
> (c)   is not a person to whom the seller is likely to be prepared to sell the property.
>
> Nothing in this subsection authorises the doing of anything which constitutes an unlawful act of discrimination.

The Responsible Person therefore has a discretion as to the people he must provide with a HIP and the seller can exercise some control over the supply of the information about his property by giving instructions that bring the agent within the scope of s.156(4). There is nothing in the section or the Regulations that requires the Responsible Person to tell the potential buyer why a copy HIP is being refused nor any time period in which such information must be relayed.

It is, however, important to note the rider to this subsection. Discriminatory behaviour can cover a wide range of actions and conduct so care must be taken to ensure that a refusal to provide a HIP is made on lawful grounds only. Nonetheless, there is a basis upon which the distribution of HIPs can, in practice, be curtailed.

These grounds do not provide a basis for refusing a request if 'the responsible person knows or suspects that the person making the request is an officer of an enforcement agency' (s.156(5)). Estate agents will wish to be familiar with the policy and procedures of the enforcement officers for their area in order to train their staff to be prepared and to respond to a request. The topic of enforcement is dealt with more fully in **Chapter 8**.

A seller who is regarded as a Responsible Person does not have a duty to provide the HIP if there is also another Responsible Person; i.e. an estate agent who is marketing the property. The seller does not, in these circumstances, have to provide a copy of the HIP so long as he reasonably believes that the estate agent has a compliant pack. However, there is an obligation to inform the potential buyer requesting a copy of the HIP that this can be obtained from the estate agent who is responsible (s.156(6) and (7)).

5.5.2   Cost

The potential buyer is not entitled to receive a paper copy of the HIP entirely free of charge. Section 156(8) provides that: 'The responsible person may charge a sum not exceeding the reasonable cost of making and, if requested, sending a paper copy of the pack or document.'

The charge to be levied must be reasonable for preparing a copy of the HIP and this is not intended to allow the cost of compiling the HIP to be passed on. The charge can be made for a paper copy but not for an electronic copy. Postage could be added if the buyer asks for the HIP to be to be sent to him or his adviser or if that is the way in which the estate agent decides to organise delivery of copy HIPs. That procedure would seem to be particularly appropriate for unregistered land where the HIP is likely to be substantial and take time to copy and check. There would be nothing to prevent an estate agent from requiring all potential buyers to register with and pay a registration fee to his agency when applying to receive the HIP details of a property. There are no provisions in relation to the sale of property equivalent to those in the Accommodation Agencies Act 1953 which prohibit charges for registration or for giving out details for rental properties. It also seems possible for the copy of the HIP to be 'rented' out upon request and that a condition could be imposed for its return at the end of the rental period.

5.5.3   Timing

The request for a copy of the HIP need not be met if, before the 14–day period from the date of the request expires, the property is sold or taken off the market or the Responsible Person, being an estate agent, has his instructions withdrawn or terminated:

> If the responsible person ceases to be responsible for marketing the property before the end of the permitted period (whether because the property has been taken off the market or sold or for any other reason), he ceases to be under any duty to comply with the request.
>
> (s.156(10))

We have seen that s.156(4) (para.5.5.1) sets out other grounds upon which the Responsible Person may refuse to provide a copy of the HIP. To safeguard his position the estate agent should obtain prior instructions identifying the categories of applicant to whom a pack can be provided or he could, within the permitted 14–day period, obtain instructions about a specific request. In either case, estate agents will be entitled to request from buyers and then verify much more information than they may have done in the past. Buyer registration would be prudent for a number of reasons. Details requested would include:

- identification – such as is needed to comply with the money laundering legislation;
- financial information – to enable the agent to ascertain whether the potential buyer can afford the property in question;
- details of any connected and dependent transaction; and
- details of any 'in principle' mortgage offer.

All are relevant and can cause delays once an offer has been made and accepted.

Assuming that, during the 14–day period, clearance is obtained from the seller, two further requirements can be imposed:

- a request for payment – the HIP would not have to be provided until payment was received; and
- in addition, the buyer may have to meet the terms of s.157(3), namely:

    > The potential buyer may be required to accept any terms specified in writing which –
    >
    > (a)   are proposed by the seller or in pursuance of his instructions; and
    > (b)   relate to the use or disclosure of the copy (or any information contained in or derived from it).

Such terms could limit dissemination of the content of the HIP and protect the confidentiality of the information. Whilst some of its content may be available publicly the HIP clearly brings much data together within a valuable and verified dossier. The content of the HCR will, of course, be of interest to other estate agents in the local market and buyers may be in contact with them to discuss other available properties.

If another agent is shown a copy of a HIP in breach of a confidentiality agreement that agent may introduce the buyer to an alternative property that he is marketing – the unlawfully disclosed HIP being used to make comparisons favourable to the property he is marketing. The disgruntled owners of the original property may well complain about a breach of any agreement or their instructions concerning confidentiality.

The required terms must be specified in writing so as to avoid any misunderstanding and must emanate from the seller. It should also be noted that these conditions are limited to the use and disclosure of the copy of the HIP – they do not permit conditions to be imposed so as to restrict the provision of the HIP to or from certain potential groups of buyers. However, the conditions in s.156(4) properly applied could enable estate agents to keep copies of the HIP away from nosy neighbours and/or property tourists or, even, for a while from their own competitors.

The timetable for providing a copy of the HIP is thus extended to the end of 14 days from the buyer complying with the conditions in s.156 (for payment) and s.157 (confidentiality) and this could add up to a period of 28 days for the Responsible Person to comply with a request. The buyer must be told of these conditions within the first 14-day period.

Where there are conditions the buyer must comply with them before the 14-day time period starts to run and, if there are two conditions to meet, the period only starts to run when both have been met.

Conditions relating to disclosure of the HIP will be important to a homeowner and privacy issues should be explored at the outset of an estate agent's instructions rather than left to be dealt with only when a request for a copy of the HIP is made by a potential buyer.

5.6   AUTHENTICITY

It is crucial to the process that information is accurately transmitted to a potential buyer. Section 158 imposes a duty to ensure that documents are authentic in situations where the HIP is produced following a request under s.156. This extends also to a situation where the HIP is shown to a buyer or inspected:

(1)   Where a responsible person provides a potential buyer with, or allows a potential buyer to inspect, any document purporting to be –

    (a)   a copy of the home information pack for the property, or
    (b)   a copy of a document (or part of a document) included in that pack,

the responsible person is under a duty to ensure that the document is authentic.

(2)   A document is not authentic for the purposes of subsection (1), unless at the time it is provided or inspected –

    (a)   it is a copy of the home information pack for the property or a document (or part of a document) included in that pack, as the case may be; and

(b)   that pack or document complies with the requirements of any regulations under section 163.

In effect, this is saying that the copy provided (or inspected) must be a copy of the document which is in the HIP for the property. Responsible Persons must ensure that copies are taken from the source document rather than copies of copies as they may be, or become, corrupted or incomplete through the copying and re-copying process.

Documents must be legible and in the case of maps, plans and drawings they must be clear. Regulation 7(2) provides some relief where an original of a document is illegible or obscured.

Section 158(4) has been included to overcome duplication so if the HIP has been provided under s.156 then it will be the 'original' document and therefore automatically authentic. Regulation 6 reiterates the requirements as to authenticity stating that copies of the HIP must be 'true' copies or if the document in the pack is an official copy then either a 'true' copy or another official copy.

5.7   QUALIFYING ACTION

Section 159 is intended as an anti-avoidance provision and states:

(1)   This section applies to a person acting as an estate agent for the seller of a residential property where –

(a)   the property is not on the market; or

(b)   the property is on the market but the person so acting is not a person responsible for marketing the property.

If the property has not yet been put on the market (or the property is on the market and the agent is not the estate agent responsible for the marketing, being perhaps a sub-agent), then there is a duty to have a pack if any 'qualifying action' is undertaken. This is any action that communicates that the property is available for sale (s.159(3)).

Not falling within the definition of a Responsible Person, an agent might seek to avoid the responsibility of having and providing a copy of the HIP. Thus, someone not responsible for marketing the property might be used by the seller to make specific overtures to interested parties who would not come within the expression 'the public' or 'a section of the public'.

In this context it should be remembered that the definition of an 'estate agent' provides that anyone taking action 'in pursuance of marketing instructions from the seller' will be treated as an estate agent under the Act, it being immaterial whether or not a person describes himself as an 'estate agent'.

By way of illustration, an estate agent or some other person could, before the property is put on the market, telephone potential buyers who have registered an interest in a property similar to the subject property, to advise them of its upcoming availability. Without s.159, this would not trigger the requirement for a HIP.

'Qualifying action' is defined as:

> ... action taken with the intention of marketing the property which –
>
> (a) communicates to any person in England and Wales the fact that the property is or may become available for sale; but
> (b) does not put the property on the market or make public the fact that the property is on the market.
>
> (s.159(3))

At the time a person undertakes a qualifying action, he must have a compliant pack (s.159(2)) and, as always, the HIP must be authentic if shown or produced for inspection (s.159(4)). The meaning of 'authentic' follows the exact wording of s.158(2) above.

5.8   SUMMARY

It is clear that a HIP is needed at the time a property is marketed or a qualifying action is taken. The Responsible Person or person carrying out the qualifying action must have a HIP that is compliant in all respects with the Act – a non-compliant HIP is not a HIP for the purposes of the Act – and the estate agent must be in a position to provide a copy if a valid request is made for one.

These obligations only cease for the estate agent when:

* he is no longer instructed by the seller;
* he takes no further steps which makes public the fact that the property is on the market *and* any similar actions which have been taken on his behalf (by employees or sub-agents) have also ceased;
* the property is taken off the market;
* the property is sold.

Various methods of marketing a property give rise to the responsibilities under the Act as suggested in the examples below:

* Seller:
  – self-placed newspaper advertisement;
  – own dedicated website;
  – home-made 'for sale' board outside house;
  – represented by agent but seller continues involvement;
  – represented by estate agent outside the jurisdiction.
* Estate agent:
  - outside the jurisdiction but place of business in England or Wales;
  - inside the jurisdiction if instructed by a seller private treaty or auction;
  - sub-agent – taking qualifying action.

- Others:*
  - direct mailing organisation;
  - Internet website provider;
  - media publisher of newspapers/magazines;
  - posters;
  - property fairs and exhibitions.

* Usually, these marketing entities will not be responsible but see the OFT Intermediaries Guidance (available at **www.oft.gov.uk**).

Key points

- Responsible Person can be seller, estate agent or person carrying out a 'qualifying action'
- Statutory duty to have HIP before marketing residential property.
- Commencement and cessation of responsibilities.
- Establish relevant FPM.
- Fix point of withdrawal of property from market.
- Statutory duty to provide a copy of HIP to buyers and TSOs.
- Right to charge for paper copy of HIP.
- Electronic copy only where the buyer agrees.
- The HIP must be authentic and the buyer must be given an up-to-date copy.
- Estate agent's discretion to refuse a copy of a HIP.
- Seller's right to protect confidentiality and limit disclosure of HIP.
- Time limits to produce a document or HIP.
- Seller's responsibilities depend on whether or not an estate agent instructed.
- Estate agent's responsibility for those acting on his behalf.

6 KEY PLAYERS

6.1 SELLER

6.1.1 The decision to sell

The seller's decision or need to sell starts off the process. Supplying the home-owners of England and Wales (14.5 million homeowners in England according to the 2003/4 *English House Condition Survey*, August 2005, available at **www.dclg.gov.uk/index.asp?id=1155269**) with the information they will need is a massive challenge. Traditionally, estate agents have been able to initiate marketing activity immediately if that was what the seller wished. That is challenged in the new HIP environment. Decisions to sell are affected by both personal and economic reasons while market fluctuations of price and sales volumes reflect economic, seasonal and political factors. The lead-time for preparation of a HIP and delay in marketing may increase market volatility with accentuated seasonal peaks and troughs as sellers adopt the optimal timing for planned sales.

The first action by a homeowner is usually a telephone call to local estate agents requesting an inspection of their property to give the seller a 'sale valuation' meaning, in this context, the price at which the property might sell, a view on its marketability and the general buoyancy of the property market. Significantly, this market appraisal is free of direct charge as residential estate agents act for sellers, in the main, on a 'no sale no fee' basis.

The seller's decision may develop over a period of time, driven by a lifestyle requirement for more or less space or amenity needs such as schools or location of healthcare. More frequently, it is a decision linked closely to a change in circumstances such as a life-changing event – birth, marriage or death. In other instances it may be the involuntary consequence of a change in employment or financial circumstances, or of divorce. Estate agents will be concerned about any delay to their ability to commence marketing, as many sales instructions from sellers currently come about as a spontaneous reaction to finding a property they want to buy rather than through a planned decision to market their property.

Many homeowners are continually 'browsing' the media for their next home without a specific timetable in mind. Most purchasers (almost 60 per cent according to the *English Home Condition Survey* (2003/4)) will borrow to fund a property purchase and it follows that, if they are already homeowners, when they find a house that they want to buy they must sell their existing property.

Within days the seller can have the benefit of a number of valuations from which to fix the asking price and proceed to appoint one or more estate agents to market the home. Typically, the estate agent or agents appointed will then prepare detailed property particulars including measurements, photographs and advertising copy on a speculative basis. Once details are approved and advertising copy placed, the property is then ready to market – this could be within less than a week of the decision to put the property on the market.

This sequence can no longer be offered – the seller will not be able to market the property without a HIP. Having decided to sell, the seller must consider the requirement for a HIP. Who will prepare and provide this and who will be the best source of the necessary advice on the process? Most estate agents will wish to offer to obtain the HIP in order to secure the sales instruction.

6.1.2   Agency contracts

With the advent of the HIP, selling a property involves the seller in a greater number of contractual relationships. The contract with any estate agent will be extended to deal with the new and additional responsibilities that go with marketing of the property for sale. The prudent or 'informed' seller may seek provisions that protect his position as regards the following:

*   the estate agent accepting all the duties of a Responsible Person;
*   responsibility for assembly of a complete and accurate HIP;
*   imposing confidentiality conditions on disclosure of the HIP;
*   retaining ownership of the HIP;
*   procedures for terminating the estate agent's retainer;
*   procedures for the property to be taken off the market temporarily;
*   marketing instructions to the estate agent to filter out buyers not fulfilling the qualifying conditions;
*   charges and fees – including any loan or credit agreement for deferred payment;
*   recourse for errors or omissions in any part of the pack and in relation to elements of the HIP such as the HCR/EPC or search reports.

Conversely, the estate agent will seek to protect his position on each of these issues (see **para.6.3**).

6.1.3   Confidentiality and restricting circulation of Home Information Packs

Sellers will need to understand that only limited protection for confidentiality of the HIP may be possible bearing in mind that there may be numerous parties interested to obtain sight of the contents of the HIP. Other estate agents may try to find out about the HCR and EPC to inform themselves for valuation purposes or to assist their own negotiations. The seller could require that all copies of the HIP that are issued must be numbered, logged and returned by the unsuccessful applicants once the property is sold. However, the circulation of electronic copies would be almost impossible to control in this way.

The owner may wish to specify the category of persons to whom a HIP can be issued upon request – so as to exclude those, for example, who are not cash buyers or who can only proceed if they sell a property they own. Alternatively, the seller could insist that any buyer demonstrates that he can finance at least 10 per cent of the purchase price by way of available cash and without any borrowing. Other conditions relating to the buyer's ability to proceed within a price range or within a given timescale appear to be lawful and if instructions are properly documented could help to protect the privacy of the property owner.

6.1.4   Engaging a Home Inspector

As originally proposed, the seller (or agent acting for the seller) will need to approach an HI. It is envisaged that if and when the HCR is made mandatory then the following procedures would be relevant. Even if the HCR proceeds initially as an authorised addition to the HIP, it is at present anticipated that the Regulations would be applied as follows.

The HI must offer standard terms of engagement with minimum prescribed terms described in Sched.5, para.2. He will inspect and prepare the HCR and if any collateral service is required by the seller by way of prior or later inspection or supervision of remedial works this must be dealt with by way of a separate contract. The owner may wish to engage a contractor directly or through the HI to remedy any defects revealed by the HCR. If remedial work is undertaken after an HCR inspection there is scope to include the details as an authorised element of the pack (see reg.9(i)). As there is clearly room for abuse of the privileged position of the HI to recommend all kinds of work for either seller or buyer and for contractors to seize a marketing opportunity, the approved certification schemes for the HI are expected to impose strict rules of conduct to regulate such ancillary activities. In addition, the HCR is to contain a declaration of any personal or business relationship between the HI and any person involved with the sale of the property (Sched.5, para.6(b)).

6.1.5   Pre-HCR inspection

At a practical level, once the HCR becomes mandatory, the seller could be well advised to have a pre-HCR inspection of the property so that any defects can be considered and estimates of repair costs obtained without any pressure or consequence. The alternative is that a defect may first be revealed by the HI and then appear in the HCR, and thence will be recorded in the central register of HCRs. Many sellers would undoubtedly feel uncomfortable about this, preferring to market their home in good order.

6.1.6   Arranging for assembly of the Home Information Pack

The seller may contract with a high street service provider such as an estate agent, HI, solicitor or lender to assemble or deliver the HIP through one or more sub-contracts. Alternatively, the seller could buy from a dedicated HIP provider, being an organisation that will procure and assemble the documents to make up the HIP.

The seller should expect a warranty that the HIP is compliant with Part 5 and the Regulations. The seller and the buyer and those advising them will each be con-cerned to know that the HIP produced is appropriate for the specific property and can be relied upon. This means that whoever assembles the HIP is likely to be made responsible for any errors or omissions.

6.1.7   Cost

Depending upon the cost of the HIP, the seller may need to take up a credit agree-ment to meet the cost of the HIP. Alternatively, he may prefer to take out a loan just for the disbursement element. Searches presently cost between £60 and £230 and it should be remembered that all elements of the HIP, apart from the statutory fees, will incur VAT. In addition, the cost of an EPC is estimated at between £150 and £250. The government had estimated the average cost of an HCR (including an EPC) at £350. Given the relatively small differential, the government hopes that the market (and consumers) will opt for the full HCR.

The definition of 'seller' includes a person acting on behalf of the owner of the property. Where there is more than one registered owner, the seller will need authority from all owners and this may be needed in irrevocable form, as it is the seller who will otherwise have to meet the abortive costs of preparing the HIP if there is a change of decision or other reason for the owner withdrawing the prop-erty from the market. Executors and trustees will normally be in a position to obtain an indemnity from an estate or fund for their commitment and any outlay.

A prudent seller should seek independent advice on what is bound to be, at least in the early days, a wide choice of alternative types of agreement for obtaining the HIP. Visiting an independent legal adviser may ultimately come to be seen as an essential first step on the road to a successful sale, but only if lawyers can develop the necessary mechanisms to manage the sale process as seamlessly as some of their more obvious competitors.

6.1.8   Timetable planning

Timing is crucial for most sellers and this encourages advance preparations for the sale. The seller (or someone acting on his behalf) will need to engage an accredited assessor to deliver an EPC and may arrange this through an HI who carries out a physical inspection to deliver an HCR. Time is also needed to obtain copies of title deeds, searches, planning information, guarantees and warranties and to obtain copies of any missing information. If the information contained in Sched.11 (and to be found in the Home Contents and Home Use Forms on which the government is consulting) is to be included in the HIP then a personal meeting may be needed between the seller and the pack provider. In the past these issues were only seriously addressed after an offer had been accepted. Timing will be an especially important consideration if the seller wishes to 'catch' a rising market or seasonally buoyant market conditions in spring and autumn.

6.2   BUYER

6.2.1   Government objectives

The declared intention behind the Act and the Labour Party manifestos of 1997 and 2001 was to 'improve' the residential property market for buyers and to eliminate gazumping. Subsequent consultation and research has moved the emphasis towards improved transparency and to assisting first-time buyers. Other longer-term objectives include improving the condition of residential property and complying with the EU Energy Directive.

The government policies are designed to assist buyers and to leave decisions so far as possible for consumers to make rather than for industry to dictate. This will create a period of uncertainty and initially result in the proliferation of channels for delivery of the HIP and ancillary services such as insurance products.

This is regarded by government as more effective and less wasteful than the present system where detailed factual information would only come into the buyer's hands through his solicitor after an offer has been accepted. Before reaching that stage the buyer might have incurred the cost of a survey/valuation as well as legal fees and other expenses.

With the introduction of a full and complete HIP the buyer would be in a position to form a clearer view of the worth of any property under consideration, especially if there is more than one property of that type on the market. By comparing the facilities and condition of each property as recorded in an HCR the buyer would be able to make an informed evaluation and then decide whether to proceed to offer and at what level to offer. Unfortunately, this objective has been lost through the change of direction that relegates the HCR to a voluntary rather than mandatory component.

6.2.2   Information available to the buyer

Currently, a prospective buyer will acquaint himself by a variety of methods with the properties available in the location of choice. Newspaper advertising and visits to local estate agent showrooms provides information about a locality and the types of property generally available. The Internet has made detailed information about most of the property currently on the market accessible for buyers, enabling them to make appointments for viewings and to download the information they require. Online photographs have reduced the number of viewings needed to achieve the average sale and the time spent before a buyer feels confident to make an offer.

By the time he approaches an estate agent in connection with a particular property or properties, it is quite likely that research resources available on the Internet, including information on local amenities and neighbourhood statistics, will have been scrutinised by the buyer. Once the type of property in the chosen area has been targeted and the properties 'currently available' viewed on local websites, the buyer is then able to view comparative price data from the Land Registry. Both general and specific information on planning and local development plans, as well as information on council tax, can also be found on local authority websites.

In addition to receiving property particulars from an estate agent outlining details of properties on the market the buyer may have access to a great deal of detailed information about properties on the market before making an offer for a particular property. Historically, the buyer's negotiating bids and offers have been based on extremely limited information. A variety of problems or obstacles often then emerge at a later stage after an offer is accepted. Leaving aside problems of 'human nature' these can arise out of survey or from title information delivered with the contract to the buyer's legal representative. In many cases delays in any linked transactions also affect the buyer's ability to proceed. If the price is renegotiated or the transaction turns out to be abortive it can then be difficult to establish the true reason why. It is typically during periods of delay that personal circumstances can change and gazumping issues may arise. The owner or agent may even actively encourage competing offers for the property in order to overcome delay, in particular if there is a disappointed under-bidder waiting in the wings. If the HIP does not contain an HCR problems on survey may still arise at a later date.

6.2.3   Inspection and supply of Home Information Packs

It is anticipated in the Act that the buyer may be permitted to inspect the HIP or just a particular document in it (s.158(1)). In such case, there is no provision enabling the seller or estate agent to make a charge and it is an implicit rather than an express right for the buyer. However, a paper copy of the HIP and any document or part of a document in it can be requested from the Responsible Person and the maximum charge to the buyer will be that of making the copy and of posting it to the buyer.

When a buyer makes a request for a copy of the HIP the estate agent has a discretion under s.156(4) to refuse to supply a copy of the HIP if the buyer does not appear to meet the lawful requirements laid down by the seller or if he cannot satisfy the agent that he is a genuine potential buyer of the property.

This may encourage the adoption of a diverse range of policies by estate agents. In some cases buyers could be asked to register their interest in buying a property or to indicate, in rather more detail than at present, the type of property they are looking for and their price range. They could be asked to provide evidence of their ability to purchase in a certain price range and show that funds are immediately or easily available if holding themselves out as a 'cash' buyer. A buyer with a dependent sale may also have to provide more details of any dependent transaction and give authority for enquiries – both initial and continuing – to be made of the estate agents and/or solicitors involved in that transaction. The buyer might be asked to agree that he will accept electronic delivery of a HIP. This could relieve the estate agent from making and delivering a paper copy to meet any subsequent request, although it does mean that control of onward circulation would then be more difficult.

The HIP for each property will contain the 'required' information and may contain additional authorised information. However, this will be different in every case according to the seller's instructions and the type of property. In most cases it is likely that a buyer will incur professional costs for dealing with any necessary additional enquiries, survey/valuation requirements and for obtaining any 'authorised' and other relevant information that is of interest but not given.

6.2.4   Lenders' requirements

It remains to be seen what requirements of the CML Lender's Handbook can be satisfied with the information contained in the HIP; it is unlikely that the 'required' documents alone will be sufficient. Overall, the buyer will need guidance as to the meaning and effect of elements of the HIP before making an offer to buy. This would be the case even where the seller's representatives produce, either within or separately from the HIP, a written summary or explanation of the HIP documents.

Most first-time buyers, having only a deposit available in cash, will need to obtain some indication of their suitability for a mortgage before submitting an offer. When proceeding to make an offer, buyers may, on advice, require the property to be withdrawn from the market so that no further HIPs are issued to any other party. In return, the seller may require a fixed timetable for exchange of contracts. Before committing to that, the buyer's legal adviser would wish to comment upon the quality of the HIP and its adequacy for the purposes of any lender's requirements. In addition, there may be aspects of any HCR provided or buyer's survey which require further investigation to ensure that later work can be carried out in accordance with the buyer's wishes and that there are no problems preventing insurance cover of the building on standard terms and for the usual risks.

6.2.5   Future expectations

In the future as the new system establishes itself, the government hopes that buyers' demands and expectations will lead the market. It is hoped that an HCR will be undertaken by sellers as a culture of disclosure takes hold.

6.3   ESTATE AGENT

6.3.1   The current situation

Most sales take place by private treaty and the procedure often starts with a home visit by the estate agent who inspects the property and gives a marketing appraisal and valuation without obligation. The estate agent is currently obliged under the Estate Agents (Provision of Information) Regulations 1991, SI 1991/859, to give details of his services including the charges and any expenses payable as well as the types of agency contract available. There are statutory definitions of sole and multiple agency, which are in use in all written agreements, though in many respects unsatisfactory. This was not expected to become subject to immediate change. The OFT estate agency report (*Estate Agency Market in England and Wales*, March 2004, (OFT 693)) endorsed the current system of negative licens ing and 'self regulation' but recommended reforms included improvement to these statutory definitions and also to introduce statutory regulation for consumer complaints if the industry did not adopt a satisfactory voluntary code binding all agents (see also the Minister for Housing and Planning's Written Ministerial Statement of 18 July 2006 at **Appendix D**).

The OFT investigation found that fees generally were charged on a 'no sale no fee' basis and had fallen from the level of 2 per cent towards 1.5 per cent over the previous 10 years. Increased competition and transparency were seen as a means of improving consumer choice and the range of services available. The marketing agreements commonly in use were found, with regional variations, to follow a standard pattern. Thus, it is at present relatively unusual in the residential market for fees to be payable for simply introducing a buyer 'ready, willing and able' to buy. By contrast, the concept of 'joint sole agents' has grown in popularity, particularly in larger conurbations where there is a wide choice of agents. The HIP could give impetus to change in the form and structure of estate agents' agreements as the reform invites agents to 'unbundle' their services and charge for work done, rather than on a speculative 'success only' basis. If HIPs are produced independently of estate agents then this might stimulate the growth of multiple listings by sellers' agents more in line with estate agency practice in the USA.

Since the advent of the Property Misdescriptions Act 1991 (PMA 1991) it has become customary for sales details to be sparse on detail. Location, price and a photograph of the property may be the only information utilised for window display. Information as to the history of the property, any building work carried out or regarding lease terms takes time to find and is difficult to verify. So, given the criminal sanction for breaches, the way in which estate agents conduct their business not surprisingly has been affected by PMA 1991. Much that Part 5 now seeks to achieve could, it is submitted, have been addressed simply by requiring certain minimum statutory disclosures by estate agents. These would have been effectively reinforced by the existing PMA 1991 legislation.

New regulation that will affect estate agents is expected in the parliamentary session commencing in October 2006.

6.3.2   The potential impact of the new legislation

Crucially, from an estate agent's point of view, the opportunity for 'Day 1' marketing is diminished with the advent of HIPs. Agents will not be permitted to contact buyers on a register or known to be looking for a particular type of property or property in a particular location or road and to book an immediate viewing before a HIP is in existence. This had in the past been a valuable tool in winning the seller's business and was used to build confidence in the agent's ability to perform and produce a buyer for the property. Where the buyer is looking for a property and has his own home to sell an agent will be keen to activate that instruction in order to secure two commission fees. The advent of HIPs will curtail the rush to value a house, compile and print property particulars and mail out to buyers who might be interested in as short a time scale as possible.

The estate agent will be forced to adopt a more measured approach to accepting certain instructions, for example, for leasehold property and new homes. Initially at least, there is bound to be an impact on the market as the time scale will lengthen for these instructions to be brought to the market. Following this period and assuming that market volumes are not permanently affected then pipelines of work in progress will stabilise. There must, however, be the possibility that uncommitted sellers will be discouraged from entering the market at all or will postpone their decision. Thus, a number of speculative sales may be eliminated in both the short and medium term.

6.3.3   Fears over damage to housing market

It had been thought that the delay in obtaining an HCR would damage the market. As it is now only an 'authorised' document an HCR could be produced after marketing has started. If it was an adverse report then it need not be added to the HIP unless further legislation is introduced to compel disclosure.

It had been expected prior to 18 July 2006 that, before and during the transitional period from 1 June to 31 October 2007, there would be a greater than average amount of property on the market to take advantage of the relaxation of the requirement to have a full HIP. The risk of damage to the market has been avoided by the relaxation of the requirement to include an HCR. Other HIP requirements may have an impact but far less of an effect upon market confidence.

6.3.4   New procedures

It is expected that for most property sales an estate agent will assume the role of the Responsible Person. The estate agent will need to prepare or be provided with the HIP before the start of marketing. The agent should adopt procedures to record requests from buyers for a copy of the HIP and to obtain the information he wants from a buyer before he issues a copy. The compliance procedures adopted by an estate agent will vary according to whether the HIP contains an

HCR rather than just an EPC, given the sensitivity and detail of information contained in the HCR.

The estate agent may wish to consider the basis on which HIPs will be made available for inspection at his offices, by appointment or on demand, and as to how staff will deploy the HIP or parts of it in the course of meetings with potential buyers. Where full HIPs with detailed information are produced or containing an HCR it may be prudent to retrieve copies of HIPs from unsuccessful buyers after a sale has been agreed, as the only persons thereafter needing to rely upon the HIP will be the actual buyer and his advisers.

As well as additional office facilities to allow space for inspection of a HIP to take place the agent may have to consider additional staffing needs and training. Depending upon the size and complexity of a HIP, preparing a copy and checking its accuracy will take time. Pagination of the HIP is permitted (Sched.1, para.2) and would simplify this process. The agent also needs to consider whether any copying charge received from a potential buyer should be placed in a client account and refunded to the seller or set against the cost of the HIP. These charges will only belong to the agent if his marketing agreement makes that clear. The estate agent may also require inspection to take place under supervision to ensure documents are not removed from the HIP or defaced and to check the suitability of the potential buyer for the property under discussion.

The estate agent's checklists should include procedures for updating of the HIP, which may be desirable so far as authorised information is concerned but will be obligatory for required documents and incomplete documentation (see regs.15, 16, 18, 19 and 20). There is no obligation to provide updated copies of HIPs that have already been distributed. This may, however, be a service that buyers will come to expect.

It is anticipated that estate agents will need to look carefully at their marketing agreements with sellers to ensure there is adequate protection for the agent and his staff in terms of clear instructions, accuracy of information and terms concerning payment of fees. Like the seller, the estate agent will need to consider his role as Responsible Person and the duties he must perform. He should also consider the following:

- an indemnity for claims deriving from misleading information given by the seller or any third-party HIP supplier;
- where the agent provides the HIP a warranty for any information supplied by the seller;
- a requirement for the seller to notify changes to information or documents in the HIP;
- a requirement for the seller to notify any change of circumstances and willingness/ability to proceed – this may cause conflict or dispute in cases where withdrawal triggers a liability to pay for the HIP;

- provisions for payment for services and the HIP including any loan agreement for deferred payment where interest is claimed (subject to the estate agent complying with any requirements of the Consumer Credit Act 1974);
- maintaining a register of HIPs and record of buyers' requests for the HIP and the number of copies provided or inspection facilities made available with dates and identification of buyers;
- conditions as to disclosure of the HIP and to obtaining its return from buyers who are not proceeding to buy the property;
- the information required from a buyer to enable the agent to decide whether a copy of the HIP should be provided and to comply with the seller's instructions;
- additional costs that may be incurred to meet requests for inspection of the HIP and to provide and send copies;
- fixing the cost of preparing copies, collecting the charges from potential buyers and agreeing whether it is client money;
- procedures for terminating the estate agent's retainer bringing to an end the Responsible Person obligations;
- procedures to halt marketing in the event of the property being taken off the market temporarily or on termination of the seller's instructions;
- terms for handling complaints;
- terms of indemnity insurance to protect against claims for inaccurate or misleading information; and
- retention of the HIP for six months after a sale, withdrawal from the market or termination of instructions so as to comply with the enforcement procedures in s.167(3).

6.3.5   Claims

The estate agent will want to be protected from claims arising out of the HIP and for arrangements to exist for these to be passed on to the supplier of the HIP or the subcontractor who prepares any component part of it, such as the search reports, EPC or HCR. The estate agent will not wish to have responsibility for errors and omissions over which he has no control and which may not fall within his area of expertise. Regulation 32 provides limited protection for estate agents in relation to a penalty charge notice so long as he has reasonable grounds to believe that the HIP is compliant.

Whilst trade associations may provide their members with precedent documentation and guidelines, care will be needed in relation to non-standard circumstances – special conditions or requirements will need separate consideration.

If the estate agent is part of a large organisation, the HIP may be prepared through or by that organisation's marketing department. If not, the agent will have to weigh up the competing benefits and drawbacks of being the producer of the HIP rather than just a conduit for its preparation. In circumstances where the HCR is mandatory many independent estate agents view the potential difficulties and complexities to outweigh the prospect of a small financial return. At best, the HIP is regarded as an add-on to the marketing service and its cost would be too high to be absorbed within the selling fee structure. Most agents would therefore prefer to be given a completed HIP with a disk from which copies can be run off as needed and rely upon an indemnity from the HIP provider against claims. Most agents would also require a support service from the HIP provider to deal with buyers' questions about the HIP documents. If the agent wishes or is required to handle any questions in-house then a summary or report on the HIP would be needed. Care will be needed to ensure that buyers are not given additional information verbally that may at a later date be alleged to have been relied upon. Where the HCR is not mandatory, the estate agents may favour in-house production or advise a seller to seek searches, title documents and other required elements through their solicitor while the estate agent prepares the index, sale statement and the property particulars following his usual inspection to measure and value.

6.3.6 Production of the Energy Performance Certificate

The EPC must be produced by an accredited assessor, and many estate agents may consider acquiring accreditation, details of which are awaited. The production of the EPC depends on the collection of data from the home and applying the calculation tools approved by the Building Research Establishment and the Department for the Environment, Food and Rural Affairs.

6.4 HOME INSPECTOR

Not all surveyors will be HIs, nor all HIs, surveyors. It had been anticipated that the first wave of HIs would be qualified surveyors who, through their experience, were able to acquire the additional HI qualification after a short period of additional training and examination. Members of RICS having their professional qualification can, through the 'Safe As' scheme, obtain the qualification of DipHI. The HI must belong to and be licensed by an approved certification scheme under Part 7 of the Regulations. New proposals may emerge that will enable qualified surveyors to undertake continuing professional development (CPD) or other additional training in order to authorise them automatically and without further examination to be licensed to carry out an HCR.

A number of training organisations are offering courses to train non-surveyors for the DipHI qualification. Course details are available on the Internet (see www.assetskills.org, www.abbeqa.co.uk and www.pirltd.org.uk).

The HI who prepares an HCR will have responsibility for mistakes/negligent errors to a seller, a buyer and a lender as well as to the person who commissions the report. In the past a surveyor would be instructed by the buyer/lender to carry out the survey/valuation with no responsibility to the seller. His professional indemnity insurance policy was available to meet legitimate claims brought by those entitled to rely upon the report. The terms on which the new type of indemnity cover is offered extends protection as required by the Regulations.

The HCR does appear, in some respects, to be similar to the traditional Homebuyers Report and Valuation but there are new and additional requirements to be met in relation to the EPC. New regulations will be issued to deal with the terms on which an EPC is to be offered, as it will be a stand-alone requirement at the introduction of HIPs. There will be scope to limit responsibility by recommending that further or expert advice be obtained in respect of any aspect of a building where there is cause for concern. The minimum limit of indemnity insurance cover is £1,000,000 for each and every claim with a maximum excess of £2,500.

The HI will have to carry out the HCR in accordance with the terms of a fixed form of contract provided by his certification scheme and this will contain the minimum statutory terms set out in para.2 of Sched.5. He will be subject to codes of conduct that will regulate his duties and responsibilities including possible conflicts of interest and the way in which the inspection will be conducted.

It will be made clear by the code of conduct of any certified scheme that care will be needed to avoid both real and perceived conflicts of interest (see **para.4.5**). HIs will have to separate any work over and above the HCR remit into a separate contract whether it is with the seller, the buyer or the lender. Areas for ancillary work include the seller's need for estimates of the cost of any remedial work and, for the buyer, a valuation of the property and estimate of the cost of any work to meet a buyer's specific needs. The HI may be asked to provide similar information for a proposed lender.

If the HCR is reinstated to a mandatory requirement, demand could be anticipated for pre-HCR inspections and advice. If these are widely marketed and competitively priced many potential sellers could want to call for such an appraisal of their property's health and well-being. Failing this, an adverse HCR would appear on the register as a continuing black mark against the property that could affect the saleability of the property and not just the price. Buyers are often wary of a property that is revealed as suffering from potential subsidence or damp problems. The seller may prefer to have any remedial work carried out in accordance with his own timescale and at a price he can negotiate, rather than under pressure from a buyer. In the past, the discovery of a problem such as subsidence or damp has often resulted in a price reduction attributed to the cost of the remedial work.

Any work carried out by the HI or any surveyor outside the terms of reference of an HCR should limit the scope of responsibility to a named person rather than accept the wide range of responsibility in the HCR (and the Contracts (Rights of Third Parties) Act 1999) to buyers and lenders in addition to the seller.

6.5   LENDERS

The CML has indicated that some of its members agree 'in principle' to accept an HCR in place of their usual survey requirement in some cases, but this is neither certain nor the universal position. Detailed infrastructure would need to be in place before approbation could be given. It remains to be seen to what extent conveyancers would be required to evaluate any HCR in the HIP under the requirements of the CML Lenders' Handbook. Whilst the HCR is considered by the government to be 'robust' and an improvement on the RICS Homebuyers Report and Valuation it does not provide a valuation of the property other than for insurance purposes.

The government expect that over time the valuation assessment for most standard properties will be undertaken otherwise than by physical inspection and as lenders gain confidence in the use of property price databases and their own knowledge banks to support the valuation decision. However, until automated valuation models (AVM) become the norm, lenders will require a valuation that will, as now, be paid for by the buyer. Lenders may wish to employ HIs to carry out the valuation. For the foreseeable future valuations will be required where the loan to value ration exceeds 70 per cent. In July 2006 a research paper commissioned by the CML, *Mortgage Lenders, HIPs and the Future of Valuations*, stated:

> AVMs, however, are unlikely to become the default valuation method. After five years, lenders estimate that AVMs will account for about 40% of valuations with a physical inspection accounting for about half. Drive by and desk top valuations will make up the remainder

It appears to be assumed by government that lenders will rely upon credit scoring of their mortgage applicants and make lending decisions based on the strength of the covenant rather than looking primarily to the value of the property offered as security for the loan. There is an obvious paradox in that the HI cannot provide the seller with a valuation as part of the HCR but the same person may do so for the buyer and buyer's lender.

One major negative for the lender (and defaulting borrowers) is the situation following repossession where the lender will have to provide a HIP for a subsequent sale. This will take time to prepare and may offer less information compared to other properties on the market. This may affect the price achieved and will add to the cost of sale and thereby increase the debt of the borrower. A similar problem would arise were the market to suffer 'negative equity' problems as in the early 1990s or where the owner has overborrowed.

As more homes come to be inspected and registered, the standard of maintenance and physical condition might improve thus reducing one element of the risk from the lender's point of view. This is now a more distant prospect as a result of the change announced in July 2006.

6.6   PROPERTY DEVELOPERS

As discussed in **para.2.6** different obligations apply in respect of new homes both where being sold 'off-plan' and 'under construction'. In place of an HCR a report in the form specified by Sched.7 to the Regulations is needed. In addition, a predicted energy performance certificate will be required. No time scales are imposed so neither of these has to be completed within the three months prior to marketing.

If the property becomes physically complete before the sale is completed or after marketing has begun, then, in accordance with reg.19, as it presently stands, the following are required:

(i)   an EPC in substitution for the predicted certificate;
(ii) a new homes warranty complying with Sched.6 to the Regulations with the warranty terms and a cover note.

If there is no Sched.6 warranty, an HCR is required. All other components of the HIP will need to be available for each new home. At the time of writing these provisions await amendment.

If a developer is marketing a large number of homes, it is feasible that the developer will prepare, so far as possible, a generic pack with title documents, searches, Sched.7 reports and an EPC that is acceptable for all properties at the FPM for the development, with the result that this information could be seriously out of date by the time when the last property is sold.

6.7   SOLICITOR

6.7.1   Acting for the seller

Solicitors face a challenge in meeting the demand from clients who will need both a HIP and advice across a spectrum of issues concerning detailed aspects of the new home-selling process. Where commercial HIP providers supply a HIP to an estate agent enabling the agent to get on with the marketing work, many solicitors could be excluded from acting for former clients. Although the HIP provision could theoretically be sold as a stand-alone service it seems, in such circumstances, highly probable that the person preparing the HIP will seek and obtain the instructions for the conduct of the conveyancing on the subsequent sale.

Commercial HIP providers will decide whether to operate exclusively in the business to business (b2b) market or whether they are equipped to deal with the end consumer. It is here that solicitors have a telling advantage if clients are fully aware of their services. Solicitors habitually take responsibility in a direct client relationship and there are many choices and decisions to be made in dealing with various aspects of the pack that benefit from face-to-face consultation with an accessible solicitor.

The main change brought about by the HIP is the shift in point of time for the publication of information about a property that is for sale. Where details of the title, property information and local searches have hitherto been provided after acceptance of an offer, this work is now moved to the pre-marketing stage. There are additions such as the EPC (and possibly the HCR) to consider and also advice about the degree of additional information that it is appropriate to include as authorised information. Some sellers in certain situations may need the HIP to be as comprehensive as possible so as to avoid delays at a later stage. In most cases, however, the balance struck in the Regulations favours a minimal pack and this could, in the majority of cases, turn out to be largely irrelevant or disconnected from the subsequent conveyancing process which starts when agreed terms have been struck between the seller and buyer.

The legal work for the HIP involves obtaining and checking information and documents and then assembling them with an index and sale statement. These can follow the form and format of the suggested forms that are the subject of further consultation. They do not have to – they just need to contain the prescribed information found in the relevant schedules. These can be prepared by a seller acting for himself or by anyone else on behalf of the seller, but both documents are important and carry potential liability if incomplete or inaccurate. In the case of search reports previously undertaken by the buyer's representative and at the cost of the buyer they must be obtained for the seller in the form required by Scheds.8, 9 and 10 to the Regulations.

However, as matters presently stand, it is unlikely that the buyer's legal representative can be justified in not carrying out separate searches at the appropriate time for the purpose of exchanging contracts. This will remain the position so long as the date for search reports remains fixed by reg.14(2). The age limit of three months at the FPM translates into the fact that searches could be much older than that by the date an offer is made and accepted and later still by the time an exchange of contracts takes place. There is no standard mechanism for updating or extending the protection of an existing official search of the local land charges register or local authority enquiries.

Since the HIP must be complete at FPM (subject to limited exceptions) there will be pressure to act quickly if the seller wishes marketing to begin right away. In the case of leaseholds there are likely to be delays whilst information is obtained from third parties such as accountants or managing agents. Legal issues arise if any defects in the lease are uncovered that require deeds of variation, rectification or indemnity. Early discovery of title problems for both freehold and leasehold property may enable issues to be resolved if timing allows. In some cases, and for speed, an indemnity insurance policy may be arranged in order to reduce uncertainty and delay at a later stage. In the case of leaseholds and commonholds much of the detailed information that will be wanted by a buyer has been placed in the category of authorised information. This is intended to slim down the main requirements for the pack and speed the initial pack production in such cases.

The provision of relevant information about the use of the property can be provided within the provisions of Sched.11 to the Regulations and can follow the form available at **www.communities.gov.uk** (see also **Appendix G**) (subject to ongoing consultation). The topics listed do not correspond exactly to the questions on the Law Society Sellers' Property Information Form but it is believed that the information can be supplied in this format.

Adopting the analogy of auction packs, the seller's solicitor may be expected by his client to advise on possible defects in title and to consider what steps might be taken, before marketing, to remedy anything which may prejudice a sale. Delays arising at a later date may be particularly irritating to a seller who has incurred the costs of the HIP and therefore mistakenly takes the view that the sale will proceed without any queries or delay.

Estate agents (and sellers) will be concerned to know how any queries from a buyer on material in the HIP will be handled. There may be time-consuming explanations needed and if not given competently there is an exposure to complaints and liability for giving inaccurate or misleading information from which both sellers and agents will want protection. Solicitors may be asked to provide summaries and explanations of the HIP either within it as an authorised document under reg.9(c) or separately. Such work, if carried out as part of the solicitor's legal practice, will be covered by his professional indemnity (PI) insurance. Care must be taken to identify who is the client and to ensure that where any documents are updated, removed or replaced, the summary or explanation is amended.

With the aid of well-directed marketing strategies, solicitors may be able to encourage clients to come to them first before the process starts in order to obtain advice on various aspects of the HIP, its preparation and the nature of the contractual relationships that are needed with agents, the HI and any other service provider introduced by an estate agent. This will take place long before a contract with a buyer for the sale of their property becomes relevant.

The terms of the estate agent's marketing agreement will need to be explained and appreciated by sellers especially if it contains, quite properly, protective clauses in connection with the agent's fees and role as Responsible Person. Other aspects on which advice might be needed are:

- the role of the Responsible Person and any indemnity requested by the estate agent from the seller;
- additional information required from a potential buyer to avoid requests for a pack from those who are not genuine potential buyers;
- whether it is necessary for the seller to be advised of the number of copies of the pack provided or inspection facilities made available to potential buyers;
- conditions as to disclosure of the HIP and to obtaining its return from buyers who are not proceeding with a purchase;
- procedures for terminating the estate agent's retainer so as to bring to an end the Responsible Person obligations and obtain possession of the original HIP and free from claims of copyright;

- arrangements for temporary withdrawal of the property from the market;
- procedures to protect a seller from suddenly finding himself in the role of Responsible Person;
- the obligation to advise anyone who requests a HIP as to who can supply this.

If the estate agent is not preparing the HIP but is engaging a HIP provider, sellers will need to be educated as to the possible implications. There are issues as to how future choice and decisions may be restricted regarding the use of an alternative estate agent or change of solicitor and issues about potential liability for any quality failure. The terms of any copyright in the HIP and linkage to the terms for payment for the HIP also need consideration. Further, there may be obligations that could arise as a result of the cross-selling of other products such as insurance and services such as building or utility supplies. There may also be a need to explain to the seller the disclosure of any referral payments passing between any of the parties involved in the sale. Sellers will need guidance as to the usefulness of authorised documents and especially the pricing of additional components such as optional search reports.

The solicitor can offer the service of being the HIP provider and arrange for the preparation of the EPC and/or HCR on behalf of the seller. In this case the solicitor may be exposed to a claim in respect of the negligence of the HI but it is expected that this will come within the terms of the HI's standard indemnity policy. As HIs are required by their regulating bodies to hold cover, any claims are likely to be passed on to their insurers.

The solicitor would need to work to an agreed timetable to carry out the 'required' searches and any appropriate 'authorised' searches and make disclosure of title documents. The solicitor's PI insurance (a minimum of £2 million from 1 October 2005) gives the Responsible Person comfort from an 'indemnity against claims' point of view. The estate agent's fee position would not be compromised by the solicitor carrying out the work – it is what he largely does now, but in a different order.

It can be envisaged that the seller would ask the solicitor to organise the EPC and/or HCR and possibly also recommend an estate agent for marketing of the property. Arguably, the choice of the HI by a solicitor would be more disinterested than a selection made by the estate agent. In Denmark the independence of the HI proved to be a matter of some contention, with the result that the law was changed. The appointment of the HI has now been removed from the estate agent's control and the seller must appoint the HI directly.

The estate agent may well need a summary of the HIP for his own use and, if permitted by the solicitor, for giving to buyers. Clearly, responsibility will attach to this most useful and necessary guide to the HIP. As stated earlier, it can either form part of the HIP or be provided separately (reg.9(c)). Solicitors will need to take care to limit their exposure to claims if they become involved in this aspect.

Changes to the Solicitors' Practice Rules 1990 are needed so that solicitors, when acting as estate agents, have recourse to the necessary approved redress scheme should a client make a complaint. It is also hoped that the Solicitors' Practice Rules will be relaxed to enable solicitors to compete for instructions on level terms with market competitors. Failing this, solicitors may look to form alternative business models for providing pack services under the Solicitors Separate Business Code. The guidance to the Solicitors' Practice Rules may be modified on a number of topics including Practice Rule 6. As an example, Practice Rule 6(3)A presently requires a solicitor who is instructed by a seller client to deal with more than one purchaser to notify the potential purchaser(s) of the existence of other negotiations and states that 'each prospective purchaser must be notified each time a decision is taken to deal with any further prospective purchaser'. Obviously, the fact that more than one prospective purchaser asks for a HIP could lead to a breach of this rule as it stands today. **Appendix H** sets out the Law Society's guidance as issued by the Ethics Committee of the Regulation Board as an initial and draft response. Changes are also expected to be made to the Law Society's National Conveyancing Protocol and Standard Conditions of Sale.

6.7.2   Acting for the buyer

The solicitor acting for a buyer is, in future, more likely to be consulted prior to the conclusion of the initial price negotiations. This may well involve explanation or advice concerning aspects of the HIP. These could relate to the age of documents and adequacy of search reports and omission of authorised or other relevant documents and information. If there is an HCR it may contain notes to conveyancers that need to be examined and checked. After a draft contract is issued the work of evaluation and reporting is unchanged. A decision can be taken as to whether it is necessary or prudent to commission up-to-date local searches. Those supplied in the HIP will be checked critically for their age and scope. This issue will need to be most carefully considered as the buyer's solicitor remains responsible to the buyer and the lender as the doctrine of caveat emptor still applies. The client's or lender's instructions may require additional searches to be made and further enquiries to be pursued on planning or require some other detailed information to be provided. This will vary according to the buyer's particular interest and needs. It is assumed by the writer that the buyer's solicitor will be expected in every case to check the currency of title information, searches, the EPC and any disclosed HCRs. Current practice may be changed if the lenders' procedures are adapted to accept the seller's disclosures and guidance would be welcomed at an early date. There is no age limit placed on the EPC (reg.14(3)), but this may be reviewed as a result of the government's statement on 18 July 2006.

6.7.3   Acting for the lender

The report on title and the CML Lender's Handbook will come under review and reliance may come to be placed on the seller's HIP rather than the buyer's solicitor's report on title, but this potential change lies further in the future.

6.8   SPECIALIST HIP PROVIDERS

The emergence of commercial HIP providers was a phenomenon of the period up to 18 July 2006. Many organisations wanted to operate alongside traditional service providers by supplying a particular element, if not all of the content, of the HIP to enable the estate agent to market the property (for example, search companies). Others intended to establish a 'one stop shop' offering an integrated service within a single organisation or group directly to the consumer (Rightmove were a particular example of this). A third group of providers were newcomers to the property industry including utility companies, printers and internet sellers who see the house mover as an important consumer of a variety of services. A fourth group comprised software companies seeking to facilitate HIP production as the sub-contract suppliers to front-line professionals, such as solicitors.

The charges estimated for HIP assembly were projected at around £100. Any significant profit in the preparation and presentation of the information for the HIP therefore appears heavily dependent upon other income streams. These could take the form of referral fees, insurance products or other services, such as conveyancing or estate agency. Competing with HIP providers' encroachment into the market, estate agents, solicitors, surveyors and lenders will expand their offerings to develop some or all of the new services that become relevant to sellers and buyers.

The seller's HIP provider, whoever it is, can obtain information through a number of supply channels and may seek one arrangement for convenience or trial a number of ways of dealing with the requirements of the HIP. After obtaining the basic information the HIP needs to be assembled and presented for use and in this respect some assurance of quality will be essential. The seller is primarily liable for the cost even if that cost is deferred or ultimately recovered from the buyer and the efficacy of the HIP will be tested before the time for payment arrives.

There are a number of industry specialists who could decide now, or at a later date when the market has settled down to the new reforms, to move into the business of supplying HIPs to the front-line players who have the direct relationship with consumers. Estate agents could be ready buyers of this service, whether provided from the ranks of professional firms such as solicitors or from search companies or 'professional' HIP providers.

Indemnity insurance cover will become a necessity for all HIP providers in order to give comfort to estate agent customers. Conflicts of interest will need to be considered from every viewpoint especially where the provider has links to those offering other services to seller or buyer. Whilst government might not wish to regulate the new HIP provider industry, consideration will need to be given to ensuring that a seller who chooses a HIP provider is not at a disadvantage compared with a seller whose HIP is prepared by a regulated body. This means that HIP providers should be required, at a minimum, to belong to a self-regulating body that requires its members to hold indemnity insurance, to comply with codes of conduct for conflicts of interest and confidentiality and a scheme for complaints and redress.

Where HIP providers are providing a retail service they ought to be made subject to the money laundering regulations, failing which a person wishing to sell a property purchased at any time in the past with dubious funds could avoid the kind of scrutiny that estate agents, solicitors and other property professionals must carry out under those regulations. Avoidance would be too easy if an individual or company could arrange for a pack to be prepared by a non-complying HIP provider and then sell the property through private advertising.

There were, in July 2006, approximately 145 suppliers of components for HIPs of which over 40 had joined a trade association called the Association of Home Information Pack Providers (AHIPP). Its aim is to set the standards for their industry and to agree upon protocols to reduce what will otherwise be a fragmented and confusing array of offerings. A number have declared that they would no longer be involved following the announcement of 18 July but negotiations remain in progress for government 'pump priming'.

Rightmove plc published a prospectus in 2006 declaring the intention 'to become a major player in the HIPs business' and announced in early July that 400,000 sale commitments had been secured for providing HIPs. Following the government change of policy Rightmove announced on 26 July that it would discontinue its investment in HIPs as the market was unsuitable for their continued investment. The business model had looked to take advantage of their presence at a number of levels in the market as agents and surveyors, acting for themselves and as an Internet portal for competitor agents.

Other business models are not so affected, Macdonald, Dettwiler and Associates Ltd (the search provider) continues to develop a HIP solution with the Law Society (MDA Advantage), providing a suite of tools to enable solicitors to prepare packs. Legal Marketing Services (LMS), as the preferred supplier of the National Association of Estate Agents (NAEA) retains its core business introducing marketing and other services and earning commission from introducing agents and lawyers and surveyors, and will continue its involvement in the emerging HIP market. Other suppliers which are offering a niche service to a sector or which rely upon a core business in searches are also declaring that they will continue their involvement.

Key points

Seller:

- decision-making and timetable; coinciding with purchase;
- collating information about property to be sold;
- obtain pre-marketing advice and valuation;
- obtain pre-HCR inspection; consider inclusion in HIP;
- obtain EPC;

- consider terms of contract with estate agent;
- consider who will be instructed to prepare HIP and cost;
- consider portability of HIP;
- set terms for profiling buyers and distribution of HIP;
- go ahead with marketing and negotiate on offers;
- instructions for sale contract to solicitor;
- consider fees and any credit agreement.

Buyer:

- complete Internet research within chosen price and location;
- apply to lender to certify availability of loan;
- present personal information and bona fides to estate agent;
- consider timing of any related sale or other transaction;
- list property requirements and consider packs for potential properties;
- raise additional questions with estate agent and own adviser;
- seek advice on price negotiations;
- seek withdrawal of property from market when 'under offer'.

Estate agent:

- prepare new marketing agreement and terms for HIP production;
- set payment terms for different functions;
- arrange for referral of pack preparation and EPC and possible HCR;
- check all third-party contracts;
- consider terms of marketing media;
- check all new procedures for potential liability;
- set up record keeping;
- set up HIP inspection facilities;
- check termination of instructions procedures and follow-ups;
- check PI insurance;
- instigate regular staff training and updating;
- appoint compliance officer and complaints officer;
- consider how to deal with queries on HIP from buyers;
- check terms of membership of redress scheme.

Home Inspector:

- consider terms of engagement with seller and with estate agents for EPC/HCR;
- consider terms for work outside HCR;
- check terms of PI insurance;
- attend training for CPD;
- set up procedures to identify conflicts of interest;
- training on code of conduct;
- appoint compliance and complaints officers.

Lenders:

- consider information needed in addition to HIP and EPC/HCR;
- instigate valuation procedures;
- consider repossessions policy;

Property developers:

- consider in-house HIP preparation documentation;
- investigate out-sourcing of HIPs provision;
- provide Sched.7 report and predicted EPC;
- arrange approved warranty scheme under Sched.6 and EPC.

Solicitors:

- educate and train clients and staff;
- develop marketing material for HIP services;
- consider professional rules for contract races and complaints;
- offer pre-marketing advice on new contractual arrangements for sellers;
- prepare procedures for advising buyers on HIPs;
- consider separate business models.

HIP providers:

- decide whether b2b or b2c (business to business or business to consumer);
- agree relationship with estate agent;
- arrange referrals to HI and lawyer;
- consider liabilities to others – seller-buyer-agent;
- arrange 'umbrella' insurance;
- consider money laundering protection;
- consider complaints handling;
- consider supply contracts and referral arrangements.

7 PREPARING THE HOME INFORMATION PACK

7.1 PACK PREPARATION IN GENERAL

Before 18 July 2006 it had been widely advertised by commercial HIP suppliers that a straightforward HIP could be assembled in five days. MacDonald, Dettwiler and Associates Ltd (MDA Advantage), the Law Society's chosen provider, confirms this for freehold registered properties. It is difficult, however, to make any accurate estimate for leasehold property, for the creation of new interests and for unregistered land where a longer period for preparation will be needed. Owners of unregistered land may be advised to register title before attempting to put the property on the market. Knowing that marketing cannot commence until a HIP has been prepared, the seller must decide how to compile the HIP and who is to compile it for him. Although an HCR is no longer mandatory some period of time will be needed to organise an EPC. Local searches take unpredictable periods to obtain but marketing may commence without them.

Under the present system the seller's first port of call is a local estate agent, except in the case of larger country properties where a specialist agency may be the recognised venue for price appraisal and marketing advice. It is expected that all agents will wish to offer HIP preparation as part of their service and it will be either 'in-house' or 'bought in'. If the estate agent arranges for the preparation and delivery of the HIP then contractual safeguards are needed for the protection of both parties. The estate agent can refer the sourcing of HIP components and assembly to an outside HIP provider company. There will be a multitude of variants and AHIPP are seeking to establish common standards for its member organisations. They are characterised as 'HIP providers' but many have primary expertise as software suppliers or search companies with systems that can source the information 'required' for the HIP which they have grafted onto an organisation for HIP assembly. It seems unlikely that such organisations will market their services directly to the public, preferring to remain in the b2b arena. Distribution of ready-made packs to front-line providers such as agents, solicitors and surveyors presents a large target market estimated at 1.5 million packs per annum. There could, however, be offers of HIPs or HIP elements such as the EPC directly to consumers via the Internet made by mainstream providers or intermediaries. In these circumstances the Consumer Protection (Distance Selling) Regulations 2000, SI 2000/2334 as amended, will apply. Guidance was issued by the OFT on 12 September 2006 (see the 'Business information' section of OFT website (**www.oft.gov.uk**)).

Sellers may consult a solicitor or be referred for the preparation of the HIP to a solicitor working in a collaborative relationship with an estate agent. Marketing organisations that promote HIP schemes can simply refer incoming instructions to prepare a HIP to a member firm of solicitors.

In most high street locations there is, at present, no single professional service that is equipped, by itself, to offer a 'one-stop' shop producing all relevant elements of the HIP and so outsourcing will in most cases be needed to procure one or more of the following:

- the HCR and EPC, both of which require a physical inspection by an HI or accredited assessor;
- local authority searches and enquiries that are subject to new rules as to transparency of terms and consumer protection (a personal search may be chosen by the seller as the cheapest and quickest source of reports);
- drainage and sewerage enquiry reports from the water authority but also available from search providers;
- official copies of title registers and documents obtained from the Land Registry; and
- an index map search.

If information is to be provided in respect of the matters specified in Sched.11, input is needed from the seller and certain information may have to be obtained from third-party sources. Planning information held by the local planning authority and in some cases by regional bodies is one example, and estate management information held by landlords or their managing agents is another.

Some information is available speedily from a search portal such as the NLIS hub. The OFT report (*Property Searches: A Market Study*, September 2005 (OFT 810)) recommends that electronic access be extended and be made available to more operators, and two new licences have now been authorised. Local Authorities as a whole have yet to respond positively which results in a 'postcode lottery' when search information is required.

7.2   ESTATE AGENTS

Estate agents can commission and collate much of the information for the seller. Some agents will recognise that this additional work carries with it both responsibility and cost. In addition, they will be concerned that sellers may only be prepared to pay the disbursement element incurred in the work, expecting the time spent in preparing the HIP to be included within the agency commission. If that were on the usual speculative 'no sale no fee' basis it would not be attractive to most independent estate agents. However, some estate agents may see an opportunity to move towards structured fees payable in respect of a menu of distinctive and separated services.

The HIP comprises a variety of documents which do not originate from any single organisation. The person assembling the HIP may therefore have little or no control over delay caused by any other supplier involved in the process. Organisations offering a 'one stop shop' may advertise the HIP as if it is the product of a seamless process but the reality is otherwise.

For a seller wishing to dispose of a property in the spring, when historically the property market has been buoyant, preparation of the HIP may need to be put in hand early in the year. This is especially the case if the seller decides to take the precautionary step of a pre-HCR inspection to reduce the risk of an adverse HCR or buyer's survey on the property. Marketing will generally require a longer lead-time and be more of a planned process than in the past.

There has been much criticism from the pressure group SPLINTA (Sellers' Pack Law Is Not The Answer) whose main contention is that the liquidity of the market depends heavily on impulse transactions. These are encouraged within the current system and will no longer be sensible, or even feasible, in the context of a 'full' HIP.

On 27 June 2006 research was published by Oxford Economic Forecasting (OEF) whose study considered the economic impact of a reduction in housing transactions arising from the imposition of a compulsory HIP on a largely discretionary market (*The Impact of Home Information Packs*). Two scenarios were assessed, representing small and medium percentage falls: firstly, a 10 per cent reduction in housing transactions in the first year following the introduction of HIPs, gradually rising by 1 per cent per annum over the next four years; and, secondly, a 25 per cent reduction in year one, rising at 2 per cent per annum over the next four years.

The report indicated that unemployment would rise and GDP and net revenue to the government would fall, even taking into account that new VAT will be generated on HIPs. The conclusions in this report were not contradicted by any government statement but were followed by the 18 July 2006 statement which demonstrated a change of approach in implementation (see **Appendix D**). Having regard to the emphasis placed on the EPC from 9 June 2006 and after the Regulations were announced on 14 June 2006 it is apparent that the timeline for implementation could not be met in relation to HIs and their certification schemes.

7.3   HOME INSPECTORS

The HI's role was crucial to the original scheme that included a mandatory HCR. Although HIs were unlikely to have the time or inclination to prepare the whole HIP, larger groupings and panel organisations for surveyors did envisage offering the full range of HIP preparation services so that sellers and agents could access all necessary services through them. (Examples are Habitus and Blue Box Partners owned by Allied Surveyors plc.) The DipHI qualification will authorise the holder to prepare the EPC.

7.4   SEARCH COMPANIES

Personal search companies are developing systems to deliver their components quickly and at a reasonable cost. They are aware of the market demand for an updating feature or insurance products to extend the life of the information provided in a search. Many see the opportunity to grow their role in support of estate agents and to offer assembly of the HIP.

7.5   HIP PROVIDER ORGANISATIONS

Where commercial organisations take the lead role it is expected that a small number of qualified and skilled professionals may be employed to supervise the assembly of large numbers of HIPs for onward distribution. There are difficulties with this approach where 'personal' information is required from the seller. For example, a new homes warranty (compliant with Sched.6) issued when a new property is first sold, will be relevant for up to 10 years. It will need to be disclosed if there is a sale within the warranty period as it is a 'required' document (see reg.8(i)). It is likely to be held by the seller or by the solicitor or lender who holds any deeds. This will also be the case with any detailed drawings or plans for alterations or other works carried out (authorised for inclusion under reg.9(c), (m) and (n)). Information on commonhold and leaseholds such as regulations, insurance and management information may be obtainable from third parties, but the seller will, in most cases, need to play a part in the provision or verification of information. It is intended that 'required' information should only extend to that which a commonhold or leasehold seller already has or can easily obtain. Replacing mislaid information as to regulations, commonhold community statements and commonhold assessment and service charge statements and accounts, proposed works and details of managing agents would need input or authority from the seller in any case where duplicates are needed and a fee will be incurred.

Over-arching portal type HIP provider companies may emanate from search providers, utility companies or from lenders. Others are start-up companies who may seek to supply the HIP to estate agents at a low cost. The driver to this business model is that volume will keep prices down. The organisation can commission the EPC and HCR by instructing a freelance or employed licensed HI. The introduction of this work holds out the prospect of referral fee income. They also have the potential to generate referral fee income for selling 'cases' to solicitors for the work at the 'post-offer' stage even if the solicitor's involvement has not been required before that time. They will need to acquire search reports and obtain copy title documents from the Land Registry. Since it is not a requirement to provide the information in Sched.11, it may be possible to compile the HIP without direct contact with the seller at least for a 'second-hand' registered freehold property more than 10 years old.

This does not seem feasible for the sale of unregistered land. It is unlikely that in most cases a HIP will have an adequate level of disclosure to enable the buyer's advisers to make any meaningful saving of time. By reducing the standard HIP requirements the Regulations compromise the desired objective of speeding the process to an early exchange of contracts.

Companies may acquire more prominence if and when they engage in aggressive marketing. By advertising directly to sellers and offering to complete the HIP in advance of marketing, they would be in a position to refer business to other professionals later in the process. Personal information could be acquired online without any direct or personal contact and in those circumstances, as mentioned in **Chapter 6**, there are questions as to whether these new entrants should remain outside the regulatory net that covers solicitors and HIs as well as aspects of estate agent activity. They do not have the duties and obligations that have to be met by the current stakeholders such as compliance with money laundering regulations, the setting up of complaints and redress schemes or standards requiring client confidentiality and conflict-free services. It remains to be seen whether the new industry becomes self-regulating in any meaningful way.

As described in **Chapter 4**, the major innovation to the house selling and buying process brought about by the legislation was the requirement for an HCR and EPC – all other information is currently produced during the process between the seller's solicitor and the buyer's solicitor. Apart from introducing the HCR/EPC the essence of the reform is a change in sequencing, to encourage complete information disclosure at the pre-marketing stage rather than post-offer and acceptance.

7.6   SOLICITORS

Solicitors are the professionals best placed to become over-arching pack advisers and providers. The solicitor acting for the seller should 'know' his client and be aware of the additional information that a buyer will seek. He will either already hold or can obtain the necessary background documents and apply for other information and searches needed. A degree of professional judgment is needed to anticipate any title defects and other queries that a buyer might raise. The practice of using indemnity insurance policies to repair defective titles and leases might be reduced rather than increased if time allows for proper investigation and research into the title deeds and into the history of any problems that are identified. This outcome is far from certain, as the market will be shaped by the marketing developed by the volume HIP providers and the growth of referral businesses.

The solicitor can commission the EPC and/or HCR on instructions from the seller. He can also co-ordinate assembly of the HIP and ensure the elements have the longest possible shelf life and issue to the seller and estate agent an authentic copy in hard copy form, on a CD or online. Perhaps the biggest advantage in using a solicitor to compile the pack is the security and protection afforded to the Responsible Person – whether seller or the estate agent – by his expertise, professionalism and obligation to maintain professional indemnity insurance.

In addition, an early visit to a solicitor would enable sellers to obtain advice on all contractual aspects mentioned in **Chapter 6**. There is the marketing agreement with an estate agent to consider as well as the meaning and effect of the minimum standard terms and conditions of the HI and the standard terms in contracts with personal search providers (see **Chapter 3**). In addition, having prepared the HIP, the solicitor will be able to deal swiftly with any additional enquiries raised by or on behalf of a potential buyer and then link seamlessly to the conveyancing processes that should follow acceptance of an offer.

Guidance may be needed by a number of parties to any transaction as to the meaning of the HIP and its contents as well as the implications for any later negotiations with interested parties.

Solicitors' estate agencies that offer a property-selling service are well placed to meet the requirements of sellers by providing the HIP to a professional standard. Changes to the Solicitors' Practice Rules 1990 will be canvassed to take account of the new regime and initial, draft guidance has already been issued by the Law Society's Regulation Board (see **Appendix H**). A particular area of difficulty is the number of situations in which a solicitor who prepares a HIP might later find himself unable to act for an existing client who emerges as a buyer for that property. It is not the case that a commercial HIP provider would be considered disqualified from acting in similar circumstances.

7.7   SELLERS

There is nothing in the Act or the Regulations that prevents a seller preparing the HIP for his own sale. The required documents have been reduced in number and scope and, if the seller is prepared to invest the time, a DIY pack is a possible route for a seller. It is likely that self-help books will be published to guide the seller through the procedures. High street bookshops and stationers, as well as online publishers, may market products similar to the DIY wills, tenancy and divorce packs that are now on sale.

As well as investing the time to compile the HIP, the seller may have to fund expenses for the various components instead of enjoying the option of deferred payment that commercial HIP providers will offer.

There may also be drawbacks if the seller decides to instruct a marketing agent. The agent will have responsibility for the HIP and may be concerned as to compliance issues – an additional charge may be incurred for due diligence on the HIP before an estate agent will agree to act and become a Responsible Person. It is improbable that the defence in reg.32 (see **Chapter 8**) would cover an estate agent marketing with a DIY pack unless the agent could show that he had carried out his own due diligence.

7.8   INCOMPLETE PACKS

One of the main objections to the HIP which was raised by estate agents was the delay caused to first day marketing. It is envisaged, particularly with common-hold and leasehold property, that there could be delays in marshalling some of the required and authorised content that may be of relevance to a buyer. The fact that all the information required will have been provided at some point in time to the owner of the property will not avoid the need in most cases to apply to managing agents or to landlords. They have no statutory obligation to respond within the timescales that most sellers will require for bringing a property to the market. Legislation is being considered to meet this situation.

Regulation 15 provides some leeway by allowing a property to be marketed pro-vided that certain steps are taken and any missing information is included 'as soon as practicable'. Much may depend upon the particular component that is missing at the point the property would otherwise be marketed. A discerning seller or agent may want to ensure that buyers have all the necessary information possible. This, it is hoped, will assist them in making the decision to buy and cut down on delay and disappointment otherwise caused when information is pro-duced after an offer has been made and accepted. If a component of the HIP is added after an offer is accepted and then forwarded to a buyer during the con-veyancing process a change of mind or a delay in agreement of any term may be the result.

In an effort to meet this valid objection special rules were introduced through the Regulations to allow a property to be marketed with an incomplete HIP. However, these are complex and involve a 14-day waiting period so that it is debatable whether the relaxation will be much used.

The rules relating to documents that are unavailable are found in regs.15 and 16 and refer to documents unavailable at the FPM.

Firstly, reg 15(2) requires that 'all reasonable efforts and enquiries' must have been taken and made by the Responsible Person to obtain all 'required' docu-ments before the FPM. If any document is unavailable at that point but is expected to be available at a later date the HIP will be regarded as compliant even though not complete provided that:

- all reasonable efforts continue to be made to obtain the missing document(s);
- at least 14 days have elapsed between the date when the request for the missing document was made and the FPM.

Under reg.15(2)(b), the document must be included in the HIP as soon as pos-sible. For any document that is included under reg.15 the FPM is the date of its initial inclusion.

So that there can be no abuses or mistakes about this concession on compliance, reg.15(4) sets out in great detail that any request must be properly addressed, in the correct form, contain all necessary information and either include any payment required for the document or an undertaking to pay it. Regulation 16 provides that the day a request is delivered is the day it (or if it is made in more than one part, the last part) is served on the recipient or is received (or would be received in the normal course of post) by post at the recipient's address or left at the recipient's address or is sent by electronic communication. If the request is sent by more than one method the 14-day period starts to run from the first day of service.

If a property is marketed with an incomplete HIP under this regulation, the index must give details by stating what document is missing and what steps are being taken to obtain it. Once it arrives and is included in the HIP, that fact must also be noted on the index.

The index, sale statement, official copies from the Land Registry, index map search and Sched.7 report must be in the HIP at the FPM; they cannot be added later (reg.15(1)(b)).

7.9   UNOBTAINABLE DOCUMENTS

The rules relating to documents that are 'unobtainable' are dealt with under reg.17 (see **para.3.7**). Again, all reasonable efforts must have been made to establish that the document cannot be obtained.

7.10   AGE OF DOCUMENTS (REGULATION 14)

Certain mandatory HIP documents must be dated no earlier than three months prior to the FPM. All other HIP documents can be older than that although the most recent version available must always be included.

The following documents must therefore be replaced if they are older than three months at the FPM:

- official copies of the property title interest;
- search of the index map;
- HCR (if it becomes mandatory); and
- search reports.

At present there is no date requirement in respect of the EPC or for authorised documents. If the HCR is added to the list of authorised documents then provision will need to be made as to its age at the FPM.

7.11   UPDATING HOME INFORMATION PACKS

The Regulations provide a mechanism for 'updating' both 'required' (regs.18 and 19) and 'authorised' (reg.20) documents. Updating required documents must take place if the Responsible Person amends (e.g. a sale statement), obtains (e.g. a search) or creates a further version of a 'required' HIP document. The new version must be included in the HIP and the old removed. In the case of a property that becomes physically complete after the FPM then within 14 days after that event the report under Sched.7 must be removed and be replaced with either an HCR or a Sched.6 warranty and cover note with a separate EPC (reg.19).

Updating 'authorised' documents is optional. If a new version of a document is added to the HIP, the document it supersedes must be removed.

Where any updating occurs, the date of inclusion of the new version is the FPM for that document until such time as the pack as a whole acquires a new FPM.

The only document that should never be removed is the HCR. There are exceptions where:

- it is non-compliant with Sched.5 (reg.11);
- it was prepared for a previous seller (reg.11);
- at the FPM, original or subsequent, it is more than 12 months old.

The index must record all details of updating.

7.12   PAYMENT FOR THE HOME INFORMATION PACK

Under the new legislation most homeowners will, for the first time, have to incur liability for pre-marketing costs. These costs were estimated by the government (*Contents of the Home Information Pack: A Consultation Paper* (March 2003, ODPM), Appendix P) at the figure of £665. The figures were updated in the Regulatory Impact Assessment dated 9 June 2006 to approximately £710. VAT will be payable in addition save in respect of statutory fees. The government maintained that on a sale and purchase the costs remain broadly neutral. However, the estimates did not take into account the range of fees likely to be charged for HCRs depending on values and/or size of property or time taken. Personal search fees may increase with the new requirement for indemnity insurance and any formal redress schemes to deal with complaints. The Land Registry has already increased its fees for producing official copies from 7 August 2006 under the Land Registry Fee Order 2006, SI 2006/1332.

The omission of the requirement for the HCR and its replacement with a standalone EPC may reduce the government's estimated fees for that element by £100 to £250. On the other hand the buyer will, as before, be left to decide whether to pay for his own survey.

The seller will have to fund the costs of preparing the HIP or at least commit to this along with the cost of obtaining searches, the EPC/HCR and leasehold information. Whilst, contractually, a contribution towards this cost might be recoverable from the buyer it is more likely, even in buoyant market conditions, to be 'hidden' within the final negotiated sale price.

It had been mooted by successive government ministers that the property industry would be prepared to fund costs for a seller by deferring payment until completion of the sale. However, with 30,000 properties a week going onto the market (rather than the 40,000 mentioned by Lord Rooker in the House of Lords on 3 November 2004) that would have required substantial capital and cash flow – the bulk of the cost of the HIP comprising fees for the HCR and charges for searches. Even with no abortive transactions and working on a three-month deferment, this worked out at a funding requirement of around £180m, assuming a market of 30,000 properties a week with a cost of £500 per property for a period of 12 weeks.

It is probable that HIP providers or those providing parts of the HIP will have to assist sellers in meeting these costs by agreeing instalment payments or deferred payment terms or accepting payment by credit card. Mortgagees would be in a position to help sellers by making a loan for repayment when the mortgage is redeemed or simply adding the loan to the mortgage debt if the transaction proves abortive.

With the plethora of unsecured loans currently advertised most property owners would be able to find a way to fund payment of the HIP. Some may do so in the hope of obtaining a refund or contribution from the buyer of the property. However, in reality, most will want an arrangement that means there is no up-front cost and that the final cost is hidden within the final transaction charges. This arrangement could easily be accommodated by property selling solicitors who operate as a Solicitors' Estate Agency Ltd (SEAL) or by solicitor property selling agencies.

For sellers who are also buying a property it was argued that the costs would be mitigated to the extent that their outlay as buyers may be reduced. Currently, buyers are required to fund the cost of local searches and any survey and it remains to be seen if the HIP alters that situation. The position also seems likely to remain unchanged in the short term in that a buyer who needs mortgage finance will be required to pay a lender's valuation and survey fee.

The government's original proposals could have given rise to a similar situation to that which developed in personal injury litigation where loans were marketed to claimants who then found that the cost of the credit was bundled with marketing charges and other expenses. These offers were poorly understood, as shown by the cases now coming before the courts (see *The Accident Group Test Cases* [2003] EWHC 9020). In the case of property transactions there is similar scope for the sale of additional insurance products that may not represent value for money. Without the compulsory HCR there seems to be less risk of this development at this stage.

It is unlikely that individual estate agents or other participants in the process would be willing to become involved in loan arrangements – a consumer credit licence may be needed and the formalities of the Consumer Credit Acts of 1974 and 2006 followed. That might involve additional record keeping and other consumer protection measures such as 'cooling off' periods.

7.13   OWNERSHIP OF THE HOME INFORMATION PACK

7.13.1   Copyright issues

Who will own the pack? Bearing in mind the definition of the HIP as 'a collection of documents relating to the property or the terms on which it is or may become available for sale' (s.148(2)) this is not a simple question. There will be a number of documents obtained by different people and so ownership may not be straightforward.

Copyright can be asserted by the author of each component part, in the overall 'typographical arrangement' of the HIP, or by the commissioner (the person who asks and pays) for each constituent element to be produced. It must be remembered, however, that the HI is given little control over copyright in the HCR since wide powers are given to allow copying, lending and adaptation of the HCR (Sched.5, para.2). Similar measures may be introduced in respect of the stand-alone EPC for which, at present, there is very little regulatory provision.

Neither the Act nor the Regulations has thrown light on the question of copyright in the HIP nor has the government provided guidance, leaving the matter to be construed according to the general law of copyright. The legislation dealing with copyright (and other intellectual property rights) is contained in the Copyright, Designs and Patents Act 1988.

Copyright is commonly understood to exist only in work of a creative nature such as a book, a musical composition or a piece of visual art but in fact it extends to all original works, including those that come into being in the business arena such as advertisements, manuals and brochures. It will also protect databases, trade secrets, business plans and computer software (see **Appendix C**).

Protecting intellectual property ensures that it cannot be used or copied without the owner's permission. However, copyright, unlike a patent or trademark, is not registrable and it comes into being automatically as soon as the work takes a physical form such as being written down. Because it is not registrable, steps need to be taken to indicate that a piece of work is original and 'belongs' to a certain person or persons. The copyright symbol '©' is widely recognised and, if attached to work together with the date and name of the copyright owner, usually ensures that others know the work is copyright and should not be used, distributed or copied without permission.

Copyright usually belongs to the originator of the work unless another, to whom it then belongs, has commissioned it. The question of ownership of the HIP and copyright is examined taking the 'required' constituent elements in turn.

7.13.2   Ownership of the Home Condition Report

Someone on behalf of the seller, if not the seller himself, will have commissioned this report and either paid or be liable to pay for the inspection by the HI and production of the report. On the face of it, therefore, the HCR will 'belong' to the person who contracts for it rather than the seller and not the HI who originated it. However, Part 5 requires the HCR to be registered, which will in effect make it a public document, even though access will be limited to authorised persons. The Regulations at paragraphs.2(e) and (f) of Sched.5 contain express provisions requiring that the contract with the HI must permit copying and renting or adapting or otherwise communicating a report.

7.13.3   Ownership of searches

For letters, copyright resides with the writer/sender and not the recipient. The information contained in a search report 'belongs' to the body from which it was obtained, more often than not a statutory or statute-regulated authority. The hard return copy of the search report will belong, however, to the person who has paid for the information to be put in this written form. Schedule 7, para.4 provides that the Responsible Person may copy or issue a copy of a search report contained in a HIP.

7.13.4   Ownership of warranties and guarantees

These will belong to the seller if a payment has been made to obtain the benefit of the guarantee or warranty and the certificate that is a record of any rights.

7.13.5   Title documents and deeds

Where title information is obtained from the Land Registry a licence will be needed before reproduction of copies takes place for commercial benefit and licence from Ordnance Survey is needed for the copying of plans. The Guidance indicates that the Land Registry permits copies to be reproduced to purchasers and other relevant parties as part of the pack but the permission does not extend for any other purpose. Copyright in unregistered deeds belongs to the owner.

7.13.6   Ownership of the Home Information Pack as a whole

Taking the HIP as a whole, where various elements are contained within another document then copyright may exist in the 'typographical arrangement' – the form in which the HIP is put together. Any summary or interpretation or special layout for other documents alongside the HIP will give copyright to the producer of that document.

7.14   THE RELEVANCE OF OWNERSHIP

The ownership of the entire HIP is vital to the seller, who should be wary of any offer to prepare the HIP in return for or on condition that copyright remains with that provider. Control of an up-to-date HIP is needed in order to market the property and the person with ownership of copyright could therefore prevent others from copying or using the HIP without permission or payment.

If the seller wishes to withdraw from using one firm of estate agents and instruct another he will need to own the HIP and the copyright in it, so that he can withdraw it and deliver it to newly appointed agents. This assumes that it is complete and accurate and that another agent will accept responsibility for it. Otherwise, a fresh HIP will be needed in any event. It is suggested that this may be an underlying driver for reg.21, which gives a seller the right to ask for a copy of the HIP or any HIP document to ensure 'the accuracy' of the HIP. Without this regulation, a seller might not have access to a copy of the HIP to enable him to change selling agents.

Where a second estate agent is instructed concerns may arise about the quality or completeness of the HIP and that agent may seek an indemnity from the seller unless he is instructed to prepare a fresh HIP. It should be remembered that whilst reg.32 gives protection to the Responsible Person where he has reasonable grounds to believe a document complies with the Regulations this protection does not cover the index or sale statement. In reality, a second agent will always need to consider carrying out his own due diligence.

In summary, the seller would be best advised to own the HIP and, if he wants it to be transferable from one estate agent to another, he needs to ensure that it has been prepared to the correct standard, is authentic and will protect all parties who may need to rely on it. A HIP prepared by the seller's solicitor with the protection of the minimum PI cover should be of considerable reassurance to others involved in the transaction.

Key points

- Register unregistered land before marketing.
- Rectify title defects where possible or obtain insurance.
- List possible HIP providers – in-house/out-sourced.
- Collaboration with other professionals.
- Consider payment for the HIP – cost of HCR/EPC and searches.
- Assess costs involved – budget outlay for no sale/no fee.
- Advise on copyright – elements and the whole.
- Consider ownership by seller necessary for portability.

8 ENFORCEMENT

This chapter discusses the enforcement provisions contained in Part 5, together with the issue of who enforces the obligations and how. It considers who is at risk and the sanctions for default, as well as possible defences and the appeal procedures.

8.1 ENFORCEMENT OFFICERS

Section 166(1) provides for the appointment of enforcers, as 'Every local weights and measures authority is an enforcement authority for the purposes of this Part'. The task of ensuring that, where relevant, every property on the market is backed up with a compliant pack comes within the remit of local TSOs. At some point guidance as to the practical implementation of the role of TSOs is likely from the Local Authorities Coordinators of Regulatory Services (LACORS). This body was set up in 1978 to coordinate the enforcement activities of trading standards and provides advice to support local authority regulatory services.

Trading Standards Officers are already the enforcement agents for PMA 1991, which 'regulates' the marketing of all property by estate agents, and they also enforce other aspects of EAA 1979. There appears to have been a recent increase in the number of disciplinary cases concerning estate agents that have been referred to the OFT, which suggests an upturn in attention to enforcement. A failure to properly monitor and enforce the new regime would bring the system into disrepute and give compliant organisations cause for criticism.

Whilst welcoming the new legislation in a Press Release dated 23 November 2004, LACORS expressed some disappointment:

> LACORS welcomes the introduction of these Home Information Packs which should help protect consumers by providing better information on the properties they are purchasing. However, in order to achieve the most effective framework we believe that local trading standards authorities should be able to use criminal penalties to ensure effective compliance. That said, we will continue to work with the Office of the Deputy Prime Minister to ensure that the civil remedies in the Act are used to best advantage.

On 18 July 2006 LACORS issued a further statement through its chairman Councillor Geoffrey Theobald OBE, who said:

> We have several concerns about how local authorities trading standards are expected to enforce the Home Information Packs. Firstly, Trading Standards traditionally regulate businesses, not individual private house sellers. Furthermore, the government is not giving local authorities criminal powers to investigate any alleged breaches (which they have for other consumer protection provisions), and are only proposing that local authorities can impose a civil fixed penalty charge of £200, which would have to be chased via the civil courts if it was not paid. LACORS has said from the outset that this is inappropriate as it would cost too much money to make it worthwhile pursuing such cases. This means that there is no real incentive for estate agents or sellers to ensure there is a correct Home Information Pack because the likelihood of proceedings being taken against them is very low.
>
> These views have been made clear to DCLG throughout numerous discussions and responses to consultations but our voice remains unheard. At this time, when the government is being urged to review the proposals on other grounds, and when all government departments are being asked to consider proposals for 'better regulation', we would like DCLG to consider our representations again.

LACORS appear to have rejected the argument that the new legislation offers a new tool for enforcement of existing legislation. The rationale for this proposition is that the information required for the HIP will need to be compliant with PMA 1991, which provides that:

> where a false or misleading statement about a prescribed matter is made in the course of an estate agency business . . . otherwise than in providing conveyancing services, the person by whom the business is carried on shall be guilty of an offence under this section.
>
> (PMA 1991, s.1)

The accuracy of the content of the HIP is therefore of concern to estate agents who are responsible for any statements of information in relation to matters falling within any of the 33 specified categories under the Property Misdescriptions (Specified Matters) Order 1992, SI 1992/2834 (see **Appendix C**).

Section 154 of the Act states:

> Where a residential property is on the market, a person responsible for marketing the property is subject to the duties relating to home information packs that are imposed by sections 155 to 158 until his responsibility ceases.

It is the function of the TSOs to enforce in their area:

(a) the duties under ss.155–159 and 167(4), and
(b) any duty imposed under s.172(1).

The duties in ss.155–159 relating to possession of a HIP have been discussed in **Chapter 5**. The duty under s.167(4) is to produce a copy of the HIP to an enforcement officer upon request and s.172(1) requires all estate agents to belong to an approved redress scheme (see **Chapter 10**).

Local enforcement authorities are expected to publish details of the procedures they will follow to fulfil the payment and review aspects of their role. They are likely, in practice, to adopt procedures to first 'advise' and then 'warn' before taking the prosecution route. Multiple breaches of the legislation by estate agents could be followed by reports to the OFT and other disciplinary action leading to a banning order. It remains to be seen whether their enforcement powers will only be activated on complaint or whether they will take a pro-active monitoring role. It seems likely that many complaints may come from solicitors acting for buyers or disappointed buyers.

The role of enforcement officers is supported by s.169, which makes it a criminal offence to obstruct an enforcement officer carrying out his duties under s.167 (the power to require production of a HIP or document or part document in a HIP) and/or to impersonate an enforcement officer either by purporting to exercise the powers to require such production or purporting to issue a penalty charge notice (PCN). Such offences will be dealt with summarily by a magistrates' court and the penalty will be a fine not exceeding Level 5 on the standard scale, which is currently £5000.

A request from an enforcement officer must be met within seven days 'beginning with the day after that on which it is imposed' (s.167(4)). This is subject to relief in subsection (5) to the extent that:

> A person is not required to comply with such a requirement if he has a reasonable excuse for not complying with the requirement.

It is difficult to visualise many situations apart from *force majeure* which, in these days of speedy technology, would excuse compliance, although extreme personal circumstances may provide a basis for some latitude on the time limit.

Whilst s.156 gives the estate agent a discretion to refuse a copy of the HIP to someone who would not be a potential buyer of the property, it is to be noted that the discretion is not available, if 'the responsible person knows or suspects that the person making the request is an officer of an enforcement agency'.

The HIP that is subject to inspection is described in s.167(6). When a request is made to a Responsible Person the HIP to be produced is the one he is required to have at the time of the request. If the request is made of a person whose duty has come to an end, the HIP is the one he was required to have when last subject to the duty.

This means that HIPs must be kept up to date and, most importantly, the pack index must show all revisions that have been made over the period from the commencement of marketing. Schedule 1 to the Regulations requires that amendment to the index to be made whenever a document is removed from or added to the HIP. Unobtainable documents must be noted in the index. Where the HIP is incomplete when marketing begins the relevant document must be added as soon as it is available and again this must be noted on the index.

The TSO can require a seller or estate agent to produce for inspection a copy of the HIP or any document in it and take copies for examination. This includes copies of electronically held content (s.167). But it is as well to remember that, under PMA 1991, the enforcement officer has power to enter premises to seize relevant books and documents (PMA 1991, Schedule, para.4). These powers are usually exercised only after one or more serious complaints have been lodged and after prior investigations have been carried out.

The enforcement officer will apply a series of tests to verify that:

- the Responsible Person holds an authentic copy of the HIP;
- the HIP is complete and contains all the 'required' elements;
- the HIP does not contain any material that is not 'required' or 'authorised';
- the content is not misleading and thus also compliant with PMA 1991;
- changes to the HIP have been recorded in the index; and
- where the HIP is incomplete there is compliance with regs.15, 16 and 17 relating to unavailable and unobtainable documents.

Parallel obligations are imposed on persons who, while they may not be the estate agent, nevertheless carry out a 'qualifying action' (s.159(2)).

The next question to consider is the powers available upon discovery of a breach. Section 168(1) outlines the sanction:

(1) An authorised officer of an enforcement agency may, if he believes that a person has committed a breach of –

(a) any duty under sections 155 to 159 and 167(4), or
(b) any duty imposed under section 172(1),

give a penalty charge notice to that person.

8.2   PENALTY CHARGE NOTICES

8.2.1   Issue of penalty charge notice

A penalty charge notice (PCN) can be issued in the event of a breach of the obligation to:

- have a HIP compliant with the Regulations;
- produce a copy of the HIP (or allow inspection) on request from a potential buyer;
- produce the HIP on request from an enforcement officer within seven days; or
- belong to a redress scheme in the case of an estate agent.

For a notice to be effective there are numerous technical requirements and advisers will need to scrutinise notices carefully in case they may be open to challenge:

(1) A penalty charge notice given to a person under section 168 by an officer of an enforcement authority must –

(a) state the officer's belief that that person has committed a breach of duty;

(b) give such particulars of the circumstances as may be necessary to give reasonable notice of the breach of duty;

(c) require that person, within a period specified in the notice –

(i)   to pay a penalty charge specified in the notice; or

(ii) to give notice to the enforcement authority that he wishes the authority to review the notice;

(d) state the effect of paragraph 8;

(e) specify the person to whom and the address at which the penalty charge may be paid and the method or methods by which payment may be made; and

(f) specify the person to whom and the address at which a notice requesting a review may be sent (and to which any representations relating to the review may be addressed).

(Sched.8, para.1)

Note that the PCN is addressed to a person – from this it appears that there will be dual responsibility; responsibility resting with an employer as well as an employee. This mirrors the position under PMA 1991. Many estate agents, especially those with multiple branches or in corporate ownership have instigated the appointment of a compliance officer for PMA 1991 and for money laundering requirements. It makes equal sense to ensure careful compliance with the HIP regime to protect personnel from unintended breaches and exposure to the consequences. Minor or occasional breaches are more likely to be excused where a business can show that procedures, along with relevant training, have been put in place and suitable records can be produced.

Penalty charge notices and any other notices mentioned in Sched.8 to the Act may be given by post and may be given to the secretary or clerk of a corporate body and, in the case of a partnership, to any partner or any person who has control of or manages the partnership business.

The time limit for the issue of a PCN is six months from the date of the breach or, if a continuing breach, from the last day on which the breach was committed.

8.2.2   Payment of penalty charge notice

The period for payment of the PCN will not be less than 28 days after the day the notice is given (para.1(c)) and the charge payable will be prescribed from time to time under regulations made by the Secretary of State but will not exceed £500 (para.2). Regulation 31 has fixed the penalty charge at £200. This can be revised by a future statutory instrument. Some may say this is not a stringent enough charge but it should be remembered that the issue of a PCN to an estate agent may result in disciplinary action by the OFT. This can include warning and banning notices and inhibit an estate agent's right to work. The enforcement authority has power to extend the time for payment in its discretion if it considers there are grounds to do so. The PCN can be withdrawn if the authority considers it should not have been given (para.4).

It is suggested by the guidance and some commentators that the penalty charge can be applied for each day of breach. A notice must relate to the commission of an offence and so, to enable a TSO to issue multiple notices, proof would be needed that there was a breach on each occasion that a notice is issued. Could this be proved other than by a daily visit to the premises and would the TSOs have the resources for this? The intention of the Regulations has not been made clear but a Responsible Person does appear to be at risk of multiple notices if no steps are taken to remedy a breach or withdraw the property from the market following upon an inspection by a TSO.

8.2.3   Withdrawal or review of penalty charge notice

In deciding whether to withdraw the PCN the authority will have to decide if it is satisfied:

(a)   that the recipient committed the breach of duty specified in the notice;
(b)   that the notice was given within the time allowed by section 168(2) and complies with the other requirements imposed by or under this Schedule; and
(c)   that in the circumstances of the case it was appropriate for a penalty charge notice to be given to the recipient . . .

(Regulations, Sched.8, para.5(3))

The recipient of a PCN has the right to request a review. Notice must be given within the payment period (Sched.8, para.5). On receipt of a review request the enforcement authority must consider the representations made and surrounding circumstances to reach the decision whether to withdraw or confirm the PCN. Notice of the decision must then be sent to the appellant and, if the decision is to confirm the PCN, then notification of the right of appeal to the county court must be given.

8.2.4   Appeal against penalty charge notice

When notified by the authority that the PCN is confirmed, the recipient has 28 days from the day after the confirming notice is given to appeal against the PCN to the county court. In line with its general jurisdiction, the county court has power to extend the time for appealing against the notice.

Although no information is yet available as to the procedure to be followed for such an appeal, it will be by way of a rehearing and the court may either uphold or quash the notice. In the event that a PCN is withdrawn (by the authority) or quashed (by the county court) any payment made under the PCN will be repaid.

Evidence must be produced in any recovery proceedings by way of a certificate which:

(a)   purports to be signed by or on behalf of the person having responsibility for the financial affairs of the enforcement authority; and

(b) states that payment of the penalty charge was or was not received by a date specified in the certificate . . .

(Regulations, Sched.8, para.9)

8.2.5   Additional regulations

Further and additional regulations may be made by the Secretary of State,
including changes to the form of PCN and other notices mentioned in Sched.8 to
the Regulations; circumstances in which a PCN should not be given and/or the
methods by which penalty charges can be paid.

8.3   CRIMINAL SANCTIONS

A breach of PMA 1991 carries a possible criminal sanction. Estate agents, including both the employer and employees, are indirectly exposed to an additional liability that has not been widely recognised. The fine on summary conviction is a
maximum of £5,000. Conveyancing services are excluded from these sanctions
and are defined in PMA 1991, s.1(5)(g) as meaning:

> preparation of any transfer, conveyance, writ, contract or other document in that
> connection with the disposal or acquisition of an interest in land and services ancil-
> lary to that, but this does not include anything done as mentioned in section 1(1)(a)
> of the Estate Agents Act 1979.

8.4   SOLICITORS PREPARING HOME INFORMATION PACKS

Section 1(1) of EAA 1979 in effect defines marketing activity as things done with
a view to introducing a seller or buyer to someone who wishes to acquire or sell,
as the case may be. It suggests that any work done by a solicitor preparing a HIP
may be within the exemption for conveyancing services. It should be remembered
that failures to comply with PMA 1991 that result in a prosecution would be of
particular concern to solicitors who would become exposed also to the risk of
disciplinary proceedings following any conviction. See also the initial, draft
guidance from the Law Society's Regulation Board at **Appendix H**.

8.5   DEFENCE OF 'REASONABLE BELIEF'

There are defences available to an estate agent under PMA 1991. These are based
on 'due diligence', meaning that suitable in-house procedures for verifying
information can be shown to be in place or that there has been reasonable reliance
on an outside source of information. When dealing with the information in the
HIP there is a clear benefit for the estate agent if able to rely upon a solicitor's
authentification of pack content.

In the case of the EPC/HCR the signature of the HI or accredited surveyor will render him responsible for his report but if there is a conflict with other content of the HIP that would not be his direct responsibility.

Regulation 32 provides a defence similar to that available under PMA 1991. Sanctions are not applicable where the contents of the HIP (other than the index and sale statement) do not comply with any requirement of the Regulations and the Responsible Person has reasonable grounds to believe that the document does comply. In other words, if it is reasonable the Responsible Person may rely upon a document produced by another person. This could be the case for the EPC/HCR and search reports where third parties are responsible and for documents produced by the seller's legal adviser.

8.6 RECORDS

The enforcement provisions under Part 5 suggest that recording and archiving procedures should be put in place.

In s.167(1) the words 'to be or have been subject to the duty ...' suggest that estate agents will not be able to dispose of the HIP for a property as soon as it is sold or withdrawn from the market or the minute their instructions are terminated as the enforcement officer can require production where the agent appears 'to have been subject to the duty' which refers to the past.

There is, however, a time limit for the retention of records, in that:

> A requirement under this section may not be imposed more than six months after the last day on which the person concerned was subject to the duty under section 155 or 159(2) in relation to the property (as the case may be).
>
> (s.167(3))

So, to be safe, it might seem to be prudent for estate agents to set up a procedure of retaining HIPs for nine months after the relevant obligations cease. However, under PMA 1991 there is potential for liability for a period of three years after an offence is committed (s.5) which means that in practice it will be prudent to retain records concerning verification and due diligence procedures for that longer period.

8.7 BUYER'S PRIVATE ACTION

Section 170 of the Act grants to a buyer 'the right of a private action'. It applies where a person has committed a breach of duty under s.156 by failing to comply with a request from a potential buyer for a copy of a prescribed document. A 'prescribed document' is for these purposes a document that is required to be included in the HIP by regulations under s.163.

This section enables a potential buyer who has to obtain his own version of a prescribed document to recover from the Responsible Person any reasonable fee paid or payable by him for so doing, provided that both the following conditions are satisfied:

- the property is on the market or the potential buyer and the seller are trying to agree the sale and purchase of the property (subsection (3)); and
- the potential buyer has not previously been provided with an authentic copy of the prescribed document in question (subsection (4)).

It should be noted that a copy of a prescribed document is not authentic for these purposes unless:

(a)   it is a copy of a document included in the home information pack for the property as it stands at the time the copy is provided to the potential buyer; and
(b)   the document so included complies with the requirements of any regulations under section 163 at that time.

(s.170(5))

The intention is that whenever such a document is requested and provided, the potential buyer is entitled to the latest updated version of the HIP and such document or documents must comply with all regulations made.

Section 170(8) reduces room for prevarification and misunderstanding by clarifying that;

It is immaterial for the purposes of this section that the request in question did not specify the prescribed document but was for a copy of the home information pack or a part of the pack which included (or ought to have included) that document.

The duty to hold a HIP for every residential property on the market and to provide authentic copies of the HIP or documents or part(s) of documents in it is a statutory duty and therefore one of strict liability.

Therefore, any breach will give rise to a remedy even if it is accidental and unintentional. There might be a defence to an allegation of breach where marketing is begun prematurely and before a HIP is ready if the estate agent could show that what occurred was unintentional.

The buyer who is refused a HIP may be able to recover the cost of obtaining the information in the HIP by other means. The claim could extend to professional fees and other search fees and expenses of obtaining an EPC. The costs incurred would give rise to a civil claim presumably in the Small Claims Court as the amount would be likely to be under the £5,000 limit. This means that no legal costs incurred in the legal action would be recoverable.

The buyer would presumably engage his legal adviser to obtain the information he needs in order to pursue his interest in the property and so those legal costs would form part of the claim. There are possible defences to a claim. If it emerged that the Responsible Person was entitled to refuse the HIP the claim would fail if that reason for refusal was bona fide and had been disclosed. This area is uncertain, as there is no obligation or time limit stipulated in the legislation for a refusal to be notified to the potential buyer making the request.

It is not clear whether the statutory remedy specified in s.170 exhausts the remedies open to a potential buyer or the actual buyer of the property. **Chapter 9** discusses the scope for other possible claims.

Key points

- Check local TSO guidelines and policy.
- Assess TSO powers and methods of enforcement.
- Appoint internal compliance officer.
- Set up procedures for record keeping.
- Set up training for personnel.
- Set up buyer registration procedures.
- Check time limits on receipt of any PCN.
- Check format of PCN.
- Timetable review/appeal procedure on receipt of PCN.
- Consider defences.

9 REMEDIES

The Act specifies only a limited set of sanctions and remedies. These include the PCN that may be issued against sellers and estate agents and the right of private action for buyers considered in **Chapter 8**. There will be an infrastructure of schemes for receiving and handling complaints against estate agents and HIs, and these are discussed in **Chapter 10**. Those jurisdictions do not appear to contemplate redress by way of substantial compensation for financial loss. However, a participant in the process may conceivably sustain losses in the form of wasted expenditure. Mistakes by a Responsible Person or HI could be made in the content of the HIP or in the handling of their responsibilities.

Claims could, in a general context, arise under three heads: contract, tort and statutory breach. These are considered in turn and then applied to the participants in the residential property selling and buying process.

9.1   CONTRACT CLAIMS

A contract is a legally binding promise or set of promises between two or more parties incorporating the elements of offer and acceptance with sufficient consideration and an intention to create legal relations. In the case of contracts for the sale of interests in land the Law of Property (Miscellaneous Provisions) Act 1989 requires that all the terms to be relied upon by the parties must be in writing. The 4th edition of the Law Society Standard Conditions of Sale makes no reference to HIPs. Accordingly, unless the parties agree express provisions to include references to disclosure of the HIP and possibly warranties concerning the contents of the pack, the HIP will have no direct impact upon contractual terms.

The compilation of a HIP will entail a number of contractual arrangements to which the usual contractual principles may be of relevance.

A claim for breach of contractual terms may be based upon non-performance of express or implied terms and conditions of the agreement.

More complex claims could arise for allegations such as mistake and misrepresentation. Defences to claims may turn upon questions as to capacity of the parties and enforceability and whether defences such as mistake are applicable.

'Mistake' could arise under three heads:

- common – when both parties share the same mistake over a fundamental element of the contract;
- mutual – where the parties have been negotiating at cross-purposes with the result that there is no genuine agreement; or
- unilateral – as in common mistake save that just one party is mistaken but the other is aware of this.

There could be frustration of a contract when, due to the fault of neither party, a change in circumstances makes a contract impossible to perform, illegal or radically different from what the parties had agreed. A contract would not be frustrated merely because it has become too expensive, in either time or money, to perform.

Exclusion clauses and disclaimers in contracts need to be considered. These are subject to consumer protection under the Unfair Contract Terms Act and the Unfair Contract Terms Act Regulations (see **Appendix C**). The statutory terms contained in the Regulations for providers of HCRs and search reports suggest that exclusion clauses and disclaimers would be regarded as 'less favourable terms' (Regulations, Sched.5, para.5 and Sched.8, para.9) with the result that their inclusion would make the HCR and search report non-compliant with the knock-on effect of making the HIP non-compliant.

Remedies for a breach of contract range from common law damages to equitable remedies of specific performance, injunction or rescission. Damages are compensatory and intended to put the 'innocent' party in the financial position he would have been had there been no breach – they are not punitive. Damages can be awarded for financial loss, damage to property, personal injury and for loss of enjoyment.

Losses claimed must not be too remote and must have been within the contemplation of both parties, when the contract was made, as a probable result of a breach. The claimant has a duty to mitigate his loss and must avoid taking steps that would increase such loss.

A court order for specific performance of the contract will usually only be made where an award of damages is an insufficient remedy. This is frequently recognised to be the case in connection with the sale of land. As this is a discretionary remedy it will not be available if the claimant has behaved in a less than honest manner. Nor will it be ordered if to do so would involve the court in excessive supervision or if the contract was one for personal services. Failure to comply with an order for specific performance is a contempt of court punishable by imprisonment.

'Misrepresentation' may arise from a false statement of a material fact made during contract negotiations by one of the parties to the contract inducing the other to enter into the agreement. There are three recognised types of misrepresentation to consider:

- fraudulent – a deliberate or reckless false statement;
- negligent – where the maker of the statement believes it is true but this belief is not based on reasonable grounds; and
- innocent – the maker of the statement both believes it is true and has reasonable grounds for this belief.

The remedy available depends on the type of misrepresentation committed. Fraudulent misrepresentation can be remedied by rescission of the contract and damages; negligent by rescission and/or damages under Misrepresentation Act 1967, s.2(1) (or under the tort of negligence); and innocent by rescission only or damages in lieu of rescission under Misrepresentation Act 1967, s.2(2).

An estate agent who makes an offending statement does not have direct personal liability in contract but might be sued for breach of warranty of authority or for deceit if the facts show that the false statement was intentionally made. A seller sued for misrepresentation because of a statement made on his behalf by his agent may look to have recourse against the agent in contract or tort.

9.2   CLAIMS IN TORT

Rights and obligations in tort arise under the common law and are generally concerned with a loss caused by a positive act or omission that causes damage or injury rather than economic loss. A claim is potentially available against any class of person and generally requires some element of fault, such as negligence, on the part of the wrongdoer.

Negligence will give rise to a claim where the claimant can prove:

- he was owed a duty of care; and
- that duty was breached; and
- there is a causal link between the breach and the damage suffered by him; and
- the damage caused was reasonably foreseeable.

The extension of the tort to cover negligent misstatement arose in 1964 in the seminal case of *Hedley Byrne & Co Ltd* v. *Heller* [1964] AC 465. This showed that the extent of a duty of care can be wide and arise from a careless statement. A special relationship must exist for this type of claim and such a relationship requires four conditions to be met.

1. The person making the statement is aware of the type of transaction envisaged by the person affected by it.
2. The maker of the statement communicates directly to the claimant or knows that the advice would be communicated to a discernable class which includes the claimant.
3. The person making the statement envisages that the claimant would act on the advice.
4. It is reasonable for the claimant to have relied on that advice.

To prove that there has been a breach of a duty of care the claimant will need to show a failure to reach the standard of care, which would have been attained by a reasonable person in the particular circumstances, thus adopting an objective test.

The causal link must be proved and satisfy the 'but for' test. So, if it were not for the defendant's actions, would the claimant have suffered the loss? A material contribution will not be enough and the chain of causation may be broken by an intervening event such as action by the claimant. The damage that follows must be reasonably foreseeable and within a broad class of foreseeable risk. The principle was applied in relation to estate agents in *Computastaff* v. *Ingledew Brown and Bennison Garrett* [1983] 2 EGLR 150.

Contributory negligence can provide a complete or partial defence to a claim in tort extinguishing or reducing the damages claim. The chain of causation may also be broken by supervening events. So, in *McCullagh* v. *Lane Fox & Partners* [1996] 1 EGLR 36, the estate agent's detailed particulars that contained a written disclaimer were held to override a prior statement that was made in relation to the description of a property by reference to the plot size.

The scope for liability for surveyors was fixed in *Smith* v. *Eric S Bush* [1990] 1 AC 831 (see **para.9.9.2**). Solicitors who negligently failed to pursue a request for sight of a building regulation approval were liable for the loss sustained by the claimants who acquired a defective property (*Cottingham* v. *Attey Bower and Jones* [2000] Lloyd's Rep PN 591, Ch Div per Rimer J.).

The HIP itself must not contain any disclaimers.

9.3 BREACH OF STATUTORY DUTY

These claims arise from breach of duties that have been created by legislation such as claims for unfair dismissal under employment legislation or for breach of copyright without permission under the Copyright, Designs and Patents Act 1988. The legislation places a statutory duty on an individual or entity, breach of which may give rise to a claim for damages and, in some cases, result in a criminal, professional or trade sanction.

Consumers in general have, in recent years, benefited from increased statutory protection under legislation such as PMA 1991, the Contracts (Rights of Third Parties) Act 1999, the Consumer Protection Act 1987, the Consumer Credit Act 1974, the Distance Selling Regulations 2000 and 2005, the Unfair Contract Terms Act 1977 and Unfair Contract Terms Regulations 1999. However, there is not always a right for an individual to bring a claim simply because of breach of a duty imposed under the statute.

The question of whether a claim for damages can arise for the breach of a statutory duty has been answered judicially in a number of different ways over a period of time, in relation to different types of statutory obligation. Generally, the existence of a duty is a pre-condition to recognising a cause of action and a mere statutory prohibition is not enough. The question is whether there is an intention to confer rights on third parties and of discerning the intention of parliament on an issue where it is not resolved by statutory words. The decision in *Pepper* v. *Hart* [1993] 1 All ER 42 enables the court to consider *Hansard* in order to construe the intentions of parliament. Sometimes wording may be left open to presumption or for judicial interpretation. Lord Diplock in *Lonrho Limited* v. *Shell Petroleum Co Limited* [1982] AC 173 set out the principle of first looking for the intention of the legislature and then of applying a general disinclination to infer a tort. He said that where an Act creates an obligation and provides for enforcement of perform-ance in a specific and specified manner then performance cannot be enforced in another manner. In other words, statute may prescribe a given remedy for a breach of a statutory duty and make it clear that this is the only claim that is pos-sible. There are two admitted exceptions to this principle – one where the statute creates a public right, and another where a particular member of the public suffers direct and substantial damage different from that which was common to all the rest of the public.

In relation to Part 5 there is a possibility that statutory duties might give rise to the potential for private claims. Each of the participants in the sale of a home could benefit from or be exposed to claims arising from the application of these general principles.

9.4   LIABILITIES AND RIGHTS OF PARTIES

Potentially, the new legislation could have extended additional rights to sellers, buyers and potential buyers, lenders and to any 'other person involved in the sale of the property who is not a party to the contract' (s.163(8)(c)). However, the Regulations have clarified and narrowed the ambit of this to a certain extent. Schedule 5, which regulates HCRs and contains compulsory terms for the con-tract under which the HCR is prepared, states in para.3 that the contract must allow for the statutory terms to be enforced not just by the parties to the contract but also the seller, a buyer or potential buyer of the property interest and a mort-gage lender. There is no similar requirement for a stand-alone EPC at the time of writing. In relation to search reports and enquiries there is a similar specific requirement in para.5 of Sched.8.

It could have been anticipated that the position following s.163 would have been for regulations to provide that the entire HIP could be relied on by anyone involved in the sale.

Part 5 creates a number of statutory duties the breach of which give rise to con-sequences set out in the statute. The extent to which other remedies may also be available is discussed below.

9.5   SELLER

9.5.1   Liabilities/obligations

Under Part 5 the seller who is a Responsible Person must have a compliant HIP in his possession or under his control and be able to provide a copy upon request from a potential buyer or TSO. He must also comply with the record-keeping obligation under s.167.

The seller can delegate these responsibilities by appointing estate agents to market the property for him but, if he does so, will remain responsible unless he ceases to take steps himself to market the property and he must then have reasonable grounds to believe that his agent has a HIP and can produce copies on request. The seller must also direct any requests he receives for a HIP to the estate agent who is responsible for the marketing.

Any interval that arises between the termination of one estate agent's retainer and the appointment of another will cause the seller to become the Responsible Person with all the obligations and duties that follow (unless the property is withdrawn or taken off the market).

The obligation to have a HIP includes the obligation to update required documents (regs.18 and 19) and to ensure accuracy and completeness of its content.

Any breach by failing to comply with these duties can result in the issue by the TSO of a PCN. In addition to liability imposed by Part 5, the seller is exposed to possible claims under the general law.

The HIP is not a contract. It constitutes an 'invitation to treat' rather than an 'offer' capable of acceptance. Its contents may be ascribed a status by the terms of any subsequent contract. It may be treated as containing representations or warranties that are enforceable by the buyer under the terms of a written contract in the event that there is an error or omission. This could reduce the force of caveat emptor that might otherwise defeat a buyer's claim. Alternatively, the scope of any disclosure at the marketing stage could be excluded or limited by the terms of the written sale agreement designed to protect the seller and the seller's agents.

Although a seller has no personal liability under PMA 1991, he must ensure that any information he provides for the HIP is accurate and not misleading. If he fails, by making an inaccurate statement or omitting material information, he may thereby induce a buyer to enter into a contract to buy the property. This could give rise to a claim for misrepresentation and for damages or rescission of the contract. In the past sale agreements have habitually provided that such liability is limited or excluded.

Quite separately, the seller could face an action for negligent misstatement, irrespective of whether the buyer proceeds to contract. This might arise where the buyer claims the loss of opportunity/bargain because of some inaccuracy in the content of the HIP or arising from information that is misleading. Alternatively, it might be based on an oral representation made in conjunction with the delivery of the HIP. In either event this could arise from an error in the HIP production process. For example, the requirement to update the HIP may not be undertaken thus leaving out some material addition that puts the buyer to some otherwise avoidable expense.

If there is a material inaccuracy or misrepresentation in the HIP the buyer or any other affected person might complain to one of the complaints schemes set up for estate agents and for the HIs. They, in turn, might have recourse to the seller for any compensation payment where they have relied upon disclosures or information from the seller.

Whilst the new system is as yet untried, it is not hard to imagine claims being brought against a careless or reckless seller. If a buyer discovers incorrect or misleading information in the HIP he obtains from the estate agent and withdraws from negotiations, the estate agent might also consider a claim for loss of commission on the sale and for payment in respect of the HIP where credit has been provided or this payment has been deferred. Such a claim might be enlarged to include loss of other business should a buyer's confidence in the agent be so damaged that he has no further interest in viewing other properties through the agent and removes his instructions elsewhere for the marketing of his own property for sale. Whilst such claims may seem far-fetched they are conceivable, particularly where higher priced property is involved.

9.5.2   Rights

The seller has certain rights under the legislation and may need to obtain advice concerning these in order to protect his position. The certification schemes for HIs will set out procedures to enable inaccuracies in HCRs to be rectified. It is intended that a homeowner/seller should be able to apply for an incorrect HCR to be removed from the register (reg.33(f)(iii)). The Act does not specifically provide for any compensation or refund of costs incurred in this event.

Regulations have made provision for contracts relating to HCRs and search reports to be enforceable by sellers, buyers, potential buyers and lenders whether or not a party to the contract.

Where a seller is faced with a claim as described in **para.9.5.1** much will then depend upon the terms and conditions contained in any agreement made between the seller and the chosen pack provider or professional or other advisers. Such agreements may be subject to implied terms as well as express terms. The HI's responsibility under paras.3 and 5 of Sched.5 may not be reduced and for others it is likely that contracts could contain specific indemnity clauses to anticipate situations where information is discovered to be incomplete, misleading or false.

The seller can give instructions to his estate agent outlining, subject to the laws against discrimination, the categories of people to whom he would not be prepared to sell his property. He also has an explicit right to give instructions to his estate agent as to the use and disclosure of the HIP to potential buyers (s.156(4)).

Sellers may well be concerned for personal security reasons to know that the distribution of the HIP is recorded and limited to potential buyers who have registered their personal details.

Breach of these or any specific instructions (perhaps to protect confidentiality) may prompt a seller to make a claim in damages against the estate agent either under a contract or as a breach of the statutory duty under this legislation. More probably, however, disgruntled sellers will lodge complaints against the estate agent either through the TSO or to the relevant complaints scheme. The estate agent will then have to explain his systems and any errors or mistakes that may have occurred.

The seller will have contractual rights against his estate agent, his solicitor and any HIP provider for negligent performance of their professional duties although this will depend upon the specific terms of their respective contracts of engagement. Professional rules inhibit exclusion clauses for solicitors and the Unfair Contract Terms Act 1977 and Regulations made thereunder and the Unfair Terms in Consumer Contracts Regulations 1999 give some protection to the consumer in b2c contracts. These considerations do not apply in business to business b2b transactions where the parties are considered to have more equal bargaining powers.

Where a seller does not pay for the HIP in advance or upon delivery then credit terms may be offered and in those cases the requirements of consumer credit legislation must be complied with. More commonly, it is likely that HIP suppliers will offer deferred payment terms and frontline professionals may agree to accept payment by credit card.

9.6 BUYER

9.6.1 Liabilities/obligations

The legislation is intended to mitigate the cost to buyers of making expensive mistakes in purchase negotiations and wasting expenses on abortive transactions.

At first sight, it might appear that the new regime brings only advantages to a buyer. However, obligations usually go hand in hand with rights. Whilst there are no explicit obligations imposed on buyers, some are likely to emerge in practice under the new regime.

The first step a buyer usually takes is to research the properties being advertised for sale on the Internet and in local newspapers, and then to contact estate agents marketing properties of interest to arrange a viewing. Under the new system agents may well request buyers formally to register their interest in purchasing a property. Buyers may be asked, before being given access to the detailed property information in the pack, for more information than in the past as to particular requirements, the price band in which they are searching and their ability to afford a property at a given price. If a buyer has a dependent sale he may be asked to waive confidentiality so that the agent can check progress up and down a chain of transactions. Being economical with the truth could render a buyer vulnerable to a claim for loss of bargain, loss of sale and/or loss of commission if the information given turns out to be misleading or wrong.

The new regime, if it had proceeded with a compulsory HCR, might have put a buyer under more time pressure to exchange contracts within a fixed timescale than previously. If a HIP was a complete disclosure/due diligence document, similar to those issued to buyers of new homes now, two weeks to obtain a mortgage offer and exchange might have become the norm. With no restriction on the number of HIPs in circulation, buyers might have felt pressured if there were other buyers waiting in the wings to take their place in case of delay. Although reg.3 permits a property to be withdrawn from the market for more than 28 days to allow an exchange of contracts to take place, buyers are likely to be put under pressure to perform within an agreed timetable.

The requirement for estate agents to comply with the Money Laundering Regulations 2003 has been modified to the extent that buyers do not have to be scrutinised but, if more information becomes available, this may raise suspicions that should not be ignored by estate agents.

A copy of the HIP may be produced to a buyer subject to stipulated terms as to its use and return and as to whether it can be copied to others. It is clearly possible that buyers may give false information or breach restrictions on use of the HIP and these would give rise to possible actions if any direct loss or damage could be proved.

9.6.2   Rights

The Act gives a potential buyer the right to an authentic copy of the HIP or any document or part of a document contained in the HIP. If this is denied and if the buyer is then forced to commission any part of the HIP he can claim, from the Responsible Person, the reasonable fees for doing so (s.170). There will be a defence, however, if the estate agent can show that he withheld the pack on one of the statutory grounds set out in ss.156 or 157.

A buyer or potential buyer may in future be given additional rights under s.163(8)(c) to enforce the terms of a contract to which the buyer is not a contracting party. Presently, this right is most likely to be exercised in respect of any HCR that has failed to disclose a defect following which the buyer incurs costs of further investigation or of remedial works (Sched.5, para.3). A buyer may also be able to claim indemnity for losses in respect of errors or omissions in search reports commissioned and contained in the HIP (Sched.8, para.5).

Section 172 requires that estate agents belong to a redress scheme but this presently awaits a commencement order. An estate agent redress scheme will give the buyer a forum to air grievances and, depending upon the powers given to these schemes by the Secretary of State, to obtain compensation without actually having to meet the standards of proof required for negligence claims. The complaints and redress schemes to be set up for HIs will also provide a procedure for dealing with complaints about the HCR and/or the HI. The blueprint for this is contained in the DCLG Certification Scheme Standards (**para.4.4**) and envisages a comprehensive and thorough complaints regime and requires monitoring of internal complaints processes (**para.10.2.1**).

Where a buyer proceeds to purchase a property his rights will be limited by the terms of the sale contract and advisers will need to consider how to safeguard rights of action in respect of information relied upon and contained in the HIP.

Most of the duties created by the Act are absolute but complaints could arise out of the exercise of a discretion by a seller or seller's estate agent (s.156(4)). It may be alleged that the agent acted unreasonably in situations where intention is relevant. If a buyer claims to have lost the opportunity to purchase a particular property because of the failure of a Responsible Person to provide a HIP, this could give rise to a more substantial claim than s.170 of the Act allows. The approach of the courts may be to examine whether the Act intended to provide a specific remedy for the mischief in question and not to allow any new head of claim to emerge.

9.7   ESTATE AGENT

9.7.1   Liabilities/obligations

Under this legislation, and in consequence of the processes that it introduces, estate agents and those acting as estate agents will be exposed to a range of new possible claims, fines and offences.

Under Part 5 it is a matter of substance and not form or nomenclature as to who is an estate agent and those carrying out a 'qualifying action' are also subject to the obligations of a Responsible Person.

Estate agents have duties under the general principles of common law that relate to agents and those they deal with, including buyers. At all times they remain fiduciary agents for sellers and therefore have a greater duty of care to their clients than a non-fiduciary agent (*Kelly* v. *Cooper* [1993] AC 205). This case acknowledges the difficulty in the common situation where estate agents have multiple clients and therefore there is potential for conflicts of interest to arise.

Legislation relating to estate agents requires 'prescribed information' under the Estate Agents (Provision of Information) Regulations 1991, SI 1991/859 to be given to clients before terms of engagement and instructions are accepted. This relates to the level of fees to be charged and the type of agency arrangement (i.e. sole or multiple agency) to be put in place. Agents have obligations to report, in writing, any offers received for the seller's property to the seller.

Estate agents are subject to a wide variety of general consumer legislation including statutes and regulations that regulate advertising, consumer credit, distance selling and money laundering.

The Property Misdescriptions Act 1991 introduced from 1993, when it came into operation, raised the spectre of criminal sanctions against estate agents. The Property Misdescriptions (Specified Matters) Order 1992, SI 1992/2834, sets out in Sched.1 a list of 33 specified matters which, if misrepresented or untrue, could render an estate agent liable to investigation by TSOs and the possibility of a criminal conviction both for the individual estate agent who breached the Act and, also, for the employer. Certain of these 33 specified matters are listed in **Appendix C**. The result has been to discourage estate agents from including anything in the property particulars above and beyond that which is absolutely necessary to sell a property. The HIP regime could have the same effect – less information being more likely to avoid breaches.

The HIP regime requires full and frank information and, accordingly, estate agents who prepare and/or publish a pack could find themselves liable both under this legislation and PMA 1991 legislation for the same 'mistake'. Under PMA 1991 an estate agent has a statutory defence if it can be shown he believed the information was accurate and 'due diligence' can be demonstrated. Careful consideration must therefore be given by agents as to how they might avoid or mitigate potential liability in the preparation of a HIP. If subcontracted with the benefit of safeguards and indemnities, this would give a measure of protection.

The estate agent's major responsibility under Part 5 is to have a compliant HIP and to be able to provide an authentic paper (or electronic) copy on request from a buyer or TSO. The estate agent should also seek full instructions from the seller client as to the exercise of the discretion to provide or refuse copy packs and also in relation to the confidentiality of the contents of packs by potential buyers (ss.156(4) and 157).

The exercise of this discretion could expose estate agents to claims from potential buyers who have been refused a copy of the HIP. Allegations might be made that the estate agent came to the decision on wrong information, misunderstood information or even unlawfully discriminated thus depriving a potential buyer of the opportunity of buying a property and thereby suffering a 'loss of bargain'.

As a result, it is anticipated that estate agents will adopt procedures to log how many HIPs are distributed and to whom. This could be used to demonstrate that the exercise of the discretion was reasonable in all the circumstances and to enable all HIPs provided to be retrieved from unsuccessful bidders for a property. A log will also enable the estate agent to meet the record keeping and retention obligations under s.167.

Failure to comply with these requirements and that of belonging to an approved redress scheme can render an estate agent liable to the issue of a PCN and of that offence being reported to the OFT who could impose further sanctions including a prohibition order – preventing the person acting as an estate agent (EAA 1979, s.3).

The estate agent is also required by reg.21 to provide the seller with a copy of the HIP 'for the purposes of ensuring the accuracy of the home information pack'.

9.7.2   Rights

The estate agent has the right to charge for a paper copy of the HIP (and any postage), a right to impose conditions before a copy of the HIP is provided and to cease to have the duties of the Responsible Person when instructions are terminated or the property is withdrawn from the market or sold There is also the right, but only if the buyer agrees, to provide a copy of the HIP in electronic form – however, this might not become as widespread as originally thought as electronic delivery will make it virtually impossible to control distribution and/or retrieval of the HIP and must be provided without charge.

More importantly, if the estate agent is not the HIP producer but 'buys' this in from a HIP provider or is provided with a HIP by the seller's solicitor he is likely to seek an indemnity to protect him against claims for misstatement or other errors contained in the HIP.

The estate agent also has a right of review and appeal in respect of a PCN.

9.8   PACK PROVIDERS

9.8.1   Liabilities/obligations

The liabilities of these newcomers to the property industry will depend to an extent on whether they set out to service the business market of professional agents or the consumer market of homeowners. If it is their intention to sell their expertise in compiling HIPs to estate agents then they will be expected to accept responsibility and offer protection from claims.

If it is their intention to market directly to the public these would be consumer relationships and pack providers will have to meet the obligations of consumer protection legislation such as the Unfair Terms in Consumer Contracts Regulations 1999, the Consumer Protection (Distance Selling) Regulations 2000 and the Consumer Credit Act 1974, as mentioned above. At present, they are not included within the net of regulated providers under the Money Laundering Regulations 2003. This may change in the future as it is expected that the government would wish them to meet these obligations to the same extent as estate agents.

It is to be expected that, as a self-regulating industry, voluntary standards will be extended requiring members to hold indemnity insurance and set up complaints and redress schemes. AHIPP has stated that it intends to introduce a code of practice for accreditation by the OFT.

It is more problematic to know whether quality standards will be set and whether conduct rules will be as restrictive as those for professionals, especially in relation to conflicts of interest. It is anticipated that dedicated HIP provider organisations will need to develop additional income streams from referral fees and the sale of ancillary products such as insurance and loans.

9.8.2   Rights

Home Information Pack suppliers do not have any specific rights under Part 5 as the promoters of the Act did not foresee their emergence as players in the field, expecting the role of HIP provider to be taken up by the existing participants such as estate agents and solicitors.

Their rights will be contractual and the fairness of their contract terms will be assessed according to how they proceed. There is concern that they will seek to provide packs and promote, on a referral fee basis, the services of the HI and the other professionals involved in a transaction such as the selling agent and conveyancer.

9.9   HOME INSPECTORS

9.9.1   General

The future role of HIs has been thrown into doubt by the ministerial statement of 18 July 2006. It is presently envisaged that HCRs produced on a voluntary basis should meet the standards set by the legislation but this will, of course, be open to future amendment.

HIs are to be licensed by the approved certifying bodies to produce HCRs and EPCs and have established an organisation to articulate their interests. The National Association of Licensed Home Inspectors (NALHI) presently only has a small number of members. Many points of concern could arise from matters that are not dealt with in the HCR either because they are outside its scope or because the HI reports a matter in need of further or specialist investigation. This could be a source of dissatisfaction and complaint.

9.9.2   Liabilities/obligations

The HI's terms of engagement are set out in Sched.5 to the Regulations. This prescribes the terms that must be included in the contract for the preparation of an HCR (para.2) and the contract must not include terms less favourable to the seller, buyer, potential buyer or lender. Terms may be added relating to payment of any fees and charges.

The liability of the HI is extended to sellers, buyers, potential buyers and lenders (Sched.5, para.3) but otherwise limited by reg.11 once there is another report on the same property for another seller. In other respects the terms of the contract will determine the scope of liability. The potential liability for allegations of negligence is open to a wide class of potential claimants with a wide range of possible claims.

HIs will need to be able to show that they acted in accordance with the rules of conduct of the certification scheme of which they are a member especially in relation to conflict of interest allegations.

Generally, it is to be assumed that the measure of damages where negligence causes loss will be the same as in the case of surveyors and for other professionals. Thus, in the cases of *Smith* v. *Eric Bush* and *Harris* v. *Wyre Forest District Council* [1990] 1 AC 831 a report and valuation carried out for a lender was shown to and relied upon by a buyer. The buyer in each case relied upon the report and suffered loss because of defects in the property which were negligently omitted.

Although contractual terms for the survey excluded liability the House of Lords held that such clauses offended the Unfair Contract Terms Act 1977 and were not effective. The person giving the advice was aware of the nature of the transaction under contemplation and that reliance would be placed upon the advice and information. The claimants were entitled to rely upon the advice subject only to any specific disclaimer that may have been addressed to them.

The extent to which an adviser may be liable for any loss under this principle has been the subject of many cases where alternative approaches have been canvassed. Sometimes, damages for financial loss equating to diminution in value have been awarded and in other cases financial loss has been limited to the cost of remedial work.

The legal principles concerned have been summarised recently by Mr Justice Lawrence Collins in *Greymalkin Ltd* v. *Copleys (a firm)* [2004] PNLR 44 between paras 72 and 78 of his judgment, as follows:

72 If a person is under a duty to take reasonable care to provide information on which someone else will decide upon a course of action, he is responsible only for the consequences of the information being wrong. If he is under a duty to advise whether or not a course of action should be taken, and is negligent, he is responsible for all the foreseeable loss which is a consequence of that course of action having been taken: *South Australia Asset Management Corp* v *York Montague Ltd* 1997 AC 191, at 214. The distinction was applied, e.g., in *Dent* v *Davis Blank Furniss* 2001 Lloyd's Rep PN 534.

73 Where a claimant claims that he has suffered loss by entering into a transaction as a result of negligent advice or information provided by the defendant, the first question is whether the claimant can establish that the defendant's negligence caused him to enter into the transaction. The claimant must then go on to show what (if any) part of his loss is attributable to the defendant's negligence: *Allied Maples Group Ltd* v *Simmons & Simmons* 1995 1 WLR 1602; *Bristol & West Building Society* v *Mothew* 1998 Ch 1; *Bogteng* v *Hughmans* 2002 Lloyd's Rep PN 449; *Dent* v *Davis Blank Furniss* 2001 Lloyd's Rep PN 534.

74 Consequently the fact that the claimant would not have purchased the property but for the defendant's negligence does not mean that the defendant is necessarily liable for all the consequences which would not have happened but for the negligence: *South Australia Asset Management Corp* v *York Montague Ltd* 1997 AC 191,

at 214; *Cottingham* v *Attey Bower & Jones* 2000 Lloyd's Rep PN 591. The defendant is liable to compensate the claimant for the foreseeable consequences of the fact that it purchased as a result of the negligence.

75   A solicitor is generally under a duty to provide specific information or advice and not to advise on the wisdom of transactions in general, and the loss for which he is responsible will normally be limited to the consequences of the specific information being inaccurate: for a recent example see *Cottingham* v. *Attey Bower & Jones* 2000 Lloyd's Rep PN 591.

76   As Sir Thomas Bingham MR (as he then was) said in *Reeves* v *Thrings & Long* 1996 1 PNLR 265 at 278 (in a judgment in which he dissented on liability): 'The assessment of damages is ultimately a factual exercise, designed to compensate but not over-compensate the plaintiff for a civil wrong he has suffered. While this is not an area free of legal rules, it is an area in which legal rules may have to bow to the peculiar facts of the case.' So also Cooke P (as he then was) said in *McElroy Milne* v *Commercial Electronics Ltd* 1993 1 NZLR 39, 41:

> . . . in the end assessment of damages is a question of fact: . . . there is no such thing as a rule, applicable to all cases: . . . the ultimate question as to compensatory damages is whether the particular damage claimed is sufficiently linked to the breach of the particular duty to merit recovery in all the circumstances.

77   In *County Personnel (Employment Agency) Ltd* v *Alan R. Pulver & Co* 1987 1 WLR 916, 925–926, Bingham LJ reviewed the principles governing the assessment of damages in cases where a solicitor's negligence has led to a client acquiring defective property. This judgment has been applied on numerous occasions both at first instance and in subsequent decisions of the Court of Appeal. Bingham LJ made the following points: (a) the diminution in value rule appears almost always, if not always, to be appropriate in cases where property is acquired following negligent advice by surveyors and solicitors; (b) that was not, however, an invariable approach, at least in claims against solicitors, and should not be mechanistically applied in circumstances where it may appear inappropriate; (c) consequently the court may make a more general assessment, taking account of the 'general expectation of loss', and in other cases the measure of damage may properly include the cost of making good the error of a negligent adviser; (d) while the general rule is that damages are to be assessed as at the date of breach, the rule should not be mechanistically applied in circumstances where assessment at another date may more accurately reflect the overriding compensatory rule. See also *Reeves* v *Thrings & Long* 1996 1 PNLR 265, 278; *Oates* v *Pitman & Co* 1998 PNLR 683, 694–695; *Gregory* v *Shepherds* 1996 PNLR 769, 782.

78   The diminution in value approach has been applied in the context of solicitors' negligence in *Ford* v *White & Co* 1964 1 WLR 885; *Dent* v *Davis Blank Furniss* 2001 Lloyd's Rep PN 534; *Shaw* v *Fraser Southwell* 1999 Lloyd's Rep PN 633; and *Oates* v *Pitman & Co* 1998 PNLR 683.

9.9.3   Conflicts of interest

Conflicts could come in many shapes and sizes (see **para.4.5**). Whilst there is the obvious difficulty that the HI will have to balance the interests of all the parties who will be relying upon his report he must also take care not to carry out reports or other work for people who may have a personal relationship with him or some other connection through previous or current work commitments. Where the HI is an employee or has some close tied relationship to an estate agent or HIP provider then other disclosures must be made to sellers and buyers who might otherwise feel that there is not fair dealing because of a financial interest or relationship that has not been disclosed.

Paragraph 6(b) of Sched.5 addresses this potential problem by requiring the HCR to record 'whether the home inspector has any personal or business relationship with any person involved in the sale of the property'. At first sight this looks to be a comprehensive protection for the consumer but the words 'involved in the sale' are limiting. An HI tied in any way to a lender or solicitor would not necessarily have to disclose this since, at the time of his appointment, there would be no involvement 'in the sale' – lenders only get involved when there is a buyer, long after the HCR will have been prepared. This might, at a later date, be extended to read 'involved in the sale or purchase of residential property and the funding of such purchases'.

HIs will rely on, and be guided in practice by, the terms on which their professional indemnity insurance is available. This is a prerequisite for licensing by their chosen certifying body. Their certification scheme must also have a complaints scheme which will have built into it procedures for dealing with failures in service provision that fall short of negligence but nevertheless cause loss or other damage to a consumer.

Buyers will wish to be able to make claims against the HI if a defect in a property is not disclosed by the HCR although it will not generally be possible where the defect is a 'hidden' or latent one. This aspect has been addressed in Denmark by latent defects insurance that is compulsory and the cost of which is shared by the seller and the buyer.

If the buyer proceeds with a purchase and then has to meet unexpected costs for remedial works there could be recourse to the HI. While there is no cap on the excess negotiated by an HI with his insurer, the minimum terms require the insurer to protect claimants above a threshold of £2,500. The HCR originally contained a *de minimis* provision to exclude claims of less than £1,000. This has now been omitted.

Whilst an approved scheme must contain procedures for rectifying an error in an HCR (reg.33(f)(iii)), it is not clear whether a seller will be entitled to a refund of the fee paid.

9.9.4   Rights

HIs do not seem to have any specific rights set out in Part 5. They must abide by their codes of conduct regarding conflicts of interest and breaches can give rise to claims and/or complaints. They may be called in to carry out property health checks and may become involved in remedial work by sellers and buyers. They may be asked by prospective lenders to give valuation advice even though, as HIs, they will not do so for the seller.

9.10   SOLICITORS

9.10.1   Challenges for the future

For solicitors the substance of work to be done may not be changing but the new sequencing of work challenges the viability of existing business models. To meet this challenge the types of service traditionally provided to sellers and estate agents will need to be augmented. Inevitably, the new opportunities increase exposure to potential claims along with new responsibilities. The Law Society's Regulation Board has issued initial, draft guidance (see **Appendix H**).

There are a number of possible new areas of work:

* property selling;
* producing HIPs;
* advising both buyers and sellers on HIPs;
* advising estate agents and HIs; and
* advising sellers who act for themselves instead of instructing an estate agent.

9.10.2   Liabilities/obligations

Whether acting for a seller or buyer, solicitors' obligations to clients are an amalgam of the general law and the Solicitors' Practice Rules 1990.

The first and foremost obligation of solicitors before starting to act is the retainer letter under Practice Rule 15 setting out the basis on which the solicitor is acting and the procedure for complaints. The solicitor has a general duty of care to a client and the specific duties that arise from the solicitor/client relationship such as confidentiality and avoidance of conflict. In certain limited cases these are overridden by duties to the court and duties under specific legislation such as the Money Laundering Regulations 2003.

In the context of the HIP legislation the role of the solicitor has expanded beyond simply acting for seller, buyer or lender. Instructions may be received from agents, HIP providers, HIs or other marketing intermediaries. In each case the solicitor's conduct must be determined by first asking the question 'who is the client?' Even where the instructions come from an agent it is likely that the agent's principal will be considered to be the 'real' client.

Negligence claims are met by the solicitor's PI insurance and compensation fund arrangements while the provisions of Courts and Legal Services Act 1990, s.37A relating to inadequate professional services can provide redress of up to £15,000 from 1 January 2006. This can apply where negligence is not proved but loss/damage or distress and inconvenience has been sustained as a result of the solicitor's lack of care or breach of the duty of care in the delivery of work to the expected standard.

If the solicitor is acting in the role of estate agent (as defined in Part 5) he will be required to meet the same obligations and liabilities as an 'estate agent' as described in s.149. Whilst not liable to the PMA 1991 obligations when acting purely in the capacity of conveyancing solicitor, the solicitor can be liable if acting as estate agent as defined in Part 5. Solicitors planning to become engaged in Part 5 activities through any kind of centralised operation advising or acting for clients (other than face-to-face in the traditional manner) will also have to be aware of the ambit of the Consumer Protection (Distance Selling) Regulations 2000 and 2005. Regard will also have to be had to the Unfair Terms in Consumer Contracts Regulations 1999 and the recent EU Directives on unfair terms in consumer contracts. Guidance was issued by the OFT on 12 September 2006 (see the 'Business information' section of the OFT website (**www.oft.gov.uk**)).

A solicitor acting as an estate agent will need to belong to a complaints and redress scheme for estate agents (although it is possible that the Law Society's complaints regime will be 'approved' under this legislation) and be subject to any such other rule changes as the Law Society may introduce to meet the new legislation.

Where solicitors prepare the HIP for sellers or estate agents then responsibilities will flow from that contract under its express or implied terms and solicitors will need to be aware of the potential exposure of their client to claims as described in this chapter.

The general position of solicitors in respect of liability for loss consequent upon negligent advice is summarised in the extract from *Greymalkin Limited* v. *Copleys* (*a firm*) [2004] PNLR 44 (see **para.9.9.2**). This is particularly relevant where the solicitor prepares a summary of the HIP or any document in the pack. A health warning would be appropriate indicating that no reliance should be placed upon general statements and that case-specific advice should be obtained (reg.9(c)). See **para.9.2** regarding disclaimers.

9.10.3   Rights

No special rights appear in Part 5 but this new regime does give solicitors the opportunity to proactively advise their clients who are planning to sell or buy residential property and at an earlier stage in negotiations than at present. The new types of contractual relationship with the HI and HIP provider could drive up demand for new advisory services.

Solicitors are well placed to prepare the HIP. Working within traditional local markets with local estate agents they should be able to ensure that the HIPs provided to potential buyers are compliant and appropriate. On a national scale the potential for the growth of online conveyancing services is enhanced by the add-on of HIP preparation that can be undertaken for sellers before they come to make a final decision to start marketing or even choose a selling agent.

Pre-sale planning is also set to grow in importance and those who choose to market themselves without an estate agent will in all probability still rely upon legal advice from a solicitor or licensed conveyancer.

The role of the buyer's solicitor will also evolve as points of difference between different types of property will be more clearly demarcated and the implications of that for a subsequent sale will become of increased importance to buyers.

9.11   NEWSPAPERS, MAGAZINES AND INTERNET SERVICE PROVIDERS

These media do not on the face of it have direct responsibility under Part 5 (see s.150).

At present, as sub-contractors, they accept and publish advertisements for residential properties from someone representing the seller. The existence of advertising is arguably 'with a view to effecting the introduction to the seller of a person wishing to buy the property' and unless in receipt of direct instructions from the seller they are not considered to be Responsible Persons.

If, however, their role is one that fits the definition of 'marketing instructions' in s.150(2)(b) they will be treated as an estate agent. So, if they do 'anything in the course of a business in England and Wales in pursuance of marketing instructions from the seller' (s.150(1)), this would constitute the advertising intermediary into an estate agent. The OFT 2005 Intermediaries Guidance clarifies the position.

9.12   ALL PARTICIPANTS IN THE PROCESS

Everyone involved in property transactions could be exposed to a claim for breach of copyright if they copy, distribute or otherwise disseminate packs or information contained in HIPs in which they do not have copyright or the permission of the copyright owner to reproduce the HIP or any part of it. The importance of copyright and ownership of the HIP has been considered in **Chapter 7**.

Authors will be concerned to control and license use of their reports and information and limit the class of distributors who are licensed to use or reproduce it. Sellers will clearly be advised to have ownership but HIP providers will wish to put ownership under restrictions until the HIP is paid for.

The estate agent as the front-line publisher of the HIP will work to limit exposure for republishing work produced and authored by others but will want to assert rights in textual arrangements. This would prevent competitors from copying and using the work done by the first estate agent who wins the marketing instructions.

Whether any of the participants will wish to become involved in pursuing claims under any of the above will depend on the cost and time that might be involved. Even though the small claims court might beckon, most people who have dipped their toe into litigation know that the time and money that needs to be expended in pursuing a claim can quickly become out of proportion with the 'wrong' that needs to be redressed. It is to be hoped therefore that redress schemes to be set up under the regulations for this legislation will be simple and have sufficient bite to make the process work and thus gain the confidence of all participants.

> **Key points**
>
> - Check all contractual arrangements for 'appropriate' exclusions and limitations.
> - Check that clauses are not void for breach of the Unfair Terms in Consumer Contracts Regulations 1999 (as amended).
> - Check indemnity insurance policy cover for Responsible Person and others.
> - Aim for accuracy and completeness.
> - Avoid verbal assurances that could override contents of HIP.
> - Sellers to ensure that the HIP is portable.
> - Buyers to be prepared to make full and frank disclosure of financial position.
> - Buyer to be prepared to move quickly.
> - Estate agents to instigate record keeping and HIP tracking procedures.
> - Estate agents to ensure they are members of an approved redress scheme.
> - HIP providers to consider the Money Laundering Regulations 2003, set industry standards of conduct and offer a redress/complaints scheme.
> - HIs to set clear policy on conflicts and taking on work additional to EPC/HCR.
> - HIs to check indemnity insurance terms and excess.
> - Solicitors to consider duties under Part 5 and adapt for new business models.
> - Solicitor estate agents to check duties under PMA 1991.
> - Check copyright and ownership of HIP.

10 COMPLAINTS AND REDRESS

The HIP is primarily consumer protection legislation for buyers and so it should not come as a surprise to learn that Part 5 opens up additional pathways to redress by complaint against estate agents and others. Faced with new regulation that adds to the burden of PMA 1991 and the Money Laundering Regulations 2003, estate agents have little option but to establish training and compliance procedures with a view to raising standards and avoiding the damage that can easily be suffered by an otherwise successful business.

10.1 ESTATE AGENTS

10.1.1 General

New complaints and redress schemes are to be established and all those acting as estate agents under Part 5 must belong. Section 172 provides that:

(1) The Secretary of State may by order require every estate agent to be a member of an approved redress scheme.
(2) Acting as estate agent for the seller of a residential property in contravention of such an order is a breach of duty under this Part.

This introduces a major reform of the regulation of residential estate agents. Until now estate agents have been self-regulating, subject only to the provisions of EAA 1979 and its subordinate legislation. In that legislation estate agents are widely defined to include buyers' agents as well as sellers' agents. The provisions also apply to commercial property. Under the system of what is termed 'negative licensing' a limited number of obligations are imposed by statute in relation to core aspects of agency practice such as the establishment of client accounts and various conduct rules. Enforcement is through the powers of the OFT to ban persons who are convicted of certain offences or who breach particular statutory provisions. The enforcement powers have now been strengthened by Part 8 of the Enterprise Act 2002 which enables action to be taken to protect consumer interests through 'stop' orders where there is infringement of consumer legislation. This may have led to the increasing number of undertakings from estate agents and, in some cases, banning orders.

The Estate Agents (Provision of Information) Regulations 1991, SI 1991/859 established detailed requirements for letters of engagement and for information about fees and charges that must be given to clients (note OFT press release, 18 July 2006, No.116/06). However, provisions relating to the introduction of minimum standards of competence contained in EAA 1979, s.22 have never been triggered. Many practitioners and organisations involved in the industry continue to lobby for a full licensing system in order to improve standards and to counteract adverse publicity. This is frequently attracted by the misdemeanours of those who, without qualifications, have the capital to set up as an estate agency business and then operate free from the constraints of any code of conduct. Trade associations such as NAEA have rules of conduct but these do not have statutory force and apply only to members.

The OFT Report, *Estate Agency Market in England and Wales* (March 2001 (OFT 693)) contains the comment:

> Quality of service can be improved by either setting higher standards for estate agents, or by requiring agents to provide compensation for poor service, thereby providing them with the incentive to ensure good service.

The report noted a high level of consumer dissatisfaction with agency services, with over 20 per cent of buyers and sellers complaining about a specific matter. Other problems associated with complaints were noted and many issues such as doorstep selling and unfair marketing practices were acknowledged as going largely undetected. The report made recommendations for a statutory redress scheme to be prepared in case a voluntary code for the industry did not work.

The government stated repeatedly in 2005 and 2006 that it intends to introduce further legislation applying to all agency work but the requirement in Part 5 for residential estate agents to belong to an approved redress scheme will be implemented to ensure that, for the purpose of HIPs, all estate agents do register with one redress scheme or another. This can be introduced by a ministerial order if the broader legislation mooted is not prepared in time for the start of the HIP regime. The Queen's Speech 2006 may include wider reform within its proposals for legislation against unfair commercial selling practice.

It is not yet clear whether registration of any redress scheme will be personal or corporate or a mixture of the two with an employer registering and being required to identify those members of staff to be included in the registration.

The new HIP redress system will be limited firstly to persons selling residential property as estate agents and secondly will relate only to complaints arising from duties in respect of the HIP. The establishment of schemes dealing with complaints will doubtless encourage tighter controls on market practice and promote the importance of training and education generally.

Thus, a prerequisite of acting as an estate agent under Part 5 will be membership of a redress scheme. Failure to belong will be a breach of duty under the Act leading to the service of a PCN (s.168(1)) and, more importantly, to an exercise of powers of referral to the OFT. The OFT has powers under the Estate Agents (Undesirable Practices) No.2 Order 1991, SI 1991/1032 both to warn estate agents about their business practices and, if necessary, to prohibit an individual or organisation from acting as an estate agent (EAA 1979, ss.3 and 4).

It is not yet clear how many schemes will seek to be approved. Under s.172(3) 'the Secretary of State must be satisfied that he has approved one or more redress schemes such that every estate agent who is (or will be) subject to the duty imposed by the order is eligible to join an approved redress scheme'.

A reference to EAA 1979 in s.172(3) makes it clear that persons who are banned from operating as estate agents are not eligible to join a scheme.

10.1.2   Ad hoc selling

The wide definition of 'estate agent' in Part 5 means that persons other than full-time dedicated estate agents may need to join a scheme for periodic or irregular transactions. This could affect letting agents and management agents who undertake occasional sales. Solicitors may find it necessary to join if they undertake sales and marketing work and if the Law Society's general redress scheme is not approved or does not seek accreditation under this legislation. Generally, however, the scheme may operate as a deterrent to 'dabblers' and restrict the number of operators in the market place.

10.1.3   Existing schemes

The Secretary of State may provide that certain categories of estate agents such as those already members of the RICS or any other body with a complaints and redress system will not have to comply separately with the s.172(1) requirement. This alternative is set out in s.172(4). It remains to be seen whether solicitors acting as estate agents who are already subject to the Law Society Consumer Complaints Scheme are exempt from joining a separate scheme. The NAEA has made membership of their association subject to compulsory membership of the Estate Agents Ombudsman Scheme (OEA) with effect from April 2006.

The requirement to belong to a scheme is absolute, but a scheme is only obliged to act in relation to 'relevant complaints of a prescribed description'. A 'relevant complaint' is defined as:

. . . a complaint against an estate agent which –

  (a) is made by a person who at the material time is the seller or a potential buyer of a residential property; and
  (b) relates to an act or omission affecting the complainant in the course of the estate agent's activities in relation to a home information pack that is (or will be) required for that property (including the giving of advice as to whether such a pack is required).

(s.172(6))

As it stands, a statutory redress scheme need only have a remit to act on complaints which relate to the estate agent's duties under this legislation and not generally. Nothing further has yet emerged regarding 'a prescribed description' and regulations are still awaited that may overtake this scheme.

A substantial volume of complaints can be anticipated. Initially, the number may be inflated by misunderstandings of the estate agent's duties or the scope of the contents of the HIP. Complaints could relate to the content of the HIP where this is believed to be incomplete or misleading. There is potential overlap with the TSO's powers to enforce. Additionally, it will be interesting to see how the complaints regime will engage with issues that might otherwise be actionable through the courts. It is to be expected that the required standard of proof may fall below the 'balance of probabilities' test that would be required in court. The provisions of the Solicitors Act 1974 as amended in relation to inadequate professional services may be regarded as setting a precedent for this (Solicitors Act 1974, s.37A).

Where buyers are refused a copy of the HIP and the agent purports to exercise powers under ss.156 and 157 there could be challenges from disgruntled buyers and allegations of discriminatory behaviour may be raised.

Section 172(5) allows existing redress schemes to be approved. They would not be required to deal exclusively with 'relevant complaints'. This could include schemes that are open to agents who do not sell residential property such as commercial or letting agents and schemes with authority to investigate other complaints so long as the members agree to this extended jurisdiction. Schemes that impose limitations such as time limitations for complaints to be made will be able to seek and obtain approval – such terms of reference would not operate as an automatic bar. Different standards may therefore apply across the market.

By way of example the existing OEA scheme requires members to first exhaust their internal procedure for handling complaints under its Code of Practice before a referral can be made.

Section 172 defines a redress scheme as being 'a scheme under which certain relevant complaints may be investigated and determined by an independent person' (generally referred to as 'the ombudsman') and an approved redress scheme as 'a redress scheme that is for the time being approved under section 173'.

Section 172(7) puts any ombudsman on a par with other statutory ombudsmen in allowing enquiries and process to take place without threat of being sued for defamation.

Before giving approval, the Secretary of State must be satisfied with the organisation of a scheme and that its provisions give effect to the aspirations of this legislation. A redress scheme will not be approved unless it makes satisfactory provision about the matters set out in s.173(3) including:

(a)   the matters about which complaints may be made (which may include non-compliance with the provisions of a code of practice or other document);

(b) the ombudsman's duties and powers in relation to the investigation and determination of complaints (which may include power to decide not to investigate or determine a complaint);

(c) the provision of information by the ombudsman to –

    (i) persons exercising functions under other schemes providing a means of redress for consumers; and

    (ii) the Secretary of State or any other person exercising regulatory powers in relation to the activities of estate agents.

The Secretary of State will wish to ensure that there is a proper balance between the interests of the members of the scheme and the interests of the consumer. He will also require assurance that any scheme has clear rules as to the type of complaint the scheme will consider (including breaches of a code of practice thereby signposting it might be a good idea to have one); that the ombudsman has the appropriate powers to deal with complaints (and not unduly limit his jurisdiction); and making provisions for the ombudsman to share information with other schemes presumably to ensure that recalcitrant agents do not switch redress schemes either in an attempt to avoid liability or their previous defaults coming to light.

The rules and requirements for setting up a scheme will be decided by the Secretary of State and notice must be given to the Secretary of State of any changes made to any approved scheme. As a corollary to his powers to approve a redress scheme the Secretary of State has powers to withdraw approval. If the Secretary of State decides to withdraw approval of a scheme, notice of the decision, with reasons, must be given to the person administering the scheme. The withdrawal of approval will take effect, and the scheme cease to be approved, on the date specified in the notice. On receipt of such a notice, the person administering the scheme must pass a copy to every member of the scheme so that they can transfer to another approved scheme and avoid a breach of s.172(1).

Under s.173(2)(c) a redress scheme is required to provide information about any complaint to any regulator of estate agents. This will include the OFT (s.175), which has powers under the EAA 1979 to prohibit 'unfit' persons from acting as estate agents. The OFT can also serve warning notices on agents. This is not, however, a sanction for use against sellers who are members of the public. Professional bodies such as the Law Society can be expected to make new rules in due course for the discipline of its members.

Also, the OFT *must* be notified of:

(a) any penalty charge notice given by an officer of the authority under section 168;

(b) any notice given by the authority confirming or withdrawing a penalty charge notice; and

(c) the result of any appeal from the confirmation of a penalty charge notice.

(s.175(2))

(See also **Chapter 8** on enforcement.)

This means that the OFT will in future maintain a record relating to the conduct of estate agents under Part 5 as well as under EAA 1979. Obviously, these records will be assessed when deciding whether to prohibit a person from acting as an estate agent or serving a warning notice on them. To prohibit a person acting as an estate agent or restricting their estate agent activities the OFT must be satisfied, *inter alia*, that the estate agent has been convicted of one (or more) of the specified offences or been guilty of discrimination in the course of estate agency work or failed to meet obligations under EAA 1979, s.3).

Section 175(3) specifically provides that a breach of any duty under Part 5 will be regarded as if it were a breach of EAA 1979.

Recent OFT cases show an increasing appetite for enforcement as can be seen by perusal of its website (see www.oft.gov.uk/news). Reports of the making of pro hibition and warning orders are published on the site together with a note advising that a public register of Prohibition and Warning Orders is kept by the OFT at the Consumer Credit Licensing Bureau. Offences that carry such penalties can be found in the Estate Agents (Specified Offences) No.2 Order 1991, SI 1991/1091. This sets out a list of the offences enabling the OFT to make an order if it considers a person is unfit to carry on estate agency work. An order can be made if a person is convicted of an offence involving dishonesty, breach of certain provisions of EAA 1979 or of another specified Act or engaged in an undesirable practice and if the director considers the person is unfit to carry on estate agency work.

The current OEA scheme is a voluntary one and for that reason was considered inadequate especially as it covered only about 40 per cent of estate agents. In September 2005 it received stage 1 recognition under the OFT Consumer Codes Approval Scheme (CCAS). The scheme has a Code of Practice with which members must comply and the code covers market appraisals of properties, terms of business including instructions, commission and termination, marketing and advertising, canvassing, viewings and access to premises, offers, discrimination, clients' money, conflicts, exchange of contracts and completion, compliance and monitoring and in-house complaints handling and referrals to the OEA. The code, a consumer guide to the scheme, and an explanation of the procedures for complaints can be found on the OEA's website (www.oea.co.uk).

The OEA is only able to deal with complaints against member agents made by individuals who are actual or potential buyers or sellers of residential property in the UK (the scheme covers, with certain amendments, both Scotland and Northern Ireland) and after the relevant in-house complaints procedure has been exhausted. The code imposes relatively short time limits for the in-house complaints procedure and requires the notification of a decision on the complaint to include information about the possibility of a referral to the OEA. Members of this voluntary scheme must submit to and assist the OEA in any investigation into a complaint and must comply with any award made.

If there is a referral to the OEA the complaint is assigned to a case officer who may call for the agent's file and an explanation of or comment on the complaint. The OEA aims to conclude a referral within 3–4 months of the complaint being received.

In addition to being able to find for or against the complainant, the procedure also allows for a 'negotiated solution'. So, where an offer to settle the complaint has been made by the estate agent and has not been accepted, the OEA may, while not giving advice on acceptance or otherwise, indicate that the offer is considered 'not unreasonable'.

The procedure for appeals against a decision is that the complaint and the decision are passed for fresh consideration by a different case officer who will discuss the complaint and the original decision with the OEA. There is a four-week time limit within which an appeal must be lodged.

This voluntary scheme indicates the type of redress scheme that the government may wish to approve although it may prefer future schemes to have more 'teeth' to deal with defaulters rather than leaving all disciplinary activities to the OFT.

10.2   HOME INSPECTORS

10.2.1   General

The Act introduced the new property profession of HI and s.164(5) indicated that schemes under which HIs would operate would be required by the Regulations to incorporate a procedure to deal with 'the resolution of complaints against members of the scheme'.

Regulations 33–35 deal with approved certification schemes for HIs. Regulation 33(c) repeats the requirement for bodies to provide a complaints and redress scheme and, in para.33(f)(ii), requires details of the complaints procedure to be included in the HCR itself rather than in any contract to prepare the same. This may appear odd but is necessary because of the possibility that the contract for the inspection and preparation of the HCR will not be between the seller and the HI but with an estate agent, pack provider or someone else on the seller's behalf. Whilst it is possible that a seller may see such a contract, the buyer and lender almost certainly will not.

Regulation 34(b) also imposes a duty on the certification bodies to produce a code of conduct for HIs, breach of which will, no doubt, give rise to redress in some form.

No further detail relating to these complaints and redress schemes can be found in the Regulations but are detailed instead in the DCLG Certification Scheme Standards (Parts 1 and 2) which can be accessed at the HIP website (**www.homeinformationpacks.gov.uk/certification-scheme.aspx**). Standard 5 of this document deals with consumer complaints and is divided into two parts – minimum operational standards and performance standards.

It is intended that each HI will deal with a complaint in the first instance under his, or his employer's, complaints handling process. If the complaint cannot be resolved at this level it will be 'escalated' to the Certification Scheme for consideration. Even if a complaint is resolved by the HI or his employers written notice must be given to the Scheme of all and any complaints. HIs must maintain a separate 'complaint history' which must be available for inspection at any time by the certification scheme or schemes of which he is a member and whether or not the complaint is resolved.

The complainant can request that the complaint be 'escalated' at any time and there is no charge to the complainant for doing so. The scheme may operate any form of alternative dispute resolution it deems appropriate for complaints handling and will be required to have a formal relationship with an independent third party to whom a complaint that cannot be resolved by the scheme will be passed for adjudication. The decision of any adjudicator will be binding on the HI but not on the complainant.

Schemes will be required to review both resolved and unresolved complaints (presumably by adopting regular monitoring of HIs) and will be required to meet performance targets for complaint handling at all levels, including adjudication and arbitration, as agreed with DCLG who will operate as a regulator with, possibly, powers to fine schemes for failing to meet standards where the failure is not serious enough to warrant withdrawal of approval (see **para.4.2**). A final sting in the regulatory tail is that schemes are to consider referring all customer complaints to its disciplinary process, the outline of which is discussed in **para.10.2.4**. At the time of writing it is not yet clear what scheme will be introduced for persons qualified to deliver the EPC.

10.2.2   Adjudication

The Performance Standards in Part 2 of Standard 5 outline powers that must be given to the independent third-party adjudicator. The adjudicator will decide whether the complaint reveals that the HI has fallen below the required standard of technical competence and, if so, will have power to award compensation in a stated sum to be paid by the HI to the complainant and/or to report the HI to the disciplinary arm of his certification scheme. Where a service complaint rather than a complaint concerning technical competence is upheld the adjudicator can order the HI to pay a stated sum to compensate for any material loss, stress and inconvenience.

10.2.3   Consumer rights

The certification schemes are required to ensure that consumers are made aware that their legal rights are not affected by participation in the complaints resolution process – it is assumed that a statement to this effect will be one of the additional terms included in the HCR. Records and regular review of all complaints are required to meet the performance standards and schemes will be monitored for compliance in addition to filing performance reports with the DCLG. The HI must make all complaint files available for inspection by his certifying body and these bodies will be subject to spot checks as to their analysis of complaints as well as their handling. They will also be required to include information about complaints in their annual accounts – both qualitative and quantative. If the scheme incorporates any additional, and therefore voluntary, standards, information about these must be kept separate from the compulsory standards.

10.2.4   Disciplinary

Standard 6 defines the requirements for disciplinary processes in certification schemes and again is divided between minimum operational standards and performance standards.

Referral of an HI to the disciplinary process will follow if there is a breach of the Code of Conduct, where a complaint is upheld or where deemed appropriate following investigation, monitoring or auditing of the conduct and/or work of the HI.

10.2.5   Disciplinary panel

Schemes are required to publish a list of the sanctions that can follow a referral and to set up an independent disciplinary panel to adjudicate as part of the disciplinary process in the event that there is the possibility of suspension or withdrawal of membership or if requested by the HI.

The following are broadly the minimum standards required. The panel should operate separately and independently from the scheme itself and should comprise at least three people, one of whom should be a qualified HI and the other two lay members with no expertise in home inspections. The panel will have power to suspend HIs and will be required to review suspensions at least every six months. Power should be given to the panel to convene at short notice where it is considered appropriate to do so.

10.2.6   Panel procedure

The Performance Standards in Part 2 of Standard 6 set out the procedure for disciplinary panels and include requirements that:

- the HI has a right to attend and make representations at any hearing with full legal representation;
- all documents be made available to the HI for examination;
- at least 28 days' notice of any hearing be given with details of the allegations to be considered and copies of any evidence the certification scheme will be using at the hearing;
- a tariff of sanctions be publicised that may include power to issue a formal warning, impose conditions on the HI's membership of the scheme such as retraining, impose a fine and/or suspend or withdraw membership;

- records be kept of the disciplinary process;
- HIs are advised of the panel's powers but not implying that it is a court of law;
- the process is fairly applied and that cognisance is taken of laws relating to discrimination, data protection and human rights;
- disciplinary processes are carried out in private unless otherwise requested although findings will be published;
- performance reporting information will be submitted to the DCLG including agreed targets to include the number of disciplinary cases heard in the reporting period and an analysis of awards made as a result; as with complaints these performance standards must be kept separate from any voluntary ones;
- records relating to monitoring these standards will be made available to the DCLG and assistance given to enable spot checks of the processes, the accuracy of reports and the number of disciplinary processes;
- annual reports will include details of the qualitative and quantitative aspects of the disciplinary process; and
- the names of HIs whose membership has been withdrawn or suspended be given to other certification schemes.

Certification schemes will also be required to have procedures and panels to deal with registration and memberships appeals (Standard 7) and to require lifelong learning (continuing professional development) by HIs (Standard 8).

HIs are required to have indemnity insurance to meet claims and redress awards, as has been discussed in **Chapter 4**.

It should be noted that this scheme was devised for the HCR and, at the time of writing, proposals are awaited to deal with the stand alone EPC.

10.3   LAWYERS

The Law Society, the Council for Licensed Conveyancers and the Institute of Legal Executives have relatively similar procedures for dealing with complaints, redress and disciplinary matters. The respective websites for these bodies contain details of complaints procedures. The inadequate professional services process for solicitors may order compensation of up to £15,000 for a complaint that falls short of professional negligence but fails the professional standards of service expected. Further changes to disciplinary process for all lawyers are expected if the Legal Services Bill becomes law as this will establish an Office for Legal Complaints on a profession-wide basis.

10.4   SEARCH PROVIDERS

The required contents of a search report carried out by a personal search company are set out in para.1 of Sched.8. Such a report must contain the name of the persons liable for any error in the records searched, the interpretation of the records searched and the recording of the interpretation of the records searched.

It must also contain 'a description of such complaints or redress procedures as exist in relation to the search report'. Although there is no absolute requirement to set up such schemes, there will doubtless be pressure from customers of such services that will bring about a need to establish them.

Search companies are required to have indemnity insurance to meet any claims as discussed in **Chapter 3**.

10.5   PACK PROVIDERS

The Act makes no provision for HIP providers to be regulated as their appearance was not foreseen by the legislators and there is presently no requirement for them to be insured or to offer a complaints or redress procedure. The trade association, AHIPP, is expected to produce a code of practice to show a degree of self-regulation. As with CoPSO, the trade body for search companies, the problem will be to engage with all members of the industry whilst membership remains voluntary.

Key points

Estate agents:

■   belong to a redress scheme – find a scheme to join;
■   consider a code of practice in a voluntary scheme and benchmark against this;
■   prepare in-house complaints procedure;
■   appoint a complaints officer;
■   check OFT case reports of warning and prohibition orders to note activities that bring disciplinary action.

Others:

■   consider redress and complaints scheme for HIs;
■   consider redress and complaints scheme for search providers;
■   consider redress and complaints scheme for HIP suppliers;
■   search companies to ensure adequate training for employees;
■   consider terms of insurance cover and terms as to minimum claims and maximum excess.

11 THE DRY RUN

Late in the passage of the legislation the government conceded that the new system would benefit from a 'Dry Run' of all aspects of the scheme and July 2006 was discussed as a possible start date. No indication was given at that time as to the basis on which any formal trialing would take place and doubts were expressed as to whether it would leave enough time for the pilot to take place for three to six months and for the results to be evaluated before the planned commencement, then targeted for 1 January 2007. There was also concern that objections to the regime generally or arising from problems uncovered as a result of the Dry Run would delay the start date of the new system.

The government statement of 18 July 2006, deferring the introduction of the HCR as a compulsory element of the HIP, announced that fresh proposals concerning the Dry Run would be published along with a fresh regulatory impact assessment of the new proposals.

11.1 HISTORY

Readers may recall that a pilot scheme took place in Bristol in 1999, lasting for about eight months. This involved 13 estate agency firms with a total of 31 branches, along with six firms of solicitors, two licensed conveyancers, six local surveying firms and the in-house legal department of the house builder, Beazer Homes. Sellers packs were issued (including 30 on new homes) to 189 vendors and buyers were found for 99 properties. Exchange of contracts proceeded on 90 properties, nine failed between offer/acceptance and exchange of contracts while 25 were withdrawn from the market. There were three sellers who withdrew from the scheme and, by the end of the pilot, 62 properties were still on the market seeking a buyer (see **www.communities.gov.uk**).

The pilot encouraged participation by making the HIP free of cost to any seller who marketed through an estate agent who was a member of the OEA scheme, which was then voluntary (changed for members of NAEA from April 2006). Post pilot research suggested that the HIPs were a success giving transparency and certainty and that HIPs could be assembled in less than 10 working days.

Concerns, however, remained on a number of aspects and local participants and observers of the pilot have levelled many criticisms.

11.2   TIMELINE

In March 2006 the government published the timeline proposed in the run up to the commencement date, which was confirmed to be 1 June 2007. This envisaged 'the launch of a series of geographical industry led trials' ('Home Information Pack Programme: Timeline', DCLG news release, 16 March 2006). These were intended to run as a continuing Dry Run alongside the attainment of other staging posts. They were to include government approval in September 2006 of the first certification schemes for HIs and the establishment of a contract for setting up the central HCR register. (It is not yet known when this register will be operational.) The DCLG news release envisaged that, from November 2006 to June 2007, lenders would be able to use the HCR for valuation purposes cutting down on the need for on-site valuations and producing the first evidence of savings for consumers. The Dry Run then envisaged was different from that which certain parliamentarians thought they had negotiated.

Some informal trials have taken place continuously as estate agencies have offered clients a free or voluntary pack and they have reported a reasonable level of participation and success. Few of these packs have included an HCR. However, the overall success and value of any Dry Run will depend upon the size and scope of the sample of transactions that will be monitored and how any problems that emerge are addressed.

11.3   COMPULSORY DRY RUN

There have been calls for the Dry Run to be compulsory, arguing that this can be the only way to truly evaluate the working of the scheme and to highlight any deficiencies. Consideration was given to a compulsory trial in a specific geographic area but this and most other suggestions have been rejected as impractical.

Whatever pilots do take place, the main component that may be missing is the one that is crucial to the new system as a whole and which is, unfortunately, the most expensive element in the HIP – the HCR.

11.4   DELAYS

Estate agents were (and remain) particularly worried about the time needed to assemble a HIP once the scheme becomes compulsory. They are concerned that there will be external bottlenecks if local authorities find themselves short of resources when required to produce high volumes of searches.

The HCR was expected to be a cause of delay in collating the pack because of a shortage of qualified HIs. These qualified and registered professionals may need up to three years to qualify. Conversion courses became available in late 2005 for qualified surveyors who needed to undertake short conversion and induction training being already experienced and holding relevant surveying or building qualifications. These have had poor uptake. Other training courses have so far yielded only about 235 qualified HIs although 4,500 were stated to be in training on 18 July 2006 (*Hansard*, 20 July 2006, col.14).

11.5   AIMS OF THE DRY RUN

In April 2005, the aims of the Dry Run were stated by an ODPM working group to be:

– to enable the industry to put into operation the Home Information Pack processes and systems they have developed since summer 2005;
– to enable the industry to test the certification scheme arrangements for home condition reports (HCR) under operational conditions – in particular flows of information to and from the electronic databank of HCRs;
– to enable the industry to test systems for compiling Home Information Packs quickly in order to avoid delaying commencement of the marketing process;
– to help give the industry time to become accustomed to the home information pack process and ensure that their systems are ready for the mandatory scheme;
– to help prepare the home buying and selling public for a revised process where key information will be available to them up front at the start of the process to assist their decisions and negotiations, rather than after terms have been negotiated/agreed;
– to enable government and industry to identify and address any outstanding problem areas that might otherwise put at risk a successful implementation of home information packs;
– to inform the Secretary of State's use of the flexibility contained in the Housing Act 2004 to fine tune home information packs by regulations (for example, if a particular pack item cannot be compiled quickly and causes a log jam, to allow this to be included in the pack later, thereby avoiding holding up the marketing).

ODPM Working Group Minutes

For the Dry Run to meet these aims the scheme in all of its component parts would, in effect, need to be up and running. These would include:

• the regulations to be made under the Act prescribing the contents of the HIP; the form of prescribed documents (if any); any special provisions for certain types of property; HI certification and registration schemes; the HCR register and details of any properties to be excluded from the HIP obligations;
• the various stakeholders in residential property transactions being ready to prepare and deal with the HIP and the new process;
• the existence of an estate agent's redress scheme;
• the existence of one or more approved certification schemes for HIs; and
• the existence of the HCR database for registration of HCRs.

Many practitioners firmly believe it is particularly important that the new elements comprising the HCR with its registration arrangements and the HI accreditation schemes should be fully operational. This is a radically new process that realistically, will have teething problems and could be the cause of delays and complaints. In relation to sellers, it will be important to assess how they react when they are informed that their home needs to have work undertaken before it can be successfully marketed. The speed and accuracy of reports will be a key to the confidence of buyers and lenders and thus can affect the success of the reforms.

11.6   PUBLIC EDUCATION

The government had hoped that, in conjunction with its publicity campaign, the Dry Run would educate the public to see the benefit of the scheme for all participants. The plan was for a single commencement date although it was always conceivable that parts of the new process could better be introduced by progressive stages enabling markets to adjust over time. Deferring the introduction of the HCR was always worth consideration and has belatedly been decided.

11.7   VOLUNTARY DRY RUN

The Dry Run is voluntary but it was hoped by government that all players in the industry would want to take advantage of the learning opportunity and so encourage their clients to participate. This ignored the unwillingness of clients to incur non-mandatory costs and was unrealistic in its expectation that property professionals would underwrite the costs as a training exercise. With the incidence of chains most professionals regard a Dry Run that is not compulsory as lacking credibility.

The Central Stakeholder Group (CSG), which includes representatives of all parties engaged in the home selling and buying process (i.e. lenders, lawyers, estate agents, surveyors, the Land Registry and consumer groups), have repeatedly expressed strong concerns that the Dry Run must be a valid and credible test of the scheme. A number of these participants pointed out that the industry needed certainty about the pack before being expected to make the investment, in both time and money, to put the new processes and procedures in place. By way of example, the RICS and others pointed out the difficulty in seeking to persuade someone to sign up, pay for and attend a three-year course to train as an HI without certainty that the scheme would go ahead on a fixed date or at all.

The CSG has suggested that the Dry Run needs to address such objectives as:

- whether there is sufficient capacity to provide for the operation of HIPs and, in particular, the availability of HIs to meet the initial need for pre-marketing HCRs;

- the speed with which adjustments can be made to meet problems or delays as the Dry Run progresses;
- the testing of *all* elements of the HIPs process; and
- the overall present and future planned changes to other government agencies such as the Land Registry and how they will link in with the new process.

A consultant's report commissioned by the ODPM in June 2005 cited the following 'success criteria' to form the basis of the Dry Run:

- Provide sufficient HIs by ensuring that demand exists within the industry for members wishing to be certified;
- Identify the implications of HIPs for different house price bands, at different volumes of activity, for freehold, leasehold and new build, for registered and non-registered land and to understand how behaviours may change as a consequence of the implementation of HIPs;
- Identify the impact of HIPs in both rural and urban areas and in areas of high, medium and low demand, and on lending decisions;
- Identify specific process and procedural difficulties with the compilation of a HIP; any areas of particular difficulty; the overall impact on any given property chain; and issues regarding status of the HIP and the need to refresh it during the sales process/transaction;
- Understand whether training needs associated with the Databank have been fully addressed;
- Understand whether the access issues associated with the Databank have been fully addressed;
- Identify whether all HIPs have been compiled consistently throughout the Dry Run sample and whether a consistent message has been conveyed by and/or understood equally by the whole sector;
- Identify the implications of non-standard scenarios, for example where there is a change of intermediary during the sales process; and
  Provide the facility to enable information needs and flows to be fully understood.

The Databank referred to is the proposed register for HCRs (provided for in s.165 of the Act) and, understandably, concern has been expressed that the registers of HCRs will be able, from day one, to deal with registrations of reports and 'authorised-only' access procedures with suitable security and efficiency.

11.8   PROPOSED DRY RUN

These objectives put the government under pressure to ensure that the system could be operationally effective by 1 June 2007. To address the uncertainty and to encourage the main players to engage in the process the government stated that a Dry Run would take place from 1 July 2006 (or possibly earlier to enable time for evaluation of the successful implementation of the various elements) and run for a minimum of six months. There were suggestions that the Dry Run could be extended incrementally by adding areas and types of properties to the scheme as the tests progressed, thereby avoiding the impact of a 'big bang' on the date for mandatory implementation.

For the evaluation of the Dry Run to be of value, clear measurable objectives would need to be set and contingency arrangements developed where the Dry Run did not provide the assurances necessary to support implementation of the mandatory scheme. It would be important to identify reasons for failures particularly if due to a process or format problem or the lack of interest and participation of any sector or sectors of the market. For the Dry Run to be a 'success' there is a need for all parties in the process to co-operate and share information openly.

The ODPM's external consultant's report concluded that:

> The dry run would need to operate in a real environment and enable all systems and processes to be tested to provide appropriate assurance and the confidence to progress to full implementation;

> All aspects of the dry run needed to be in place to enable testing. This could be achieved incrementally. For the databank this would represent mandatory aspects required for implementation, but not necessarily the desirable elements;

> In order for the dry run to be voluntary, there would be a need for all stakeholders to undertake considerable marketing effort to raise awareness and illustrate the benefits of participation. Given the likely time and cost to achieve this, there would be a high risk that the timing for full implementation would be prejudiced. Therefore the dry run should have a mandatory element;

> The sample size will need to be sufficiently large to provide for assessment against all the success criteria identified by the group (although these might yet need to be prioritised). Further work should be undertaken to calculate the optimum size of the sample necessary to provide for the level of assurance required; and how the sample should be calculated;

> The dry run model design must provide for the necessary sample size and may be driven by geography, time and other factors;

> The dry run should begin as soon as possible, building incrementally towards full implementation.

11.9   WHERE ARE WE NOW?

The government announcement of 18 July 2006 threw the plans for the Dry Run into disarray. Three phases were outlined in the updated regulatory impact assessment published on 14 June 2006 and set out at paras.199–205 (see **www.opsi.gov.uk/si/em2006/uksiem_20061503_en.pdf**). Incomplete half HIPs were to be gradually replaced by full packs containing the HCR prepared by registered HIs who would in the final phase be able to register the reports on their certifying bodies' registers and through them on the central register.

These plans are now to be disregarded and fresh proposals are awaited.

On 21 September 2006 a DCLG news release announced that government funding of £4 million is to be allocated for pilot testing of HIPs in November 2006.

Key points

■ Dry Run is a legislative concession.
■ The Bristol pilot.
■ The timeline.
■ Compulsory/voluntary Dry Run.
■ Aims and objectives of:
   – ODPM working groups;
   – Central Stakeholder Group;
   – consultant's report.
■ New proposals awaited.

12 THE FUTURE

One hardly needs a crystal ball to realise that the progress towards an introduction date for the HIP has brought a period of uncertainty for property professionals. Those who currently provide services are under threat as traditional roles are circumvented or remodelled.

Practitioners know that early disclosure is just one possible pill to be swallowed if the government's aim to make homebuying and selling easier, cheaper and more transparent is to become a reality. Many of the project's initial objectives such as increased speed and reduced cost are in doubt. Rather than being a cost-neutral change as argued by government, the view is widely held that the expense incurred in moving home is likely to increase.

In return for any change to the status quo, sellers as well as buyers will expect to see some tangible benefits. However, in the short term, rather than being cut out of the process, the professions are crucial to making the new system work. The roles of solicitors, agents and surveyors will evolve but the transition to new business models may be shaped by other external changes (see draft Legal Services Bill, Cm 6839 at **www.dca.gov.uk**).

One important and necessary outcome from the HIP project should be improved public understanding and ownership of the buying and selling process, and with it a cultural shift that will bring a more informed and therefore more rational approach to buying a home.

At the heart of the original HIP proposal lies the proposition that no decision by a homeowner to sell can be made and actioned in one step; the decision, however prompted, needs to be more carefully planned. This is necessary in order to commence marketing at the optimum time to coincide with the seller's needs with regard to finding a property to move to and other considerations to fit in with the domestic or business agenda. This is illustrated by the traditional peak for completion and home moves seen in July, which accommodates school terms and coincides with annual summer holidays.

In the past finding a property has often preceded the decision to sell – especially where a dream home has been spotted whilst browsing on the off chance. In future, homeowners may well need to plan the sale of their current home in advance of finding a new property to buy.

If fully implemented with the HCR then most buyers, once they have experienced the process, may understand better the importance of keeping an up-to-date file containing relevant information on their new home – adding, as they arise, planning permissions with plans, a new guarantee or warranty for a boiler or local information relating to amenities and the local environment. In addition, records containing fuller details including estimates, invoices and guarantees for work done to remedy 'defects' would become more commonplace. Overall, the quality of information made available on the sale of a home should improve. Other service offerings associated with moving will be adapted to accommodate the new paradigm. Arguably, it is in this context that, over time, homeowners may achieve savings in expense and future outlay.

If the HIP, as it is adopted in practice, proves valuable it is possible that in future, buyers will, even in the case of excluded property, be advised to seek the information and disclosures that would be available to any other home being marketed for sale. Property sellers may respond and develop a positive approach whereby rather than seeking refuge in the exclusions they may adopt the HIP for all types of residential property irrespective of whether they fall strictly within the defined categories.

Ultimately, each home will have a 'log book'; a history of owners' information gleaned from each period of ownership giving a far better picture for new prospective owners. The risks for the buyer would thereby be reduced, along with a reduction in the risk of unwelcome surprises and unbudgeted costs cropping up in the weeks after the move. The information may be stored on external databases that are developed to mirror the HCR register.

The HIP, in whatever form it is introduced, is likely to undergo continuous amendment and development. It is possible that certain authorised information will, over time, become compulsory and that the doctrine of caveat emptor will face gradual erosion as a result. The refinement and introduction of the HCR is now held out as the first likely example of this and new searches, particularly in relation to environmental matters such as flood risk and ground stability, are under development.

To learn from the Danish experience (the system from which the DCLG 'borrowed' a number of elements) there may be a need to refine the Regulations to deal with problems as they arise, particularly with the HCR. The conflict of interest rules and the quality of reports by HIs is crucial to buyer confidence. The market may develop new insurance products, such as insurance for latent defects, to give more consumer confidence. This was introduced in Denmark and has undergone some changes with the result that it is now compulsory and the price is shared equally between the seller and the buyer.

For selling property new media may develop which could bring about a change in marketing methods. At present it is believed that less than 10 per cent of all property is sold privately. If selling a home on the Internet or through a card in a local business's window can save fees in the region of 1 per cent of the purchase price (plus VAT) some people may be tempted to try it. Computers are now in most homes and most of us (or our children) are capable of operating word processing, digital photography and website design programmes. These skills enable sellers to prepare their own property particulars and photographs and to up-load them to customised websites on the Internet. Despite this, there will always be a section of the market that is excluded by age, disability, poverty or lack of education and who will need access to services delivered in an acceptable way appropriate to their needs.

Fixing an asking price for a home is also becoming easier – prices at which properties last sold have been available from the Land Registry since 2000 and there are numerous websites that give information on property value according to street and postcode. If it is in a metropolitan area, most buyers are able to get a good idea as to the value of their target home. Sellers (and their agents) will have a great deal less room for manoeuvre in terms of setting unrealistic asking prices. This is particularly the case if they wish to find a buyer within a timescale that meets the shelf life of the HIP. In future it may become popular to advertise the asking price for a property at 'offers invited in excess of £xx'. One development that could be prompted by the focus on energy efficiency is that buyers may begin to compare the relative cost of outgoings between what seem comparable properties. In Denmark, property outgoings on a monthly basis must be disclosed by the marketing agent in their equivalent of the HIP.

Buyers will have access to HIPs for comparable properties and, once HCRs are widely adopted, they will be able to take a more informed view of what they are planning to buy, how much they should offer and whether to make their offer conditional on withdrawal of the property from the market or subject to remedy of a defect disclosed in the HCR.

How might the role of estate agents be affected? There are, in practice, many services provided by estate agents that sellers generally find tedious, time consuming and unattractive to carry out themselves. Accompanying prospective buyers on viewings is heavy on time and a sensitive stage in the process. By holding keys to the property estate agents are able to free owners' time for work and at weekends as well as for holidays. Viewings with an independent agent usually encourages more productive buyer interest which can be followed up at a later date.

With the advent of HIPs estate agents are likely to keep full details of any prospective buyer who has requested a HIP and can check on their suitability before allowing viewing or arranging for a HIP to be issued. Whilst historical property price information may be available on various websites, the local estate agent should always have more up-to-date information and will know the local market. Having visited many properties, distinctions on matters of detail will be drawn and the existence of chains, which for the time being are unaffected, means that sudden changes of situation affecting both sellers and buyers will for a long time make the estate agent invaluable.

The government, having studied the Danish system, may have started with the vision of an extended role for agents as providers not only of the HIP but also the sale contract and all enquiries leading to an exchange of contracts. However, it should be pointed out that estate agents in Denmark undergo six years of training – four academic years at university and two practical years as a trainee in an estate agent's office – before they are qualified and then bonded and annually licensed to practice.

It is likely that the market for HCRs, if and when introduced, will separate and stratify. Specialist surveyors and engineers will be needed to advise on problems and defects identified by the HCR. As more HIs qualify, many may develop ancillary services either in relation to providing mortgage valuations or in offering pre-marketing condition reports to prospective seller clients. The cost of the HI's indemnity insurance cover is, of course, critical to the way the HI will operate in practice and how useful the HCR becomes. Under the Danish system these reports are not regarded as of great value but that may be the result of local factors and the modernity and well-maintained condition of much of the metropolitan housing stock. In Denmark, until recently, the appointment of the HI was under the control of the estate agent but public perception of bias brought about a change. The estate agent can now only recommend an HI and the seller must appoint and pay the HI directly.

Lenders, having changed their procedures to accommodate the introduction of the HIP, will be likely to develop further new procedures. Accessing the central database for HCRs on property being offered as security for a loan and obtaining copy HIPs for title information might encourage lenders to relax the requirements for separate reports on title and formal valuations. The system may rely more heavily upon the credit scoring of borrowers and the strength of personal covenant rather than the security value of the property. This would be the case particularly if house loans became transferable. As confidence develops and time lags shorten chain-breaking schemes may become more feasible. Bridging finance should become more easily available and competitively priced.

The existence of housebuying and selling chains has been identified as a major source of failed transactions. With the greater transparency, homeowners and banks may become more prepared to consider taking out second mortgages or bridging loans and the costs involved may be reduced. The risks of bridging finance would be reduced by fixed or low interest rates and shortened disposal timetables.

Denmark has no chains – the market there is sufficiently buoyant for seller-buyers to be confident in proceeding to commit to a purchase before they have sold an existing property. However, it should also be borne in mind that the mortgage regime is markedly different, as most house loans are for 30 years at a fixed rate.

Further down the line, property could become a more liquid asset capable of quick and easy valuation, thus enabling instant dealing to become possible. This might enable contracts to be traded literally over the counter. These would operate as options with three-month delivery dates – with payment being made against delivery of possession.

Protocols will be needed to further streamline the process with faster and wider access being given to information held on registers at local authorities, government agencies and public undertakings and utilities. This will facilitate the gathering of information to prepare the HIP. Again, the Internet, with appropriate safeguards, may open up the repositories of such information to the public generally.

E-conveyancing is already changing Land Registry practice. Progress is still hampered by security issues but once these are resolved the land registration processes from preparation of the HIP until completion will become instantaneous. For procedures prior to exchange of contracts the transaction matrix is still under development.

At the time of writing the draft Legal Services Bill has been the subject of consultation by a joint committee of both Houses of Parliament. It contains measures to introduce alternative business structures under the regulation of a new Legal Services Board. At some point in the future it is conceivable that professional and commercial providers of services might combine to offer a one-stop service for the consumer. In relation to house selling and buying this would herald a supermarket-style offering of estate agency, surveying and conveyancing services under one roof. The report by Lord Hunt's committee has, however, cast doubt on the efficacy and benefit of some of the Bill's proposals for change. The report, which was published on 25 July 2006, can be accessed online (see **www.publications.parliament.uk/pa/jt/jtlegal.htm#reports**).

Current professional rules governing solicitors in relation to conflicts of interest and confidentiality would need to undergo considerable revision before solicitors would be able to participate. However, the Council for Licensed Conveyancers does in terms permit more than one party to be represented by a licensed conveyancer in the same transaction although the market does not widely embrace this as a norm or an acceptable procedure.

If the HIP reforms were to be developed over time and take root within a new culture then it is possible that chains of transactions would speed up and then shorten. This, together with greater transparency of information and objectivity, would then reduce the potential for conflicts of interest between sellers and buyers. As the speed of transactions increased this could, subject to cost factors, encourage growth in the number of market transactions.

It will be interesting to see a review of the new system with an impact assessment after 12 months to gauge whether there has been any cultural shift in the property market and the effect on volume and sale prices. The spreading of the new direct costs involved and the differences in other professional fees and expenses will need to be monitored closely. Changes proposed in Scotland introducing a seller's survey will provide an interesting comparison.

The role of the consumer preparing a DIY pack has not been widely discussed and, though possible, is not expected to be popular. Once the market has adjusted to the availability of a HIP much will depend upon the professionalism with which the information is produced. This, at least in the early days, favours the objectivity of a third-party provider.

The existence of the HIP will make information about the properties on offer more visible and better defined. That should have the effect of deterring non-serious buyers and uncommitted sellers. Sellers who are not decided on their plans will be reluctant to incur potential expense. The one thing the HIP cannot do is remove the uncertainty of human affairs which will continue to cause some transactions to fail, although insurance for abortive transactions or schemes for self-insuring could mitigate these risks. Such insurance may become more widely available as volumes grow and risks are more easily defined and assessed than in the past.

If the HIP regime speeds up the time taken to exchange contracts then break-downs in a chain of dependent transactions will become less frequent. If there is a problem, it should also be easier to bring in another potential buyer to fill the gap as needed. The HIP will have ensured that reliable information is immediately to hand to enable a replacement transaction to be put together.

What are the downsides? Human ingenuity is such that new reasons for delays may appear. House prices may well dip rather than rise with the transparency of the HIP and the cost of the HIP itself is bound to rise after any initial 'special offers', intended to acquire market share or dominance, have run their course. Whilst some search prices may fall other components of the HIP will rise towards a price that reflects the cost, including expertise, involved. It is unlikely that HIP provision will be the truly mechanical and commoditised exercise that some envisage. The cost to the consumer is a debate that has not at the time of writing been concluded.

Initially, the market will stimulate new providers to advertise cut-price or even free HIPs. These may turn out to be suitable for an estate agent's marketing needs but not for the diligence procedures required by a buyer's solicitor. By itself, the HIP does nothing to safeguard the buyer's position at the point of sale.

Where non-compliant with the Act the estate agent will be exposed to potential liability from the TSO and also from complaining sellers, buyers and lenders. HIP providers may seek to create a margin of profit by cross-selling insurance products or introducing the professional advisers to the case and derive an income stream from referral payments. These hidden costs are likely, ultimately, to be passed on to the consumer.

In this quest for certainty the only certainty appears to be that the future remains distinctly uncertain.

POSTSCRIPT

On 18 July 2006 the housing minister, Yvette Cooper, announced that the HCR would be introduced on a voluntary basis and that revised arrangements would be made for the Dry Run. A further and revised regulatory impact assessment is to be published.

Since 14 June 2006 when the Regulations were laid in parliament the government has been heavily promoting its 'green' credentials. The EPC has been highlighted as an essential element in the HIP. The EU Directive only requires this at point of sale and, as in Northern Ireland, this can be introduced independently of the HIP. Within the Regulations the requirement for the EPC gives rise to problems consequential upon removal of references to the HCR and these will need to be resolved by way of fresh drafting to make explicit the terms on which the EPC may be produced and whether the withdrawal of the compulsory HCR affects the position on the sale of new homes.

The HIP is for the time being left standing with the fig leaf of local searches, and yet these remain as unsatisfactory as were the arrangements for the HCR. The government has proved unable to persuade local authorities to reform their procedures and adopt electronic delivery or to provide a timely and cost-effective service. The regulation of personal search companies depends upon the HIP legislation and yet, within the context of HIPs, there is no incentive or compulsion upon buyers to accept the seller's searches, which may be inadequate or out of date.

The 'half HIP', if it goes ahead, could offer the worst of all worlds, being of questionable benefit to a buyer whilst adding to the costs of the seller. The remaining elements of the HIP lack credibility in that the reforms of personal search reports have not been tested in the market and a buyer cannot be forced to rely upon sellers' search reports. No buyers' costs are saved and if the cost of the EPC is shifted onto buyers then these costs could be increased.

The lending industry has stated that it needs a longer period in which to develop its new tools for processing loans without a physical inspection.

The number of trained HIs remains low and qualified surveyors are reluctant to convert until the new certifying bodies are established and the full cost implications are known.

The terms for setting up and operating the new central database have not been concluded and until such structures are in place the widespread lack of confidence will remain.

The government, having broken free from the trap of its commitment to the original timeline, now faces the difficulty that, without significant pump priming, a voluntary system remains unlikely to attract many followers.

The industry of HIP providers is angry as delay and uncertainty causes financial jeopardy and the consumer lobby believes it has been abandoned. Estate agents remain fearful that the requirement to have a HIP before the commencement of marketing still poses a threat to market stability.

Whilst a voluntary system may stand little chance of success the imposition of a requirement upon estate agents to publish basic information about any property offered for sale would be popular and relatively easy to enact. Further, introducing the licensing of estate agents would be welcomed widely amongst agents themselves and would drive up conduct and performance standards.

Sadly, the inflexibility of government thinking in relation to the FPM and its failure to come to grips with local authorities in relation to search reports seems much to blame for the waste of resources caused by the long-drawn-out programme of reform.

The HCR, even if it is an improvement upon current practice, has no popular appeal with the electorate but, if introduced and used by buyers' surveyors, may gain recognition. Reform by coercion has not succeeded but good sense has not yet entirely prevailed.

The 'Perfect Storm' is reduced to a storm in a teacup.

Appendix A
HOUSING ACT 2004, PART 5 AND SCHEDULE 8

PART 5

HOME INFORMATION PACKS

Preliminary

148 Meaning of 'residential property' and 'home information pack'

(1) In this Part –

'residential property' means premises in England and Wales consisting of a single dwelling-house, including any ancillary land; and

'dwelling-house' means a building or part of a building occupied or intended to be occupied as a separate dwelling (and includes one that is being or is to be constructed).

(2) References in this Part to a home information pack, in relation to a residential property, are to a collection of documents relating to the property or the terms on which it is or may become available for sale.

149 Meaning of 'on the market' and related expressions

(1) In this Part references to 'the market' are to the residential property market in England and Wales.

(2) A residential property is put on the market when the fact that it is or may become available for sale is, with the intention of marketing the property, first made public in England and Wales by or on behalf of the seller.

(3) A residential property which has been put on the market is to be regarded as remaining on the market until it is taken off the market or sold.

(4) A fact is made public when it is advertised or otherwise communicated (in whatever form and by whatever means) to the public or to a section of the public.

150 Acting as estate agent

(1) A person acts as estate agent for the seller of a residential property if he does anything, in the course of a business in England and Wales, in pursuance of marketing instructions from the seller.

(2) For this purpose –

'business in England and Wales' means a business carried on (in whole or in part) from a place in England and Wales; and

'marketing instructions' means instructions to carry out any activities with a view to –

(a) effecting the introduction to the seller of a person wishing to buy the property; or

(b) selling the property by auction or tender.

(3) It is immaterial for the purposes of this section whether or not a person describes himself as an estate agent.

Responsibility for marketing residential properties

151 Responsibility for marketing: general

(1) References in this Part to a responsible person, in relation to a residential property, are to any person who is for the time being responsible for marketing the property.

(2) Sections 152 and 153 identify for the purposes of this Part –

(a) the person or persons who are responsible for marketing a residential property which is on the market ('the property'); and

(b) when the responsibility of any such person arises and ceases.

(3) Only the seller or a person acting as estate agent for the seller may be responsible for marketing the property.

(4) A person may be responsible for marketing the property on more than one occasion.

152 Responsibility of person acting as estate agent

(1) A person acting as estate agent becomes responsible for marketing the property when action taken by him or on his behalf –

(a) puts the property on the market; or

(b) makes public the fact that the property is on the market.

(2) That responsibility ceases when the following conditions are satisfied, namely –

(a) his contract with the seller is terminated (whether by the withdrawal of his instructions or otherwise);

(b) he has ceased to take any action which makes public the fact that the property is on the market; and

(c) any such action being taken on his behalf has ceased.

(3) Any responsibility arising under this section also ceases when the property is taken off the market or sold.

153 Responsibility of the seller

(1) The seller becomes responsible for marketing the property when action taken by him or on his behalf –

(a) puts the property on the market; or

(b) makes public the fact that the property is on the market.

(2) That responsibility ceases when the following conditions are satisfied, namely –

(a) there is at least one person acting as his estate agent who is responsible for marketing the property;

(b) the seller has ceased to take any action which makes public the fact that the property is on the market; and

(c) any such action being taken on the seller's behalf has ceased.

(3) In this section the references to action taken on behalf of the seller exclude action taken by or on behalf of a person acting as his estate agent.

(4) Any responsibility arising under this section also ceases when the property is taken off the market or sold.

Duties of a responsible person where a property is on the market

154 Application of sections 155 to 158

(1) Where a residential property is on the market, a person responsible for marketing the property is subject to the duties relating to home information packs that are imposed by sections 155 to 158 until his responsibility ceases.

(2) Each of those duties is subject to any exception relating to that duty which is provided for in those sections.

(3) The duty under section 156(1) is also subject to any condition imposed under section 157.

155 Duty to have a home information pack

(1) It is the duty of a responsible person to have in his possession or under his control a home information pack for the property which complies with the requirements of any regulations under section 163.

(2) That duty does not apply where the responsible person is the seller at any time when –

    (a) there is another person who is responsible for marketing the property under section 152; and

    (b) the seller believes on reasonable grounds that the other responsible person has a home information pack for the property in his possession or under his control which complies with the requirements of any regulations under section 163.

156 Duty to provide copy of home information pack on request

(1) Where a potential buyer makes a request to a responsible person for a copy of the home information pack, or of a document (or part of a document) which is or ought to be included in that pack, it is the duty of the responsible person to comply with that request within the permitted period.

(2) The responsible person does not comply with that duty unless –

    (a) he provides the potential buyer with a document which is –

        (i) a copy of the home information pack for the property as it stands at the time when the document is provided, or

        (ii) a copy of a document (or part of a document) which is included in that pack,

    as the case may be; and

    (b) that pack or document complies with the requirements of any regulations under section 163 at that time.

(3) In subsection (2) 'the home information pack' means the home information pack intended by the responsible person to be the one required by section 155.

(4) That duty does not apply if, before the end of the permitted period, the responsible person believes on reasonable grounds that the person making the request –

    (a) is unlikely to have sufficient means to buy the property in question;

    (b) is not genuinely interested in buying a property of a general description which applies to the property; or

    (c) is not a person to whom the seller is likely to be prepared to sell the property.

Nothing in this subsection authorises the doing of anything which constitutes an unlawful act of discrimination.

(5) Subsection (4) does not apply if the responsible person knows or suspects that the person making the request is an officer of an enforcement authority.

(6) That duty does not apply where the responsible person is the seller if, when the request is made, the duty under section 155 does not (by virtue of subsection (2) of that section) apply to him.

(7) But where the duty under this section is excluded by subsection (6), it is the duty of the seller to take reasonable steps to inform the potential buyer that the request should be made to the other person.

(8) The responsible person may charge a sum not exceeding the reasonable cost of making and, if requested, sending a paper copy of the pack or document.

(9) The permitted period for the purposes of this section is (subject to section 157(5)) the period of 14 days beginning with the day on which the request is made.

(10) If the responsible person ceases to be responsible for marketing the property before the end of the permitted period (whether because the property has been taken off the market or sold or for any other reason), he ceases to be under any duty to comply with the request.

(11) A person does not comply with the duty under this section by providing a copy in electronic form unless the potential buyer consents to receiving it in that form.

157 Section 156 (1) duty: imposition of conditions

(1) A potential buyer who has made a request to which section 156(1) applies may be required to comply with either or both of the following conditions before any copy is provided.

(2) The potential buyer may be required to pay a charge authorised by section 156(8).

(3) The potential buyer may be required to accept any terms specified in writing which –

(a) are proposed by the seller or in pursuance of his instructions; and

(b) relate to the use or disclosure of the copy (or any information contained in or derived from it).

(4) A condition is only effective if it is notified to the potential buyer before the end of the period of 14 days beginning with the day on which the request is made.

(5) Where the potential buyer has been so notified of either or both of the conditions authorised by this section, the permitted period for the purposes of section 156 is the period of 14 days beginning with –

(a) where one condition is involved, the day on which the potential buyer complies with it by –

(i) making the payment demanded, or

(ii) accepting the terms proposed (or such other terms as may be agreed between the seller and the potential buyer in substitution for those proposed),

as the case may be; or

(b) where both conditions are involved, the day (or the later of the days) on which the potential buyer complies with them by taking the action mentioned in paragraph (a)(i) and (ii).

158 Duty to ensure authenticity of documents in other situations

(1) Where a responsible person provides a potential buyer with, or allows a potential buyer to inspect, any document purporting to be –

(a) a copy of the home information pack for the property, or

(b) a copy of a document (or part of a document) included in that pack,

the responsible person is under a duty to ensure that the document is authentic.

(2) A document is not authentic for the purposes of subsection (1) unless, at the time when it is provided or inspected –

(a) it is a copy of the home information pack for the property or a document (or part of a document) included in that pack, as the case may be; and

(b) that pack or document complies with the requirements of any regulations under section 163.

(3) In subsection (2) 'the home information pack' means the pack intended by the responsible person to be the one required by section 155.

(4) The duty under this section does not apply to anything provided in pursuance of the duty under section 156.

Other duties of person acting as estate agent

159 Other duties of person acting as estate agent

(1) This section applies to a person acting as estate agent for the seller of a residential property where –

   (a) the property is not on the market; or

   (b) the property is on the market but the person so acting is not a person responsible for marketing the property.

(2) It is the duty of a person to whom this section applies to have in his possession or under his control, when any qualifying action is taken by him or on his behalf, a home information pack for the property which complies with the requirements of any regulations under section 163.

(3) In subsection (2) 'qualifying action' means action taken with the intention of marketing the property which –

   (a) communicates to any person in England and Wales the fact that the property is or may become available for sale; but

   (b) does not put the property on the market or make public the fact that the property is on the market.

(4) Where a person to whom this section applies provides a potential buyer with, or allows a potential buyer to inspect, any document purporting to be –

   (a) a copy of the home information pack for the property; or

   (b) a copy of a document (or part of a document) included in that pack;

   it is his duty to ensure that it is an authentic copy.

(5) A document is not authentic for the purposes of subsection (4) unless, at the time when it is provided or inspected –

   (a) it is a copy of the home information pack for the property or a document (or part of a document) included in that pack, as the case may be; and

   (b) that pack or document complies with the requirements of any regulations under section 163.

(6) In subsection (5) 'the home information pack' means the home information pack intended by the person to whom this section applies to be the one required by subsection (2).

Exceptions from the duties

160 Residential properties not available with vacant possession

(1) The duties under sections 155 to 159 do not apply in relation to a residential property at any time when it is not available for sale with vacant possession.

(2) But for the purposes of this Part a residential property shall be presumed to be available with vacant possession, at any time when any of those duties would apply in relation to the property if it is so available, unless the contrary appears from the manner in which the property is being marketed at that time.

161 Power to provide for further exceptions

The Secretary of State may by regulations provide for other exceptions from any duty under sections 155 to 159 in such cases and circumstances, and to such extent, as may be specified in the regulations.

162 Suspension of duties under sections 155 to 159

(1) The Secretary of State may make an order suspending (or later reviving) the operation of any duty imposed by sections 155 to 159.

(2) An order under this section may provide for the suspension of a duty to take effect only for a period specified in the order.

(3) A duty which is (or is to any extent) revived after being suspended under this section is liable to be suspended again.

Contents of home information packs

163 Contents of home information packs

(1) The Secretary of State may make regulations prescribing –

    (a) the documents which are required or authorised to be included in the home information pack for a residential property; and

    (b) particular information which is required or authorised to be included in, or which is to be excluded from, any such document.

(2) A document prescribed under subsection (1) must be one that the Secretary of State considers would disclose relevant information.

(3) Any particular information required or authorised to be included in a prescribed document must be information that the Secretary of State considers to be relevant information.

(4) In this section 'relevant information' means information about any matter connected with the property (or the sale of the property) that would be of interest to potential buyers.

(5) Without prejudice to the generality of subsection (4), the information which the Secretary of State may consider to be relevant information includes any information about –

    (a) the interest which is for sale and the terms on which it is proposed to sell it;

    (b) the title to the property;

    (c) anything relating to or affecting the property that is contained in –

        (i) a register required to be kept by or under any enactment (whenever passed); or

        (ii) records kept by a person who can reasonably be expected to give information derived from those records to the seller at his request (on payment, if required, of a reasonable charge);

    (d) the physical condition of the property (including any particular characteristics or features of the property);

    (e) the energy efficiency of the property;

    (f) any warranties or guarantees subsisting in relation to the property;

    (g) any taxes, service charges or other charges payable in relation to the property.

(6) The regulations may require or authorise the home information pack to include –

    (a) replies the seller proposes to give to prescribed pre-contract enquiries, and

    (b) documents or particular information indexing or otherwise explaining the contents of the pack.

(7) The regulations may require a prescribed document –

(a) to be in such form as may be prescribed; and

(b) to be prepared by a person of a prescribed description on such terms (if any) as may be prescribed.

(8) The terms mentioned in subsection (7)(b) may include terms which enable provisions of the contract under which the document is to be prepared to be enforced by –

(a) a potential or actual buyer;

(b) a mortgage lender; or

(c) any other person involved in the sale of the property who is not a party to that contract.

(9) The regulations may –

(a) provide for the time at which any document is to be included in or removed from the home information pack; and

(b) make different provision for different areas, for different descriptions of properties or for other different circumstances (including the manner in which a residential property is marketed).

(10) In this section 'prescribed' means prescribed by regulations under this section.

164 Home condition reports

(1) Regulations under section 163 may make the provision mentioned in this section in relation to any description of document dealing with matters mentioned in section 163(5)(d) or (e) (reports on physical condition or energy efficiency) which is to be included in the home information pack.

(2) In this section 'home condition report' means a document of that description.

(3) The regulations may require a home condition report to be made by an individual who is a member of an approved certification scheme following an inspection carried out by him in accordance with the provisions of the scheme.

(4) The regulations shall, if the provision mentioned in subsection (3) is made, make provision for the approval by the Secretary of State of one or more suitable certification schemes (and for the withdrawal by him of any such approval).

(5) The regulations shall require the Secretary of State to be satisfied, before approving a certification scheme, that the scheme contains appropriate provision –

(a) for ensuring that members of the scheme are fit and proper persons who are qualified (by their education, training and experience) to produce home condition reports;

(b) for ensuring that members of the scheme have in force suitable indemnity insurance;

(c) for facilitating the resolution of complaints against members of the scheme;

(d) for requiring home condition reports made by members of the scheme to be entered on the register mentioned in section 165;

(e) for the keeping of a public register of the members of the scheme; and

(f) for such other purposes as may be specified in the regulations.

(6) Subsection (5)(d) only applies where provision for a register of home condition reports is made under section 165.

(7) The regulations may require or authorise an approved certification scheme to contain provision about any matter relating to the home condition reports with which the scheme is concerned (including the terms on which members of the scheme may undertake to produce a home condition report).

(8) Nothing in this section limits the power under section 163 to make provision about home condition reports in the regulations.

Register of home condition reports

165 Register of home condition reports

(1) Where the provision mentioned in section 164(3) is made in relation to an approved certification scheme, regulations under section 163 may make provision for and in connection with a register of the home condition reports made by members of the scheme.

(2) The regulations may provide for the register to be kept –

    (a) by (or on behalf of) the Secretary of State; or

    (b) by such other person as the regulations may specify.

(3) The regulations may require a person wishing to enter a home condition report onto the register to pay such fee as may be prescribed.

(4) No person may disclose –

    (a) the register or any document (or part of a document) contained in it; or

    (b) any information contained in, or derived from, the register,

except in accordance with any provision of the regulations which authorises or requires such a disclosure to be made.

(5) The provision which may be made under subsection (1) includes (without prejudice to the generality of that subsection) provision as to circumstances in which or purposes for which a person or a person of a prescribed description –

    (a) may (on payment of such fee, if any, as may be prescribed) –

        (i) inspect the register or any document (or part of a document) contained in it;

        (ii) take or be given copies of the register or any document (or part of a document) contained in it; or

        (iii) be given information contained in, or derived from, the register; or

    (b) may disclose anything obtained by virtue of provision made under paragraph (a).

(6) The purposes which may be so prescribed may be public purposes or purposes of private undertakings or other persons.

(7) A person who contravenes subsection (4) is guilty of an offence and liable on summary conviction to a fine not exceeding level 5 on the standard scale.

(8) Nothing in this section limits the power to make regulations under section 163.

Enforcement

166 Enforcement authorities

(1) Every local weights and measures authority is an enforcement authority for the purposes of this Part.

(2) It is the duty of each enforcement authority to enforce –

    (a) the duties under sections 155 to 159 and 167(4), and

    (b) any duty imposed under section 172(1),

in their area.

167 Power to require production of home information packs

(1) An authorised officer of an enforcement authority may require a person who appears to him to be or to have been subject to the duty under section 155 or 159(2), in relation to a residential property, to produce for inspection a copy of, or of any document included in, the home information pack for that property.

(2) The power conferred by subsection (1) includes power –

    (a) to require the production in a visible and legible documentary form of any document included in the home information pack in question which is held in electronic form; and

    (b) to take copies of any document produced for inspection.

(3) A requirement under this section may not be imposed more than six months after the last day on which the person concerned was subject to the duty under section 155 or 159(2) in relation to the property (as the case may be).

(4) Subject to subsection (5), it is the duty of a person subject to such a requirement to comply with it within the period of 7 days beginning with the day after that on which it is imposed.

(5) A person is not required to comply with such a requirement if he has a reasonable excuse for not complying with the requirement.

(6) In this section 'the home information pack' means –

    (a) where a requirement under this section is imposed on a person at a time when he is subject to the duty under section 155 or 159(2), the home information pack intended by him to be the one he is required to have at that time; or

    (b) in any other case, the home information pack intended by the person concerned, when he was last subject to the duty under section 155 or 159(2), to be the one he was required to have at that time.

168 Penalty charge notices

(1) An authorised officer of an enforcement authority may, if he believes that a person has committed a breach of –

    (a) any duty under sections 155 to 159 and 167(4), or

    (b) any duty imposed under section 172(1),

give a penalty charge notice to that person.

(2) A penalty charge notice may not be given after the end of the period of six months beginning with the day (or in the case of a continuing breach the last day) on which the breach of duty was committed.

(3) Schedule 8 (which makes further provision about penalty charge notices) has effect.

169 Offences relating to enforcement officers

(1) A person who obstructs an officer of an enforcement authority acting in pursuance of section 167 is guilty of an offence.

(2) A person who, not being an authorised officer of an enforcement authority, purports to act as such in pursuance of section 167 or 168 is guilty of an offence.

(3) A person guilty of an offence under this section is liable on summary conviction to a fine not exceeding level 5 on the standard scale.

170 Right of private action

(1) This section applies where a person ('the responsible person') has committed a breach of duty under section 156 by failing to comply with a request from a potential buyer of a residential property for a copy of a prescribed document.

(2) If the potential buyer commissions his own version of the prescribed document at a time when both of the conditions mentioned below are satisfied, he is entitled to recover from the responsible person any reasonable fee paid by him in order to obtain the document.

(3) The first condition is that –

    (a) the property is on the market; or

    (b) the potential buyer and the seller are attempting to reach an agreement for the sale of the property.

(4) The second condition is that the potential buyer has not been provided with an authentic copy of the prescribed document.

(5) A copy of a prescribed document is not authentic for the purposes of subsection (4) unless –

   (a) it is a copy of a document included in the home information pack for the property as it stands at the time the copy is provided to the potential buyer; and

   (b) the document so included complies with the requirements of any regulations under section 163 at that time.

(6) In subsection (5) 'the home information pack' means the home information pack intended by the responsible person to be the one required by section 155.

(7) In this section 'prescribed document' means a document (being one required to be included in the home information pack by regulations under section 163) which is prescribed by regulations made by the Secretary of State for the purposes of this section.

(8) It is immaterial for the purposes of this section that the request in question did not specify the prescribed document but was for a copy of the home information pack or a part of the pack which included (or ought to have included) that document.

Supplementary

171 Application of Part to sub-divided buildings

(1) This section applies where –

   (a) two or more dwelling-houses in a sub-divided building are marketed for sale (with any ancillary land) as a single property; and

   (b) any one or more of those dwelling-houses –

      (i) is not available for sale (with any ancillary land) as a separate residential property; but

      (ii) is available with vacant possession.

(2) This Part applies to the dwelling-houses mentioned in subsection (1)(a) (with any ancillary land) as if –

   (a) they were a residential property, and

   (b) section 160 were omitted.

(3) Subsection (2) does not affect the application of this Part to any of those dwelling-houses which is available for sale (with any ancillary land) as a separate residential property.

(4) In this section 'sub-divided building' means a building or part of a building originally constructed or adapted for use as a single dwelling which has been divided (on one or more occasions) into separate dwelling-houses.

172 Power to require estate agents to belong to a redress scheme

(1) The Secretary of State may by order require every estate agent to be a member of an approved redress scheme.

(2) Acting as estate agent for the seller of a residential property in contravention of such an order is a breach of duty under this Part.

(3) Before making such an order the Secretary of State must be satisfied that he has approved one or more redress schemes such that every estate agent who is (or will be) subject to the duty imposed by the order is eligible to join an approved redress scheme.

For this purpose 'estate agent' does not include a person who is (by virtue of a prohibition imposed by or under the Estate Agents Act 1979 (c. 38)) unable lawfully to act as estate agent for the seller of a residential property.

(4) An order under this section may –

    (a) exclude estate agents of a prescribed description from any duty imposed under subsection (1);

    (b) limit any duty so imposed so that it applies only in relation to relevant complaints of a prescribed description.

(5) Nothing in this section is to be taken as preventing an approved redress scheme from providing –

    (a) for membership to be open to persons who are not subject to any duty to belong to an approved redress scheme;

    (b) for the investigation and determination of complaints, other than those in relation to which such a duty applies, made against members who have voluntarily accepted the jurisdiction of the scheme over such complaints;

    (c) for the exclusion from investigation and determination under the scheme of any complaint in such cases or circumstances as may be specified in the scheme.

(6) In this section and sections 173 and 174 –

'approved redress scheme' means a redress scheme that is for the time being approved under section 173;

'estate agent' means a person who acts as estate agent for sellers of residential properties for which a home information pack is (or will be) required under this Part;

'redress scheme' means a scheme under which certain relevant complaints may be investigated and determined by an independent person (referred to in those sections as 'the ombudsman'); and

'relevant complaint' means a complaint against an estate agent which –

    (a) is made by a person who at the material time is the seller or a potential buyer of a residential property; and

    (b) relates to an act or omission affecting the complainant in the course of the estate agent's activities in relation to a home information pack that is (or will be) required for that property (including the giving of advice as to whether such a pack is required).

(7) For the purposes of the law relating to defamation, proceedings under an approved redress scheme in relation to the investigation and determination of a complaint which is subject to an order under this section are to be treated in the same way as proceedings before a court.

173 Approval of redress schemes

(1) If the Secretary of State considers that a redress scheme (including one made by him or in pursuance of arrangements made by him) is satisfactory for the purposes of section 172, he may approve it for those purposes.

(2) In determining whether a redress scheme is satisfactory the Secretary of State shall have regard to –

    (a) the provisions of the scheme;

    (b) the manner in which the scheme will be operated (so far as can be judged from the facts known to him); and

    (c) the respective interests of members of the scheme and of sellers and potential buyers of residential properties.

(3) A redress scheme may not be approved unless it makes satisfactory provision about the following matters (among other things) –

    (a) the matters about which complaints may be made (which may include non-compliance with the provisions of a code of practice or other document);

(b) the ombudsman's duties and powers in relation to the investigation and deter-mination of complaints (which may include power to decide not to investigate or determine a complaint);

(c) the provision of information by the ombudsman to –

(i) persons exercising functions under other schemes providing a means of redress for consumers; and

(ii) the Secretary of State or any other person exercising regulatory functions in relation to the activities of estate agents.

(4) An application for approval of a redress scheme shall be made in such manner as the Secretary of State may determine, accompanied by such information as the Secretary of State may require.

(5) The person administering an approved redress scheme shall notify the Secretary of State of any change to the scheme as soon as practicable after the change is made.

174 Withdrawal of approval of redress schemes

(1) The Secretary of State may withdraw his approval of a redress scheme.

(2) But before withdrawing his approval, the Secretary of State shall serve on the person administering the scheme a notice stating –

(a) that he proposes to withdraw his approval;

(b) the grounds for the proposed withdrawal of approval; and

(c) that representations about the proposed withdrawal may be made within such period of not less than 14 days as is specified in the notice.

(3) The Secretary of State shall give notice of his decision on a proposal to withdraw approval, with his reasons, to the person administering the scheme.

(4) Withdrawal of approval has effect from such date as may be specified in that notice.

(5) The person administering the scheme shall give a copy of a notice under subsection (3) to every member of the scheme.

175 Office of Fair Trading

(1) An enforcement authority may notify the Office of Fair Trading of any breach of duty under this Part appearing to the authority to have been committed by a person acting as estate agent.

(2) An enforcement authority shall notify the Office of Fair Trading of –

(a) any penalty charge notice given by an officer of the authority under section 168;

(b) any notice given by the authority confirming or withdrawing a penalty charge notice; and

(c) the result of any appeal from the confirmation of a penalty charge notice.

(3) The Estate Agents Act 1979 (c. 38) applies in relation to a person who has commit-ted a breach of duty under this Part in the course of estate agency work (within the meaning of that Act) as it applies in relation to a person who has engaged in a practice such as is mentioned in section 3(1)(d) of that Act in the course of such work.

176 Grants

(1) The Secretary of State may make grants towards expenditure incurred by any person in connection with –

(a) the development of proposals for any provision to be made by regulations under section 163;

(b) the development of schemes which are intended to be certification schemes for the purposes of any provision made or expected to be made in regulations under section 163 by virtue of section 164; or

(c)   the development of a register for the purposes of any provision made or expected to be made in regulations under section 163 by virtue of section 165.

(2)   A grant under this section may be made on conditions, which may include (among other things) –

(a)   conditions as to the purposes for which the grant or any part of it may be used; and

(b)   conditions requiring the repayment of the grant or any part of it in such circumstances as may be specified in the conditions.

177 Interpretation of Part 5

(1)   In this Part –

'ancillary land', in relation to a dwelling-house or a sub-divided building, means any land intended to be occupied and enjoyed together with that dwelling-house or building;

'long lease' means –

(a)   a lease granted for a term certain exceeding 21 years, whether or not it is (or may become) terminable before the end of that term by notice given by the tenant or by re-entry or forfeiture; or

(b)   a lease for a term fixed by law under a grant with a covenant or obligation for perpetual renewal, other than a lease by sub-demise from one which is not a long lease;

and for this purpose 'lease' does not include a mortgage term;

'potential buyer' means a person who claims that he is or may become interested in buying a residential property;

'sale', in relation to a residential property, means a disposal, or agreement to dispose, by way of sale of –

(a)   the freehold interest;

(b)   the interest under a long lease;

(c)   an option to acquire the freehold interest or the interest under a long lease;

and 'seller' means a person contemplating disposing of such an interest (and related expressions shall be construed accordingly).

(2)   Any reference in the definition of 'sale' to the disposal of an interest of a kind mentioned in that definition includes a reference to the creation of such an interest.

(3)   A document which is not in electronic form is only to be regarded for the purposes of this Part as being under the control of a person while it is in the possession of another if he has the right to take immediate possession of the document on demand (and without payment).

(4)   A document held in electronic form is only to be regarded for the purposes of this Part as being in a person's possession or under his control if he is readily able (using equipment available to him) –

(a)   to view the document in a form that is visible and legible; and

(b)   to produce copies of it in a visible and legible documentary form.

178 Index of defined expressions: Part 5

In this Part, the expressions listed in the left-hand column have the meaning given by, or are to be interpreted in accordance with, the provisions inserted in the right-hand column.

Expression	Provision of this Act
Acting as estate agent for the seller	Section 150
Ancillary land	Section 177(1)
Control of documents	Section 177(3) and (4)
Dwelling-house	Section 148(1)
Enforcement authority	Section 166
Home information pack	Section 148(2)
Long lease	Section 177(1)
Make public	Section 149(4)
Possession of electronic documents	Section 177(4)
Potential buyer	Section 177(1)
Putting on the market	Section 149(2)
Remaining on the market	Section 149(3)
Residential property	Section 148(1)
Responsible person	Section 151(1)
Sale (and related expressions)	Section 177(1)
Seller (and related expressions)	Section 177(1)
The market	Section 149(1)

*****

SCHEDULE 8

PENALTY CHARGE NOTICES UNDER SECTION 168

1   A penalty charge notice given to a person under section 168 by an officer of an enforcement authority must –

(a)   state the officer's belief that that person has committed a breach of duty;

(b)   give such particulars of the circumstances as may be necessary to give reasonable notice of the breach of duty;

(c)   require that person, within a period specified in the notice –

   (i)   to pay a penalty charge specified in the notice, or

   (ii)   to give notice to the enforcement authority that he wishes the authority to review the notice;

(d)   state the effect of paragraph 8;

(e)   specify the person to whom and the address at which the penalty charge may be paid and the method or methods by which payment may be made; and

(f)   specify the person to whom and the address at which a notice requesting a review may be sent (and to which any representations relating to the review may be addressed).

2   The penalty charge specified in the notice shall be of such amount (not exceeding £500) as may be prescribed for the time being by regulations made by the Secretary of State.

3   (1) The period specified under paragraph 1(c) must not be less than 28 days beginning with the day after that on which the penalty charge notice was given.

   (2) The enforcement authority may extend the period for complying with the requirement mentioned in paragraph 1(c) in any particular case if they consider it appropriate to do so.

4   The enforcement authority may, if they consider that the penalty charge notice ought not to have been given, give the recipient a notice withdrawing the penalty charge notice.

5   (1)   If, within the period specified under paragraph 1(c) (or that period as extended under paragraph 3(2)), the recipient of the penalty charge notice gives notice to the enforcement authority requesting a review, the authority shall –

    (a)   consider any representations made by the recipient and all other circumstances of the case;

    (b)   decide whether to confirm or withdraw the notice; and

    (c)   give notice of their decision to the recipient.

    (2)   A notice under sub-paragraph (1)(c) confirming the penalty charge notice must also state the effect of paragraphs 6(1) to (3) and 8(1) and (3).

    (3)   If the authority are not satisfied –

    (a)   that the recipient committed the breach of duty specified in the notice;

    (b)   that the notice was given within the time allowed by section 168(2) and complies with the other requirements imposed by or under this Schedule; and

    (c)   that in the circumstances of the case it was appropriate for a penalty charge notice to be given to the recipient,

they shall withdraw the penalty charge notice.

6   (1)   If after a review the penalty charge notice is confirmed by the enforcement authority, the recipient may, within the period of 28 days beginning with the day after that on which the notice under paragraph 5(1)(c) is given, appeal to the county court against the penalty charge notice.

    (2)   The county court may extend the period for appealing against the notice.

    (3)   Such an appeal must be on one (or more) of the following grounds –

    (a)   that the recipient did not commit the breach of duty specified in the penalty charge notice;

    (b)   that the notice was not given within the time allowed by section 168(2) or does not comply with any other requirement imposed by or under this Schedule; or

    (c)   that in the circumstances of the case it was inappropriate for the notice to be given to the recipient.

    (4)   An appeal against a penalty charge notice shall be by way of a rehearing; and the court shall either uphold the notice or quash it.

7   If the penalty charge notice is withdrawn or quashed, the authority shall repay any amount previously paid as a penalty charge in pursuance of the notice.

8   (1)   The amount of the penalty charge is recoverable from the recipient of the penalty charge notice as a debt owed to the authority unless –

    (a)   the notice has been withdrawn or quashed, or

    (b)   the charge has been paid.

    (2)   Proceedings for the recovery of the penalty charge may not be commenced before the end of the period mentioned in paragraph 5(1).

    (3)   And if within that period the recipient of the penalty charge notice gives notice to the authority that he wishes the authority to review the penalty charge notice, such proceedings may not be commenced –

    (a)   before the end of the period mentioned in paragraph 6(1), and

    (b)   where the recipient appeals against the penalty charge notice, before the end of the period of 28 days beginning with the day on which the appeal is withdrawn or determined.

9   In proceedings for the recovery of the penalty charge, a certificate which –

    (a)   purports to be signed by or on behalf of the person having responsibility for the financial affairs of the enforcement authority; and

    (b) states that payment of the penalty charge was or was not received by a date specified in the certificate;

is evidence of the facts stated.

10 (1) A penalty charge notice and any other notice mentioned in this Schedule may be given by post.

  (2) Any such notice may be given–

    (a) in the case of a body corporate, to the secretary or clerk of that body; and

    (b) in the case of a partnership, to any partner or to a person having control or management of the partnership business.

11 The Secretary of State may by regulations make provision supplementary or incidental to the preceding provisions of this Part, including in particular provision prescribing –

  (a) the form of penalty charge notices or any other notice mentioned in this Schedule;

  (b) the circumstances in which penalty charge notices may not be given;

  (c) the method or methods by which penalty charges may be paid.

Appendix B
HOME INFORMATION PACK REGULATIONS 2006 SI 2006/1503

Made	*9th June 2006*
Laid before Parliament	*14th June 2006*
Coming into force	
for the purposes of Part 7	*6th July 2006*
for all other purposes	*1st June 2007*

CONTENTS

PART 5 – EXCEPTIONS

22. Meaning of 'non-residential premises'
23. Exclusion from meaning of 'non-residential premises'
24. Exception for seasonal and holiday accommodation
25. Exception for mixed sales
26. Exception for dual use of a dwelling-house
27. Exception for portfolios of properties
28. Exception for unsafe properties
29. Exception for properties to be demolished
30. Exception – 1st June 2007 to 31st October 2007

PART 6 – ENFORCEMENT

31. Amount of penalty charge
32. Exclusion of penalty charges for content of pack documents

PART 7 – APPROVED CERTIFICATION SCHEMES

33. Approval of certification schemes
34. Terms of approved certification schemes
35. Withdrawal of approval from certification schemes

SCHEDULE 1 – Home information pack index
SCHEDULE 2 – Sale statement
SCHEDULE 3 – Commonhold information
SCHEDULE 4 – Leasehold information
SCHEDULE 5 – Home condition report
SCHEDULE 6 – Exception from home condition report for specific new homes warranties
    PART 1 – General
    PART 2 – Arrangements for entering into specific new homes warranties
    PART 3 – Minimum cover for specific new homes warranties
    PART 4 – Limits on cover for specific new homes warranties
SCHEDULE 7 – Report on a home not physically complete
SCHEDULE 8 – General provision on searches and search reports
    PART 1 – All search reports (other than official search certificate of the local land charges register)
    PART 2 – Specific required search reports
    PART 3 – Authorised search reports
SCHEDULE 9 – Local enquiries
    PART 1 – General
    PART 2 – Enquiries
SCHEDULE 10 – Drainage and water enquiries
    PART 1 – General
    PART 2 – Enquiries and responses
SCHEDULE 11 – Additional relevant information

The Secretary of State makes the following Regulations in exercise of the powers conferred by sections 161, 163, 164 and 250(2) of and paragraphs 2 and 11(b) of Schedule 8 to the Housing Act 2004.

Under section 250(3) of that Act, the Secretary of State has consulted the National Assembly for Wales in relation to residential properties in Wales.

PART 1 – CITATION, COMMENCEMENT AND INTERPRETATION

Citation and commencement

1.   (1)   These Regulations may be cited as the Home Information Pack Regulations 2006.
    (2)   These Regulations shall come into force for the purposes of Part 7 on 6th July 2006 and for all other purposes on 1st June 2007.

Interpretation – general provisions

2.   (1)   In these Regulations –

'the 2004 Act' means the Housing Act 2004;

'appropriate local land charges register' means the register described in section 4 of the Local Land Charges Act 1975;

'approved certification scheme' means a certification scheme approved by the Secretary of State under regulation 33 of these Regulations and from which such approval has not been withdrawn under regulation 35;

'the Chief Land Registrar' means the person appointed by the Lord Chancellor under section 99(3) of the Land Registration Act 2002;

'conservation area consent' means the consent described in section 74(1) of the Planning (Listed Buildings and Conservation Areas) Act 1990;

'developer' means a person who has built, converted, or is building or converting the property;

'edited information document' means, where the Chief Land Registrar has designated a document an exempt information document, the edited copy of that document lodged under rule 136(2)(b) or 138(4) of the Land Registration Rules 2003;

'energy performance certificate' means the certificate required by Council Directive 2002/91/EC whose form and content complies with any enactment which implements that Directive;

'exempt information document' means the original and copies of a document so designated under rule 136(3) of the Land Registration Rules 2003;

'first point of marketing' must be construed in accordance with regulation 3;

'home information pack' in relation to a property, means –

    (a)   where a duty arises under section 155(1) of the 2004 Act, the home information pack intended by the responsible person to be the one required by that subsection; and

    (b)   where a duty arises under section 159(2) of that Act, the home information pack intended by the person to whom that section applies to be the one required by that subsection;

'home information pack index' means the document required by regulation 8(a);

'home inspector' means a person who is a member of an approved certification scheme;

'individual register' means the register so named in rule 2 of the Land Registration Rules 2003, the contents and arrangement of which are described in rules 3 and 4 of those Rules;

'lease' means a long lease except in regulation 8(g), regulation 23(b)(i), paragraph 3(l) of Schedule 3 and paragraph 3(a) of Schedule 4;

'listed building consent' means a consent under section 8(1), (2) or (3) of the Planning (Listed Buildings and Conservation Areas) Act 1990;

'occupant' includes a potential occupant;

'pack document' means a document (or part of a document) required or authorised by these Regulations to be included in the home information pack;

'planning permission' means a permission (granted or deemed to be granted) under Part 3 of the Town and Country Planning Act 1990;

'premises' includes buildings and land;

'property' means the residential property in respect of which a duty arises under section 155(1) or 159(2) of the 2004 Act;

'property interest' means the freehold interest (including a freehold estate in commonhold land) or the leasehold interest in the property that the seller is proposing to sell;

'records' includes documents, registers, files and archives, kept in any form;

'register of title' means the register kept by the Chief Land Registrar pursuant to section 1 of the Land Registration Act 2002;

'registered estate' means a legal estate the title to which is entered in the register of title, other than a charge the title to which is entered in that register;

'sale', includes the potential sale of a property interest;

'sale statement' means the document required by regulation 8(b);

'search' means an inspection or investigation (whether manual or electronic) of records;

'service charge' has the same meaning as in section 18 of the Landlord and Tenant Act 1985; and

'title plan' means the plan so named in rule 5(a) of the Land Registration Rules 2003.

(2) In these Regulations, any expression relating to commonhold land must be construed in accordance with –

(a) Part 1 of the Commonhold and Leasehold Reform Act 2002 if it is also used in that Act; or

(b) the Commonhold Regulations 2004 where those Regulations further define or elaborate upon an expression used in Part 1 of that Act,

and in relation to commonhold land, references to common parts are to those that relate to the property and the commonhold of which the property forms part.

(3) For the purposes of these Regulations –

(a) the property is physically complete if its building or its conversion for residential purposes has been completed; and

(b) where a question arises as to whether the property is physically complete, it must be considered physically complete if it –

(i) is wind and weather proof;

(ii) is safe and sanitary in relation to its occupants or visitors;

(iii) has facilities for the supply of space heating, hot and cold water and electricity; and

(iv) has washing and drainage facilities.

(4) In these Regulations, references to the amendment or revision of a document include its modification or variation.

(5) In these Regulations, references to a number of days or months are to a consecutive period of such days or months.

Interpretation – first point of marketing

3. (1) Subject to the provisions specified in paragraph (2), a reference in these Regulations to the 'first point of marketing' is to the first time a duty arises under section 155(1) or 159(2) of the 2004 Act in relation to the sale of the property interest.

(2) The provisions referred to in paragraph (1) are –

(a) regulations 15(3), 18(3) and 20(3); and

(b) the following paragraphs of this regulation.

(3)   The first point of marketing remains the time identified in paragraph (1) where the property is taken off the market for 28 days or less before being put back on the market.

(4)   Except in the circumstances described in paragraph (5), where the property is taken off the market for more than 28 days before being put back on the market –

   (a)   a further first point of marketing arises in relation to the sale; and

   (b)   that first point of marketing is the time at which it is put back on the market.

(5)   The first point of marketing remains the time identified in paragraph (1) where the property –

   (a)   is taken off the market for any period of time because the seller accepts an offer to buy the property; and

   (b)   is then put back on the market within 28 days of that offer being withdrawn or its acceptance repudiated.

PART 2 – HOME INFORMATION PACK: GENERAL PROVISIONS

Required, authorised and excluded documents

4.   (1)   Under these Regulations, a home information pack –

   (a)   must include –

      (i)   the documents required under regulation 8 (including that regulation as modified by regulation 10); and

      (ii)   the particular information so required to be included in a pack document; and

   (b)   may include –

      (i)   the documents authorised under regulation 9 (including that regulation as modified by regulation 10); or

      (ii)   the particular information so authorised to be included in a pack document.

   (2)   A home information must not include any other documents or information in a document.

   (3)   A copy of a home information pack, or of a pack document provided to a potential buyer pursuant to section 156(1) of the 2004 Act, must be separated and clearly distinguished by the responsible person from documents or information which are –

   (a)   provided to a potential buyer in close proximity to the pack or pack document; and

   (b)   neither required nor authorised by these Regulations to be included in the pack.

The home information pack

5.   (1)   Except where an official copy of a document is required or authorised by these Regulations to be included in the home information pack, the pack must be composed of original documents or true copies of them.

   (2)   For the purposes of these Regulations, a copy of a document containing a map, plan or drawing –

   (a)   which is in the seller's possession, under his control, or to which he has reasonable access; and

(b) in which colours are used to mark boundaries or other features,

is a true copy if those colours are reproduced with sufficient accuracy to enable them to be identified.

Copies of a home information pack

6. The copies of a home information pack or pack document provided or produced under section 156 or 167 of the 2004 Act must be –

(a) true copies of the home information pack or pack document; or

(b) where a pack document is an official copy, a true copy of it or another official copy.

Comprehension of documents

7. (1) Subject to paragraph (2), pack documents and true copies of documents made in accordance with regulation 6 –

(a) must be legible; or

(b) in the case of maps, plans or drawings, must be clear.

(2) Paragraph (1) does not apply where, despite all reasonable efforts and enquiries by the responsible person –

(a) the only version of a pack document available is one which is illegible or unclear (either in whole or in part); and

(b) that document is to be included under any of the following provisions –

(i) regulation 8(d)(ii);

(ii) regulation 9(f);

(iii) regulation 8(e) or 9(g); or

(iv) regulation 8(f) or 9(h).

(3) Pack documents must be in –

(a) English, where the property is in England; or

(b) English, Welsh or a combination of English and Welsh, where the property is in Wales.

PART 3 – CONTENTS OF HOME INFORMATION PACKS

Required pack documents

8. Subject to regulations 10, 11, 12 and Part 4, the home information pack must include the following –

(a) an index to the home information pack complying with Schedule 1 (the home information pack index);

(b) a document complying with Schedule 2 (the sale statement);

(c) if the property interest is or includes the whole or part of a registered estate –

(i) an official copy of the individual register relating to that estate; and

(ii) an official copy of the title plan relating to that estate;

(d) if the property interest is or includes the whole or part of an estate, the title to which is not entered in the register of title –

(i) a certificate of an official search of the index map issued under rule 145(4) of the Land Registration Rules 2003 in relation to the parcel of land to which the property interest relates; and

(ii) such other documents on which the seller can reasonably be expected to rely in order to deduce title to that estate for the purposes of its sale;

(e) if the property interest is or includes the whole or part of a freehold estate in commonhold land –

(i)   the documents described in paragraph 1 of Schedule 3; and

(ii)   documents consisting of or containing information about the matters described in paragraph 2 of that Schedule;

(f) if the property interest is or includes the whole or part of a leasehold interest –

(i)   the documents described in paragraph 1 of Schedule 4; and

(ii)   documents consisting of or containing information about the matters described in paragraph 2 of that Schedule;

(g) if the property interest is or includes the whole or part of an interest in dwelling-houses to which Part 5 of the 2004 Act applies by virtue of section 171(2) of that Act, such leases or licences –

(i)   to which the dwelling-houses are subject or are expected to be subject at the time of, or following completion of the sale of the property interest; and

(ii)   as have not been included in the pack under paragraph (f) of this regulation;

(h) if the property is physically complete on or before the first point of marketing, either or both of the following –

(i)   a home condition report which complies with Schedule 5; or

(ii)   the terms of a new homes warranty which has not commenced, which otherwise complies with Schedule 6 and to which the property is expected to be subject, together with the document described in paragraph 4 of that Schedule (cover note);

(i) a new homes warranty which complies with Schedule 6 –

(i)   where the property is the subject of such a warranty; and

(ii)   it has not expired at the first point of marketing;

(j) such other home condition reports complying with Schedule 5 as have been completed in respect of the property within the 12 months preceding the first point of marketing;

(k) if the property is physically complete before the first point of marketing, the energy performance certificate for the property where –

(i)   a home condition report complying with Schedule 5 is not included in the pack under paragraph (h)(i) or (j) of this regulation; or

(ii)   such a certificate is obtained in addition to such a report which is so included and is dated later than such a report;

(l) if the property is not physically complete before the first point of marketing, a document complying with Schedule 7 (report on a home not physically complete);

(m) a search report which relates to the property and which records the results of a search of all parts of the appropriate local land charges register –

(i)   in the form of an official search certificate, in the case of an official search made pursuant to section 9 of the Local Land Charges Act 1975; or

(ii)   in any other form but which complies with Parts 1 and 2 of Schedule 8 in the case of a personal search made pursuant to section 8 of that Act;

(n) a search report which –

(i)   complies with Parts 1 and 2 of Schedule 8 and with Schedule 9; and

(ii)   records the results of a search of records held by or derived from a local authority (local enquiries); and

(o) a search report which complies with Parts 1 and 2 of Schedule 8 and with Schedule 10 (drainage and water enquiries).

Authorised pack documents

9.   Subject to regulations 10, 11, 12 and Part 4, the home information pack may include documents consisting of or containing any of the following –

(a)   an accurate translation in any language of any pack document;

(b)   an additional version of any pack document in another format, such as Braille or large print;

(c)   a summary or explanation of any pack document;

(d)   information identifying the property including a description, photograph, map, plan or drawing of the property;

(e)   information about a pack document, about information contained within a pack document or about the home information pack, relating to –

(i)   its source or supply; or

(ii)   complaints or redress procedures arising from it;

(f)   if the property interest is or includes the whole or part of a registered estate, official copies of any documents referred to in the individual register, including any edited information documents derived from such exempt information documents as are referred to in the register;

(g)   if the property interest is or includes the whole or part of a freehold estate in commonhold land, information which –

(i)   relates to one or more of the matters described in paragraph 3 of Schedule 3; and

(ii)   would be of interest to potential buyers of the property interest;

(h)   if the property interest is or includes the whole or part of a leasehold interest, information which –

(i)   relates to one or more of the matters described in paragraph 3 of Schedule 4; and

(ii)   would be of interest to potential buyers of the property interest;

(i)   documentary evidence of such safety, building, repair or maintenance work as has been carried out in relation to the property since the date of any home condition report included in the pack under regulation 8(h)(i) or 8(j);

(j)   any warranty, policy or guarantee for defects in the design, building, or completion of the property, or its conversion for residential purposes;

(k)   one or more of the following search reports, which comply with Parts 1 and 3 of Schedule 8, which record the results of a search relating to the property and which relate to any of the following matters –

(i)   information held by or derived from a local authority, and dealing with matters supplementary to those contained in the search reports required by regulation 8(m) or 8(n);

(ii)   common land;

(iii)   rights of access to, over or affecting the property interest;

(iv)   ground stability, the effects of mining or extractions or the effects of natural subsidence;

(v)   actual or potential environmental hazards, including the risks of flooding or contamination from radon gas or any other substance;

(vi)   telecommunications services;

(vii)   sewerage, drainage, water, gas or electrical services;

(viii)   the potential or actual effects of transport services, including roads, waterways, trams and underground or over-ground railways; or

(ix)   liabilities to repair or maintain buildings or land not within the property interest;

(l)   where it would be of interest to potential buyers of the property interest, a document which –

(i)   records the results of a search relating to other premises in the vicinity of the property; and

(ii)   would otherwise be a report of the type required by regulation 8(m), 8(n) or 8(o) or authorised by paragraph (k) of this regulation, if references in those provisions and in Schedules 8, 9 and 10 to 'property', 'land' and 'land on which the property is or will be situated' were references to those other premises;

(m)   any documents referred to in a search report included in the pack under regulation 8(m), 8(n), 8(o) (subject to paragraph 2(4)(b) of Schedule 10) or paragraphs (k) or (l) of this regulation; and

(n)   information which –

(i)   relates to one or more of the matters described in Schedule 11; and

(ii)   would be of interest to potential buyers of the property interest.

Creation of interests

10. (1) Subject to regulation 12 and Part 4, where the sale involves –

(a)   the whole or part of a commonhold unit, which at the first point of marketing has not been registered by the Chief Land Registrar as a freehold estate in commonhold land; or

(b)   a leasehold property interest, which at the first point of marketing has not yet been created,

regulations 8 and 9 apply as respects that freehold estate or leasehold interest, as modified by this regulation.

(2) Where paragraph (1)(a) applies –

(a)   the sale statement must be completed as if the freehold estate had been registered by the Chief Land Registrar;

(b)   regulations 8(c), 8(d) and 9(f) apply as if for 'is or includes' in each paragraph, there were substituted 'to be registered as a freehold estate in commonhold land arises from';

(c)   paragraphs 1 and 2 of Schedule 3 do not apply;

(d)   regulation 9(g) and paragraph 3 of Schedule 3 must be construed by reference to the information expected to be relevant to the interest to be registered as a freehold estate in commonhold land; and

(e)   the home information pack must include documents consisting of or containing information which relates to the matters described in paragraph 4 of Schedule 3.

(3) Where paragraph (1)(b) applies –

(a)   the sale statement must be completed as if the leasehold interest had been created;

(b)   regulations 8(c), 8(d) and 9(f) apply as if for 'is or includes' in each paragraph, there were substituted 'is to be created from';

(c)   paragraphs 1 and 2 of Schedule 4 do not apply;

(d)   regulation 9(h) and paragraph 3 of Schedule 4 must be construed by reference to the information expected to be relevant to the interest to be created; and

(e)   the home information pack must include documents consisting of or containing information which relates to the matters described in paragraph 4 of Schedule 4.

Prohibitions relating to home condition reports

11. (1) A home condition report complying with Schedule 5 must not be included in the home information pack if it was not completed for the purposes of the sale by the seller of the property interest.

    (2) No pack document may be described as a 'home condition report' unless it complies with Schedule 5.

Exclusion of advertising information

12. (1) Information advertising or marketing goods or services must not be included in a pack document –

    (a) by a responsible person;

    (b) at his request; or

    (c) with his permission.

    (2) In paragraph (1), 'information advertising or marketing goods or services' does not include –

    (a) trade names used to describe the materials used in the building of any premises;

    (b) the information described in paragraph 1(h) of Schedule 8 (description of how relevant search documents can be obtained); or

    (c) the information described in paragraphs 12, 19 and 20 of Schedule 10 (names of sewerage and water undertakers and those billing for sewerage and water services).

PART 4 – ASSEMBLY AND ACCURACY OF HOME INFORMATION PACKS

Time at which pack documents are to be included

13. (1) Subject to regulations 15 and 17, the documents required by these Regulations to be included in the home information pack under regulation 8 (including that regulation as modified by regulation 10) must be included before the first point of marketing.

    (2) The pack documents authorised by these Regulations to be included in the home information pack under regulation 9 (including that regulation as modified by regulation 10) may be included at any time.

Age of pack documents when first included

14. (1) The following pack documents must be dated no earlier than three months preceding the first point of marketing –

    (a) official copies included in the home information pack under regulation 8(c), 8(e) and 8(f); and

    (b) a certificate of an official search of the index map included in the pack under regulation 8(d)(i).

    (2) The pack documents included under regulation 8(h)(i), 8(m), 8(n) and 8(o), (home condition reports and search reports) must be completed no earlier than three months preceding the first point of marketing.

    (3) All other pack documents –

    (a) may be completed or dated earlier than three months preceding the first point of marketing; and

    (b) with the exception of home condition reports included under regulation 8(j), must be such versions of the documents as can reasonably be assumed to be the most recent to the first point of marketing.

(4) Where –

   (a) a pack document has been amended at any time before its inclusion in the home information pack; and

   (b) the amendment is not incorporated in the document,

that amendment must be included in the pack.

Required pack documents which are unavailable before the first point of marketing

15. (1) This regulation applies –

   (a) where regulation 17 does not apply; and

   (b) to the pack documents required to be included in the home information pack under any of paragraphs (d)(ii) to (o) of regulation 8, except paragraph (l) (report on a home not physically complete).

(2) If, despite all reasonable efforts and enquiries by the responsible person, a pack document to which this regulation applies cannot be obtained by him before the first point of marketing, but he believes on reasonable grounds that it is likely to become available afterwards –

   (a) the home information pack complies with the requirements of these Regulations where –

      (i) he continues to use all reasonable efforts to obtain the document; and

      (ii) the first point of marketing occurs no earlier than the end of the period of 14 days starting with the day a request for the document is delivered; and

   (b) the document must be included in the home information pack as soon as reasonably practicable.

(3) The time the document is included under paragraph (2)(b) becomes the first point of marketing for that document –

   (a) for the purposes of any provision of these Regulations that requires the age or currency of a pack document to be determined by reference to a period preceding the first point of marketing; and

   (b) until such time (if any) as a further first point of marketing arises in relation to the sale under regulation 3(4).

(4) In paragraph (2)(a)(ii) –

   (a) the reference to a request is to a request properly addressed to a person who usually provides or is likely to provide such a document, and which is –

      (i) made in such form;

      (ii) contains all such information; and

      (iii) includes such payment or an undertaking to make such payment,

as is usually necessary to obtain that document; and

   (b) the reference to the day a request for a document is delivered shall be construed in accordance with regulation 16.

Delivery of documents under regulation 15

16. (1) Subject to paragraphs (2) and (3), the day a request for the document is delivered is for the purposes of regulation 15(2)(a)(ii), depending on the method of delivery –

   (a) the day the request is served personally on the intended recipient;

   (b) the day it would be delivered to the intended recipient's address in the ordinary course of post or (if sooner), the day on which it is proved to have been actually delivered;

   (c) the day it is left at the intended recipient's address;

(d)   the second day after it is left at the document exchange of the person making the request or (if sooner), the day on which it is proved to have been actually delivered; or

(e)   the day it is sent by fax or electronic communication to the intended recipient's address or (if later), the day on which it is proved to have been actually delivered.

(2)   Subject to paragraph (3), where a request for a document is delivered to the Chief Land Registrar, the day the request is delivered is for the purposes of regulation 15(2)(a)(ii), the day it is delivered in accordance with, or under, the Land Registration Act 2002 –

(a)   personally;

(b)   by post, and is the day it would be delivered to the Chief Land Registrar in the ordinary course of post or (if sooner), the day on which it is proved to have been actually delivered;

(c)   by document exchange, and is the second day after it is left at the document exchange of the person making the request or (if sooner), the day on which it is proved to have been actually delivered;

(d)   orally; or

(e)   by telephone, fax or other electronic method.

(3)   Where a request for a document –

(a)   is made in parts, the day the request is delivered is the day the last part is delivered;

(b)   is delivered more than once, the day the request is delivered is the first day on which a request is delivered; and

(c)   is delivered using more than one method of delivery, the day the request is delivered is the first day on which a request is delivered.

(4)   In paragraph (1)(a), a document is served personally –

(a)   on an individual by leaving it with that individual;

(b)   on a business by leaving it with an employee or owner of the business; and

(c)   on any other body of persons corporate or unincorporate by leaving it with an employee or member of that body.

(5)   References to a recipient's address –

(a)   in paragraphs (1)(b) and (c) are if the intended recipient is an individual –

(i)   to his usual or last known residence; or

(ii)   if his usual or last known residence is the property, to that address and an address (if any) at which it can reasonably be assumed he will be contacted;

(b)   in paragraph (1)(b) and (c), are if the intended recipient is a business or other body, to any principal or last known place of business from which the document requested is usually or likely to be provided; and

(c)   in paragraph (1)(e), is to any electronic address, identification or number published or provided by the intended recipient for the purposes of supplying the document requested.

Required pack documents which are unobtainable

17. (1)   The provisions of regulation 8 specified in paragraph (2) do not apply where, after making all reasonable efforts and enquiries, the responsible person believes on reasonable grounds that the document in question

(a)   no longer exists in any form; or

(b)   cannot be obtained from or created by any person.

(2)   The provisions of regulation 8 referred to in paragraph (1) are paragraphs (d)(ii), (e), (f), (g) or (i).

Updating of required pack documents

18. (1)   This regulation applies to any document included in a home information pack under regulation 8 (including that regulation as modified by regulation 10).

(2)   Where the responsible person amends such a document or obtains or creates a further version of it, he must –

(a)   include the amended document or the further version in the pack;

(b)   amend accordingly such translations, additional versions, summaries or explanations as are included in the pack under regulation 9(a), 9(b) or 9(c) or include a further version of such translations, additional versions, summaries or explanations; and

(c)   subject to paragraph (4), remove such documents as have been wholly superseded by a document included under sub-paragraphs (a) or (b).

(3)   The time the responsible person amends a document or obtains or creates a further version of it under paragraph (2) becomes the first point of marketing for that document –

(a)   for the purposes of any provision of these Regulations that requires the age or currency of a pack document to be determined by reference to a period preceding the first point of marketing; and

(b)   until such time (if any) as a further first point of marketing arises in relation to the sale under regulation 3(4).

(4)   Nothing in paragraph (2)(c) authorises a person to remove from a pack a home condition report complying with Schedule 5 (or any part of such a report), unless it has been included in contravention of regulation 11.

Inclusion of home condition reports or energy performance certificates following physical completion

19. (1)   If the property is not physically complete before the first point of marketing, and becomes so after that time, but before the sale is completed, the responsible person must include in the home information pack –

(a)   either or both of the following –

(i)   a home condition report which complies with Schedule 5; or

(ii)   the terms of a new homes warranty which has not commenced, which otherwise complies with Schedule 6 and to which the property is expected to be subject, together with the document described in paragraph 4 of that Schedule (cover note); and

(b)   the energy performance certificate for the property where –

(i)   a home condition report complying with Schedule 5 is not included in the home information pack under paragraph (1)(a)(i); or

(ii)   such a certificate is obtained in addition to such a report which is so included and is dated later than any such report.

(2)   A document required to be included in the pack under paragraph (1)(a) or (b) must be so included within the period of 14 days starting with the day the property becomes physically complete.

(3)   Where such documents are included, a document included in the pack under regulation 8(l) (report on a home not physically complete) must be removed.

Updating of authorised pack documents

20. (1)   This regulation applies to any document included in a home information pack under regulation 9 (including that regulation as modified by regulation 10).

(2) A responsible person may –

(a) include an amended document or further version in the pack; and

(b) subject to paragraph (4), remove such documents as have been wholly superseded by a document or version included under sub-paragraph (a).

(3) The time the responsible person includes the amended document or further version under paragraph (2)(a) becomes the first point of marketing for that document –

(a) for the purposes of any provision of these Regulations that requires the age or currency of a pack document to be determined by reference to a period preceding the first point of marketing; and

(b) until such time (if any) as a further first point of marketing arises in relation to the sale under regulation 3(4).

(4) Nothing in paragraph (2)(b) authorises a person to remove from a pack a home condition report complying with Schedule 5 (or any part of such a report), unless it has been included in contravention of regulation 11.

Seller's check of the home information pack

21. If he is not the seller, the responsible person must provide the seller with a copy of any of the pack documents which the seller has requested him to provide for the purposes of ensuring the accuracy of the home information pack.

PART 5 – EXCEPTIONS

Meaning of 'non-residential premises'

22. (1) In this Part 'non-residential premises' includes –

(a) premises where the most recent use of the premises, is or was primarily non-residential; and

(b) any dwelling-house where it is clear from the manner in which it is marketed that it is due to be converted for primarily non-residential use by the time its sale is completed, and all the relevant –

(i) planning permissions; and
(ii) listed building consents,

exist in relation to the conversion.

(2) For the purposes of this Part, where a question arises as to whether premises are –

(a) non-residential premises; or
(b) residential property by virtue of being ancillary land,

the premises may be treated as non-residential premises if the conditions in paragraph (3) are met.

(3) The conditions referred to in paragraph (2) are that –

(a) the total area of the land is 5 hectares or more; and

(b) the most recent use of the land is or was primarily for one or more of the following purposes –

(i) horticulture or cultivation;
(ii) the breeding or keeping of animals or livestock; or
(iii) the use of land as grazing land or woodlands.

Exclusion from meaning of 'non-residential premises'

23. In this Part, 'non-residential premises' do not include –

(a) premises due to be converted to a dwelling-house by the time the sale of the property interest is complete; or

(b) a dwelling-house or a building ancillary to a dwelling-house used for either or both of the following purposes –

(i)   letting under a lease; or

(ii) home working.

Exception for seasonal and holiday accommodation

24. The duties under sections 155 to 159 of the 2004 Act do not apply in relation to a property where –

(a) the dwelling-house which is or forms part of the property is subject to a condition imposed under section 72(1)(a) of the Town and Country Planning Act 1990 regulating the use of the dwelling-house to either or both of the following –

(i)   occupation for less than 11 months in any 12 month period; or

(ii) use only for holiday accommodation; and

(b) that regulation of the use of the dwelling-house is clear from the manner in which the property is marketed.

Exception for mixed sales

25. The duties under sections 155 to 159 of the 2004 Act do not apply in relation to a property where –

(a) it is to be sold with one or more non-residential premises;

(b) the dwelling-house which is or forms part of the property is ancillary to those non-residential premises;

(c) at the time the first point of marketing would have otherwise occurred, the seller does not intend to accept an offer to buy the property in isolation from any one of those non-residential premises; and

(d) it is clear that he would not do so from the manner in which the property is marketed.

Exception for dual use of a dwelling-house

26. The duties under sections 155 to 159 of the 2004 Act do not apply in relation to a property where –

(a) the dwelling-house which is or forms part of that property was most recently used for both residential and non-residential purposes; and

(b) the manner in which it is marketed suggests it is suitable for –

(i)   non-residential use; or

(ii) both residential and non-residential use.

Exception for portfolios of properties

27. (1) Subject to paragraph (2), the duties under sections 155 to 159 of the 2004 Act do not apply in relation to a property where –

(a) the dwelling-house which is or forms part of that property is to be sold with one or more other dwelling-houses;

(b) the dwelling-houses mentioned in sub-paragraph (a) are not dwelling-houses to which Part 5 of the 2004 Act applies by virtue of section 171(2) of that Act;

- (c) at the time the first point of marketing would have otherwise occurred, the seller does not intend to accept an offer to buy any one of those dwelling-houses in isolation from another; and
- (d) it is clear that he would not do so from the manner in which the dwelling-houses are marketed.

(2) Paragraph (1) does not apply to one or more dwelling-houses which are ancillary to a principal dwelling-house.

Exception for unsafe properties

28. The duties under sections 155 to 159 of the 2004 Act do not apply in relation to a property –

- (a) which is unoccupied;
- (b) whose condition poses a serious risk to the health or safety of its occupants or visitors; and
- (c) where the manner in which the property is marketed suggests it is unsuitable for occupation in that condition.

Exception for properties to be demolished

29. (1) The duties under sections 155 to 159 of the 2004 Act do not apply in relation to a property where –

- (a) it is clear from the manner in which the property is marketed that –
   - (i) the dwelling-house which is or forms part of the property is suitable for demolition; and
   - (ii) the resulting site is suitable for re-development;
- (b) all the relevant –
   - (i) planning permissions;
   - (ii) listed building consents; and
   - (iii) conservation area consents,

   exist in relation to the demolition; and
- (c) in relation to the re-development –
   - (i) either outline planning permission or planning permission exists, or both; and
   - (ii) where relevant, listed building consent exists.

(2) In paragraph (1)(c)(i), 'outline planning permission' means a planning permission for the erection of a building, which is granted subject to a condition requiring the subsequent approval of the local planning authority with respect to one or more of the following matters –

- (a) siting;
- (b) design;
- (c) external appearance;
- (d) means of access; or
- (e) the landscaping of the site.

Exception – 1st June 2007 to 31st October 2007

30. (1) In this regulation, 'transitional period' means the period starting with 1st June 2007 and ending with 31st October 2007.

(2) Subject to paragraph (1), a seller or a person acting as an estate agent for a seller is not a responsible person in relation to a property by virtue of action taken during the transitional period, by him or on his behalf, which makes public the fact that the property is on the market where, before that period begins –

(a)   the property was put on the market; and

(b)   further action was taken by him or on his behalf to market the property.

(3)   Subject to paragraph (4), the duties under sections 155 to 159 of the 2004 Act do not apply in relation to a property which is put on the market during the transitional period where –

(a)   it was put on the market by or on behalf of the seller before that period begins;

(b)   it remained on the market until it was taken off the market because the seller accepted an offer to buy the property; and

(c)   it is put back on the market within 28 days of that offer being withdrawn or its acceptance repudiated.

(4)   Paragraphs (2) and (3) cease to apply at the end of the transitional period.

PART 6 – ENFORCEMENT

Amount of penalty charge

31.   The amount of a penalty charge specified in a notice given to a person under section 168 of the 2004 Act (penalty charge notices) shall be £200.

Exclusion of penalty charges for content of pack documents

32.   Section 168(1)(a) of the 2004 Act does not apply to a breach of a duty under section 155(1) or 159(2) of that Act to the extent that –

(a)   the content of a pack document, other than the home information pack index and the sale statement, fails to comply with any requirement of these Regulations; and

(b)   the responsible person believes on reasonable grounds that the document does comply with that requirement.

PART 7 – APPROVED CERTIFICATION SCHEMES

Approval of certification schemes

33.   The Secretary of State shall approve one or more certification schemes, but before doing so must be satisfied that a scheme contains appropriate provision –

(a)   for ensuring that its members are fit and proper persons who are qualified (by their education, training and experience) to produce home condition reports;

(b)   for ensuring that its members have in force suitable indemnity insurance;

(c)   for facilitating the resolution of complaints against its members;

(d)   for requiring home condition reports made by its members to be entered onto a register kept pursuant to any regulations made under section 165 of the 2004 Act;

(e)   for the keeping of a public register of its members; and

(f)   for requiring all members of all certification schemes as have been approved, to make home condition reports using a standard form for the type of dwelling-house which is or forms part of the property, which –

(i)   includes the terms prescribed in paragraph 2 of Schedule 5;

(ii)   includes a statement of the procedures for the resolution of complaints against members;

(iii) includes a statement of such procedures as the certification scheme main-tains for rectifying inaccuracies in a particular home condition report; and

(iv)   includes a numerical scale for rating the conditions within the property.

Terms of approved certification schemes

34. An approved certification scheme must contain provision –

(a) for ensuring that its objects and activities are compatible with protecting, promoting and facilitating the reliability and trustworthiness of home condition reports and home inspectors, with particular reference to potential and actual buyers, sellers and mortgage lenders of residential properties;

(b) for ensuring that it produces and publishes a code as regards the conduct required of its members;

(c) for the conduct of inspections of residential properties by its members; and

(d) for ensuring that its members complete home condition reports complying with Schedule 5 using the standard form described in regulation 33(f).

Withdrawal of approval from certification schemes

35. The Secretary of State may withdraw approval from one or more certification schemes –

(a) with immediate effect, or

(b) with written notice –

(i) with effect from a date specified in the notice; or

(ii) temporarily for a period specified in the notice.

Signed by authority of one of Her Majesty's Principal Secretaries of State

Yvette Cooper

Minister of State Department for Communities and Local Government

9th June 2006

SCHEDULE 1 – HOME INFORMATION PACK INDEX (REGULATION 8(A))

Required matters

1. A home information pack index must –

(a) consist of a list of all the documents included in the home information pack;

(b) be revised whenever a document is included in or removed from the pack;

(c) where regulation 15 or 17 applies, indicate –

(i) that a document otherwise required by these Regulations is missing from the pack;

(ii) specify which document it is; and

(iii) the reason why it is missing; and

(d) where regulation 15 applies, indicate such steps as are being taken to obtain the document.

Authorised matters

2. A home information pack index may indicate where a particular pack document can be found in the home information pack.

SCHEDULE 2 – SALE STATEMENT (REGULATION 8(B))

A sale statement must state –

(a) the address or proposed address of the property;

(b) whether the property interest is –

      (i)   a freehold interest other than a freehold estate in commonhold land;

      (ii) a freehold estate in commonhold land; or

      (iii) a leasehold interest;

(c) whether at the first point of marketing –

      (i)   the property or the land on which the property is or will be situated is a registered estate; or

      (ii) the title to the property or the land on which the property is or will be situated is not entered in the register of title;

(d) the name of the seller, and the capacity in which they are selling the property;

(e) whether the property –

      (i)   is being sold entirely with vacant possession; or

      (ii) is a property to which Part 5 of the 2004 Act applies by virtue of section 171(2) of that Act; and

(f) if it is a property to which Part 5 of the 2004 Act applies by virtue of section 171(2) of that Act, the nature of any lack of vacant possession.

SCHEDULE 3 – COMMONHOLD INFORMATION (REGULATION 8(E), 9(G) AND 10(2))

Required commonhold documents

1. (1) Subject to sub-paragraph (2), the documents referred to in regulation 8(e)(i) are –

      (a) an official copy of such of the following documents, as are kept by the Chief Land Registrar –

          (i)   the individual register and title plan relating to the common parts; and

          (ii) the commonhold community statement referred to in that register;

      (b) except where they are described in the commonhold community statement, such regulations or rules as are made for the purposes of managing the commonhold by the –

          (i)   commonhold association;

          (ii) such managing agents as are appointed, or proposed by the commonhold association to manage the commonhold; or

          (iii) such other persons as manage or are likely to manage the commonhold,

      and their predecessors (if any); and

      (c) the most recent requests for payment or financial contribution where made in respect of the property, relating to the 12 months preceding the first point of marketing, towards such of the following as are relevant to the property –

          (i)   commonhold assessment;

          (ii) reserve funds;

          (iii) insurance against damage for the common parts (if made separately to the requests relating to commonhold assessment included under sub-paragraph (i)); and

          (iv) insurance for any person in respect of personal injury or death caused by or within the common parts (if made separately to the requests relating to commonhold assessment included under sub-paragraph (i)).

  (2) Except for the documents specified in paragraph (a), the documents required by

sub-paragraph (1) are only those which are in the seller's possession, under his control or to which he can reasonably be expected to have access, taking into account the enquiries that it would be reasonable to make of –

(a)   the unit-holder (unless the seller is the unit-holder); and
(b)   the persons described in sub-paragraph (1)(b)(i) to (iii) and their predecessors (if any).

Required commonhold information

2.   (1)   Subject to sub-paragraph (2), the matters referred to in regulation 8(e)(ii) are –

(a)   the names and addresses of –

(i)   such managing agents as are appointed, or proposed by the common-hold association to manage the commonhold; and

(ii)   such other persons as manage or are likely to manage the common-hold;

(b)   such amendments as are proposed to the following –

(i)   the commonhold community statement; and

(ii)   the regulations or rules described in paragraph 1(1)(b) of this Schedule; and

(c)   a summary of such works as are being undertaken or proposed, affecting the property or the common parts.

(2)   The information required by sub-paragraph (1) is only that which the seller can reasonably be expected to be aware of, taking into account the enquiries that it would be reasonable to make of –

(a)   the unit-holder (unless the seller is the unit-holder); and
(b)   the persons described in paragraph 1(1)(b)(i) to (iii) of this Schedule and their predecessors (if any).

Authorised commonhold information

3.   The matters referred to in regulation 9(g) are –

(a)   the commonhold community statement;
(b)   the rights or obligations of the unit-holder under the commonhold community statement or otherwise, including whether the unit-holder has complied with such obligations;
(c)   the rights or obligations of the commonhold association under the commonhold community statement or otherwise, including whether it has complied with such obligations;
(d)   the commonhold association and any information that might affect the unit-holder's relationship with it;
(e)   any agent of the commonhold association or other manager of the property and any information that might affect the unit-holder's relationship with such persons;
(f)   the membership of the commonhold association;
(g)   the status or memorandum and articles of association of any company related to the management of the property or the commonhold;
(h)   any commonhold assessment payable for the property, including whether payments for such assessment are outstanding;
(i)   any reserve fund levy relating to the property or the commonhold, including whether payments for such levies are outstanding;
(j)   any planned or recent works relating to the property or the commonhold;

(k) responsibility for insuring the property or the commonhold, including the terms of such insurance and whether payments relating to it are outstanding; and

(l)   any lease or licence of the property.

Creation of commonhold interests

4.   The matters referred to in regulation 10(2)(e) are –

(a) the terms of the commonhold community statement that will or is expected to apply in relation to the property interest once it has been registered as a freehold estate in commonhold land; and

(b) estimates of the payment or financial contribution likely to be required of the unit-holder within 12 months of completion of the sale of the interest towards –

(i)   commonhold assessment;

(ii)   reserve funds;

(iii) insurance against damage for the common parts (if not to be included in contributions towards commonhold assessment); and

(iv) insurance for any person in respect of personal injury or death caused by or within the common parts (if not to be included in contributions towards commonhold assessment).

SCHEDULE 4 – LEASEHOLD INFORMATION (REGULATIONS 8(F), 9(H) AND 10(3))

Required leasehold documents

1.   (1) Subject to sub-paragraph (2), the documents referred to in regulation 8(f)(i) are –

(a) the lease in the form of –

(i)   an official copy;

(ii)   any other copy; or

(iii) an edited information document if, despite all reasonable efforts and enquiries by the responsible person, it can only be obtained by him in that form;

(b) such regulations or rules as are made for the purposes of managing the property by –

(i)   the current lessor or proposed lessor;

(ii)   such managing agents as are appointed or proposed by the lessor to manage the property; and

(iii) such other persons as manage or are likely to manage the property,

and their predecessors (if any);

(c) statements or summaries of service charges supplied in respect of the property under section 21 of the Landlord and Tenant Act 1985 or otherwise, and relating to the 36 months preceding the first point of marketing; and

(d) the most recent requests for payment or financial contribution where made in respect of the property, relating to the 12 months preceding the first point of marketing, towards such of the following as are relevant to the property –

(i)   service charges;

(ii)   ground rent;

(iii) insurance against damage for the building in which the property is situated (if made separately to the request relating to service charges included under sub-paragraph (i)); and

(iv) insurance for any person in respect of personal injury or death caused by or within the building in which the property is situated (if made separately to the request relating to service charges included under sub-paragraph (i)).

(2) Except for the documents specified in paragraph (a), the documents required by sub-paragraph (1) are only those which are in the seller's possession, under his control or to which he can reasonably be expected to have access, taking into account the enquiries that it would be reasonable to make of –

    (a)   the lessee (unless the seller is the lessee); and

    (b)   the persons described in sub-paragraph (1)(b)(i) to (iii) and their predecessors (if any).

Required leasehold information

2.   (1)   Subject to sub-paragraph (2), the matters referred to in regulation 8(f)(ii) are –

    (a)   the names and addresses of –

        (i)   the lessor of the property or the building;

        (ii)   such managing agents as are appointed or proposed by the lessor to manage the property; and

        (iii)   such other persons as manage or are likely to manage the property;

    (b)   such amendments as are proposed to the following –

        (i)   the lease; and

        (ii)   the regulations or rules described in paragraph 1(1)(b) of this Schedule; and

    (c)   a summary of such works as are being undertaken or proposed, affecting the property or the building in which the property is situated.

    (2)   The information required by sub-paragraph (1) is only that which the seller can reasonably be expected to be aware of, taking into account the enquiries that it would be reasonable to make of –

    (a)   the lessee (unless the seller is the lessee); and

    (b)   the persons described in paragraph 1(1)(b)(i) to (iii) of this Schedule and their predecessors (if any).

Authorised leasehold information

3.   The matters referred to in regulation 9(h) are –

    (a)   any lease of the property, including those that are superior or inferior to the property interest;

    (b)   any licence of the property;

    (c)   any freehold estate to which the lease relates including any proposals to buy a freehold interest relating to the property;

    (d)   the rights or obligations of the lessee under the lease or otherwise, including whether the lessee has complied with such obligations;

    (e)   the rights or obligations of the lessor under the lease or otherwise, including whether the lessor has complied with such obligations;

    (f)   the lessor of the property and any information that might affect the lessee's relationship with the lessor;

    (g)   any agent of the lessor or other manager of the property and any information that might affect the lessee's relationship with such persons;

    (h)   the membership or existence of any body of persons corporate or unincorporate which manages the property or building in which the property is situated;

    (i)   the status or memorandum and articles of association of any company related to the management of the property or building in which the property is situated;

    (j)   the rent payable for the property, including whether payments for such rent are outstanding;

(k) any service charges payable in respect of the property, including whether payments for such charges are outstanding;

(l) any reserve fund relating to the property for necessary works to it or the building in which the property is situated, including whether payments to such a fund are outstanding;

(m) any planned or recent works to the property or the building in which the property is situated; and

(n) any responsibility for insuring the property or the building in which the property is situated, including the terms of such insurance and whether payments relating to it are outstanding.

Creation of leasehold interests

4. The matters referred to in regulation 10(3) are –

(a) the terms of the lease that will or is expected to be granted in order to create the property interest; and

(b) estimates of the payment or financial contribution likely to be required of the lessee within 12 months of completion of the sale of the interest towards –

(i) service charges;

(ii) ground rent;

(iii) insurance against damage for the building in which the property is situated (if not to be included in contributions towards service charges); and

(iv) insurance for any person in respect of personal injury or death caused by or within the building in which the property is situated (if not to be included in contributions towards service charges).

SCHEDULE 5 – HOME CONDITION REPORT (REGULATION 8(H)(I) AND 8(J))

Home condition reports

1. A home condition report –

(a) must be made by a home inspector following an inspection carried out by him in accordance with the provisions of such approved certification schemes of which he is a member; and

(b) must be entered onto a register kept pursuant to any regulations made under section 165 of the 2004 Act.

Terms for the preparation of a home condition report

2. A home inspector must prepare a home condition report on the following terms without exclusion or limitation –

(a) that the report will be prepared with reasonable care and skill;

(b) that the home inspector will provide in the report an objective opinion about the condition of the property;

(c) that such an opinion will be based on his inspection;

(d) that the home inspector will identify in the report such conditions within the property as appear to –

(i) be defects that are serious or require urgent attention, or both;

(ii) give rise to repair or replacement; or

(iii) give rise to further investigation;

(e) that a responsible person may copy or issue a copy of the report for the purposes of complying with –

(i) regulations 5, 6, 8(h)(i), 8(j) and 21; and

      (ii)   section 156(1), (2) and (11) of the 2004 Act; and

(f)   that any person may do one or more of the following for the purposes of a disclosure or other act authorised by regulations made under section 165 of the 2004 Act –

      (i)   copy a report;
      (ii)   issue a copy of a report;
      (iii)   rent or lend a report;
      (iv)   communicate a report; or
      (v)   make an adaptation of a report or do any of the above in relation to an adaptation.

Third party contractual rights in relation to home condition reports

3.   A home inspector must prepare a home condition report on terms enabling the provisions of the contract under which the report is prepared to be enforced in relation to the terms mentioned in paragraph 2 of this Schedule, by the following persons in their own right (whether or not they are a party to such a contract)

(a)   the seller;
(b)   a potential or actual buyer of the property interest; and
(c)   a mortgage lender in respect of the property interest.

Inclusion of additional or more favourable terms for home condition reports

4.   A home inspector may prepare a home condition report on any of the following –

(a)   terms additional to those described in paragraphs 2 and 3 of this Schedule (but without excluding or limiting them); and
(b)   terms more favourable to –

      (i)   the seller;
      (ii)   a potential or actual buyer of the property interest; or
      (iii)   a mortgage lender in respect of the property interest,

than those described in paragraphs 2 and 3 of this Schedule.

Less favourable terms

5.   Any home condition report which contains terms less favourable to –

(a)   the seller;
(b)   a potential or actual buyer of the property interest; or
(c)   a mortgage lender in respect of the property interest,

than those required by this Schedule does not comply with the requirements of this Schedule.

Completion of home condition reports by home inspectors

6.   A home condition report must be completed by a home inspector so as to contain his record of the following information –

(a)   his name;
(b)   whether he has or is likely to have any personal or business relationship with any person involved in the sale of the property;
(c)   the reference number or code against which the report is registered under paragraph 1(b) of this Schedule;
(d)   the names of such approved certification schemes as of which he is a member and in which capacity the report is made;
(e)   such membership numbers or codes as have been allocated to him by those schemes;

(f) the name and address of his employer, or if he is self-employed, the name under which he trades;

(g) the date of the inspection and the date the report is completed;

(h) the address of the property;

(i) the year of building of the property or, if this cannot be ascertained by him, his estimate of the year of building;

(j) the number of –

   (i)   storeys or levels in the property; and
   (ii) rooms on each storey or level of the property;

(k) such provision as has been made for the parking of vehicles relating to occupants of or visitors to the property;

(l) such utility services as are connected to the property and the condition of their visible parts;

(m) if the property is situated in a flat or maisonette –

   (i)   the number of storeys or levels of the building in which the flat or maisonette is situated;
   (ii) the number of flats and maisonettes in that building or, if this cannot be ascertained by him, his estimate of the approximate number of flats and maisonettes;
   (iii) whether the building contains a passenger lift to the storey or level on which the property is situated;
   (iv) the general condition of such areas that lead to the property as are common to both it and any neighbouring premises; and
   (v)   the general condition of the building in which the flat or maisonette is situated;

(n) risks to the health or safety of the property's occupants or visitors, so far as he can ascertain them;

(o) the condition of the outside parts of the property including such –

   (i)   roof coverings;
   (ii) rainwater pipes and gutters;
   (iii) chimney stacks; and
   (iv) walls, doors and windows,

   as relate to the property;

(p) the condition of the inside parts of the property including –

   (i)   roof structures accessible directly from the property;
   (ii) ceilings and floors;
   (iii) internal walls; and
   (iv) kitchen and bathroom fittings,

   and whether their appearance suggests that they have been materially affected by dampness;

(q) the general condition of such outbuildings as are part of the property;

(r) the energy performance of the property, including an energy performance certificate;

(s) whether any parts of the property to which he would normally expect to have access were not accessible to him on the day of the inspection; and

(t) any other provision required by an approved certification scheme of which he is a member and in which capacity the report is made.

Conduct of inspections

7. Nothing in this Schedule shall be construed as requiring a home inspector to –

    (a) inspect such parts of the property as are not reasonably accessible on the day of the inspection; or

    (b) move furniture, fittings or personal items at the property during an inspection.

Prohibition on personal and security information

8. A home condition report must not contain any of the following –

    (a) information or data from which another living individual can be identified from the report;

    (b) any expression of opinion about a living individual; or

    (c) information about security features at the property and, in particular, burglar alarm systems, safes or locks.

SCHEDULE 6 – EXCEPTION FROM HOME CONDITION REPORT FOR SPECIFIC NEW HOMES WARRANTIES – REGULATION 8(H)(II) AND 8(I)

PART 1 – GENERAL

Interpretation

1. In this Schedule –

    'annual increment' means a compound increase occurring each 12 months after the commencement date, the increase being based on the lower of –

    (a) the rate of inflation in re-building residential premises; or

    (b) a rate of 10% ;

    'common parts' means such common parts –

    (a) as relate to the property;

    (b) as are shared with other premises; and

    (c) as are built or converted by the developer together with the property;

    'commencement date' means the day the new homes warranty commences;

    'continuous structures' means premises that share common foundations;

    'damage' includes water ingress;

    'financial compensation' relates to the actual costs incurred in the carrying out of remedial work to the property by a person other than a warranty provider;

    'policy-holder' means –

    (a) the owner of the property for the time being; and

    (b) the party to the new homes warranty for the time being (not being a warranty provider);

    'structural features' means –

    (a) foundations;

    (b) walls bearing normal residential loads;

    (c) non load-bearing partition walls;

    (d) wet-applied wall plaster;

    (e) external render and vertical tile hanging;

    (f) load-bearing parts of roof;

    (g) tile and slate coverings to pitched roofs;

    (h) ceilings;

    (i) load-bearing parts of floors;

    (j)   staircases and internal floor decking and other floor screeds intended to support normal residential loads;

    (k)   retaining walls necessary for structural stability of the property;

    (l)   double or triple glazed panes to external windows and doors;

    (m)   under-ground drainage that the policy-holder is responsible for maintaining; and

    (n)   chimneys and flues;

'warranty period' means the period of time during which the new homes warranty exists; and

'warranty provider' is any person who does one or more of the following –

    (a)   offers the new homes warranty to an owner or potential owner of the property;

    (b)   effects the contract of insurance which is the subject of the new homes warranty;

    (c)   carries out such a contract;

    (d)   deals with such a contract as an agent;

    (e)   makes arrangements for another person (whether as principal or agent) to buy, sell, subscribe for or underwrite such a contract;

    (f)   makes arrangements with a view to a person who participates in such arrangements buying, selling, subscribing for or underwriting such a contract (whether as principal or agent);

    (g)   assists in the administration and performance of such a contract;

    (h)   advises a person (in that person's capacity as a policy-holder or potential policy-holder) on the merits of such a contract; or

    (i)   agrees to carry out any of the activities specified in sub-paragraphs (a) to (h), and

where there is more than one warranty provider in relation to a particular new homes warranty, 'warranty provider' refers to any of those persons.

New homes warranties – general

2.   (1)   A new homes warranty complies with this Schedule if it –

    (a)   is made under the arrangements described in Part 2; and

    (b)   contains, as a minimum, the terms described in Part 3, although the term described in paragraph 10 must only be included where the new homes warranty makes provision for a developer's obligations to the policy-holder.

    (2)   Any warranty dealing with any defects in the design, building, or completion of the property, which contains –

    (a)   terms additional to those described in Part 3 of this Schedule (without excluding or limiting them); or

    (b)   terms more favourable to the policy-holder than those described in Part 3,

may be regarded as complying with this Schedule.

    (3)   A new homes warranty may be regarded as complying with this Schedule if it contains –

    (a)   any of the limits described in Part 4; or

    (b)   any limits of a type described in that Part, but which are more favourable to the policy-holder.

    (4)   Any new homes warranty which contains terms less favourable to the policy-holder than those described in Part 4 does not comply with this Schedule.

    (5)   The undertakings described in Part 3 of this Schedule must be made in the new homes warranty by a warranty provider.

PART 2 – ARRANGEMENTS FOR ENTERING INTO SPECIFIC NEW HOMES WARRANTIES

Existence of insurance and regulation of warranty provider

3.   (1)   Any liability of any type arising under a new homes warranty which complies with this Schedule must be the subject of a contract of insurance against such risk to be effected by and to be carried out by persons so authorised for the purposes of the Financial Services and Markets Act 2000.

   (2)   Where a warranty provider –

   (a)   effects the contract of insurance which is the subject of the new homes warranty;

   (b)   carries out such a contract;

   (c)   deals with such a contract as an agent;

   (d)   makes arrangements for another person (whether as principal or agent) to buy, sell, subscribe for or underwrite such a contract;

   (e)   makes arrangements with a view to a person who participates in such arrangements buying, selling, subscribing for or underwriting such a contract (whether as principal or agent);

   (f)   assists in the administration and performance of such a contract;

   (g)   advises a person (in that person's capacity as a policy-holder or potential policy-holder) on the merits of such a contract; or

   (h)   agrees to carry out the activities specified in sub-paragraphs (a) to (g),

   it must be authorised to do so under the Financial Services and Markets Act 2000.

Cover notes

4.   Prior to the commencement date, a warranty provider must provide the potential policy-holder with a document confirming that –

   (a)   it has conducted a final inspection under paragraph 9(a) of this Schedule; and

   (b)   it intends to enter into the new homes warranty with the potential policy-holder.

Commencement date

5.   The commencement date for the new homes warranty must be no earlier than the day the sale of the property is completed.

PART 3 – MINIMUM COVER FOR SPECIFIC NEW HOMES WARRANTIES

Warranty period

6.   The warranty period for the new homes warranty must be at least 10 years from the commencement date.

Certificate of cover and copy of new homes warranty

7.   Under the new homes warranty, a warranty provider must provide the policy-holder with –

   (a)   a certificate confirming the existence of the new homes warranty and the commencement date; and

   (b)   a document setting out all the terms of the new homes warranty.

Transfer of cover to future owners

8.   The new homes warranty must be capable of being transferred during the warranty period –

(a) by a current policy-holder to a subsequent owner of the property; and

(b) no payment or consideration in kind must be charged to anyone for doing so.

Cover for design and building

9.   Under the new homes warranty, a warranty provider must undertake that –

(a) it has conducted reasonable checks and inspections during the building or conversion of the property and a final inspection of the property, all for the purposes of ensuring –

(i)   that the property is physically complete; and

(ii) it is designed and finished to a reasonable standard; and

(b) the inspections described in sub-paragraph (a) lead a warranty provider to believe that –

(i)   most of such structural features as exist at the property will withstand normal residential wear and tear for 60 years from the commencement date, if properly maintained; and

(ii) the building of the property meets all the statutory requirements which apply at the commencement of building work and, in particular, those of the Building Act 1984 and the Building Regulations 2000.

Developer cover

10. (1) This paragraph applies –

(a) where the new homes warranty makes provision for a developer's obligations to the policy-holder in respect of the matters described in paragraphs 11(1)(a), 11(1)(b) and 12(2)(a) of this Schedule, or any other any defects or damage to the property; and

(b) such a defect is apparent or such damage occurs at any time during the warranty period.

(2) Under such a new homes warranty, a warranty provider must undertake that –

(a) a warranty provider will meet all such obligations if the developer fails to do so (or no longer exists and has no successor), or provide financial compensation in respect of the obligations;

(b) it will provide a resolution or conciliation service –

(i)   the aim of which is to resolve any disputes between the policy-holder and the developer relating to such obligations and their timely fulfilment; and

(ii) for which no payment or consideration in kind is charged to the policy-holder;

(c) if the resolution or conciliation service described in paragraph (b) recommends that remedial work to the property should be conducted by the developer, a warranty provider will use all reasonable endeavours to ensure that the developer carries out such work;

(d) if the developer fails to carry out such remedial work (or no longer exists and has no successor), a warranty provider will carry out the work instead, or provide financial compensation for it; and

(e) if the resolution or conciliation service described in paragraph (b) does not prove satisfactory to the policy-holder, it will make available to the policy-holder another form of resolution or conciliation service which is independent to that warranty provider.

Structural defects cover to property and common parts throughout the new homes warranty

11. (1) Under the new homes warranty, a warranty provider must undertake that it or the developer will put right, arrange to put right or provide financial compensation for –

    (a) any actual destruction of or damage to the property caused by any defects –

        (i) of such structural features as exist at the property and common parts; and

        (ii) occurring during the first 10 years of the warranty period; and

    (b) any conditions caused by defects in the design, workmanship, materials or other components –

        (i) of such structural features as exist at the property and common parts;

        (ii) which cause an imminent danger of destruction or damage to the property; and

        (iii) which are apparent during the first 10 years of the warranty period.

  (2) The carrying out of the obligations described in sub-paragraph (1) may be shared between a warranty provider and the developer.

Additional defects cover for property – first two years

12. (1) This paragraph applies to such of the following as exist at the property and common parts –

    (a) electrical wiring and connections;

    (b) equipment and fixtures for the collection and distribution of gas, water, heating and ventilation;

    (c) drains;

    (d) other mechanical and electrical apparatus that are intended to be lasting –

        (i) including boilers; and

        (ii) excluding lifts;

    (e) wall partitions;

    (f) internal windows;

    (g) plaster applied to walls and ceilings;

    (h) tiling to walls, floors or ceilings;

    (i) other floor coverings that are intended to be lasting;

    (j) internal and external doors;

    (k) finishes to surfaces; and

    (l) fixtures.

  (2) Under the new homes warranty, a warranty provider must undertake that it or the developer will put right, arrange to put right or provide financial compensation –

    (a) for any –

        (i) defect in any of the items described in sub-paragraph (1); and

        (ii) damage to the property caused by such a defect; and

    (b) where such a defect is apparent or such damage occurs during the first two years of the warranty period.

  (3) The carrying out of the obligations described in sub-paragraph (2) may be shared between a warranty provider and the developer.

Cover for costs of alternative accommodation

13. Subject to paragraph 18 of this Schedule, under the new homes warranty, a warranty

provider must undertake to pay to the policy-holder (or another person as agreed with the policy-holder) all costs and expenses –

(a) that are incurred by those normally living at the property for –

    (i) the removal and storage of belongings; and

    (ii) securing alternative accommodation; and

(b) occurring due to the property becoming uninhabitable as a result of any liability on the part of a warranty provider under the new homes warranty or otherwise.

Professional fees

14. Subject to paragraph 19 of this Schedule, under the new homes warranty, a warranty provider must undertake to pay such professional and other fees –

(a) as are incurred by the policy-holder relating to the complete or partial re-building of or rectifying work to the property –

    (i) as a result of any liability on the part of a warranty provider under the new homes warranty or otherwise; and

    (ii) excluding the actual costs of carrying out such work; and

(b) for which the prior written permission of a warranty provider is sought by the policy-holder, and given accordingly.

PART 4 – LIMITS ON COVER FOR SPECIFIC NEW HOMES WARRANTIES

Permitted limits for newly built properties

15. (1) This paragraph applies to a property newly built from foundations.

  (2) The total amount of any payments, financial compensation or costs of remedial work arising under the new homes warranty may, in relation to the property, be limited to –

    (a) £500,000 plus the annual increment; or

    (b) the value of the property at the time the sale of the property was completed plus the annual increment.

  (3) Where the property forms part of a continuous structure, the total amount of any payments, financial compensation or costs of remedial work arising under all the related new homes warranties may be limited to £10,000,000 plus the annual increment in relation to all the premises which form part of the continuous structure.

Permitted limits for converted premises

16. (1) This paragraph applies to a property where the most recent use of the premises, is or was a primarily non-residential use, and it is due to be converted to a residential property by the time the sale is completed.

  (2) The total amount of any payments, financial compensation or costs of remedial work arising under the new homes warranty may, in relation to the property be limited to –

    (a) £250,000 plus the annual increment; or

    (b) the value of the property at the time the sale of the property was completed plus the annual increment.

  (3) Where the property forms part of a continuous structure, the total amount of any payments, financial compensation or remedial work arising under all related new

homes warranties may be limited to £5,000,000 plus the annual increment in relation to all the premises which form part of the continuous structure.

Permitted excesses

17. (1) Subject to sub-paragraph (2), the new homes warranty may contain either or both of the following terms –

    (a) a term requiring a contribution to be paid by the policy-holder in relation to any claims made under the new homes warranty; or

    (b) a term requiring a minimum financial value to any claims made by the policy-holder under the warranty.

  (2) The contribution or value required in each of the sub-paragraphs (1)(a) or (b) must be no more than £1,000 plus the annual increment.

Permitted limits on cover for costs of alternative accommodation

18. The costs and expenses payable by a warranty provider under paragraph 13 of this Schedule may be limited to those that are reasonably and necessarily incurred.

Permitted limits on cover for professional fees

19. The fees payable by a warranty provider under paragraph 14 of this Schedule may be limited to either or both of the following –

    (a) those that are reasonably and necessarily incurred; or

    (b) those other than fees incurred by the policy-holder in investigating or preparing a claim under the new homes warranty.

SCHEDULE 7 – REPORT ON A HOME NOT PHYSICALLY COMPLETE (REGULATION 8(L))

Report

1. A report on a home not physically complete must consist of –

    (a) a statement of the day or the predicted day on which the property is likely to be physically complete;

    (b) a statement of whether the property will be –

      (i) a house;

      (ii) a bungalow;

      (iii) a flat; or

      (iv) a maisonette.

    (c) if the property will be a house or bungalow, a statement of whether it will be –

      (i) detached;

      (ii) semi-detached; or

      (iii) terraced;

    (d) if the property will be a flat or maisonette, a statement of –

      (i) the total number of floors in the building;

      (ii) the total number of the flats or maisonettes in the building;

      (iii) whether there will be a lift to the floor on which the entrance to the property will be situated;

    (e) a statement of the approximate total useable floor area in the property (in square metres);

    (f) a description of the proposed methods of building (including any trade names for the materials described);

(g) a description of the materials used or to be used in the outside parts of the property;

(h) a description of the heating and hot-water systems to be used for the property;

(i) a description of the standards to which the garden or other land being sold with the property will be finished;

(j) a statement as to whether any land on the site has been or will be brought up to the level of the surrounding area artificially;

(k) a statement as to whether a new homes warranty complying with Schedule 6 has been offered for the building, completion or conversion of the property and whether the property will qualify for such a warranty; and

(l) if the property will not qualify for such a warranty, a statement of the name and qualifications of the person monitoring the building, completion or conversion of the property.

Attachments

2. A report on a home not physically complete must attach –

(a) a plan (to a scale of not less than 1:1250) showing the location and actual or approximate boundaries of the property (with the length of the boundaries indicated in metres) as it will be once it is completed, and marking –

(i) neighbouring buildings and structures, and surrounding land; and

(ii) the roads, public highways and footpaths that serve or will serve the property;

(b) a plan (to a scale of not less than 1:100) showing the layout and actual or approximate height, width and length (in metres) of each of the proposed rooms in the property; and

(c) a predicted energy performance certificate for the property.

SCHEDULE 8 – GENERAL PROVISION ON SEARCHES AND SEARCH REPORTS (REGULATIONS 8(M)(II), 8(N), 8(O), 9(K) AND 9(L))

PART 1 – ALL SEARCH REPORTS (OTHER THAN OFFICIAL SEARCH CERTIFICATE OF THE LOCAL LAND CHARGES REGISTER)

General requirements

1. A search report complying with this Schedule must contain the following information –

(a) the address of the premises in respect of which the search is conducted;

(b) a statement of whether the following persons have, or are likely to have, any personal or business relationship with any person involved in the sale of the property –

(i) a person who conducted the search; and

(ii) a person who prepared the search report;

(c) subject to Schedules 9 and 10, such enquiries as formed the basis of the search and the information sought;

(d) subject to paragraph 3 of this Schedule, the results of the search;

(e) the date the search was completed;

(f) a description of the records searched, and who they are held by;

(g) if the records searched are derived from other records, a description of those other records and whom those other records are held by;

(h) a description of how relevant documents can be obtained (if they are not included in the home information pack);

(i) the names and addresses of the parties to the arrangements –

    (i) under which the search was conducted; and

    (ii) if different, under which the search report was prepared;

(j) the name of the persons liable in each of the following events –

    (i) any negligent or incorrect entry in the records searched;

    (ii) any negligent or incorrect interpretation of the records searched; and

    (iii) any negligent or incorrect recording of that interpretation in the search report;

(k) a description of such complaints or redress procedures as exist in relation to the report; and

(l) the terms on which the report is made, including

    (i) the terms described in paragraphs 4, 5 and 6 of this Schedule; and

    (ii) the names of the persons who are liable to make the payments described in paragraph 6(b) and 6(c) of this Schedule.

Additional search information

2. A search report complying with this Schedule may contain or be accompanied by documents containing all or any of the following information –

(a) information which identifies the search or the search report;

(b) information which explains the results of the search, the search report or the enquiries or matters to which the results of the search relate; and

(c) information which identifies services or features local to the property, but not including any advertising or marketing information about them.

Unavailable search results

3. The results of the search included in a search report under paragraph 1(d) of this Schedule must not fail to answer such enquiries as formed the basis of the search, nor fail to give the information originally sought, unless –

(a) a record from which the answer or result could be deduced is not held by or obtainable under any circumstances from –

    (i) a local authority in the case of a search report required by regulation 8(m)(ii) or 8(n), or authorised by regulation 9(k)(i); or

    (ii) any person in the case of any other search report, and

(b) a statement is also included in the search report indicating –

    (i) that a particular result is not included; and

    (ii) the reason under sub-paragraph (a) for failing to include the result.

PART 2 – SPECIFIC REQUIRED SEARCH REPORTS

Terms for the preparation of required searches

4 Any person may prepare a report required by regulation 8(m)(ii), 8(n) or 8(o), but must do so on the following terms without exclusion or limitation

(a) that the search report will be prepared with reasonable care and skill; and

(b)   that a responsible person may copy or issue a copy of the report for the purposes of complying with any of the following provisions –

    (i)   regulations 5, 6, 8(m)(ii), 8(n), 8(o) and 21; and

    (ii) section 156(1), (2) and (11) of the 2004 Act.

Third party contractual rights in relation to search reports

5.   The person preparing a search report required by regulation 8(m)(ii), 8(n) or 8(o) must do so on terms enabling the provisions of the contract under which the report is prepared –

(a)   to be enforced in relation to the terms mentioned in paragraph 4 of this Schedule, by –

    (i)   the seller;

    (ii)   a potential or actual buyer of the property interest; and

    (iii) a mortgage lender in respect of the property interest; and

(b)   to be enforced by such persons in their own right, whether or not they are a party to such a contract.

Insurance cover for third party contractual rights

6.   The person preparing the search reports required by regulation 8(n) or 8(o) must do so on terms ensuring that –

(a)   any liability of any type arising under paragraph 5 of this Schedule is the subject of a contract of insurance against such risk effected by, and to be carried out by persons so authorised for the purposes of the Financial Services and Markets Act 2000;

(b)   any liability for financial loss arising under paragraph 5 of this Schedule will be met by financial compensation to be paid by a person (other than the persons described in paragraph 5(a)(i) to (iii) of this Schedule) who is –

    (i)   a party to the contract of insurance; or

    (ii) another person involved in the sale of the property; and

(c)   such financial compensation is paid by a person mentioned in sub-paragraph (a), if any person mentioned in sub-paragraph (b) fails to pay it (or no longer exists and has no successor).

Permitted limit on liability for financial loss

7.   The amount of the financial compensation referred to in paragraph 6(b) of this Schedule may be limited to the amount the potential or actual buyer reasonably believed to be the value of the property interest –

(a)   at the time the search report was completed; and

(b)   as used for residential purposes.

Inclusion of additional or more favourable terms for required search reports

8.   A person may prepare the search reports required by regulation 8(m)(ii), 8(n) or 8(o) on any of the following terms –

(a)   terms additional to those described in paragraphs 4, 5 and 6 of this Schedule (without excluding or limiting them); and

(b)   terms more favourable to –

    (i)   the seller;

    (ii)   a potential or actual buyer of the property interest; or

    (iii) a mortgage lender in respect of the property interest,

than those described in paragraphs 4, 5 and 6 of this Schedule.

Less favourable terms

9.   Any search report which contains terms less favourable to –

(a)   the seller;

(b)   a potential or actual buyer of the property interest; or

(c)   a mortgage lender in respect of the property interest,

than those required by this Part of this Schedule does not comply with the requirements of this Schedule.

Required searches by another name

10.   Paragraph 4 of this Schedule applies to pack documents which contain the enquiries required (or enquiries to like effect) to be contained in a search report which would be included under regulation 8(m)(ii), 8(n) or 8(o), regardless of whether one or more of the following has occurred –

(a)   they are included under regulation 9(k), Schedule 11 or another provision of these Regulations; or

(b)   they are described as a local land charges search, local enquiries or drainage and water enquiries, or given similar descriptions.

PART 3 – AUTHORISED SEARCH REPORTS

Terms for the preparation of authorised search reports

11.   The search reports authorised by regulation 9(k) and 9(l) may be made on any terms, which, in particular, may include the terms described in Parts 1 and 2 of this Schedule.

SCHEDULE 9 – LOCAL ENQUIRIES (REGULATION 8(N))

PART 1 – GENERAL

Interpretation

1.   (1)   In this Schedule –

'adoption' and related expressions mean an agreement made under section 38 of the Highways Act 1980;

'bond' means an indemnity or guarantee which is sought by a local authority as to the financial security of a developer of land;

'bond waiver' means an agreement that a local authority will not seek a bond from a developer of land;

'breach of condition notice' means a notice served under section 187A of the Town and Country Planning Act 1990;

'building preservation notice' means a notice served under section 3 of the Planning (Listed Buildings and Conservation Areas) Act 1990;

'building regulations approvals' means –

(a)   plans passed under section 16 of the Building Act 1984; or

(b)   a certificate given under regulation 21(6) of the Building Regulations 2000 (regularisation certificates);

'building regulations completion certificate' means a certificate given under regulation 17(1) of the Building Regulations 2000;

'building regulations' has the same meaning as in section 122 of the Building Act 1984;

'certificate of lawfulness of existing use or development' means a certificate issued under section 191(4) of the Town and Country Planning Act 1990;

'certificate of lawfulness of proposed use or development' means a certificate issued under section 191(2) of the Town and Country Planning Act 1990;

'compulsory purchase order with a direction for minimum compensation' means an order confirmed or made under section 50(1) of the Planning (Listed Buildings and Conservation Areas) Act 1990;

'conservation area' means either or both of the following –

    (a)   an area designated under section 69 of the Planning (Listed Buildings and Conservation Areas) Act 1990; or

    (b)   an area so designated before 31st August 1974 by other means;

'contaminated land notice' means a notice given under section 78B(3) of the Environmental Protection Act 1990;

'cycle track' means a way constituting or comprised in a highway, being a way over which the public have the following, but no other, rights of way, that is to say, a right of way on pedal cycles (other than pedal cycles which are motor vehicles within the meaning of the Road Traffic Act 1988) with or without a right of way on foot;

'development plan' must be construed in accordance with section 38 of the Planning and Compulsory Purchase Act 2004;

'direction restricting permitted development' means a direction given under article 4 of the Town and Country Planning (General Permitted Development) Order 1995;

'drainage agreement' means an agreement made under section 22(2) of the Building Act 1984;

'enforcement notice' means a notice issued under section 172 of the Town and Country Planning Act 1990;

'footpath' means a highway over which the public have a right of way on foot only, not being a footway;

'footway' means a way comprised in a highway which also comprises a carriageway, being a way over which the public have a right of way on foot only;

'frontager' means the owner or occupier of premises that abut a road, footway or footpath;

'highway maintainable at public expense' means a highway which by virtue of section 36 of the Highways Act 1980 or of any other enactment is a highway which for the purposes of that Act is a highway maintainable at the public expense;

'improvement' means the doing of any act under powers conferred by Part 5 of the Highways Act 1980 and includes the erection, maintenance, alteration and removal of traffic signs, and the freeing of a highway or road-ferry from tolls;

'land required for public purposes' means land to which paragraphs 5 and 6 of Schedule 13 to the Town and Country Planning Act 1990 relate;

'land to be acquired for road works' means land to be acquired by a public authority under any of sections 239 to 246 of the Highways Act 1980;

'listed building enforcement notice' means a notice issued under section 38 of the Planning (Listed Buildings and Conservation Areas) Act 1990;

'listed building repairs notice' means a notice served under section 48 of the Planning (Listed Buildings and Conservation Areas) Act 1990;

'mini-roundabout' means a roundabout consisting of a level or raised circular marking of a diameter of four metres or less;

'order requiring discontinuance of use or alteration or removal of buildings or works' means an order made under section 102 of the Town and Country Planning Act 1990;

'order revoking or modifying planning permission' means an order made under section 97 of the Town and Country Planning Act 1990;

'planning agreement' means an agreement made under section 106 of the Town and Country Planning Act 1990, as existing at any time before the enactment of the Planning and Compulsory Purchase Act 2004;

'planning contravention notice' means a notice served under section 171C of the Town and Country Planning Act 1990;

'planning contribution' means a contribution to be made pursuant to any regulations made under sections 46 to 48 of the Planning and Compulsory Purchase Act 2004;

'remediation notice' means a notice served under section 78E of the Environmental Protection Act 1990;

'railway' means a system of transport employing parallel rails which –

(a) provide support and guidance for vehicles carried on flanged wheels; and

(b) form a track which either is of a gauge of at least 350 millimetres or crosses a carriageway (whether or not on the same level),

but does not include a tramway;

'road hump' means an artificial hump in or on the surface of the highway which is designed to control the speed of vehicles, and references to a road hump include references to any other works (including signs or lighting) required in connection with such a hump;

'special road' means a highway, or a proposed highway, which is a special road in accordance with section 16 of the Highways Act 1980;

'stop notice' means a notice served under section 183 of the Town and Country Planning Act 1990;

'traffic calming works', in relation to a highway, means works affecting the movement of vehicular or other traffic for the purpose of –

(a) promoting safety (including avoiding or reducing, or reducing the likelihood of, danger connected with terrorism within the meaning of section 1 of the Terrorism Act 2000); or

(b) preserving or improving the environment through which the highway runs;

'tramway' means a system of transport used wholly or mainly for the carriage of passengers and employing parallel rails which –

(a) provide support and guidance for vehicles carried on flanged wheels; and

(b) are laid wholly or mainly along a street or in any other place to which the public has access (including a place to which the public has access only on making a payment);

'tree preservation order' means an order made under section 198 of the Town and Country Planning Act 1990; and

'trunk road' means a highway, or a proposed highway, which is a trunk road by virtue of section 10(1) or section 19 of the Highways Act 1980 or by virtue of an order or direction under section 10 of that Act or under any other enactment.

(2) In paragraph 8 'private sewer', 'drain' and 'disposal main' have the same meaning as in paragraph 1(1) of Schedule 10.

Enquiries

2.   (1) The search report required by regulation 8(n) must contain the enquiries set out in Part 2 of this Schedule.
      (2) Those enquiries must relate to the property.
      (3) The enquiries in paragraphs 6 to 18 relate only to matters which are not entered on the appropriate local land charges register.

PART 2 – ENQUIRIES

Planning and building decisions and pending applications

3.   What applications for any of the following relating to the property have been given, approved or rejected or are pending a decision –

      (a) a planning permission;
      (b) a listed building consent;
      (c) a conservation area consent;
      (d) a certificate of lawfulness of existing use or development;
      (e) a certificate of lawfulness of proposed use or development;
      (f) building regulations approvals; and
      (g) a building regulations completion certificate?

Planning designations and proposals

4.   What designations of land use for the property or the area, and what specific proposals for the property, are contained in any existing or proposed development plan?

Roads

5.   Which of the roads, footways and footpaths on which the property is or will be situated are –

      (a) highways maintainable at public expense;
      (b) subject to adoption and supported by a bond or bond waiver;
      (c) to be made up by a local authority who will reclaim the cost from the frontagers; or
      (d) to be adopted by a local authority without reclaiming the cost from the frontagers?

Land required for public purposes

6.   Is the property included in land required for public purposes?

Land to be acquired for road works

7.   Is the property included in land to be acquired for road works?

Drainage agreements and consents

8.   Do either of the following exist in relation to the property –

      (a) an agreement to drain buildings in combination into an existing sewer by means of a private sewer; or
      (b) an agreement or consent for a building, or extension to a building on the property to be built over, or in the vicinity of a drain, sewer or disposal main?

Nearby road schemes

9.   Is the property (or will it be) within 200 metres of any of the following –

      (a) the centre line of a new trunk road or special road specified in any order, draft order or scheme;

(b)   the centre line of a proposed alteration or improvement to an existing road involving construction of a subway, underpass, flyover, footbridge, elevated road or dual carriageway;

(c)   the outer limits of construction works for a proposed alteration or improvement to an existing road, involving –

   (i)   construction of a roundabout (other than a mini-roundabout); or

   (ii)   widening by construction of one or more additional traffic lanes;

(d)   the outer limits of –

   (i)   construction of a new road to be built by a local authority;

   (ii)   an approved alteration or improvement to an existing road involving construction of a subway, underpass, flyover, footbridge, elevated road or dual carriageway; or

   (iii)   construction of a roundabout (other than a mini-roundabout) or widening by construction of one or more additional traffic lanes;

(e)   the centre line of the proposed route of a new road under proposals published for public consultation; or

(f)   the outer limits of –

   (i)   construction of a possible alteration or improvement to an existing road involving construction of a subway, underpass, flyover, footbridge, elevated road or dual carriageway;

   (ii)   construction of a roundabout (other than a mini-roundabout); or

   (iii)   widening by construction of one or more additional traffic lanes, under proposals published for public consultation?

Nearby railway schemes

10.   Is the property (or will it be) within 200 metres of the centre line of a proposed railway, tramway, light railway or monorail?

Traffic schemes

11.   Has a local authority approved but not yet implemented any of the following for roads, footways and footpaths which abut the boundaries of the property –

(a)   permanent stopping up or diversion;

(b)   waiting or loading restrictions;

(c)   one way driving;

(d)   prohibition of driving;

(e)   pedestrianisation;

(f)   vehicle width or weight restriction;

(g)   traffic calming works including road humps;

(h)   residents parking controls;

(i)   minor road widening or improvement;

(j)   pedestrian crossings;

(k)   cycle tracks; or

(l)   bridge building?

Outstanding notices

12.   Do any statutory notices which relate to the following matters exist in relation to the property other than those revealed in a response to any other enquiry in this Schedule –

(a)   building works;

(b)   environment;

(c)   health and safety;

(d) housing;
(e) highways; or
(f) public health?

Contravention of building regulations

13. Has a local authority authorised in relation to the property any proceedings for the contravention of any provision contained in building regulations?

Notices, orders, directions and proceedings under Planning Acts

14. Do any of the following subsist in relation to the property, or has a local authority decided to issue, serve, make or commence any of the following –

(a) an enforcement notice;
(b) a stop notice;
(c) a listed building enforcement notice;
(d) a breach of condition notice;
(e) a planning contravention notice;
(f) another notice relating to breach of planning control;
(g) a listed building repairs notice;
(h) in the case of a listed building deliberately allowed to fall into disrepair, a compulsory purchase order with a direction for minimum compensation;
(i) a building preservation notice;
(j) a direction restricting permitted development;
(k) an order revoking or modifying planning permission;
(l) an order requiring discontinuance of use or alteration or removal of buildings or works;
(m) a tree preservation order; or
(n) proceedings to enforce a planning agreement or planning contribution?

Conservation areas

15. Do the following apply in relation to the property –

(a) a decision to make the area a conservation area before 31st August 1974; or
(b) an unimplemented decision to designate the area a conservation area?

Compulsory purchase

16. Has any enforceable order or decision been made to compulsorily purchase or acquire the property?

Contaminated land

17. Do any of the following apply (including any relating to land adjacent to or adjoining the property which has been identified as contaminated land because it is in such a condition that harm or pollution of controlled waters might be caused on the property) –

(a) a contaminated land notice;
(b) in relation to a register maintained under section 78R of the Environmental Protection Act 1990 –

(i) a decision to make an entry; or

     (ii)   an entry; or

(c) consultation with the owner or occupier of the property conducted under section 78G(3) of the Environmental Protection Act 1990 before the service of a remediation notice?

Radon gas

18. Do records indicate that the property is in a 'Radon Affected Area' as identified by the Health Protection Agency?

SCHEDULE 10 – DRAINAGE AND WATER ENQUIRIES (REGULATION 8(O))

PART 1 – GENERAL

Interpretation

1.   (1) In this Schedule –

'the 1991 Act' means the Water Industry Act 1991;

'the 2000 Regulations' means the Water Supply (Water Quality) Regulations 2000;

'the 2001 Regulations' means the Water Supply (Water Quality) Regulations 2001;

'adoption agreement' means an agreement made or to be made under section 51A(1) or 104(1) of the 1991 Act;

'bond' means a surety granted by a developer who is a party to an adoption agreement;

'bond waiver' means an agreement with a developer for the provision of a form of financial security as a substitute for a bond;

'calendar year' means the twelve months ending with 31st December;

'discharge pipe' means a pipe from which discharges are made or are to be made under section 165(1) of the 1991 Act;

'disposal main' means (subject to section 219(2) of the 1991 Act) any outfall pipe or other pipe which –

    (a)   is a pipe for the conveyance of effluent to or from any sewage disposal works, whether of a sewerage undertaker or of any other person; and

    (b)   is not a public sewer;

'drain' means (subject to section 219(2) of the 1991 Act) a drain used for the drainage of one building or of any buildings or yards appurtenant to buildings within the same curtilage;

'effluent' means any liquid, including particles of matter and other substances in suspension in the liquid;

'financial year' means the twelve months ending with 31st March;

'lateral drain' means –

    (a)   that part of a drain which runs from the curtilage of a building (or buildings or yards within the same curtilage) to the sewer with which the drain communicates or is to communicate; or

    (b)   (if different and the context so requires) the part of a drain identified in a declaration of vesting made under section 102 of the 1991 Act or in an agreement made under section 104 of that Act;

'licensed water supplier' means a company which is the holder for the time being of a water supply licence under section 17A(1) of the 1991 Act;

'maintenance period' means the period so specified in an adoption agreement as a period of time –

(a) from the date of issue of a certificate by a sewerage undertaker to the effect that a developer has built (or substantially built) a private sewer or lateral drain to that undertaker's satisfaction; and

(b) until the date that private sewer or lateral drain is vested in the sewerage undertaker;

'map of waterworks' means the map made available under section 198(3) of the 1991 Act in relation to the information specified in subsection (1A);

'private sewer' means a pipe or pipes which drain foul or surface water, or both, from premises, and are not vested in a sewerage undertaker;

'public sewer' means, subject to section 106(1A) of the 1991 Act, a sewer for the time being vested in a sewerage undertaker in its capacity as such, whether vested in that undertaker –

(a) by virtue of a scheme under Schedule 2 to the Water Act 1989;

(b) by virtue of a scheme under Schedule 2 to the 1991 Act;

(c) under section 179 of the 1991 Act; or

(d) otherwise;

'public sewer map' means the map made available under section 199(5) of the 1991 Act;

'resource main' means (subject to section 219(2) of the 1991 Act) any pipe, not being a trunk main, which is or is to be used for the purpose of –

(a) conveying water from one source of supply to another, from a source of supply to a regulating reservoir or from a regulating reservoir to a source of supply; or

(b) giving or taking a supply of water in bulk;

'sewerage services' includes the collection and disposal of foul and surface water and any other services which are required to be provided by a sewerage undertaker for the purpose of carrying out its functions;

'sewerage undertaker' means the company appointed to be the sewerage undertaker under section 6(1) of the 1991 Act for the area in which the property is or will be situated;

'surface water' includes water from roofs and other impermeable surfaces within the curtilage of the property;

'water main' means (subject to section 219(2) of the 1991 Act) any pipe, not being a pipe for the time being vested in a person other than the water undertaker, which is used or to be used by a water undertaker or licensed water supplier for the purpose of making a general supply of water available to customers or potential customers of the undertaker or supplier, as distinct from for the purpose of providing a supply to particular customers;

'water meter' means any apparatus for measuring or showing the volume of water supplied to, or of effluent discharged from any premises;

'water supplier' means the company supplying water in the water supply zone, whether a water undertaker or licensed water supplier;

'water supply zone' means the names and areas designated by a water undertaker within its area of supply that are to be its water supply zones for that year; and

'water undertaker' means the company appointed to be the water undertaker under section 6(1) of the 1991 Act for the area in which the property is or will be situated.

(2) In this Schedule, references to a pipe, including references to a main, a drain or

a sewer, shall include references to a tunnel or conduit which serves or is to serve as the pipe in question and to any accessories for the pipe.

Enquiries and responses

2. (1) The search report required by regulation 8(o) must contain –

(a) the enquiries set out in sub-paragraph (1) of each paragraph of Part 2 of this Schedule; and

(b) in relation to each such enquiry, a response set out in sub-paragraph (2) of each such paragraph, which must be the appropriate response in respect of the property.

(2) Where sub-paragraph (2) of each such paragraph includes alternative responses, only one of those responses may be the appropriate response.

(3) Where the search report is made using a document which reproduces all of the enquiries and responses set out in Part 2 of this Schedule, the person preparing the report must delete or strike out any such of those responses as are not appropriate.

(4) Where a response set out in sub-paragraph (2) of each paragraph of Part 2 of this Schedule –

(a) includes words highlighted in italics which request the giving of information about specified matters –

(i) the appropriate response or the search report must include the information to which those matters refer; and

(ii) where information is so included and the search report is made using a document which reproduces that response, the person preparing the report may delete or strike out the words in italics, and

(b) refers to an additional document being included, that document must accompany the search report required by regulation 8(o).

PART 2 – ENQUIRIES AND RESPONSES

Public sewer map

3. (1) Where relevant, please include a copy of an extract from the public sewer map.

(2) (a) A copy of an extract from the public sewer map is included in which the location of the property is identified;

(b) A copy of an extract of the public sewer map is included, showing the public sewers, disposal mains and lateral drains in the vicinity of the property; or

(c) No map is included, as there are no public sewers in the vicinity of the property.

Foul water

4. (1) Does foul water from the property drain to a public sewer?

(2) (a) Records indicate that foul water from the property drains to a public sewer;

(b) Records indicate that foul water from the property does not drain to a public sewer; or

(c) This enquiry appears to relate to a plot of land or a recently built property. It is recommended that drainage proposals are checked with the developer.

Surface water

5. (1) Does surface water from the property drain to a public sewer?

(2) (a)   Records indicate that surface water from the property does drain to a public sewer;

   (b)   Records indicate that surface water from the property does not drain to a public sewer; or

   (c)   This enquiry appears to relate to a plot of land or a recently built property. It is recommended that drainage proposals are checked with the developer.

Public adoption of sewers and lateral drains

6. (1) Are any sewers or lateral drains serving or which are proposed to serve the property the subject of an existing adoption agreement or an application for such an agreement?

   (2) (a)   Records indicate that in relation to sewers and lateral drains serving the development of which the property forms part –

       (i)   an adoption agreement is currently in preparation;
       (ii)   an adoption agreement exists and the sewers and lateral drains are not yet vested in the sewerage undertaker, although the maintenance period has commenced;
       (iii)   an adoption agreement exists and the sewers and lateral drains are not yet vested in the sewerage undertaker and the maintenance period has not yet commenced;
       (iv)   an adoption agreement exists and is supported by a bond;
       (v)   an adoption agreement exists and is the subject of a bond waiver; or
       (vi)   an adoption agreement exists and is not supported by a bond or by a bond waiver; or

   (b)   Records confirm that sewers serving the development, of which the property forms part are not the subject of an existing adoption agreement or an application for such an agreement; or

   (c)   The property is part of an established development and is not subject to an adoption agreement.

Public sewers within the boundaries of the property

7. (1) Does the public sewer map indicate any public sewer, disposal main or lateral drain within the boundaries of the property?

   (2) (a)   The public sewer map included indicates that there is a public sewer, disposal main or lateral drain within the boundaries of the property;

   (b)   The public sewer map indicates that there are private sewers or lateral drains subject to an existing adoption agreement within the boundaries of the property; or

   (c)   The public sewer map indicates that there are no public sewers, disposal mains or lateral drains within the boundaries of the property. However, it has not always been a requirement for such public sewers, disposal mains or lateral drains to be recorded on the public sewer map. It is therefore possible for unidentified sewers, disposal mains or lateral drains to exist within the boundaries of the property.

Public sewers near to the property

8. (1) Does the public sewer map indicate any public sewer within 30.48 metres (100 feet) of any buildings within the property?

   (2) (a)   The public sewer map included indicates that there is a public sewer within 30.48 metres (100 feet) of a building within the property;

   (b)   The public sewer map indicates that there is a public sewer or lateral drain subject to an existing adoption agreement within 30.48 metres (100 feet) of a building within the property; or

(c)   The public sewer map indicates that there are no public sewers within 30.48 metres (100 feet) of a building within the property. However, it has not always been a requirement for such public sewers to be recorded on the public sewer map. It is therefore possible for unidentified sewers or public sewers to exist within the boundaries of the property.

Building over a public sewer, disposal main or drain

9.   (1)   Has a sewerage undertaker approved or been consulted about any plans to erect a building or extension on the property over or in the vicinity of a public sewer, disposal main or drain?

(2)   (a)   Records indicate that a sewerage undertaker has approved or has been consulted about plans to erect a building or extension on the property over or in the vicinity of a public sewer, disposal main or drain;

(b)   Records indicate that a sewerage undertaker has rejected plans to erect a building or extension on the property over or in the vicinity of a public sewer, disposal main or drain; or

(c)   There are no records in relation to any approval or consultation about plans to erect a building or extension on the property over or in the vicinity of a public sewer, disposal main or drain. However, the sewerage undertaker might not be aware of a building or extension on the property over or in the vicinity of a public sewer, disposal main or drain.

Map of waterworks

10.   (1)   Where relevant, please include a copy of an extract from the map of waterworks.

(2)   (a)   A copy of an extract from the map of waterworks is included in which the location of the property is identified;

(b)   A copy of an extract of the map of waterworks is included, showing water mains, resource mains or discharge pipes in the vicinity of the property; or

(c)   No map is included, as there are no water mains, resource mains or discharge pipes in the vicinity of the property.

Adoption of water mains and service pipes

11.   (1)   Is any water main or service pipe serving or which is proposed to serve the property the subject of an existing adoption agreement or an application for such an agreement?

(2)   (a)   Records confirm that in relation to water mains and service pipes serving the development, of which the property forms part –

(i)   an adoption agreement is currently in preparation;

(ii)   an adoption agreement exists and the water mains or service pipes are not yet vested in the water undertaker;

(iii)   an adoption agreement exists and is supported by a bond; or

(iv)   an adoption agreement exists and is not supported by a bond; or

(b)   Records confirm that water mains or service pipes serving the property are not the subject of an existing adoption agreement or an application for such an agreement.

Sewerage and water undertakers

12.   (1)   Who are the sewerage and water undertakers for the area?

(2)   *Give company name and address* is the sewerage undertaker for the area, and *give company name and address* is the water undertaker for the area.

Connection to mains water supply

13. (1) Is the property connected to mains water supply?
    (2) (a)   Records indicate that the property is connected to mains water supply;
         (b)   Records indicate that the property is not connected to mains water supply
               and water is therefore likely to be provided by virtue of a private supply; or
         (c)   This enquiry relates to a plot of land or a recently built property. It is
               recommended that the water supply proposals are checked with the
               developer.

Water mains, resource mains or discharge pipes

14. (1) Are there any water mains, resource mains or discharge pipes within the
         boundaries of the property?
    (2) (a)   The map of waterworks indicates that there are water mains, resource
               mains or discharge pipes within the boundaries of the property;
         (b)   The map of waterworks does not indicate any water mains, resource mains
               or discharge pipes within the boundaries of the property; or
         (c)   The map of waterworks indicates that there is a water main subject to an
               existing adoption agreement within the boundaries of the property.

Current basis for sewerage and water charges

15. (1) What is the current basis for charging for sewerage and water services at the
         property?
    (2) (a)   The charges are based on actual volumes of water measured through a
               water meter ('metered supply');
         (b)   The charges are based on the rateable value of the property of £ *give
               rateable value* and the charge for the current financial year is £ *give amount
               of charge*;
         (c)   The charges are made on a basis other than rateable value or metered sup-
               ply. They are based on *give basis for charges* and are £ *give amount of charge*
               for each financial year.
         (d)   Records indicate that this enquiry relates to a plot of land or a recently built
               property.

Charges following change of occupation

16. (1) Will the basis for charging for sewerage and water services at the property change
         as a consequence of a change of occupation?
    (2) (a)   The basis for the charges will change and will be based on an unmeasured
               supply;
         (b)   The basis for the charges will change and will be based on a metered
               supply;
         (c)   The basis for the charges will change and will be based on *give basis for
               charges*;
         (d)   The basis for the charges will change and will be based on rateable value;
         (e)   There will be no change in the current charging arrangements as a
               consequence of a change of occupation; or
         (f)   Records indicate that this enquiry relates to a plot of land or a recently built
               property. It is recommended that the charging proposals are checked with
               the developer.

Surface water drainage charges

17. (1) Is a surface water drainage charge payable?

(2) (a)   Records confirm that a surface water drainage charge is payable for the property at £ *give level of charge* for each financial year; or

(b)   Records confirm that a surface water drainage charge is not payable for the property.

Water meters

18. (1)   Please include details of the location of any water meter serving the property.

(2) (a)   Records indicate that the property is not served by a water meter; or

(b)   Records indicate that the property is served by a water meter, which is located –

(i)   within the dwelling-house which is or forms part of the property, and in particular is located at *give details of location*; or

(ii)   is not within the dwelling-house which is or forms part of the property, and in particular is located at *give details of location*.

Sewerage bills

19. (1)   Who bills the property for sewerage services?

(2) (a)   The property is billed for sewerage services by *give company name, billing address, enquiry telephone number and website address*; or

(b)   The property is not billed for sewerage services.

Water bills

20. (1)   Who bills the property for water services?

(2) (a)   The property is billed for water services by *give company name, billing address, enquiry telephone number and website address*; or

(b)   The property is not billed for water services.

Risk of flooding due to overloaded public sewers

21. (1)   Is the dwelling-house which is or forms part of the property at risk of internal flooding due to overloaded public sewers?

(2) (a)   Records confirm that the property is at risk of internal flooding due to overloaded public sewers (following an actual flooding event or otherwise) and a report is included describing –

(i)   this and the action proposed by the sewerage undertaker to remove the risk;

(ii)   who will undertake this action and when; and

(iii)   whether mitigation measures have been installed to reduce the risk of flooding to the property;

(b)   An investigation is currently being carried out by the sewerage undertaker to determine if the property should be recorded on a register as being at risk of internal flooding due to overloaded public sewers, and a report is included describing –

(i)   the action proposed by the water undertaker to remove the risk; and

(ii)   who will undertake the action and when; or

(c)   The property is not recorded as being at risk of internal flooding due to overloaded public sewers.

Risk of low water pressure or flow

22. (1)   Is the property at risk of receiving low water pressure or flow?

(2) (a)   Records confirm that the property is recorded on a register kept by the water undertaker as being at risk of receiving low water pressure or flow, and a report is included describing –

        (i)   the action proposed by the water undertaker to remove the risk; and

        (ii)   who will undertake the action and when;

(b)   An investigation is currently being carried out by the water undertaker to determine if the property should be recorded on a register as being at risk of receiving low water pressure or flow, and a report is included describing –

        (i)   the action proposed by the water undertaker to remove the risk; and

        (ii)   who will undertake the action and when; or

(c)   Records confirm that the property is not recorded on a register kept by the water undertaker as being at risk of receiving low water pressure or flow.

Water quality analysis

23. (1) Please include details of a water quality analysis made by the water undertaker for the water supply zone in respect of the most recent calendar year.

    (2) (a)   The analysis confirmed that all tests met the standards prescribed by the 2000 Regulations or the 2001 Regulations; or

        (b)   The analysis confirmed that tests met the standards prescribed by the 2000 Regulations or the 2001 Regulations, except that *give number* tests of *give total number* tests failed to meet the standard for nitrate;

        (c)   The analysis confirmed that tests met the standards prescribed by the 2000 Regulations or the 2001 Regulations, except that *give number* tests of *give total number* tests failed to meet the standard for lead;

        (d)   The analysis confirmed that tests failed to meet the standards of the 2000 Regulations or the 2001 Regulations in relation to both nitrate and lead, and these are *give further details of such tests*; or

        (e)   The analysis records confirmed that tests failed to meet the standards of the 2000 Regulations or the 2001 Regulations in relation to another substance or substances, and these are *include further details*.

Authorised departures from water quality standards

24. (1) Please include details of any departures –

        (a)   authorised by the Secretary of State under Part 6 of the 2000 Regulations from the provisions of Part 3 of those Regulations; or

        (b)   authorised by the National Assembly for Wales under Part 6 of the 2001 Regulations from the provisions of Part 3 of those Regulations.

    (2) (a)   There are no such authorised departures for the water supply zone; or

        (b)   The Secretary of State or the National Assembly for Wales has authorised a departure from the standards prescribed by the 2000 Regulations or the 2001 Regulations, in the water supply zone, and –

           (i)   the departure permits the water undertaker or water supplier to supply water that does not meet the standard for *give substance* whilst remedial action to restore normal water quality is taken;

           (ii)   the maximum permitted departure is up to *give number* micrograms per litre; and

           (iii) the measures taken to restore normal water quality are due to be completed by *give approximate month and year*.

Sewage treatment works

25. (1) Please confirm the distance from the property to the nearest boundary of the nearest sewage treatment works.

    (2) The nearest sewage treatment works is *give distance in kilometres or miles* to the

give direction of the property. The name of the nearest sewage treatment works is *give name.*

SCHEDULE 11 – ADDITIONAL RELEVANT INFORMATION (REGULATION 9(N))

The matters referred to in regulation 9(n)(ii) are –

(a) the property's contents, fixtures or fittings;
(b) any information provided by the Chief Land Registrar relating to the property;
(c) equitable interests in the property;
(d) rights of access to or over –

    (i) the property (not including any ancillary land); or
    (ii) land outside the property;

(e) rights of access to or over any ancillary land to the property including –

    (i) obligations to maintain such land; or
    (ii) whether any payments for maintaining such land are outstanding;

(f) obligations to maintain the boundaries of the property;
(g) communications from any public authority or person with statutory functions, that affect or might affect the property, including whether any request made by them (under any enactment or otherwise) has been complied with;
(h) acquisition of any land by a public authority or person with statutory functions that affects or might affect the property;
(i) standards of safety, building, repair or maintenance to which the property, its contents or the building in which it is situated ought to comply, and whether such standards have been complied with;
(j) the property's suitability or potential suitability for occupancy by a disabled person;
(k) the energy performance of the property;
(l) alterations or other works relating to the property and whether

    (i) any necessary permissions for such alterations or works have been obtained; and
    (ii) relevant consultations have been conducted;

(m) use or occupation of the property or use or occupation of other premises which affects or might affect the property;
(n) insurance policies, warranties, certificates or guarantees for the property or its contents;
(o) utility services connected to the property;
(p) potential or actual environmental hazards that might affect the property or its occupants; and
(q) taxes, levies or charges relating to the property.

EXPLANATORY NOTE

(This note is not part of the Regulations)

The main purpose of these Regulations is to prescribe the documents to be included in home information packs and the circumstances in which they are included (Parts 1 to 4 of the Regulations). The duties to have a home information pack which complies with these Regulations are found in sections 155 to 159 of the Housing Act 2004 ('the home information pack duties'). In general, the duties apply to a 'responsible person' as described in sections 151 to 153 of the Housing Act 2004.

The Regulations make a distinction between 'required' documents which must be included in home information packs and 'authorised' documents which may be included. A pack must not include any documents not required or authorised (regulation 4) and advertising information must not be included in pack documents in the circumstances described in regulation 12. Part 2 of the Regulations makes provision about the source and clarity of documents included in an original home information pack, and in copies of a pack.

Regulations 8, 9 and 10 are the regulations that set out which documents are required and authorised to be included in packs. The required documents specified in regulation 8 include an index, a sale statement, title information, additional information for common-hold and leasehold properties, information about the physical condition and energy efficiency of the property and property searches. Schedules 1 to 10 to the Regulations make further provision about these documents, and in some cases prescribe minimum terms for the documents or the terms on which they must be provided in order to comply with the Regulations. Not all documents are required in every case, and regulation 8 further describes the circumstances in which a document is required.

Regulation 9 describes the information authorised to be included in a home information pack. This information may be included in a separate document or within a required document. Authorised information includes translations, Braille versions, summaries or explanations of pack documents, additional title information or information relating to commonhold and leasehold properties and additional information about physical condition. It includes further property searches and searches relating to other premises may be included. Schedule 11 to the Regulations specifies additional relevant information which may be included. Regulation 10 deals with the required information for new properties where the legal commonhold or leasehold interest being sold has not yet been registered or created.

Part 4 of the Regulations deals with the assembly and accuracy of home information packs. Required documents must be included before the first point of marketing which is defined in regulation 3 as the time a duty under sections 155(1) or 159(2) of the Housing Act 2004 first arises. Certain title information, home condition reports and required property searches should be no older than 3 months at the first point of marketing (regulation 14). Regulation 3(3) and 3(5) describe the circumstances in which putting the property back on the market will not result in a new first point of marketing. Regulations 15 and 17 deal with the event that certain required documents are unavailable or unobtainable before the first point of marketing. Regulation 15(2) provides that a home information pack complies with the Regulations if a responsible person continues to use all reasonable efforts to obtain a document and the first point of marketing does not occur 14 days before the day a request for a document is first delivered.

Regulations 18 to 20 deal with the circumstances in which the pack or pack documents must or may be updated, and the effect of regulation 21 is that a responsible person must provide a seller with a copy of any pack documents requested by him for the purposes of checking their accuracy.

Part 5 of the Regulations makes exceptions from the home information pack duties. These exceptions relate to seasonal accommodation, sales mixed with sales of non-residential premises, dwelling-houses used for both residential and non-residential purposes, portfolios of residential properties, unsafe properties and properties to be demolished. The exception under regulation 30 deals with a transitional period starting on 1st June 2007 and ending on 31st October 2007. It ensures that where a responsible person makes public that a property is on the market during the transitional period, a person does not become a responsible person if it was put on the market before the period, providing further action was taken to market the property. It also deals with the circumstances where the home information pack duties do not arise by putting the property on the market during the transitional period, providing the property was first put on the market before the period and an offer to buy the property was withdrawn (or its acceptance repudiated).

Part 6 of the Regulations specifies that the level of penalty charge for penalty charge notices which may be given by enforcement authorities is £200 (for a breach of a home information pack duty). Regulation 32 specifies that penalty charge notices do not apply where the content of a pack document fails to comply with these Regulations, but a responsible person believes on reasonable grounds that it does.

Additionally, the Regulations require home condition reports (which must be included in home information packs in the circumstances described in regulation 8(h)) to be made by members of a certification scheme (home inspectors) approved by the Secretary of State under Part 7. Before approving a scheme, the Secretary of State must be satisfied that a scheme contains appropriate provision for the matters described in regulation 33.

A full regulatory impact assessment of the effect that this instrument will have on businesses has been prepared and placed in the libraries of both Houses of Parliament. Copies of the regulatory impact assessment and guidance related to these Regulations are available at the Department for Communities and Local Government's website and/or from its Home Buying and Selling Reform Division [. . .].

Appendix C
SUMMARY OF RELATED LEGISLATION

ESTATE AGENTS ACT 1979 (EAA 1979)

EAA 1979 defines estate agency work and this is different from the definition in Part 5. It covers all types of property agency work including commercial and agricultural and acting for buyers. Work of any type falling within the definition is 'estate agency work' whether or not payment is made or the instructions to act are in writing.

EAA 1979 gives limited regulatory status to the OFT granting it power to prohibit any person from doing estate agency work if it is considered that the person is unfit to carry on estate agency work generally or of a particular description or that person has committed a breach of a legal obligation specified under EAA 1979. A 'warning' as to future conduct can be given if it is considered that the 'offence' under consideration is a first offence and is not an offence of discrimination or a criminal offence. This is applied to HIPs through HA 2004, s.175(3).

Under EAA 1979 anything done by an employee is treated as done by the employer as well, whether or not the employer knew or approved of the action in question. The employer's only defence is that reasonable steps were taken to prevent the employee from so transgressing. It is understood that similar 'double jeopardy' will pertain in respect of 'offences' relating to the HIPs legislation.

Section 18 of EAA 1979 sets out specific information that the estate agent must give any client before entering into an estate agency contract with the client. The information must be given in writing and before the client has entered into any commitment to the estate agent.

In addition to the possibility that a breach of this requirement could lead to a prohibition order, failure to comply also means that the estate agent cannot recover fees without a court order – the court on hearing such a claim for fees may dismiss or reduce the agent's claim so as to compensate the client for any prejudice suffered by the failure to comply.

ESTATE AGENTS (PROVISION OF INFORMATION) REGULATIONS 1991, SI 1991/859 (INFORMATION REGULATIONS)

These Regulations require the terms 'sole agency', 'sole selling rights' and 'ready, willing and able' to be clearly explained in writing if they are used by the agent in relation to the client's liability to pay fees. The regulations specify the wording to be used in this connection and do not permit any material alterations or additions to the prescribed text.

Estate agents are required to advise clients in writing (and at the same time as giving information about fees or other charges) of any services being offered or intended to be offered to any prospective buyer. This requirement must also be met if such services are to be offered by a 'connected person' or by any other person where the estate agent might derive a financial benefit from the fact that the service is being provided. A 'connected person' (the definition for which is also important in relation to the obligation of an estate agent to notify a client if he or a connected person has an interest in a transaction) is defined as meaning:

- the estate agent's employer or principal;
- any employee or agent of the estate agent; or
- any associate of the estate agent or person mentioned above.

'Associate' has a very wide meaning and includes spouses, relatives, spouses or relatives of a business associate as well as business associates. Prompt written disclosure must be made to a client if the estate agent personally has or seeks to acquire an interest in the land being sold or in the proceeds of sale, or if a connected person is so interested.

Negotiations must not be started until such written disclosure has been made.

Offers must be promptly notified to the client in writing. What constitutes an offer is not defined. With the likelihood that a number of HIPs will be in circulation at any one time estate agents will need to take care to report bids.

Once an offer has been made there is a continuing obligation to give written notification to the seller client of all and any services requested by the buyer. This is a separate obligation to that set out above which is required at the beginning of the relationship.

Disclosure of personal interest must always be made promptly and in writing and this obligation covers a prospective interest.

The Estate Agents (Accounts) Regulations set out detailed rules for dealing with deposits and other 'client money' breach of which is a criminal offence. These rules may be extended to apply to deposits which agents may hold on account of payments for HCRs and searches in the event that an estate agent takes on the role of pack provider. They may also apply to payments made by buyers for a copy of the pack.

Provisions in these Regulations to require minimum standards of competence and a prohibition on unqualified persons acting as estate agents have never been activated.

PROPERTY MISDESCRIPTIONS ACT 1991 (PMA 1991)

PMA 1991 with its criminal sanctions has caused estate agents to restrict the information contained in property sales details so as to reduce the scope for mistakes. With its statutory instrument, the Property Misdescriptions (Specified Matters) Order 1992 (SI 1992/2834), this legislation is similar in purpose to the Trade Descriptions Act 1968 making it a criminal offence to publish misleading property descriptions. It does not, however, create any statutory or separate right for a person to claim damages or to avoid contractual obligations.

PMA 1991 only applies to statements made in the course of an estate agency business defined in much the same way as in EAA 1979. It applies to all types of property and not just residential property.

The scope of PMA 1991 is wide in that it applies to solicitors when acting as estate agents and to statements made in the course of a property development business. It does not, however apply to sellers of land, other than developers, where the seller is a private individual, a partnership or corporate entity.

Statements can be by words or pictures, in writing or oral and, in an estate agent's office might be made by any employee – the liability is not just confined to negotiating staff.

The offence is committed each time a misstatement is made or defective set of property particulars is sent out.

PMA 1991 does not, however, 'punish' the failure to publish information, which is why the Act has brought about a reduction in the amount of information. PMA 1991 only applies to statements made about 'prescribed' matters namely those contained in the 1992 Order including, *inter alia*:

- location or address;
- availability of and proximity to services;
- accommodation, measurements, sizes;
- fixtures and fittings;
- price;
- tenure or estate;
- length of lease;
- length of time land has been available for sale either generally or by or through a particular person;
- amount of any ground rent or other charge such as service charge;
- whether there is any tenancy of the land;
- council tax payable;
- planning position;
- restrictive covenants, easements or rights of way.

This is not an exhaustive list and readers should consult the Order in its entirety.

Disclaimers to exclude, avoid or reduce liability are not mentioned in PMA 1991 and accordingly are dealt with under the general law that requires them to be 'as bold, precise and compelling as the (trade) description itself and must be as effectively brought to the notice of the person (to whom the goods may be supplied)' – thus small print will not be effective.

A disclaimer will be of no effect in any event if the statement is made while knowing it to be untrue or being reckless as to its veracity. The offence is one of strict liability in that the prosecuting authority does not need to prove either an intention to deceive or negligence.

As with EAA 1979, liability under PMA 1991 falls both on the employer and the individual who made the misstatement. The employee's liability is separate from that of the employer who, provided he was not negligent and neither knew nor connived at the making of the misstatement, may have a defence of 'due diligence' as outlined below.

The sanction is a criminal one being on summary conviction at the magistrates' court a fine not exceeding the maximum (currently £5,000) but on conviction on indictment at the Crown Court an unlimited fine. A conviction under this Act can lead to a prohibition order being made by the OFT.

Section 2 of PMA 1991 provides a statutory defence if the defendant can show 'that he took all reasonable steps and exercised all due diligence to avoid committing the offence'.

To succeed, the estate agent has to show that:

- positive action was taken to avoid breach of the Act;
- a system of controls existed in the estate agency; and
- the system was properly monitored

These are not hard-and-fast rules as each case is considered on its merits taking into account all factors including the size of the firm involved.

If an estate agent bases his due diligence defence upon reliance on information obtained from another, PMA 1991 requires the agent to show that such reliance was reasonable in all the circumstances. The court will look at steps actually taken to check the information;

what steps might reasonably have been taken to so check and whether there was any reason to disbelieve the information relied upon. A prudent estate agent should keep a note of sources of information.

TSOs are the front line enforcers of the Act and they have powers 'at all reasonable hours' to enter on commercial premises to carry out their obligations. Refusal to allow entry could result in a warrant being obtained. They can also require the production of documents, books and/or computer records which they can then remove. Privileged documents are not covered by this power but the agent's files dealing with a transaction will be covered and can be removed.

It is a criminal offence to obstruct a TSO and to give false answers to questions either knowingly or recklessly. The TSO has authority to administer a caution and a person charged under the PMA 1991 who intends to defend the charge on the basis of an 'act or default of another' or 'reliance on information supplied by another' must give the prosecuting authority seven days' notice of this defence together with all possible information in support including the name of the other person relied upon.

It is anticipated that enforcement procedures under Part 5 will be similar in practice to PMA 1991 enforcement.

CONSUMER CREDIT ACT 1974 (CCA 1974)

This legislation came into force over 30 years ago to protect against unscrupulous and unfair lending and hiring or leasing of goods. It only covers b2c transactions and the DTI are currently consulting as regards the stepped implementation of the Consumer Credit Act 2006 that amends the 1974 legislation (see DTI website for updates – www.dti.gov.uk).

A licence issued under the CCA 1974 is required if a business wishes to, *inter alia*:

- sell on credit;
- lend money;
- arrange credit for others;
- offer hire purchase terms;
- collect debts;
- advise on people's credit standing;

to individuals, although a licence would not be required if the only 'credit' being given was that of allowing a customer to pay a bill in four or fewer instalments within a year and if within the exemptions provided by the CCA.

It is a criminal offence to trade without a licence and all professions or trades are businesses for licensing purposes even if no charge is made for the services offered or if the trading entity is a non-profit making organisation. Conviction can render the offender liable to a fine, imprisonment or both. In addition to the criminal sanction, arrangements falling into licensable categories cannot be enforced by a business who should, but does not, have a licence.

This legislation needs to be considered by those who plan to provide packs and to give or arrange credit for sellers to meet the costs of compiling the pack – in particular the cost of the HCR and searches.

DATA PROTECTION ACT 1998 (DPA 1998)

DPA 1998 came into force on 1 March 2000 replacing the Data Protection Act 1984. It extends protection by prescribing the rules to govern the holding and handling of information about individuals. DPA 1998 is enforced by an independent Information Commissioner.

DPA 1998 deals with the processing of personal data relating to individuals such as clients, customers, suppliers and employees. It regulates all record keeping including computer-based records, paper records and health and public authority records.

'Processing' includes wide-ranging activities such as collecting, recording, holding, dissemination, disclosure and destruction of information.

DPA 1998 sets out eight core principles for all data processors who are the keepers of records. Individuals whose information may be collected and held must be advised of the record keepers' 'privacy policy'. The core principles must be observed throughout the data-holding period, not just at the collection point. These core principles are:

1. that personal data shall be processed fairly and only if at least one of the pre-conditions is met, i.e. the individual has given consent or the processing is necessary for performing a contract to which that individual is a party; and, in the case of 'sensitive data' one of the additional preconditions has been met, i.e. consent or a necessary legal obligation requires the data processing;
2. that personal data is only to be collected for one or more specified purposes and is not to be subject to further processing incompatible with the original specified purpose;
3. that the personal data collected shall be relevant and adequate and not excessive in relation to the purpose for which it is processed;
4. that it shall be accurate and kept up to date;
5. that it shall not be kept for longer than is necessary;
6. that personal data will be processed in accordance with DPA 1998;
7. that appropriate measures will be taken to prevent unlawful or unauthorised processing and accidental loss, damage or destruction of personal data;
8. personal data shall not be transferred outside the European Economic Area unless to a territory that has a similar level of protection.

Individuals are granted a number of rights under DPA 1998 in relation to their personal data:

*   to request information as to what data is being kept, the purpose for which it is being kept, who has or can have access to it and the source of the personal data;
*   to prevent processing that is likely to cause substantial distress or damage;
*   to object to their data being used for a direct marketing purpose;
*   to veto automated decisions about them;
*   to compensation for breaches of DPA 1998.

Those who keep records in property transactions should take care to ensure that any notes or other records kept on individual clients do not contain any comments that they would not wish the client to see or which are unlawful such as discriminatory remarks.

Under DPA 1984 data processors were required to register with the Data Protection Registrar. Under DPA 1998 there is a notification procedure that requires a data controller to send a list of the types of information held to the Information Commissioner together with the requisite fee.

As with other related legislation, breaches of this Act, including data processing without notification, carries criminal sanctions and directors and officers of a limited company can be held personally liable.

With the additional record keeping required under the HIP legislation extra care will need to be taken regarding the holding and processing of data and all estate agents will need to 'notify'.

CONTRACTS (RIGHTS OF THIRD PARTIES) ACT 1999 (CRTPA 1999)

Section 163(8)(c) of HA 2004 gave effect to this legislation in express terms giving additional rights to sellers, buyers, potential buyers, lenders and to any 'other person involved in the sale of the property who is not a party to the contract'. This, however, was only to apply where so provided in the regulations. In the regulations issued so far such rights are restricted to certain documents and to specified parties.

CRTPA 1999 dilutes the doctrine of privity of contract – the rule that only parties to a contract can enforce that contract. The Act enabled this after it came into force on 11 November 1999.

CRTPA 1999 allows a third non-contracting party to a contract to enforce a term of that contract where:

* the contract expressly provides that right; or
* the contract purports to confer a benefit on the third party – unless it is clear from the contract that there was no intention to allow the third party to enforce the contract.

The Act does not, however, allow contracting parties to impose obligations on non-parties to the contract. To acquire the right to enforce a contract under CRTPA 1999 the third party must be expressly identified by name as a member of a class or by a particular description – he does not, however, have to be in existence at the time the contract is made.

The contrast to the arrangements for third-party enforcement of HIPs is that under CRTPA 1999 it is possible for contracting parties to exclude third-party rights or limit enforcement by third-parties generally or with regard to particular terms of the contract.

Where a third party's rights under a contract have 'crystallised' the contracting parties can neither rescind nor vary the contract without the third party's consent unless they have given themselves that right in the contract.

'Crystallisation' is effective if:

* the third party has communicated agreement to the term in question to the contracting party against whom the third party would enforce the contract;
* that contracting party is aware that the third party has relied on the term in question; or
* the contracting party should reasonably be expected to have foreseen that the third party would rely on the term and has done so.

The remedies available to a third-party enforcer are the same as for a contracting party (subject to the terms of the contract) thus an exclusion or limitation of liability term will also operate against a third party. The third party cannot pray in aid the Unfair Contract Terms Act 1977 that restricts, in section 2(2), exclusion or limitation of liability for negligence.

The same defences as are available in enforcement proceedings brought by a contractual party can be raised against a third party – unless the contract states otherwise.

It should be noted that not all contracts are subject to this legislation – in particular there is no right for a third party to enforce a contract of employment against an employee or any term in a worker's contract or in any agency worker's contract. Contracts relating to bills of exchange, promissory notes and other negotiable instruments are excluded, as are certain contracts of carriage.

MONEY LAUNDERING REGULATIONS 2003, SI 2003/3075 (MLR 2003)

The Money Laundering Regulations 2003 support the Proceeds of Crime Act 2002 (PCA 2002) and the Anti-terrorism, Crime and Security Act 2001 (ATCSA 2001) and follow the EU Second Directive 91/308/EEC.

From 1 March 2003 these Regulations extended the scope of the legislation by defining the regulated sectors to include estate agents and high value dealers being those accepting cash payments of £10,000 or more.

Both employees and employers have obligations under these Regulations.

Put simply, money laundering is the processing of money generated by illegal activity so that it acquires the appearance of 'clean' funds. Property transactions are susceptible to being used to churn or invest the proceeds of crime. In the past, insufficient attention had been given to the source of the funds used to purchase a property where it is then sold and turned into liquid funds.

Now, the sale of a property may provoke enquiry or suspicion as to the source of the funds originally used for the purchase. Bringing estate agents into the remit of the Regulations brings to the intelligence-gathering authorities more information that may assist in tracing the sources of money triggered by crime. In July 2006 a solicitor was convicted and imprisoned along with estate agents where a house was sold at an undervalue (*R v. Davis Pattison and Griffiths* – not yet reported).

Businesses covered by these regulations are required to set up procedures to ensure that they comply. The sanctions are a criminal conviction carrying a prison sentence, a fine or both. The following are necessary steps to implement:

* identification procedures for anyone who wishes to enter into a business relationship whether it is intended to be continuous or on a one-off basis;
* record-keeping procedures;
* internal reporting procedures – reports of suspicion to be made to a specific person in the organisation with responsibility for compliance – a money laundering reporting officer (MLRO);
* internal controls to ensure an early warning system for the company;
* training of employees to ensure they, as the front-line interface with clients, are aware of the regulations and the obligations under it.

PCA 2002 applies to all firms operating in the UK including those who act for clients/customers overseas. It created three specific offences:

1. 'Assisting' – dealing with a matter on behalf of someone where one either knows or suspects that the person is involved in criminal conduct or has benefited financially from such conduct. Ignoring a potential problem can open up the possibility of being accused of the offence – it is necessary to show that it was not reasonable either to know, suspect or be aware of the criminality behind the transaction. Disclosure to the company's MLRO or to the National Criminal Intelligence Service (NCIS) must be made.
2. 'Tipping off' – great care must be taken regarding this offence which is committed if an investigation is prejudiced by a person under suspicion being informed that a disclosure has been made whether to the company's MLRO or to NCIS directly or that an investigation is under way or proposed. It is a further offence to conceal, destroy or falsify documents relevant to such an investigation.
3. 'Failing to report' – suspicions of money laundering must be reported as soon as practical to avoid the commission of this offence. Initially, the suspicion should be

reported internally and the MLRO must then make the decision whether to report the matter to NCIS.

The sanctions for these offences are up to 14 years in prison for assisting; up to 5 years for tipping off or failing to report plus a fine.

ATCSA 2001 has equivalent offences and has added terrorist fundraising, using money or property for terrorist purposes and making funds or services available to someone who has committed an act of terrorism or attempts to do so.

The reporting requirements are more stringent than under PCA 2002 so any suspicion should be reported immediately. These reporting obligations override client confidentiality but care should be taken as to the relevance of information disclosed to protect against a civil claim from an innocent client whose activities were reported. As with the tipping off offence, no indication must be given to the client (or anyone else) that a report is being made or an investigation being undertaken.

The procedures listed above may give rise to suspicions, for example, where there is difficulty or undue delay in identification documents being provided or large sums of cash are produced or one source of funding is substituted for another.

Where suspicions arise over a particular transaction it should be reported and care needs to be taken not to 'tip off' the client/customer. If the matter is referred by the MLRO for the company to NCIS consent must be obtained from NCIS to continue with the transaction – there is a danger here of inadvertent 'tipping off' if steps in a transaction have to be delayed while NCIS consider the matter. They have seven working days to do so. If they refuse consent, a further period of 31 days must lapse before the transaction can be continued unless, during that time, NCIS obtain a court order preventing further action. NCIS will react quickly if they are told of the urgency when a report is made and the reasons for urgency.

There are specific rules for record keeping and identity verification and these should be incorporated into the procedures mentioned above.

Solicitors must now routinely comply with these Regulations. Estate agents are required to do so for sellers not buyers and pack providers may be required to do so too if they supply packs directly to the public.

Guidance has been given by the courts in *Bowman* v. *Fels* [2005] EWCA Civ 226 and this better defines areas where legal privilege may be claimed and come to the aid of the solicitor/client relationship. The Law Society has issued revised guidance following this decision including guidance for transactional lawyers that can be accessed at their website (www.lawsociety.org.uk).

THE CONSUMER PROTECTION (DISTANCE SELLING) REGULATIONS 2000 (DSR 2000) (AMENDED FROM 6 APRIL 2005 BY THE CONSUMER PROTECTION (DISTANCE SELLING) (AMENDMENT) REGULATIONS 2005, SI 2005/689

These Regulations give consumers protection and certain rights when they shop for either goods or services 'at a distance' and apply when goods are sold or services are provided other than by 'face to face' contact for example:

- by the Internet;
- by mail order catalogues;
- by mail order through newspapers or magazines;

- by interactive television;
- by fax;
- by telephone;
- by text messaging.

However, they do not apply to financial services (as these are regulated by other legislation); b2b contracts; vending machine transactions; contracts for the sale of land (but do apply to rental agreements with consumers) or auction sales whether of goods or services. Nor do the information and cancellation provisions apply to contracts for, *inter alia*, accommodation. The right to cancel does not apply, unless otherwise agreed, to contracts for such items as personalised goods, perishable goods, newspapers and periodicals.

Where these regulations apply clear information must be provided so that the consumer can make an informed decision whether to buy. Information that is required includes:

- seller's business name and, if advance payment is required, postal address;
- description of goods or services;
- price inclusive of all and any taxes;
- delivery costs if applicable;
- payment arrangements;
- arrangements including the date for delivery of goods or services;
- details as to how long an offer or price is valid;
- the cost of any premium rate charges – telephone, fax or Internet;
- if substitute goods will be supplied where the goods ordered are unavailable;
- and, if so, the cost of returning unsuitable goods in the event of cancellation;
- the minimum duration of any long-term contract for the provision of a service;
- cancellation rights.

When any such order is received from a consumer the seller must send written confirmation to include when and how the consumer can exercise the right to cancel; whether the consumer is required to return the goods; who is responsible for the cost of returning or recovering the goods; a geographical contact address and details of any after-sales service or guarantee.

This confirmation must be provided no later than the date on which the goods are delivered or where services have been purchased, during the performance of the contract.

Unless agreed with the consumer, the goods must be delivered or the service provided within 30 days after the day on which the consumer sent the order.

If it appears that this requirement cannot be met, the consumer must be advised before the expiry of the period and unless the consumer agrees an extension his money must be refunded within the next 30 days. A consumer cannot be required to agree an extension.

These Regulations amend the Unsolicited Goods and Services Act 1971 to rescind any rights the seller might have in respect of unsolicited goods and services. Consumers may retain such goods or dispose of them with no liability to the sender. Demanding payment for unsolicited goods is an offence.

One of the main rights under these Regulations is an unconditional right to cancel. This allows the consumer time to examine the goods and/or consider the services to be provided. If a consumer wishes to cancel, notice must be given to the seller:

(a) for goods, seven working days from the day after that on which the goods are received by the consumer;
(b) for services, seven working days from the day after that on which the consumer agrees to proceed with the contract for services.

Failure to provide consumers with written confirmation of all information required can result in cancellation periods being extended to a maximum of three months and seven working days. If the missing information is provided within the extended period, it comes to an end seven working days beginning with the day after the full written information was received by the consumer. This position has been clarified by the 2005 amendment that adds the following provision:

> Where the performance of the contract has begun with the consumer's agreement before the expiry of the period of seven working days beginning with the day after the day on which the contract was concluded and the supplier has not complied with regulation 8 on or before the day on which performance began, but provides to the consumer the information referred to in regulation 8(2) in good time during the performance of the contract, the cancellation period ends –
>
> (a)   on the expiry of the period of seven working days beginning with the day after the day on which the consumer receives the information; or
>
> (b)   if the performance of the contract is completed before the expiry of the period referred to in sub-paragraph (a), on the day when the performance of the contract is completed

If a consumer cancels a contract he must ensure that reasonable care is taken of any goods received and must return them (if so stated in the contract) or make them available for collection. The consumer's money must be refunded as soon as possible and no later than 30 days after receiving the notice of cancellation.

If the consumer is to be charged for the direct cost of returning the goods this must be made clear as above. In the event that payment for the goods or services was to be under a related credit agreement, cancellation of the main contract also has the effect of cancelling the credit agreement.

The OFT and TSOs are charged with enforcing these regulations. Although the Regulations are stated not to cover contracts for the sale of 'land' it is considered they do cover the preparation of marketing materials and therefore the preparation of HIPs.

UNFAIR CONTRACT TERMS ACT 1977 (UCTA 1977) AND UNFAIR TERMS IN CONSUMER CONTRACTS REGULATIONS 1999, SI 1999/2083 (UTCCR 1999)

UCTA 1977 was designed to give protection to consumers from exemption clauses relied upon by businesses seeking to avoid liability. It applies only to exclusion, limitation of liability clauses and indemnity clauses. Any attempt by a business to exclude liability for death or personal injury due to negligence is void. Damage to property can be excluded or restricted only if the term is reasonable and the Act contains guidelines for assessing the reasonableness of such terms. The burden of proving that a term is reasonable falls on the party seeking to rely on it. The reasonableness test is applied when considering a clause in standard terms of business where one of the parties is a consumer – the greater negotiating power of the business is thus construed in favour of the consumer. UCTA 1977 provides that a clause seeking to exclude liability imposed by the Sale of Goods Act is void as against a consumer and subject to the 'reasonable' test where it is a b2b contract.

UTCCR 1999 extended the protection for consumers to apply to any term in a b2c contract that has not been individually negotiated save for the main subject matter of the contract and the price, although there is a requirement that these meet the obligation to be couched in plain and intelligible language.

Any term that is not regarded as fair is not binding on the consumer. Again, there are guidelines as to what is and is not 'fair'. Generally, a term will be unfair if it 'causes a significant imbalance in the parties' rights or obligations under the contract, to the detriment of consumers'. UTCCR 1999 also require standard terms to be in plain and intelligible language and if the meaning of a term is unclear it will be construed in favour of the consumer. The Regulations also contain a list of terms that might be regarded as unfair.

However, these Regulations do not make any term void *ab initio*. In addition the burden of proving that a term is unfair has shifted to the consumer. The Regulations do, however apply to all types of consumer contract including property and also allow various bodies to take action to prevent the use of unfair terms. They do not, however, apply to business or private contracts.

The OFT is the main enforcement agency for UCTA 1977 and UTCCR 1999 but it will not determine what is or is not a fair term or whether there is a right to compensation. The OFT will consider complaints about terms and can seek an injunction from the court to prevent its use. Only the court can decide on the fairness or otherwise of a term.

Certain other 'qualifying bodies' also have powers under this legislation such as utility regulators, the Information Commissioner, the Consumers Association, the Financial Services Authority and all trading standards authorities. Professional bodies such as the Law Society also describe the terms that would be regarded as unfair through their professional practice rules.

The use by businesses of standard terms and conditions for the provision of services can fall foul of these regulations and needs to be carefully considered particularly if it is hoped to exclude or limit liability in negligence. This provision will be relevant for any organisation providing HIP services for consumers.

COPYRIGHT, DESIGNS AND PATENTS ACT 1988 (CDPA 1988)

Copyright is a 'property' right that subsists in certain types of work and by force of statute gives the copyright owner exclusive rights over the owner's work. This synopsis only considers copyright topics being the rights defined in legislation to copy, to distribute and to publish.

CPDA 1988 recognises nine categories of copyright works. In relation to HIPs, two are of interest – literary works and the right to protect a typographical arrangement of a published edition of a work.

Copyright comes into existence automatically when a 'qualifying' person creates an 'original' work, and cannot be protected by a patent or trademark. Three conditions need to be satisfied for copyright to subsist. The work must:

- have been created by a qualifying person;
- first be published in or transmitted from a qualifying country; and
- be in a material form

A literary work includes such mundane written work as the instructions on a box containing flat pack furniture, the list of ingredients on a breakfast cereal box, a draft lease or a database on a computer. The typography right covers the layout of editions of published 'literary' works whether or not these works themselves have copyright protection. Thus, in the context of HIPs there will be copyright in the HCR and in the layout of the pack when its disparate parts are assembled to form the pack.

It must not be forgotten that there is no copyright in an idea itself although it subsists in the tangible expression of the idea, i.e. the draft manuscript of a book, preparatory ideas for a computer programme, an advertisement or a database.

The 'originality' requirement only relates to a 'literary' work not the typographical right. To be regarded as original a work does not need to be inventive – it must originate from the author who must have expended some skill and judgment in its creation. The EU has issued directives in relation to databases and computer programmes that actually set a higher standard for these to be regarded as original in that they must be as a result of the author's intellectual creation rather than the 'sweat of the brow' test which needed only to show 'skill, labour and judgement'.

The requirement that for an original work to be capable of being copyright it must be recorded in some tangible form is known as 'fixation'.

The basic rule is that copyright in a work belongs to the creator, the author. This is displaced by CDPA 1988, s.11(2) which provides that, where a person creates a work in the course of employment, the employer is the owner of the copyright – unless, of course, there is an agreement to the contrary. Such an agreement can be expressed in writing, or be oral or implied from a course of action. The author is the person who writes the work unless the writer is merely taking dictation when the speaker is the author.

This may appear straightforward and common sense but complications arise when there is joint authorship – a situation that will be common in connection with HIPs where the pack is a number of documents forming the whole. The fact of the level of contribution will be crucial.

In the case of documents comprising the HIP, the seller should ensure that copyright has been assigned to him in return for the payment made or for which he is liable.

MINISTER FOR HOUSING AND PLANNING'S WRITTEN MINISTERIAL STATEMENT, 18 JULY 2006

I am today setting out further details of the government's implementation strategy and dry run for home information packs (HIPs).

The aims of the HIPs programme

The aims of the Government's reforms to the home buying and selling process are threefold:

(i) to provide home owners with important energy efficiency information about their homes to help them cut fuel bills and carbon emissions. This is vital as homes account for 27 per cent of Britain's carbon emissions. Energy performance certificates will provide clear information about the energy efficiency of homes and how that can be improved. The Energy Saving Trust estimates that following the advice in energy performance certificates could save the average home owner up to £300 a year on their fuel bills The Government believe it is important to implement these as early as possible given the importance of reducing carbon emissions.

(ii) to benefit consumers by cutting waste and duplication, speeding up home sales and reducing the number of failed transactions, which at present cost consumers around £350 million a year in wasted costs.

(iii) to encourage and support long-term transformation of the home buying and selling industry by introducing greater transparency and competition to drive down costs and incentivise better service and clearer redress for consumers.

Testing

There are three main components to home information packs: searches and other legal documents; energy performance certificates; and the home condition surveys that make up the other component of a full home condition report. It is essential that all aspects of home information packs are properly tested before full implementation. We need to be sure that consumers understand, value and can utilise the information that HIPs provide; that the assumed benefits will be realised; and that the different operating systems underpinning HIPs will work effectively.

As part of our ongoing programme of implementation, we have already successfully tested more than 14,000 HIPs with searches, but largely without home condition reports, in the dry run so far. Over the course of the summer we propose to undertake further consumer research on home condition reports; to study in greater detail the 250 HIPs that have been produced to date with some kind of survey; and to look to see what more we can learn from experience in other countries where HIPs have been introduced successfully or are currently being proposed. From the autumn the emphasis of our implementation programme will switch to the testing of energy performance certificates and home condition reports. Working with the industry and with consumers, we are proposing to support a series of area-based trials and we will test proposals such as allowing sellers to start marketing their homes if they have already commissioned their HIP rather than having to wait up to 14 days. There will be independent assessment and monitoring of all aspects of the dry run.

Roll out

It is also important that reforms are introduced on a timetable and as part of a programme that maximises the benefits for consumers and the environment. As part of the development of the dry run, we have engaged in detailed consultation with a wide range of stakeholders and have gathered substantial information on the progress of implementation so far. As a result, we have concluded that there would be significant risks and potential disadvantages to consumers from a mandatory 'big bang' introduction of full home condition reports on 1 June 2007. In particular:

- Further testing is needed to ensure that home condition reports deliver the assumed benefits for consumers and that the operating systems that support them work smoothly. Design work on the dry run has made it clear that this cannot be completed in time for the results to be taken into account in by 1 June.
- A recent report from the Council of Mortgage Lenders identified the real possibility that some lenders might not be fully geared up to use HCRs until 2008–09. In particular the industry's plans for bringing in automated valuation models means that many lenders will not have them in place by June 2007 and so will continue to seek separate mortgage valuation surveys where they could have relied on a home condition report.
- There are concerns about the number of inspectors that will be in place in time for June next year.

Moreover, because of our commitment to addressing climate change we do not want to jeopardise the successful introduction of energy performance certificates at the earliest possible opportunity by pursuing the 'big bang' mandatory introduction of full home condition reports at the same time.

We believe that progressive market-led take-up of full HCRs could strongly benefit consumers. Bearing in mind our commitment to the early introduction of energy performance certificates, combining an energy performance certificate and a full home condition report at the same time is likely to offer significant additional benefits to buyers and sellers. In particular, sellers offering full home condition reports should be more likely to benefit from swifter sales and suffer fewer transaction failures, as accepted offers are much less likely to be re-opened as a result of new information coming to light. In addition, once automated valuation models are in place, home condition reports should mean buyers get cheaper and swifter valuations and mortgage offers. We therefore believe that there will be a significant incentive for consumers to top up their HIPs voluntarily to include full home condition reports and that this is a product that the market can and should deliver.

Therefore we have concluded that:

- HIPs will be introduced with searches and other key documents from 1 June 2007.
- Energy performance certificates will be included in HIPs on a mandatory basis from 1 June 2007.
- We will work with the industry to facilitate market-led take-up of full HCRs. As part of this approach, we will explore with the sector a wide range of options to enable a

successful and innovative market for HCRs, including options for supporting the provision of necessary systems, effective demonstration projects for HCRs, and will consider the case for pump-priming funding. This market-led approach has the added benefit of giving industry more flexibility to innovate and adapt to consumer preferences.

- This means that the remaining aspects of home condition reports will not be made mandatory from June next year, but HCRs will be authorised documents that sellers will be able to include in their packs.

- Mandatory HCRs will remain on the table if the industry fails to make a success of the roll out of HCRs.

As part of the next phase of reform of we will also be setting out our plans for an ombudsman scheme for estate agents to strengthen consumer protection as well as further proposals to review competition and transparency in the industry to the benefit of consumers.

We believe that these arrangements will ensure that home information packs are implemented in a way that maximises benefits for consumers and the environment and successfully enables the long-term transformation of the home buying and selling market.

Appendix E
SAMPLE HOME CONDITION REPORT

HOME CONDITION REPORT

52 Hazelwood Drive,
St Albans
AL4 OUW
Hertfordshire
United Kingdom

Report reference number (RRN) **1234–6789–1234–6789–1234**
Inspection date **9 June 2006**

SAMPLE

Home Information Pack: Certification Schemes Standards – Part 2: Technical Standards

52 Hazelwood Drive St Albans Herts AL4 0UW United Kingdom
9 June 2006   RRN: 1234–6789–1234–6789–1234

Contents

HOME CONDITION REPORT

Home Condition Report Look and feel (Sample)

52 Hazelwood Drive St Albans Herts AL4 0UW United Kingdom   Introduction
9 June 2006   RRN: 1234–6789–1234–6789–1234

Introduction and terms on which report is prepared

To market your home for sale you must have a home information pack that
includes a home condition report. This Home Condition Report is produced
by a Home Inspector, who is a member of [Scheme Name]
(a government-approved certification scheme).

The Home Inspector must provide an objective opinion about the condition
of the property which the buyer, the seller and the buyer's mortgage
company must be able to rely on and use.

To become a member of [Scheme Name] and be able to produce
home condition reports, a Home Inspector has to:

• pass an assessment of skills, in line with National Occupational Standards;
  and

• have insurance that provides cover when a Home Inspector is negligent.

The Home Inspector must follow the necessary standards and [Scheme
Name's] code of conduct.

A Home Condition Report is not valid unless it has been produced by a
Home Inspector who is a member of a government-approved scheme and
it has been entered on the Register of Home Condition Reports.

The Home Condition Report is in a standard format and is based on these
terms, which set out what you should expect of both the Home Inspector
and the home condition report. You and the Home Inspector cannot amend
these terms.

Any other services the Home Inspector may provide are not covered
by these terms and so must be covered by a separate contract.

If you have any complaint about this report, you can complain by
following the complaints procedure, which is explained in more detail
at the end of this document.

HOME CONDITION REPORT

Page 3 of 29

Home Information Pack: Certification Schemes Standards – Part 2: Technical Standards

52 Hazelwood Drive St Albans Herts AL4 0UW United Kingdom
9 June 2006   RRN: 1234–6789–1234–6789–1234

Introduction

What this report tells you

This report tells you:
• about the construction and condition of the home on the date it was inspected; and
• whether more enquiries or investigations are needed.

The report's main aim is to tell you about any defects that need urgent attention or are serious. It also tells you about things that need further investigation to prevent damage to the structure of the building.

The report gives 'condition ratings' to the major parts of the main building (it does not give condition ratings to outbuildings). However, the report does not mention minor defects that do not need building work to put them right.

The report contains an energy performance certificate that tells you about the energy and environmental performance of the home, and suggests any improvements that you can make.

What this report does not tell you

This report does not tell you the value of your home or cover things that will be considered when a valuation is provided, such as the area the home is in or the availability of public transport or facilities.

It does not tell you about any minor defects that would not normally have any effect on a buyer's decision to buy.

• This report does not warn you about any health and safety risks to people using or visiting the property, unless repair or building work is needed to avoid the risk.

• The report does not give advice on the cost of any repair work or the types of repair which should be used.

• The report is not an asbestos inspection under the Control of Asbestos at Work Regulations 2002.

If you need advice on subjects that are not covered by the home condition report, you must arrange for it to be provided separately.

HOME CONDITION REPORT

Home Condition Report Look and feel (Sample)

What is inspected?

The Home Inspector inspects the inside and outside of the main building and all permanent outbuildings, and the parts of the gas, electricity and water and drainage services that can be seen.

The Inspector gives each part of the structure of the main building a condition rating, to make the report easy to follow. The condition ratings are as follows.

Condition rating	Definition
1	No repair is currently needed. Normal maintenance must be carried out.
2	Repairs or replacements are needed but the Home Inspector does not consider these to be serious or urgent.
3	These are defects which are either serious and/or require urgent repair or replacement.
NI	Not inspected (See important note below)

Important note
The inspection is 'non-invasive'. This means that the Home Inspector does not take up carpets, floor coverings or floorboards, move furniture or remove the contents of cupboards. Also, the Home Inspector does not remove secured panels or undo electrical fittings.

The Home Inspector will say at the start of sections D, E and F of the report if it was not possible to inspect any parts of the home that are normally reported on. If the Home Inspector is concerned about these parts, the report will tell you about any further investigations that are needed. The Home Inspector does not report on the cost of any work to correct defects or how repairs should be carried out.

 HOME CONDITION REPORT

Home Information Pack: Certification Schemes Standards – Part 2: Technical Standards

52 Hazelwood Drive St Albans Herts AL4 0UW United Kingdom
9 June 2006   RRN: 1234–6789–1234–6789–1234

Section A General Information

52 Hazelwood Drive St Albans AL4 0UW Hertfordshire United Kingdom

Property reference number:	45275
Home Inspector's name:	Lorem Ipsum
Home Inspector's membership number:	12345
Company name:	Lorem Ipsum
Company address and postcode:	Lorem ipsum 7 Lorem ipsum street, 122 345
Company email:	Lorem@email.com
Company telephone number:	123456789
Company fax number:	123456789
Date of the inspection:	24 April 2006
Report reference number:	1234
The report reference number of any other Home Condition Reports written for this property in the last 12 months: (Reports prepared for previous sellers are excluded).	1234–1234–1234–1234–1234

Lorem ipsum Lorem ipsum Lorem ipsum

HOME CONDITION REPORT

Home Condition Report Look and feel (Sample)

52 Hazelwood Drive St Albans Herts AL4 0UW United Kingdom
9 June 2006   RRN: 1234–6789–1234–6789–1234

Section B Summary

Section B Summary

Date of the inspection:	Lorem ipsum
Full address and postcode of the property:	Nemo enim ipsam voluptatem quia voluptas sit
Weather conditions:	Nemo enim ipsam voluptatem quia voluptas sit
The state of property when inspected:	Nemo enim ipsam voluptatem quia voluptas sit
Approximate year when the property was built:	Nemo enim ipsam voluptatem quia voluptas sit
Approximate year when the property was extended:	xxxx
Approximate year when the property was converted:	xxxx
Type of property:	voluptatem quia voluptas sit

HOME CONDITION REPORT

Page 7 of 29

Home Information Pack: Certification Schemes Standards – Part 2: Technical Standards

52 Hazelwood Drive St Albans Herts AL4 0UW United Kingdom
9 June 2006   RRN: 1234–6789–1234–6789–1234

Section B Summary

For flats and maisonettes

The Property is a [Purpose Built] flat on the [Flat Location] floor of a [Storey-Count] story block of [Total-Apartments] flat

Accommodation

Storey	Living rooms	Bedrooms	Bath/or shower	Separate toilet	Kitchen	Utility room	Conservatory	Other	Name of other
Lower ground	1								
Ground	1								
First	1								
Second	1								
Third									
Fourth									
Roof space									
Totals									

Floor Area:	The [Measurement-Type] floor area of the [Property-Type] is [Floor-Area] square metres
Reinstatement cost:	Lorem ipsum Lorem ipsum

Note: This reinstatement cost is the estimated cost of completely rebuilding the property. It represents the sum at which the home should be insured against fire and other risks. It is based on building and other related costs and does not include the value of the land the home is built on. It does not include leisure facilities such as swimming pools and tennis courts. The figure should be reviewed regularly as building costs change. **Importantly,** it is not a valuation of the property.

If the property is very large or historic, or if it incorporates special features or is of unusual construction and a specialist would be needed to assess the reinstatement cost, no cost figure is provided and the report says that a specialist is needed.

HOME CONDITION REPORT

Page 8 of 29

Home Condition Report Look and feel (Sample)

52 Hazelwood Drive St Albans Herts AL4 0UW United Kingdom   **Section B** Summary
9 June 2006   RRN: 1234–6789–1234–6789–1234

Construction

A short general description of the construction:

Nemo enim ipsam voluptatem quia voluptas sit aspernatur aut odit aut fugit, sed quia consequuntur
magni dolores eos qui ratione voluptatem sequi nesciunt. Neque porro quisquam est, qui dolorem
ipsum quia dolor sit amet, consectetur, adipisci velit, sed quia non numquam eius modi tempora
incidunt ut labore et dolore magnam aliquam quaerat voluptatem.

Main Services   Drainage ☐   Gas ☐   Electricity ☐   Water ☐

The ticked boxes indicate that mains services are present

Central Heating

Nemo enim ipsam voluptatem quia voluptas sit aspernatur aut odit aut fugit, sed quia consequuntur
magni dolores eos qui ratione

Outside facilities

Nemo enim ipsam voluptatem quia voluptas sit aspernatur aut odit aut fugit, sed quia consequuntur
magni dolores eos qui ratione voluptatem sequi nesciunt. Neque porro quisquam est, qui dolorem
ipsum quia dolor sit amet, consectetur, adipisci velit, sed quia non numquam eius modi tempora
incidunt ut labore et dolore magnam aliquam quaerat voluptatem.

HOME CONDITION REPORT

Home Information Pack: Certification Schemes Standards – Part 2: Technical Standards

52 Hazelwood Drive St Albans Herts AL4 0UW United Kingdom   **Section B** Summary
9 June 2006   RRN: 1234–6789–1234–6789–1234

Summary of ratings and condition

Section of the report	Part no.	Part name	Identifier (more than one)	Rating
D: Outside	D1	Chimney stacks	X	X
	D2	Roof coverings	X	X
	D3	Rainwater pipes and gutters	X	X
	D4	Main walls	X	X
	D5	Windows	X	X
	D6	Outside doors	X	X
	D7	All other woodwork	X	X
	D8	Outside decoration	X	X
	D9	Other external detail	X	X
E: Inside Condition	E1	Roof structure		X
	E2	Ceilings	X	X
	E3	Inside walls	X	X
	E4	Floors	X	X
	E5	Fireplaces &chimneybreasts	X	X
	E6	Built in fitments – example	X	X
	E7	Inside woodwork	X	X
	E8	Bathroom fittings	X	X
	E9	Dampness	X	X
	E10	Other inside detail	X	X
F: Services	F1	Electricity	na	X
	F2	Gas	na	X
	F3	Water	na	X
	F4	Heating	na	X
	F5	Drainage	na	X

Widespread problems that affect   Lorem ipsum
many parts of the property:

Summary of structural movement: Lorem ipsum

HOME CONDITION REPORT   Page 10 of 29

240

Home Condition Report Look and feel (Sample)

52 Hazelwood Drive St Albans Herts AL4 0UW United Kingdom
9 June 2006   RRN: 1234–6789–1234–6789–1234

Section B Summary

Recommended investigation of
defects seen or suspected:

Lorem ipsum

Page 11 of 29

Home Information Pack: Certification Schemes Standards – Part 2: Technical Standards

Section C Conveyancing and health and safety issues

Issues for conveyancers

The Home Inspector does not act as 'the conveyancer'. However, if during the inspection,
the Inspector identifies issues that the conveyancers advising the buyer and seller may need
to investigate further, the Inspector will refer to these in the report. This is to draw the issues
to the attention of others to improve the quality of the information in the home information pack.
The Inspector will not have seen the legal and other documents in the home information pack.

Roads and footpaths:	Lorem ipsum
Drainage:	Lorem ipsum
Planning and any other permission needed:	Lorem ipsum
Freehold owner consents:	Lorem ipsum Lorem ipsum
Flying freeholds:	Lorem ipsum
Mining:	Lorem ipsum Lorem ipsum
Rights of way:	Lorem ipsum
Boundaries (including Party Walls):	Lorem ipsum
Easements:	Lorem ipsum Lorem ipsum
Repairs to shared parts:	Lorem ipsum
Previous structural repairs:	Lorem ipsum
New building warranties:	Lorem ipsum Lorem ipsum
Building insurance (ongoing claims):	Lorem ipsum
Tree preservation orders:	Lorem ipsum
Property let:	Lorem ipsum

HOME CONDITION REPORT

Home Condition Report Look and feel (Sample)

52 Hazelwood Drive St Albans Herts AL4 0UW United Kingdom   **Section C** Conveyancing and health and safety issues
9 June 2006   RRN: 1234–6789–1234–6789–1234

Contaminated land and flooding

The Home Inspector assumes that the home is not built with nor contains hazardous materials and it is not built on contaminated land. However if any of these materials are found during the inspection, or if the Home Inspector finds evidence to suspect that the land may be contaminated, this will be shown on the report along with recommendations for further investigations.

Contamination: Lorem ipsum

Flooding: Nemo enim ipsam voluptatem

Health and safety risks

The Home Inspector will draw your attention to items from a set list of health and safety issues if they are seen at the property.

The Inspector does not have to identify risks which have existed in the property for a long time, and which cannot reasonably be changed. As an example, the Inspector will not draw your attention to uneven floor surfaces that have existed for decades.

HOME CONDITION REPORT

Page 13 of 29

52 Hazelwood Drive St Albans Herts AL4 0UW United Kingdom
9 June 2006　　RRN: 1234–6789–1234–6789–1234

Section D Outside condition

The inspector carried out a non-invasive inspection (see the important note on page 4 for an explanation of 'non-invasive') of the outside of the main building and permanent outbuildings. They made this inspection from various points within the boundaries of the property and from public areas such as footpaths and open spaces, using binoculars where necessary. The Inspector did not stand on walls or enter neighbouring private property. They examined roofs, chimneys and other external surfaces of the building from the ground. They inspected flat roofs to single-storey buildings from a ladder, where the surface of the roof was not more than three-metres above ground level. They did not inspect features above this level that cannot be seen from any point. Because of the risk of causing damage, the Inspector did not walk on flat roofs. They assessed rainwater fittings (gutters and downpipes) only if there was heavy rain at the time of inspection.

The Inspector looked at the overall condition and the state of repair of the outside parts of the property. The report does not reflect every minor blemish and does not point out each individual minor defect in the outside walls. However, where there are so many minor defects that together they are serious, the report will say this.

When inspecting blocks of flats, it is often difficult to see the whole outside of a building or block, and its maintenance is rarely the responsibility of one person. The Inspector only carried out a non-invasive inspection to the level of detail set out above, to the main walls, windows and roof over the flat.

The Inspector did not inspect the rest of the block to this level of detail; but instead has formed an opinion based on a general inspection of the rest of the block. They provide information about the outside and shared parts so that the conveyancer can check whether the maintenance clauses in the lease or other title documents are adequate.

The Inspector inspected the shared access to the flat together with the area where car parking and any garage for the flat are, along with the access to that area. They did not inspect other shared parts, such as separate halls, stairs and access ways to other flats in the block, the lift motor room and cleaning cupboards.

HOME CONDITION REPORT

Home Condition Report Look and feel (Sample)

52 Hazelwood Drive St Albans Herts AL4 0UW United Kingdom
9 June 2006   RRN: 1234–6789–1234–6789–1234

Section D Outside condition

| I could not inapect the [property feature], because […Justification]. |
| I could not inspect the [property feature], because […justification]. |

D1 Chimney stacks	Rating
[Name]	

D2 Roof coverings	Rating
[Name] [Comments]	

D3 Rain water pipes and gutters	Rating
[Name] [Comments]	

D4 Main walls	Rating
[Name] [Comments]	

D5 Windows	Rating
[Name] [Comments]	

D6 External doors (including patio doors)	Rating
[Name] [Comments]	

D7 All other woodwork	Rating
[Name] [Comments]	

HOME CONDITION REPORT

Page 15 of 29

Home Information Pack: Certification Schemes Standards – Part 2: Technical Standards

52 Hazelwood Drive St Albans Herts AL4 0UW United Kingdom
9 June 2006   RRN: 1234–6789–1234–6789–1234

Section D Outside condition

D8 Outside decoration	Rating
[Name] [Comments]	

D9 Other outside detail	Rating
[Name] [Comments]	

	Rating
[Name] [Comments]	

HOME CONDITION REPORT

Home Condition Report Look and feel (Sample)

Section E Inside condition

The Home inspector carried out a non-invasive inspection of all the parts of the home they could
see without causing damage. However, if the Inspector could not see a part of the home without
the risk of damage, and they suspect that there could be a problem, the report will say this and
include recommendations on the need for further investigation.

The Home Inspector checked for damp in vulnerable areas by using a moisture measuring meter.

They inspected the roof structure from inside the roof space where it was accessible but did not
move or lift insulation material, stored goods and other contents. The Inspector did not walk around
the space if there was a risk to safety (for example, where insulation covers the ceiling joists).
Instead they inspected the roof from the access point.

They opened some of the windows and all the doors. They inspected floor surfaces and under-floor
spaces where they were readily accessible. They did not move or lift furniture, floor coverings
or other contents. The Home Inspector has not commented on sound insulation or chimney flues
(or both), because it is rarely practical to do so without using specialist equipment that Home
Inspectors do not carry.

The Home Inspector inspected the inside of the flat in the same way as is described under 'The
inside of the property' in section C. However, they inspected the roof space only where they could
get safe access from within the flat itself. The Inspector did not go into the roof space if access
was only possible from the shared parts or from within another flat.

HOME CONDITION REPORT

Home Information Pack: Certification Schemes Standards – Part 2: Technical Standards

52 Hazelwood Drive St Albans Herts AL4 0UW United Kingdom   **Section E** Inside condition
9 June 2006   RRN: 1234–6789–1234–6789–1234

I could not inspect the [property feature], because [...justification].
I could not inspect the [property feature], because [...justification].

E1. Roof structure	Rating
[Name] [Comments]	
[Name] [Comments]	Rating
E2 Ceilings	Rating
[Name] [Comments]	
[Name] [Comments]	Rating
E3 Internal walls & partitions & plasterwork	Rating
[Name] [Comments]	
[Name] [Comments]	Rating
E4 Floors	Rating
[Name] [Comments]	
[Name] [Comments]	Rating

HOME CONDITION REPORT

Page 18 of 29

Home Condition Report Look and feel (Sample)

52 Hazelwood Drive St Albans Herts AL4 0UW United Kingdom
9 June 2006   RRN: 1234–6789–1234–6789–1234

Section E Inside condition

E5 Fireplaces and chimney breasts (and the outside of flues)	Rating
[Name]
[Comments]	

E6 Built in fittings (built in kitchen and other fittings, not test all the fittings)	Rating
[Name]
[Comments]	

E7 Inside woodwork (staircase, joinery, and so on)	Rating
[Name]
[Comments]	

E8 Bathroom fittings	Rating
[Name]
[Comments]	

E9 Dampness	Rating
[Name]
[Comments]	

E10 Other issues	Rating
[Name]
[Comments]	

HOME CONDITION REPORT

Page 19 of 29

Home Information Pack: Certification Schemes Standards – Part 2: Technical Standards

52 Hazelwood Drive St Albans Herts AL4 0UW United Kingdom   **Section F** Services
9 June 2006   RRN: 1234–6789–1234–6789–1234

Section F Services

Services are generally hidden within the construction of the property; for example, pipes are beneath the floors and wiring is within the walls. As a result only the visible parts of the available services can be inspected. Specialist tests were not carried out. The visual inspection does not assess the services to make sure they work properly and efficiently and meet modern standards. If any services (such as the boiler or mains water) are turned off, the Home Inspector will state that in the report and will not turn them on.

Otherwise, the Home Inspector turned on some taps on appliances and, where safe and practical to do so, lifted the covers on the drainage inspection chambers.

The Home Inspector reports only on the services covered in this section (electricity, gas, oil, water, heating and drainage). All other services and domestic appliances are not included in the reporting: for example security and door-answering systems, smoke alarms, television, cable, wireless and satellite communication systems, cookers, hobs, washing machines and fridges (even where built-in).

The report gives some general advice on safety and the importance of maintaining and servicing the home's services and appliances, particularly those providing heating and hot water.

HOME CONDITION REPORT

Page 20 of 29

Home Condition Report Look and feel (Sample)

52 Hazelwood Drive St Albans Herts AL4 0UW United Kingdom
9 June 2006   RRN: 1234–6789–1234–6789–1234

Section F Services

I could not inspect the [property feature], because [...justification].

I could not inspect the [property feature], because [...justification].

F1 Electricity	Rating

General advice
Safety warning: Periodic inspection and testing of electrical installations is important to protect your home from damage and to ensure the safety of the occupants. Guidance published by the Institute of Electrical Engineers recommends that inspections and testing are undertaken at least every 10 years and on change of occupancy. All electrical installation work undertaken after 1st January 2005 should be identified by an Electrical Installation Certificate.

[Comments]

F2 Gas/Oil	Rating

General advice
Safety Warning – GAS and OIL – Regular inspection, testing, maintenance and servicing of all heating and hot water appliances and equipment should be undertaken by a registered 'competent person' and in accordance with the manufacturer's instructions'. This is important to ensure that such equipment is working correctly to minimise the risk of fire and carbon monoxide poisoning as well as leakages of Carbon Dioxide and other greenhouse gases to the atmosphere. For further advice contact CORGI for gas installations, OFTEC for oil installations and HETAS for solid fuel installations.

[Comments] Gas

[Comments] Oil

F3 Water	Rating

[Comments]

F4 Heating	Rating

[Comments]

F5 Drainage	Rating

[Comments]

 HOME CONDITION REPORT

Page 21 of 29

Home Information Pack: Certification Schemes Standards – Part 2: Technical Standards

52 Hazelwood Drive St Albans Herts AL4 0UW United Kingdom   **Section G** Grounds (including shared parts for flats)
9 June 2006   RRN: 1234–6789–1234–6789–1234

Section G Grounds (including shared parts for flats)

The Home Inspector inspected the condition of the boundary walls, outbuildings and areas in common (shared) use

To inspect these areas the Home Inspector walked around the grounds. The report provides a summary of the general condition of any garden walls, fences, and permanent outbuildings. Conservatories with translucent or clear roofs attached to the main buildings are treated as outbuildings, as are garages and permanent store sheds. Buildings containing swimming pools and sports facilities are also treated as outbuildings, but the Home Inspector does not report on the leisure facilities, such as the pool itself and its equipment.

The Inspector did not inspect leisure facilities, landscaping and other facilities, including swimming pools and tennis courts, and non-permanent outbuildings

Comments on:

garages:	Lorem ipsum et alia
permanent sheds:	Lorem ipsum et alia
other permanent outbuildings:	Lorem ipsum et alia
other walls:	Lorem ipsum et alia
paved areas:	Lorem ipsum et alia
areas in common (shared) use:	Lorem ipsum et alia
conservatories:	Lorem ipsum et alia
other structures:	Lorem ipsum et alia

HOME CONDITION REPORT

Appendix F
SAMPLE ENERGY PERFORMANCE CERTIFICATE

HOME CONDITION REPORT

HOME CONDITION REPORT

10 Mountain Ash Avenue
Leigh-on-Sea
Essex
SS98 4YY
United Kingdom

Report reference number (RRN) **SA3675892**
Inspection date **9 June 2006**

Section H Energy Performance Certificate

10 Mountain Ash Avenue
Leigh-on-Sea
Essex SS9 4SY
United Kingdom

Dwelling type: Detached Bungalow
Home inspector's name: John Brown
Date of inspection: 9 June 2006
Date of making the report: 8 June 2206
Certificate number: 13024
Floor area: 64 sq metres

The home's performance ratings

This home has been assessed using the UK's Standard Assessment Procedure (SAP) for dwellings. Its performance is rated in terms of the energy use per square metre of floor area, energy efficiency based on fuel costs and environmental impact based on Carbon Dioxide (CO_2) emissions.

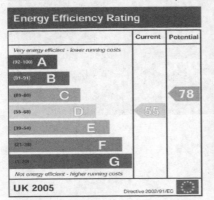

The energy efficiency rating is a measure of the overall efficiency of a home. The higher the rating the more energy efficient the home is and the lower the fuel bills will be.

The environmental impact rating is a measure of a home's impact on the environment in terms of Carbon Dioxide emissions. The higher the rating the less impact it has on the environment.

Estimated energy use, Carbon Dioxide (CO_2) emissions and fuel costs of this home

This table provides an indication of how much it will cost to provide lighting, heating and hot water to this home. The fuel costs and Carbon Dioxide emissions are calculated based on a SAP assessment of the energy use. This makes standard assumptions about occupancy, heating patterns and geographical location. The energy use includes the energy used in producing and delivering the fuels to this home. The fuel costs only take into account the cost of fuel and not any associated service, maintenance or safety inspection costs. The certificate allows one home to be compared with another, but always check the date the certificate was issued. Since fuel prices can increase over time, an older certificate may underestimate the property's fuel cost.

HOME CONDITION REPORT

10 Mountain Ash Avenue Leigh-on-Sea Essex SS98 4YY
9 June 2006   RRN: SA3675892

Section H Energy Performance Certificate

	Current	Potential
Energy use	261 KWh/m² per year	178 kWh/m2 per year
Carbon dioxide emissions	3.50 tonnes per year	2.46 tonnes per year
Lighting	£34.71 per year	£34.71 per year
Heating	£222.29 per year	£135.73 per year
Hot water	£47.25 per year	£47.25 per year

To see how this home can achieve its potential rating please see the recommended measures.

Summary of this home's energy performance related features

The following is an assessment of the key individual elements that have an impact on this home's performance rating. Each element is assessed against the following scale: Very poor/Poor/Average/Good/Very good.

Element	Description	Current performance
Main walls	Cavity (as built)	Poor
Main roof	Pitched, 150mm loft insulation	Good
Main floor	Uninsulated solid concrete (assumed)	Average
Windows	100% double glazed or better. During or post 2002	Good
Main heating	Mains gas boiler	Average
Main heating controls	Programmer, TRVs and bypass	n/a
Secondary heating	None	n/a
Hot water	From main	n/a
Lighting	Mostly low energy lighting	Good

Current energy efficiency rating	D 59
Current environmental impact rating	D 57

HOME CONDITION REPORT

10 Mountain Ash Avenue Leigh-on-Sea Essex SS98 4YY   **Section H** Energy Performance Certificate
9 June 2006   RRN: SA3675892

Recommended measures to improve this home's performance ratings

The measures below are cost effective. The performance ratings after improvement listed below are cumulative, that is they assume the improvements have been installed in the order that they appear in the table.

Lower cost measures (up to £500)	Typical savings	Performance ratings after improvement	
		Energy efficiency	Environmental impact
1 Put 150mm jacket on hot water cylinder	£25.00	D:60	D:58
2 Upgrade loft insulation to 250mm	£6.75 per year	D:62	D:60
3 Fully fill wall cavity with blown fibre	£80.00 per year	C:70	C:70
	Sub-total £86.75 per year		
Higher cost measures (over £500)			
4 Improve TRVs, programmer & boiler manager	£2.75 per year	C:71	C:70
	Total £89.50 per year		
Potential energy efficiency rating		C:71	
Potential environmental impact rating		C:70	

The further measures below could deliver even higher standards for this home.

Solar Water heating. A solar collector coupled with solar water storage reduces the fuel needed for domestic hot water.

Photovoltaics. A solar collector which generates electricity for use in the home or for sale to the National Grid.

Improvements to the energy efficiency and environmental impact ratings will usually be in step with each other. However, they can sometimes diverge because reduced energy costs are not always accompanied by reduced Carbon Dioxide emissions.

HOME CONDITION REPORT

10 Mountain Ash Avenue Leigh-on-Sea Essex SS98 4YY
9 June 2006   RRN: SA3675892

Section H Energy Performance Certificate

About the measures to improve this home's performance ratings

Lower cost measures (typically up to £500 each)

These measures are relatively inexpensive to install. Some of them may be installed as DIY projects. DIY is not always straightforward, and sometimes there are health and safety risks, so take advice from an energy advisor before carrying out DIY improvements.

1 Upgrade loft insulation to 250mm

The anticipated cost is based upon a contractor installing an additional 100mm of glass fibre or mineral wool insualtion in your loft, but it can also be installed by a capable DIY entusiast. If you choose the DIY installation then take care not to block ventialtion at the edge of the loft space as this may cause condensation. When handling the insulation always wear gloves and masks.

2 Fully fill wall cavity with blown fibre

The external walls of your home are built with a gap, called a cavity, between the inside and outside layers of the wall. Cavity Wall insulation fills this gap with an insulating material. The material is pumped into the gap through small holes, which are drilled into the outside layer of the walls (the small holes are sealed afterwards). Because this involves using specialist machinery, a professional installation company must carry out the work. The contractor will thoroughly survey your walls before commencing work to be sure that this type of insulation is right for your home, and provide a guarantee for the work.

Higher cost measures (typically over £500 each)

3 Improve thermostatic radiator valves (TRVs), programmer & boiler manager

The heating system is controlled by TRVs but does not include a room thermostat. This means the boiler continues to operate even when no heating is required – even when the TRVs have turned off the radiators, the boiler is still burning fuel and wasting your money. Ask for a thermostat to be located in the lounge and insist it switches off the boiler as well as the pump.

Further measures

Solar water heating can make a significant contribution to the supply of domestic hot water for use in the home while reducing the amount of fuel needed. This uses radiation from the sun to heat water and typically requires the installation of a collector on a southerly facing roof slope or on a free-standing tilted frame.

Solar photovoltaics are used to generate electricity from daylight for use in the home. Photovoltaic modules can be fitted on top of an existing roof structure using a properly designed support structure.

HOME CONDITION REPORT

10 Mountain Ash Avenue Leigh-on-Sea Essex SS98 4YY   **Section H** Energy Performance Certificate
9 June 2006   RRN: SA3675892

About this energy inspection

This inspection has been undertaken by a qualified Inspector who has received appropriate training to collect the correct information about the energy performance of homes. This information has been processed by a Government approved organisation to produce the energy performance certificate and the recommendations for improvements in this report. Both the Inspector and the energy performance certificate supplier are regularly monitored to ensure that their work is up to standard.

For clarification of the technical information in this energy performance certificate please contact: the Home Inspector.

About this home's performance ratings

The ratings provide a measure of the overall energy efficiency of this home and its environmental impact. Both are calculated using the Standard Assessment Procedure (SAP), which is the Government's recommended system for assessing the energy performance of dwellings. The ratings take into account the home's insulation, heating systems, hot water system, fixed lighting, ventilation, number of windows and fuels used.

Not all of us use our homes in the same way so to allow one home to be directly compared to another, energy ratings are calculated using 'standard occupancy' assumptions. Standard occupancy is based on a home in a central UK location and assumes that during the heating season the home is heated for 9 hours a day during weekdays and 16 hours a day at weekends, with the living room heated to 21°C and the rest of the house at 18°C.

The ratings are expressed on a scale of 1 to 100. The higher the energy efficiency rating the more energy efficient the home and the higher the environmental impact rating the less impact it has on the environment.

Homes which are more energy efficient use less energy, saving money and helping to protect the environment. The cost of providing lighting, heating and hot water to a home with an energy efficiency rating of 100 would be practically zero. Similarly the Carbon Dioxide emissions from lighting, heating and hot water for a home with an environmental impact rating of 100 would be practically zero.

The potential ratings shown above describe the energy performance of the home assuming all cost effective measures have been installed. For comparison a home built to the 2006 Building Regulations would typically be around the boundary of bands B and C.

HOME CONDITION REPORT

10 Mountain Ash Avenue Leigh-on-Sea Essex SS98 4YY   **Section H** Energy Performance Certificate
9 June 2006   RRN: SA3675892

This home's impact on the environment

Carbon dioxide is one of the biggest contributors to the man-made greenhouse effect. We all use energy every day – at home, at work and when we travel. To generate that energy, we burn fossil fuels (coal, oil and gas) that produce 'greenhouse' gases – particularly Carbon Dioxide – which are changing our climate and damaging the environment. The energy we use for heating, lighting and power in our homes produces over a quarter of the UK's Carbon Dioxide emissions.

The average household in the UK creates about six tonnes of Carbon Dioxide every year. There are simple steps you can take to cut Carbon Dioxide emissions and help prevent climate change. Making your home more energy efficient by adopting the suggestions in this report can help protect the environment by reducing Carbon Dioxide emissions. You could reduce your emissions even more by switching to renewable energy sources.

What can I do today?

In addition to the specific measures suggested in this report, don't forget there are many simple measures you can put into action today that will save you money, help reduce your impact on the environment and improve the comfort of your home.

For example:
- Check that your heating system thermostat is not set too high (21°C in the living room is suggested) and use the timer or programmer to ensure you only heat your home when necessary.
- Make sure your hot water is not too hot. Your cylinder thermostat shouldn't need to be set higher than 60°C/140F.
- Turn off lights when not needed and do not leave appliances on standby. Remember not to leave chargers (e.g. for mobile phones) turned on when you are not using them.

Remember to look for the energy saving recommended logo when buying energy efficient products. It's a quick and easy way to identify the most energy efficient products on the market.

For advice on how to take action and to find out about offers available to help make your home more energy efficient call 0800 512 012 or visit www.est.org.uk/myhome

10 Mountain Ash Avenue Leigh-on-Sea Essex SS98 4YY
9 June 2006   RRN: SA3675892

Section A General information

When the report is complete

All home condition reports are held on a register kept by or on behalf of the Government in accordance with regulations made under the Housing Act 2004. Under those regulations, a copy of this home condition report can be inspected on-line at [hcrportal@address] by entering its unique reference number SA3675892. Entering this number allows anyone to inspect the report so you should not give it to someone unless you are happy for them to see the report. If you give someone the reference number and wish to prevent others from inspecting the report, you should tell the recipient that you do not want the number to be further disclosed.

Home Inspector's signature
Note: Facsimile signature taken from in the database)

Inspector's licence number:	42764
Name:	John Brown
Qualifications:	FRICS
Address:	47 Long Street Leigh-On-Sea Essex SS97 3QC
Phone number:	01702 844489
Fax number:	01702 844489
E-mail address:	homeinspections@townside.co.uk
Date of making the report:	9 June 2006

What to do if you have a complaint

If you have a complaint about this Home Condition Report or the Home Inspector who carried it, out you should follow the procedures set out below.

- Ask the company who provided the report, (the company named on the front of the report) or the Home Inspector who carried it out to give you a copy of their complaints handling procedure. All companies must have a written procedure and make it available to you if you ask.
- Follow the guidance given in the document, which includes making a formal complaint.
- Companies that provide home condition reports must handle your complaint in accordance with their procedure.

You may ask [scheme name] [scheme address] to investigate the complaint if:

- your complaint is about an allegation of criminal activity;
- the company fails to handle your complaint in line with their procedure; or
- you are not happy with how they have handled your complaint.

If you are the seller and believe that the report is incorrect. You should report this to the company that provided the report (or the Home Inspector who carried out the inspection).

- If the company or the Inspector agrees that details are not correct, they will give a corrected report and ask for the inaccurate report to be removed from the register of home condition reports.
- If the company or Inspector do not agree, you may complain to [scheme name] and apply to have the report removed from the register of home condition reports.

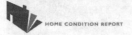 HOME CONDITION REPORT

Page 8 of 8

Appendix G
FORMS FROM DRAFT REGULATIONS

Sale statement for

~~first holder of property to be sold below and include postcode.~~

About this form:

- Under the Home Information Pack Regulations, you must provide the following information in your Home Information Pack and may use this form to do so.

- Someone can complete this form on behalf of a seller.

- If the property has not yet been completed or converted, please answer the questions as if the property is finished.

- Please answer all questions by checking the relevant box and adding any further information asked for. Where alternatives are offered, please indicate which one (or more) applies.

- The Regulations also tell you what other documents must and may be in the Home Information Pack. Guidance on the Regulations is available at www.homeinformationpacks.gov.uk

	Statement
1. The property is (or will be):	☐ Freehold ☐ Commonhold ☐ Leasehold starting (or likely to start) from and with years left on the lease
2. The title to the interest in the property being sold is:	☐ Registered at Land Registry ☐ Unregistered
3. Who is selling the property?	☐ The owner or owners ☐ A representative with the necessary authority to sell the property for an owner who has died ☐ A representative with the necessary authority to sell the property for a living owner (for example with a power of attorney) ☐ Other (please give details):
4. The property is being sold:	☐ With vacant possession ☐ Subject to occupation where one or more properties in a sub-divided building are marketed for sale as a dwelling property, but at least one is with vacant possession (for example, a house which is vacant but sold with an occupied annexe)

Home Information Pack Index for

Insert address of property to be sold below and include postcode.

About this form

- Under the Home Information Pack Regulations, you must include an index which lists all the documents included in your Home Information Pack.

- You may use this form as an index. However, under the Regulations not all the documents listed in the form have to be included in every case, and if you are not sure which documents must be included in your pack, please seek advice.

- Where a document required by the Regulations is unavailable or unobtainable, the index should indicate that the document is missing, and the reason why. Where the document can be obtained from or created by a person, or does exist, the index should indicate the steps being taken to obtain the document.

- The index to your Home Information Pack should be updated whenever the pack or a pack document is added or removed.

- Someone can complete this form on behalf of a seller.

- The Regulations also tell you what other documents must and may be in the Home Information Pack, and guidance on the Regulations is available at www.homeinformationpacks.gov.uk

PART 1 – General

Home Information Pack document	Further details about pack document, including date of documents	Included ☒	Not included or not applicable (N/I or N/A)	Reason why not included and steps being taken to obtain the document
Basic pack documents				
1. Index		☐	☐ N/I ☐ N/A	
2. Sale statement		☐	☐ N/I ☐ N/A	
Title information				
3. Land Registry individual register		☐	☐ N/I ☐ N/A	
4. Land Registry title plan		☐	☐ N/I ☐ N/A	

Home Information Pack document	Further details about pack document, including date of documents	Included ☒	Not included or not applicable (N/I or N/A)	Reason why not included and steps being taken to obtain the document
5. Land Registry copies of documents referred to in the individual register		☐	☐ N/I ☐ N/A	
6. Official search of Land Registry index map		☐	☐ N/A	
7. Deduction of title documents		☐	☐ N/I ☐ N/A	
8. Leases, tenancies or licences for properties where part of the property in a sub-divided building not sold with vacant possession		☐	☐ N/I ☐ N/A	
The physical condition of the property				
9. Home Condition Report		☐	☐ N/I ☐ N/A	
10. Uncommenced new homes warranty with cover note		☐	☐ N/I ☐ N/A	
11. Commenced new homes warranty		☐	☐ N/I ☐ N/A	
12. Other warranties		☐	☐ N/I ☐ N/A	
13. Additional Home Condition Reports for the past 12 months		☐	☐ N/I ☐ N/A	
14. Energy Performance Certificate (separate to a Home Condition Report)		☐	☐ N/I ☐ N/A	
15. Report on a property not physically complete		☐	☐ N/I ☐ N/A	
16. Evidence of safety, construction, repair or maintenance		☐	☐ N/I ☐ N/A	

Home Information Pack document	Further details about pack document, including date of documents	Included ☒	Not included or not applicable (N/I or N/A)	Reason why not included and steps being taken to obtain the document
Search reports				
17. Local land charges		☐	☐ N/I ☐ N/A	
18. Local enquiries		☐	☐ N/I ☐ N/A	
19. Additional local enquiries		☐	☐ N/I ☐ N/A	
20. Water and drainage enquiries		☐	☐ N/I ☐ N/A	
21. Radon gas		☐	☐ N/I ☐ N/A	
22. Common land		☐	☐ N/I ☐ N/A	
23. Ground stability		☐	☐ N/I ☐ N/A	
24. Mining		☐	☐ N/I ☐ N/A	
25. Other extractions		☐	☐ N/I ☐ N/A	
26. Subsidence		☐	☐ N/I ☐ N/A	
27. Environmental hazards		☐	☐ N/I ☐ N/A	
28. Flood risk		☐	☐ N/I ☐ N/A	
29. Contaminated land		☐	☐ N/I ☐ N/A	
30. Telecommunications		☐	☐ N/I ☐ N/A	
31. Utilities		☐	☐ N/I ☐ N/A	
32. Transport		☐	☐ N/I ☐ N/A	
33. Repairing liabilities		☐	☐ N/I ☐ N/A	
34. Other search reports for the property		☐	☐ N/I ☐ N/A	
35. Search reports for other properties		☐	☐ N/I ☐ N/A	

Home Information Pack document	Further details about pack document, including date of documents	Included ☒	Not included or not applicable (N/I or N/A)	Reason why not included and steps being taken to obtain the document
Other				
36. Translations of pack documents		☐	☐ N/I ☐ N/A	
37. Additional versions of any pack document in another format such as Braille or large print		☐	☐ N/I ☐ N/A	
38. Summary or explanation of any pack document		☐	☐ N/I ☐ N/A	
39. Information identifying the property including a description, photograph, map, plan or drawing of the property		☐	☐ N/I ☐ N/A	
40. Information identifying the persons involved in providing the pack document or information within a pack document		☐	☐ N/I ☐ N/A	
41. Additional relevant information		☐	☐ N/I ☐ N/A	

PART 2 – Commonhold properties

Home Information Pack document	Date of pack document	Included ☒	Not included or not applicable (N/I or N/A)	Reason why not included and steps being taken to obtain the document
42. Land Registry individual register and title plan for common parts		☐	☐ N/I ☐ N/A	
43. Land Registry copy of commonhold community statement		☐	☐ N/I ☐ N/A	

Home Information Pack document	Date of pack document	Included ☒	Not included or not applicable (N/I or N/A)	Reason why not included and steps being taken to obtain the document
44. Name and address of managing agents and/or other manager		☐	☐ N/I ☐ N/A	
45. Rules and regulations outside the commonhold community statement		☐	☐ N/I ☐ N/A	
46. Amendments proposed to the commonhold community statement, and other rules		☐	☐ N/I ☐ N/A	
47. Summary of works affecting the commonhold (current or proposed)		☐	☐ N/I ☐ N/A	
48. Requests for payment of commonhold assessment for the past 12 months		☐	☐ N/I ☐ N/A	
49. Requests for payment of reserve fund for the past 12 months		☐	☐ N/I ☐ N/A	
50. Requests for payment for insurance for the past 12 months (separate to commonhold assessment or reserve fund)		☐	☐ N/I ☐ N/A	
51. Other commonhold information (please list below):		☐	☐ N/I ☐ N/A	

Appendix C

Home Information Pack document	Date of pack document	Included ☒	Not included or not applicable (N/I or N/A)	Reason why not included and steps being taken to obtain the document
52. Proposed commonhold community statement, memorandum and articles of association (new properties)		☐	☐ N/I ☐ N/A	
53. Estimate of commonhold assessment, reserve fund and insurance payments expected during 12 months after completion (new properties)		☐	☐ N/I ☐ N/A	

Part 3 – Leasehold properties

Home Information Pack document	Date of pack document (day/month/year)	Included ☒	Not included or not applicable (N/I or N/A)	Reason why not included and steps being taken to obtain the document
54. The lease		☐	☐ N/I ☐ N/A	
55. Name and address of landlord		☐	☐ N/I ☐ N/A	
56. Name and address of managing agents or other manager		☐	☐ N/I ☐ N/A	
57. Rules and regulations outside the lease		☐	☐ N/I ☐ N/A	
58. Amendments proposed to the lease, other rules and regulations		☐	☐ N/I ☐ N/A	
59. Written summaries or statements of service charges for past 36 months		☐	☐ N/I ☐ N/A	

Home Information Pack document	Date of pack document (day/month/year)	Included ☒	Not included or not applicable (N/I or N/A)	Reason why not included and steps being taken to obtain the document
60. Summary of works affecting the property (current or proposed)		☐	☐ N/I ☐ N/A	
61. Requests for payment of service charges for the past 12 months		☐	☐ N/I ☐ N/A	
62. Requests for payment of ground rent for the past 12 months		☐	☐ N/I ☐ N/A	
63. Requests for payment for insurance for the past 12 months (separate to service charges or ground rent)		☐	☐ N/I ☐ N/A	
64. Other leasehold information (please list below):		☐	☐ N/I ☐ N/A	
65. Proposed lease (new properties)		☐	☐ N/I ☐ N/A	
66. Estimate of service charges, ground rent and insurance payments expected during 12 months after completion (new properties)		☐	☐ N/I ☐ N/A	

Home use form for

Insert address of property to be sold below and include postcode.

Part 1 – About this form and seller's check

About this form:

- Under the Home Information Pack Regulations, you must include this form in your Home Information Pack. It is not compulsory to fill it in, but doing so should help negotiations with buyers and speed up the sale.

- A buyer's legal adviser and mortgage lender are also likely to ask many of these questions during the sale, so answering them now should save time later.

- If you choose not to fill this form in, you must provide the information asked for by shaded questions elsewhere in your Home Information Pack.

- Parts 1 and 2 of this form apply to all properties. Part 3 just applies to commonhold properties and Part 4 just applies to leasehold properties.

- Someone can complete this form on behalf of a seller.

- Please cross through any questions or answers that are not relevant and use the suggested answers by checking the relevant box and adding any further information asked for. Where alternatives are offered, please indicate which one (or more) applies.

- If the property has not yet been completed or converted, please answer the questions as if the property is finished.

- The Regulations also tell you what other documents must and may be in the Home Information Pack, and guidance on the Regulations is available at www.homeinformationpacks.gov.uk

Seller's check of this form

- Someone can complete this form on behalf of a seller, but given that a buyer and mortgage lender might rely on the information in this form, it is important that the seller checks the answers to ensure that they are as truthful and as accurate as possible.

Please check the boxes below to confirm that:

☐ This form has been completed by the seller(s) or with their authority; and

☐ to the best of the seller's knowledge, the answers are true and accurate.

Part 2 – All properties

About the property being sold ("the property")	
1. Is the property a flat or a house?	☐ Flat (incl. maisonette) **or** ☐ House (incl. bungalow)
2. If it is a flat, what type of building is it in?	☐ Purpose built block ☐ Converted house **or** ☐ Conversion of commercial premises
3. Does the owner have access to any parts of the building or surrounding land along with other residents ("common parts")? Examples could include a private road, recreation area or car park:	☐ Yes ☐ No **or** ☐ Don't know If "Yes", please give details:
4. If the answer to question 3 is "Yes", are there any conditions attached or costs incurred for exercising access rights?	☐ Yes ☐ No **or** ☐ Don't know If "Yes", please give details:
5. Will the new owner have to pay a contribution to the costs of maintaining any common parts?	☐ Yes ☐ There are no common parts for the property ☐ No **or** ☐ Don't know If "Yes", please give details:
6. If you answered "yes" to question 5, who else contributes to the cost of maintaining any common parts?	☐ The person(s) listed below: ☐ No-one else contributes **or** ☐ Don't know
7. Do any buildings or surrounding land form part of the property (such as a garage or garden) for the owners' use only?	☐ Yes ☐ No **or** ☐ Don't know If "No", please give details:
8. Which services are connected to the property?	☐ Mains Water ☐ Telephone ☐ Private water supply ☐ Drainage ☐ Electricity ☐ Septic tank/cesspool ☐ Gas ☐ Broadband/digital
9. Indicate the banding the property is in for the council tax purposes: Note: The current council tax band may increase following a sale of the property if it has undergone improvements, such as an extension, since it was last assessed by the Valuation Office Agency (VOA). The current council tax bands for all domestic properties in England and Wales, together with further information, are available on the VOA's website at www.voa.gov.uk.	☐ Band A ☐ Band B ☐ Band C ☐ Band D ☐ Band E ☐ Band F ☐ Band G **or** ☐ Band H

Boundaries	
10. Facing the front of the property, who is responsible for maintaining fences, walls, hedges or anything else marking boundaries:	On the right? On the left? At the back? Other:
11. Has the seller had a dispute or are they aware of a dispute with anyone over boundaries or boundary markings?	☐ Yes ☐ No **or** ☐ Don't know If "Yes", please give details.

Access over and to the property	
12. Does the property have free running of services across adjacent land and does it have access to adjacent land for maintaining the services?	☐ Yes ☐ No **or** ☐ Don't know If "Yes", please give details:
13. Do any neighbouring homes, buildings or land have a right of access through the property?	☐ Yes ☐ No **or** ☐ Don't know If "Yes", please give details:
14. As far as the current owner is aware, has there been a dispute with anyone over access relating to the property?	☐ Yes ☐ No **or** ☐ Don't know If "Yes", please give details:

Changes to the property	
15. While the current owner has owned the property, have there been any building works to the property?	☐ Yes ☐ No **or** ☐ Don't know If "Yes", please give details:
16. If you answered "Yes" in question 15, was any planning permission, building control approval or listed building consent obtained for the works?	☐ Yes ☐ Needed but not obtained ☐ No, but work covered by approved person scheme ☐ No, not needed **or** ☐ Don't know If "Yes" or "No, but work covered by approved person scheme" please give details:
17. If you answered "Yes" in question 15, was any permission needed for the works from a commonhold association, landlord, other manager/company whose consents are required?	☐ Yes ☐ Needed but not obtained ☐ No, not needed **or** ☐ Don't know If "Yes", please give details:

Changes to the property *(continued)*

18. While the current owner has owned the property, have they needed to get any permission from a commonhold association, landlord, or other manager to make other changes to the property or to decorate it?	☐ Yes ☐ Needed but not obtained ☐ No, not needed ☐ No changes made **or** ☐ Don't know If "Yes", please give details:
19. Has planning permission, building control approval or listed building consent been obtained for any future works to the property?	☐ Yes ☐ No **or** ☐ Don't know If "Yes", please give details:
20. If the property has not yet been completed or converted, have all necessary planning permissions, building control approvals or listed building been obtained?	☐ Yes ☐ Application made ☐ Needed but not obtained **or** ☐ Not applicable If "Yes", please give details:

Use and occupation of the property

21. Would a relative, partner (including a former partner) or other person have a legal claim to any rights to the property?	☐ Yes ☐ No **or** ☐ Don't know If "Yes", please give details:
22. Is the seller aware of any complaints that have been made about the use of the property?	☐ Yes ☐ No **or** ☐ Don't know If "Yes", please give details:
23. Is the seller aware of any complaints made about neighbours' use of their properties?	☐ Yes ☐ No **or** ☐ Don't know If "Yes", please give details:

Insurance policies, warranties and guarantees

24. Please give the name of any insurer who covers the property against damage and against injury or death caused by or within the property:	The name of the insurer is **or** ☐ No such insurance currently exists for the property
25. If this is the first sale of a new home and you are not including a Home Condition Report, please include a copy an uncommenced new build warranty with a cover note:	☐ Included

Insurance policies, warranties and guarantees *(continued)*	
26. If there is a warranty of the type mentioned in question 25 and the cover has already started, you should still include it or any other type of new build warranty:	☐ Included
27. Please provide copies of any warranties or guarantees for building work, treatment or installations done to the property if these can be transferred to the new owner:	☐ Included ☐ Not available ☐ None existing **or** ☐ Don't know

Part 3 – Commonhold properties

The commonhold community statement ("CCS")	
28. Please include a copy of the CCS registered with Land Registry. If no CCS has yet been registered, include the proposed CCS:	☐ Included
29. Please include a copy of any amendments proposed to the CCS which have not yet been registered with Land Registry.	☐ Included ☐ None proposed **or** ☐ Don't know of any
30. Are there any proposals to enlarge or reduce the size of the commonhold?	☐ Yes ☐ No ☐ Don't Know **or** ☐ First sale of the commonhold If "Yes", please give details:
Relationship with the commonhold association	
31. Please include copies of any extra rules or regulations about the use of the commonhold made or that will be made by the commonhold association or its agent or manager (which apply as well as those in the commonhold community statement):	☐ Included **or** ☐ There are no extra rules or regulations made so far
32. Please include a copy of any separate amendments proposed to the rules or regulations referred to in question 31:	☐ Included **or** ☐ Don't know of any proposed
33. Name and registered address of the commonhold association:	
34. When did the seller or unit-holder last hear from the commonhold association?	☐ Date: ☐ There has been no contact with the association ☐ Don't know **or** ☐ First sale of the commonhold
35. Has the commonhold association employed an agent to manage the property or will it do so?	☐ Yes, **and** Name and current address: **or** ☐ No, **or** ☐ Don't know

Relationship with the commonhold association *(continued)*	
36. If you answered "Yes" in question 35, when did the seller or unit-holder last hear from the agent?	☐ Date: ☐ There has been no contact with the agent ☐ Don't know **or** ☐ First sale of the commonhold
37. Is there any other manager of the commonhold or will there be?	☐ Yes **and** Name and current address: **or** ☐ No **or** ☐ Don't know
38. If you answered "Yes" in question 37, when did the seller or unit-holder last hear from the manager?	☐ Date: **or** ☐ There has been no contact with the manager ☐ Don't know **or** ☐ First sale of the commonhold
39. Please include the commonhold association's memorandum and articles of association registered with Land Registry. If none have yet been registered, include the proposed versions of these documents:	☐ Included
40. Please include a copy of any amendments proposed to the memorandum and articles of association which have not yet been registered with Land Registry:	☐ Included ☐ None proposed **or** ☐ Don't know of any
41. Is the commonhold association is a member of an ombudsman scheme?	☐ Yes ☐ No ☐ Don't know If "Yes", please give details:
Commonhold assessment and reserve fund levy	
42. Is there any commonhold assessment due for the property which has not been paid?	☐ Yes ☐ No ☐ None due **or** ☐ Don't know If "Yes", please state how much:
43. Please include the most recent request for payment of commonhold assessment for the past 12 months:	☐ Included ☐ No request made **or** ☐ No payments have been made
44. Is there any reserve fund levy due for the property which has not been paid?	☐ Yes ☐ No **or** ☐ None due ☐ Don't know If "Yes", please state how much:

Commonhold assessment and reserve fund levy *(continued)*

45. Please include the most recent request for payment of reserve fund levy for the past 12 months:	☐ Included ☐ No request made **or** ☐ No payments have been made
46. While the current owner has owned the property, have there been any disputes over commonhold assessment or reserve fund levy?	☐ Yes ☐ No ☐ Don't know **or** ☐ First sale of the commonhold If "Yes" please give details:
47. At the end of the financial year are there expected to be any additional expenses due for works to the unit or the common parts which will not be covered by commonhold assessment or reserve fund levy?	☐ Yes ☐ No ☐ Don't know **or** ☐ First sale of the commonhold If "Yes", please give details:
48. If this is the first sale of the commonhold, please provide a total estimate of any commonhold assessment and reserve fund levy payable during the first 12 months of a new unit-holder's ownership:	The total is likely to be £
49. Has there been a reserve study and if so, what was its outcome?	☐ Yes **and** Date and outcome: ☐ No ☐ Don't know **or** ☐ First sale of the commonhold

Maintenance of the property

50. Are there any works affecting the unit or common parts being undertaken or are there any proposed?	☐ Yes ☐ No **or** ☐ Don't know If "Yes", please give details:
51. When was the outside of the building last maintained?	☐ Year: ☐ It has not been maintained during the unit-holder's ownership **or** ☐ Don't know
52. When were the common parts last decorated?	☐ Year: ☐ They have not been decorated during the unit-holder's ownership **or** ☐ Don't know
53. Is there or will there be a unit-holders' or residents' association of any kind?	☐ Yes ☐ No **or** ☐ Don't know If "Yes", please give details:

Insurance for the property	
54. Who is or will be responsible for insuring the unit against damage to it or injury caused by it?	☐ Commonhold association ☐ Unit-holder **or** ☐ Don't know
55. Please include copies of any request for contributions for insuring the common parts for the past 12 months:	☐ Included ☐ Payment included in commonhold assessment or reserve fund levy ☐ No request made **or** ☐ No contribution required so far

Part 4 – Leasehold properties

The lease	
56. Please include a copy of the lease of the property or the proposed lease:	☐ Included
57. Is the seller aware of any negotiations under way to extend the length of the lease?	☐ Yes ☐ No ☐ Don't Know **or** ☐ First sale of the lease If "Yes", please give details:
58. Are there any proposals by or affecting the seller or leaseholder to exercise any right to buy a freehold of the property?	☐ Yes ☐ No ☐ Don't Know **or** ☐ First sale of the lease If "Yes", please give details:
59. Is the lease held on a shared equity basis? If so, what percentage has been purchased (and is for sale)?	☐ Yes and % has already been bought from the Landlord and is now being offered for sale and % is the maximum additional equity share that can be bought from the Landlord in the future **or** ☐ No ☐ Don't know ☐ First sale of the lease **or** ☐ Not applicable
60. Is a share of the freehold interest of the building containing the property also included in the sale? If yes, will it be owned jointly with others in addition to the buyer of this property?	☐ Yes ☐ No **or** ☐ Don't Know If "Yes", please give details:

The lease *(continued)*	
60. Is a share of the freehold interest of the building containing the property also included in the sale? If yes, will it be owned jointly with others in addition to the buyer of this property?	☐ Yes ☐ No **or** ☐ Don't Know If "Yes", please give details:
61. Have the leaseholder's rights or obligations been altered other than through changes to the lease (for example by a custom or common practice)?	☐ Yes ☐ No ☐ Don't know **or** ☐ [illegible] If "Yes", please give details:
62. Please include a copy of any separate amendments to the lease and any amendments that are currently being negotiated:	☐ Included **or** ☐ None made or proposed
63. Please include copies of any leases above the lease being sold:	☐ Included ☐ Unavailable **or** ☐ Not applicable
Relationship with the landlord	
64. Is the landlord's consent needed for the sale of the lease?	☐ Yes ☐ No, none needed **or** ☐ Don't know If "Yes", please provide details of the landlord's requirement for giving consent (if known):
65. Please include copies of all the rules and regulations which affect the use and enjoyment of the property:	☐ Included **or** ☐ There are no extra rules or regulations made so far
66. Please include a copy of any separate amendments proposed to the rules or regulations referred to in question 65:	☐ Yes **and** ☐ Included **or** ☐ Don't know of any proposed
67. Name and current address of the landlord:	
68. When did the seller or leaseholder last hear from the landlord?	☐ Date ☐ There has been no contact with the landlord ☐ Don't know **or** ☐ First sale of the lease
69. Has the landlord employed an agent to manage the property or will he or she do so?	☐ Yes **and** Name and current address: **or** ☐ No **or** ☐ Don't know

Relationship with the landlord *(continued)*

70. If you answered "Yes" in question 69, when did the seller or leaseholder last hear from the agent?	☐ Date ☐ There has been no contact with the agent ☐ Don't know **or** ☐ First sale of the lease
71. Is there any other manager of the building (such as a right to manage company, resident management company or a tenants management organisation)?	☐ Yes **and** Name and current address: **or** ☐ No **or** ☐ Don't know
72. If you answered "Yes" in question 71, when did the seller or leaseholder last hear from the manager?	☐ Date: ☐ There has been no contact with the manager ☐ Don't know **or** ☐ First sale of the lease
73. If you answered "Yes" in question 72, must leaseholders become members of any management company for the building?	☐ Yes **and** memorandum and articles of association included ☐ Membership optional ☐ Membership neither required nor optional **or** ☐ There is not or will not be a management company
74. Is the landlord, agent or manager a member of a professional association?	☐ Yes ☐ No **or** ☐ Don't Know If "Yes", please give details:

Rent, service charges and reserve fund payments

75. Is there any ground rent due for the property which has not been paid?	☐ Yes ☐ No **or** ☐ None due **or** ☐ Don't know If "Yes", please state how much:
76. Please include the most recent request for payment of ground rent for the past 12 months:	☐ Included ☐ No request made **or** ☐ No payments have been made
77. Must the current leaseholder pay a service charge? A service charge is a payment in addition to ground rent which is payable, for services, repairs, maintenance, improvements or insurance or the landlord's costs of management. The amount typically varies according to the costs involved:	☐ Yes ☐ No **or** ☐ Don't know If "Yes", please state how much:
78. If you answered "Yes" in question 77, please include the most recent request for payment of service charge for the past 12 months:	☐ Included ☐ No request made ☐ Unavailable ☐ No payments have been made **or** ☐ First sale of the lease

Rent, service charges and reserve fund payments *(continued)*	
79. Are there any service charge payments due for the property which have not been paid?	☐ Yes ☐ No ☐ None due ☐ Don't know **or** ☐ First sale of the lease If "Yes", please state how much:
80. Have there been any disputes over service charge payments for the property during the leaseholder's ownership?	☐ Yes ☐ No ☐ Don't know **or** ☐ First sale of the lease If "Yes", please give details:
81. Please include any written summaries or statements of service charge costs supplied by the landlord for the past 36 months:	☐ Included ☐ None received **or** ☐ First sale of the lease
82. Is there or will there be a reserve fund included within the property?	☐ Yes ☐ No **or** ☐ Don't know If "Yes", please give details:
83. At the end of the financial year, are there expected to be any additional service charges payable for works to the property or the common parts or payment made from any reserve fund?	☐ Yes ☐ No ☐ Don't know **or** ☐ First sale of the lease If "Yes", please give details:
84. If this is the first sale of the lease, please provide a total estimate of any ground rent, service charges and reserve fund payments payable during the first 12 months of a new leaseholder's ownership:	The total is likely to be £
Maintenance of the property	
85. Are there any works affecting the unit or common parts being undertaken or are there any proposed?	☐ Yes ☐ No **or** ☐ Don't know If "Yes", please give details:
86. Are there any other large scale redecoration or works planned to the property or building?	☐ Yes ☐ No **or** ☐ Don't know If "Yes", please give details:

Maintenance of the property *(continued)*

87. When was the outside of the property or building last maintained?	☐ Year: ☐ It has not been maintained during the leaseholder's ownership **or** ☐ Don't know
88. If there are any common parts used with the property, when were these last decorated?	☐ Year: ☐ They have not been decorated during the leaseholder's ownership ☐ Don't know **or** ☐ There are no common parts
89. Is there or will there be a leaseholders' or residents' association of any kind?	☐ Yes ☐ No **or** ☐ Don't know If "Yes", please give details:

Insurance for the property

90. Who is or will be responsible for insuring the property or the building against damage to it or injury caused by it?	☐ Landlord ☐ Leaseholder ☐ Other (please specify): **or** ☐ Don't know
91. If the leaseholder should contribute to the cost of such insurance, please include copies of the request for payment made for the past 12 months:	☐ Included ☐ Payment included in service charge ☐ No request made **or** ☐ No contribution required so far

Organisation Name

Home contents form for

Insert address of property to be sold below and include postcode.

Important information

- Under the Home Information Pack Regulations, you must include this form in your Home Information Pack. It is not compulsory to fill it in, but doing so should help negotiations with buyers and speed up the sale.

- On this form you can show what the contents of the home are and whether a seller is prepared to include them in the sale. Buyers are likely to want to know this, but the replies are not legally binding. They just show what a seller's plans are and they can change their mind prior to exchange of contract.

- Someone can complete this form on behalf of a seller.

- If the property has not yet been completed or converted, please answer the questions as if the property is finished.

- Please cross through any items listed that are not at the property.

- The Regulations also tell you what other documents must and may be in the Home Information Pack, and guidance on the Regulations is available at www.homeinformationpacks.gov.uk

Home essentials

(Unless you say otherwise, the buyer will assume that the following items are included in the sale and that the seller will leave them behind once the sale is complete. Please use the comments section to say otherwise.)

	Comments		Comments
1. Central-heating systems		2. Radiators; Other wall heaters	
3. Night-storage heaters		4. Boilers; Immersion heaters	
5. Windows and window fitments		6. Double glazing	
7. Electrical installation, including cables and sockets		8. Light switches; Other light fittings	
9. Laminate flooring; Parquet flooring; Floor tiles		10. Fires; Fireplaces	
11. Extractor fans and hoods		12. Fitted kitchen cupboards; Kitchen sinks; Other fitted kitchen accessories	
13. Baths; Bathroom sinks; Showers; Toilets; Taps; Plugs; Other items		14. Fitted bathroom cupboards	
15. Fitted towel rails; Soap, toothbrush and toilet roll holders		16. Fitted shelves	
17. Fitted wardrobes; Dressing tables; Cupboards		18. Wall tiles	
19. Door and cupboard handles and knobs		20. Fitted hooks and holders	
21. Inside and outside doors and gates (not including baby and toddler gates)		22. Greenhouses	
23. Fuel stores		24. Water butts	
25. Outside lights		26. Other (please give details):	

Home furnishings

(For each item, please check one of the columns only. If your answers depend on which room or area of the property the item is in, please say so.)

	Included in the sale	To be taken with the seller	To be negotiated
27. Carpets	☐	☐	☐
28. Rugs	☐	☐	☐
29. Curtains/net curtains/palmets/blinds	☐	☐	☐
30. Curtain rails	☐	☐	☐
31. Sofas	☐	☐	☐
32. Ceiling lampshades	☐	☐	☐
33. Beds including headboards	☐	☐	☐
34. Moveable wardrobes	☐	☐	☐
35. Moveable cupboards	☐	☐	☐
36. Moveable dressing tables including any mirrors and chairs	☐	☐	☐
37. Moveable cabinets/bookcases	☐	☐	☐
38. Dining tables and chairs	☐	☐	☐
39. Other desks/tables/chairs	☐	☐	☐
40. Moveable kitchen accessories	☐	☐	☐
41. Bathroom cabinets, mirrors/shower curtains/rails	☐	☐	☐
42. Other mirrors	☐	☐	☐
43. Moveable bathroom and toilet fittings and accessories	☐	☐	☐
44. Other (please give details):	☐	☐	☐

Home appliances

(For each item, please check one of the columns only. If your answers depend on which room or area of the property the item is in, please say so.)

	Included in the sale	To be taken with the seller	To be negotiated
45. Ovens and grills	☐	☐	☐
46. Cookers/other cooking hobs	☐	☐	☐
47. Microwave ovens	☐	☐	☐
48. Fridges	☐	☐	☐
49. Freezers	☐	☐	☐
50. Dishwashers	☐	☐	☐
51. Washing machines	☐	☐	☐
52. Tumble dryers	☐	☐	☐
53. Telephone receivers and cables	☐	☐	☐
54. Aerials/satellite dishes	☐	☐	☐
55. Other (please give details):	☐	☐	☐

Outside the home

	Included in the sale	To be taken with the seller	To be negotiated
56. Dustbins	☐	☐	☐
57. Clothes lines/other clothes dryers	☐	☐	☐
58. Shed and contents	☐	☐	☐
59. Garden trees/shrubs/plants	☐	☐	☐
60. Garden furniture/ornaments	☐	☐	☐
61. Water butts	☐	☐	☐
62. Other (please give details):	☐	☐	☐

Report on a home not physically complete for

Insert address of property to be sold below and include postcode.

About this form.

- Under the Home Information Pack Regulations, you must provide the following information in your Home Information Pack if the property being sold is not yet physically complete. You may use this form to do so.

- Someone can fill in this form for you (if you are the seller).

- Not "physically complete" means properties not yet built, not physically completed or still being converted for residential purposes. If you are not sure whether the property is physically complete, you can assume it is if:

- it is windproof and weatherproof;

- it is safe and sanitary;

- it has facilities for the supply of heating to rooms, hot and cold water and electricity; and

- it has washing and drainage facilities.

- Please cross through any questions or answers that are not relevant and use the suggested answers by checking the relevant box and adding any further information asked for. Where alternatives are offered, please indicate which one (or more) applies.

- Please note that if the property becomes physically complete after marketing starts, a Home Condition Report or new homes warranty must be added to the pack. This form must then be removed from the pack.

- The Regulations also tell you what other documents must and may be in the Home Information Pack, and guidance on the Regulations is available at www.homeinformationpacks.gov.uk

	Statement
1. The property is likely to be physically complete on: (Please say whether this date is only approximate.)	☐ Approximate date
2. The property will be:	☐ a house ☐ a bungalow ☐ a flat ☐ a maisonette **or** ☐ other (please give details):
3. If the property will be a house or bungalow, it will be:	☐ detached ☐ semi-detached ☐ terraced **or** ☐ other (please give details):
4. If the property will be a flat or maisonette, the building containing it will:	☐ have a total of floors ☐ contain a total of flats or maisonettes ☐ contain a lift to the floor that the property will be on
5. Please attach a plan (to a scale of not less than 1:1250) showing the location and boundaries of the property (in metres) as it will be once it is completed. Also mark: neighbouring buildings and structures, and surrounding land; and the roads, public highways and footpaths that serve or will serve the property.	☐ attached ☐ not attached ☐ please check box if the boundaries are only approximate
6. Please attach a plan (to a scale of not less than 1:100) showing the layout and approximate height, width and length (in metres) of each of the rooms in the property:	☐ attached ☐ not attached
7. The total useable floor area in the property will be approximately:	square metres
8. Please give details of the proposed methods of construction (including any trade names for the materials described):	details: or ☐ not applicable
9. Please give details of the materials used or to be used in the outside parts of the property.	details: or ☐ not applicable
10. Please give details of the heating and hot-water systems to be used for the property.	details:
11. Please give details of the standards to which the garden or other land being sold with the property will be finished.	details:
12. Will any land on the site be brought up to the level of the surrounding area artificially?	☐ yes (please give details below): or ☐ no

	Statement
13. Please attach a predicted energy-performance certificate for the property.	☐ attached ☐ not attached
14. Has a new homes warranty been offered for the construction, completion or conversion of the property?	☐ yes (please give details below): **or** no
15. If the property will not qualify for a warranty, please give the name and qualifications of the person monitoring the construction, completion or conversion of the property:	name: address: qualifications: ☐ not applicable

LAW SOCIETY INITIAL GUIDANCE, AUGUST 2006

GUIDANCE ON PROFESSIONAL CONDUCT AND HOME INFORMATION PACKS – PROFESSIONAL ETHICS – AUGUST 2006

This guidance is issued by the Rules and Ethics Committee to assist compliance with professional conduct requirements for solicitors providing home information pack (HIP) services when the HIP regime comes into force in June 2007.

The guidance takes the form of general statements of principle, accompanied by questions and answers on specific points, but cannot anticipate all the situations which may arise. It is based on information available at present (summer 2006) including the recent Government announcement that Home Condition Reports will not initially be mandatory.

CONTENTS

1. Retainer and client care
2. Conflict of interests between solicitor and client
3. Conflict of interests between clients
4. Referral arrangements
5. Practice Rule 6A (seller's solicitor dealing with more than one prospective buyer)
6. Property selling
7. Separate businesses

1.   RETAINER AND CLIENT CARE

General principle:

Where a solicitor provides a home information pack (HIP) directly to a seller, or provides the legal component of a HIP to the seller's estate agent or other HIP provider, the solicitor will have a retainer with the seller. Practice Rule 15 and the Solicitors' Costs Information and Client Care Code 1999 will apply.

Question 1.01:

Isn't the seller's retainer with the HIP provider who instructs, and may well be paying, the solicitor, rather than with the solicitor?

Answer:

Where an estate agent markets a property with an HIP produced by an HIP provider, the estate agent and the HIP provider are agents of the seller. The nature of the seller's instructions is affected by the requirements of the Housing Act 2004 and the Home Information Pack Regulations 2006, but the relationship of agency remains.

When dealing with an agent, a solicitor's ultimate client is the principal, and not the agent. Therefore, the seller will be the solicitor's client, and all the professional conduct requirements relating to clients, such as the client care requirements, will apply. The solicitor may have a separate retainer with the agent – see question 3.04.

Question 1.02:
Can the retainer with the seller be 'limited' because it is for the provision of specific services on the HIP provider or estate agent's standard terms?

Answer:
Every retainer is 'limited' to the work the solicitor agrees to carry out for the client. The limits may be defined by the HIP provider or estate agent's terms, but there cannot be a retainer in which the solicitor owes a lower standard of professional conduct duties. For instance, the duty to act in the client's best interests (Practice Rule 1) will always apply, irrespective of the 'limits' placed on the retainer, or who is paying the solicitor – see section 1.

The HIP provider might also ask the solicitor to provide ancillary services, such as explaining the transaction or the paperwork to one or both of the parties. This too would fall within the retainer, and all the conduct duties to clients would apply.

2.   CONFLICT OF INTERESTS BETWEEN SOLICITOR AND CLIENT

General principle:
The fact that a solicitor is paid for HIP services by an estate agent or HIP provider does not in itself threaten the solicitor's independence, or create a conflict of interests between the solicitor and the seller client. However, solicitors should not participate in arrangements which threaten the solicitor's independence or which are not in the client's best interests.

Question 2.01:
How might arrangements for providing HIPs threaten the solicitor's independence or create a conflict of interests between the solicitor and client?

Answer:
HIP providers may form the link between estate agent and solicitor. Solicitors could receive instructions for HIP services through the HIP provider – see also section 4 on referrals. Solicitors could be paid by the HIP provider, or provide the HIP services free or at a discounted rate on the basis that they will be instructed by the seller in the subsequent conveyance.

The seller could pay the HIP provider immediately or defer the payment until completion of the sale, or the HIP could be free or discounted if the seller meets certain conditions. For instance, a lender/HIP provider might offer a "relocation package" including a free or discounted HIP, new mortgage on the seller's next purchase, and insurance.

When entering into an arrangement with an HIP provider, a solicitor should look at the nature of any free, discounted or deferred payment package. In itself, such a package is not a problem. But if the package seems unfair or unduly onerous for sellers, the solicitor should not enter into the arrangement.

Question 2.02:

Is a solicitor involved in the sale of the HIP and/or the HIP payment package to the seller involved in the provision of financial services?

Answer:

HIP providers will probably aim to sell the HIP and/or any payment package direct (for example, via the internet) or through an estate agent, but there could be cases where a solicitor is asked to present a package to the seller.

The sale of an HIP and/or its payment package does not in itself involve the solicitor in financial services activities. However, some of the products featuring in packages, such as a mortgage or insurance, may be regulated investments. Solicitors must consider financial services regulation depending on what they are being asked to do in respect of these products. Most solicitors are not authorised by the Financial Services Authority, and must be satisfied that they comply with the Solicitors' Financial Services (Scope) Rules 2001 when they carry on regulated activities.

Question 2.03

If the solicitor is involved in the sale of the HIP and/or the HIP payment package to the seller, does that create a conflict of interests between the solicitor and the seller?

Answer:

Solicitors involved in selling HIP/payment packages to sellers must advise clients as to their best interests. If a HIP/payment package is unfair or unduly onerous, the solicitor should not enter into the arrangement. If the terms are fair and comparable to the rest of the market, but do not suit the needs of a particular client, the solicitor must advise according to the client's need.

However, solicitors are not obliged to question clients about every detail of, for instance, their financial position in order to confirm that a package is suitable. Solicitors should bear in mind that

- sellers will be making their own judgements about HIPs/payment packages in the same way as any other financial aspect of the sale
- if a payment package contains investment elements (see also question 2.02), the restrictions in the Solicitors' Financial Services (Scope) Rules 2001 may apply. These prevent solicitors from recommending that their clients enter into particular mortgages and regulated products with an investment element (such as life policies). Solicitors are under no duty to force the client to take independent advice, but they should be aware of the restrictions in the Rules, and must refer clients to an authorised person if they do in fact require this.

3.   CONFLICT OF INTERESTS BETWEEN CLIENTS

General principle:

Practice Rule 6 applies to the provision of HIP services. Solicitors must not act for seller and buyer where there is a conflict of interest, and must comply with the requirements of Practice Rule 6(2) in relation to work done for a seller and/or a buyer.

Question 3.01:

Does the HIP regime affect conflict between seller and buyer?

Answer:

Under Practice Rule 6(2), a solicitor must not act for seller and buyer if a conflict of interest exists or arises. When providing HIP services to a seller, a solicitor's duty to potential buyers is to provide truthful and accurate information (not advice). There is no retainer or other contractual relationship between solicitor and potential buyer, and therefore no conflict with the solicitor's obligations to the seller.

However, as part of an estate agent's or HIP provider's 'packaging' of services, solicitors may be asked to offer services to buyers. Questions 3.02 and 3.03 examine situations where a solicitor might be able to act for the buyer.

Question 3.02:

Could a solicitor act for the buyer where an HIP, but no conveyancing services, has been provided for the seller?

Answer:

Where the retainer with the seller has definitely finished, the solicitor may act for the buyer, unless he or she holds confidential information about the seller which is 'material to that client's [the buyer's] matter.' (Practice Rule 16E(3)).

In most cases the solicitor will have no material information, as all the information gained from acting will be put into the HIP. But a solicitor holding other material information cannot act.

The only exception to this is where information barriers can be set up under Practice Rule 16E(4)–(6). However, this exception was designed with large firms and corporate clients in mind. Setting up appropriate information barriers will probably be beyond the scope of most firms. Also, the solicitor must act in the client's best interests. While a corporate client may feel it appropriate to accept a limitation on disclosure under Rule 16E(5), a buyer of a residential property will rarely if ever be in such a position.

Question 3.03:

Could a solicitor provide an HIP, and do the conveyancing both for the seller and also for the buyer?

Answer:

Practice Rule 6(2) allows a solicitor to act for seller and buyer only if the conditions set out in Rule 6(2) are met. The solicitor must obtain the written consent of both parties, and no conflict of interest must exist or arise.

The situation must also meet one or more of the conditions in 6(2)(b) (established clients, consideration less than £10,000, use of two separate offices of a firm, no other qualified conveyancer in the area). The provision of HIP services does not affect this, unless the solicitor has gained confidential information, as described in question 3.02.

Question 3.04:

Might a conflict of interest arise between a seller or buyer client, and an HIP provider or estate agent client?

Answer:

The arrangement with the HIP provider and/or estate agent may amount to a retainer – probably of a limited type – or there may be a duty of care and potential liabilities in tort.

Estate agents' and HIP providers' interests generally lie with the transaction proceeding quickly and obtaining their fees including any referral fees – see section 4. The buyer or seller may have different objectives – for instance, they may need independent advice about the merits of the sale or purchase, or may wish to delay the transaction to fit in with personal circumstances. Such conflicts may be unlikely, given the probably limited nature of the retainer with the estate agent and/or HIP provider. Each situation will depend upon its own facts.

4.   REFERRAL ARRANGEMENTS

General principle:

The Solicitors' Introduction and Referral Code 1990 applies to any referral arrangement under which solicitors provide HIP services.

Question 4.01:

Are referral arrangements under the Solicitors' Introduction and Referral Code 1990 (SIRC) likely to arise under the HIP regime?

Answer:

Many HIP providers are likely to receive clients direct or via estate agents, and refer them on to solicitors. This would come under SIRC. If the solicitor pays a fee for the referral, he or she must comply with SIRC section 2A.

However, HIP providers and/or estate agents may also offer solicitors' services as part of a "package" – see sections 1 and 2 – under which solicitors are paid directly by, for instance, the HIP provider. Such an arrangement would, depending on the services provided, fall under SIRC section 3 or section 3A.

5.   PRACTICE RULE 6A (SELLER'S SOLICITOR DEALING WITH MORE THAN ONE PROSPECTIVE BUYER)

General principle:

A solicitor who supplies information to an HIP provider or estate agent for the purpose of preparation of an HIP is not normally 'dealing' with prospective buyers for the purpose of Practice Rule 6A.

Question 5.01:

What amounts to 'dealing' under Practice Rule 6A?

Answer:

Whenever a solicitor is instructed to 'deal with' more than one prospective buyer, the solicitor must inform each prospective buyer, or his or her conveyancer. A solicitor who has provided information for an estate agent or HIP provider only as part of the creation of a HIP will not have 'dealt' with prospective buyers for the purpose of Rule 6A, but providing additional information to buyers, either direct or through the estate agent or HIP provider, will normally amount to 'dealing'.

6.   PROPERTY SELLING

General principle:

Where a solicitor provides estate agency services which include providing HIPs direct to sellers, the HIP services will be property selling services covered by Chapter 26 of the Guide to the Professional Conduct of Solicitors.

Question 6.01:

May a solicitor providing property selling services, including HIPs direct to sellers, also provide services for buyers?

Answer:

Under Practice Rule 6(2) a solicitor may:

- provide property selling services, including a HIP, for the seller (through either the firm or a Solicitors' Estate Agency Limited (SEAL)),
- do the seller's conveyancing, and
- provide mortgage-related services to the buyer (through either the firm or a SEAL).

A solicitor providing property selling services to the seller through a SEAL (not the firm) could:

- provide the HIP for the seller
- provide mortgage-related services for the buyer (through either the firm or the SEAL), and
- do the buyer's conveyancing.

Also, a SEAL may act for the seller (including providing an HIP) and also provide mortgage-related services for the buyer: one of the participating firms may do the seller's conveyancing, and another participating firm may do the buyer's conveyancing.

Furthermore, if any of the circumstances set out in Rule 6(2)(b) apply (established clients, consideration of £10,000 or less, representation by two separate offices, or no other qualified conveyancer in the area), a solicitor may:

- sell the property (including providing an HIP)
- provide mortgage related services, and
- act for seller and buyer in the conveyancing.

All the above is subject to compliance with the conditions set out in Rule 6(2)(a) and (c) as appropriate, in particular that no conflict of interest exists or arises between the seller and the buyer.

7.   SEPARATE BUSINESSES

General principle:

A solicitor may set up a separate business to provide HIP services, in compliance with the Solicitors' Separate Business Code 1994.

Question 7.01:

What conditions apply to a solicitor's separate business providing HIP services?

Answer:

The Solicitors' Separate Business Code (SSBC) prohibits a solicitor having a separate business which provides 'any activity reserved to solicitors'. General HIP services such as title checks, searches and the assembly and provision of the HIP, are not reserved to solicitors and could be provided through a separate business. The requirements of SSBC section 5(2) will apply to a solicitor operating such a business.

Preparing the draft contract, on the other hand, is reserved to solicitors under section 22 of the Solicitors Act 1974, and so would have to be done within the solicitor's practice. At that point, therefore, the matter would need to be transferred from the separate business to the solicitor's practice, and the safeguards in SSBC section 5(2) would apply.

Practice Rule 16E could still apply where a solicitor's separate business provided HIP services for a seller, the solicitor's practice then did the conveyancing for the buyer, and the solicitor learnt of information material to the buyer through the separate business. This is because the duty of disclosure of material information to a client applies 'regardless of the source of the information' (rule 16E(3)).

Appendix I
ESTATE AGENT'S CHECKLISTS

A. FOR DEALING WITH THE SELLER

In addition to the usual terms in an agency marketing agreement with a seller, estate agents should consider the following which assume greater importance under Part 5:

- Money laundering procedures
- Authority to sell and duration of retainer
- Advice on requirement for a HIP and transitional provisions
- Sole agency or selling rights/joint agency/multiple agency
- Provision for payment for services and for the pack including any loan agreement for deferred payment where interest is claimed (subject to complying with Consumer Credit Act requirements)
- Fix cost of preparing copies and collecting the charges from potential buyers
- Termination arrangements – notice period; recorded in writing; potentially makes seller the RP
- Retention of the pack for minimum period after a sale, withdrawal from the market or termination of instructions so as to comply with the enforcement procedures in section 167(3) (six months – but see PMA 1991)
- Return of HIP to seller on termination, subject to payment of any outstanding fees for HIP and HCR/EPC
- Authority to retain buyer's payments for copy of the HIP
- Supply to seller on termination, withdrawal or sale details of buyers with a HIP
- Retrieval of distributed HIPs on termination, withdrawal or sale
- Maintain a register of HIPs and record of buyers' requests for the pack and reporting to seller the number of copies provided or inspection facilities made available with dates and identification of buyers
- Instructions from seller as to categories of buyer he would not sell to – discrimination warning
- Instructions from seller as to confidentiality of HIP
- Instructions from seller relating to electronic copies of HIP – retrieval/ dissemination problems
- Warranty/indemnity from seller regarding truth of information in HIP
- Ownership of/copyright in HIP to belong to owner when fees paid
- Check exclusions for types of property and other disclaimers from responsibility so far as permitted
- Check DCLG guidance
- Check TSO policy
- Withdrawal by seller to trigger payment of deferred fee?
- Remind seller of right to fee – where buyer introduced by agent proceeds to exchange
- Remind seller to provide information where pack is incomplete
- Require seller to notify changes to information or documents in the pack
- Require seller to notify any change of personal circumstances and willingness/ability to proceed – possible trigger of liability to pay for the pack
- Provide copy HIP to seller for checking

- Obtain instructions whether to cease marketing on receipt of offer/continue marketing and providing copy HIPs
- Procedures to halt marketing as soon as possible in the event of the property being taken off the market temporarily for up to 28 days or termination of the seller's instructions
- Arrangements for taking property off market temporarily or after offer accepted
- Check style of marketing where property is listed under exceptions to Part 5 – Regulations 22–29) and retain audit trail
- Check that non-HIP material is provided separately and not in close proximity

B.   FOR DEALING WITH A PACK PROVIDER

- This is a b2b contract so no consumer protection is implied
- Warranty/Indemnity from pack provider for compliance of HIP and due diligence re contents
- Require a summary document
- Access to HIP needed in order to comply with ability to download/copy
- Ownership of/copyright in HIP to remain with whom?
- Terms for payment if deferred
- Indemnity insurance of pack provider/ protection from claims and statutory breach – PMA and Part 5
- Check/query any terms relating to cross-selling of products and services and referral arrangements
- Access to complaints scheme
- Consider competitive position and obtain non compete/confidentiality agreement where relevant

C.   FOR DEALING WITH A BUYER

- Money laundering procedure
- Full details as to property requirements
- Full disclosure of financial status for purchase
- Details of lawyer to be instructed and mortgage lender
- Chain details including continuing authority to check with lawyers and agents in chain
- Agreement and signature to confidentiality undertaking
- Costs that may be incurred to meet requests for inspection of the pack and to provide and send copies

Appendix J
SELLER'S CHECKLISTS

A. FOR DEALING WITH THE ESTATE AGENT/RESPONSIBLE PERSON

- Discuss types of packs appropriate to circumstances of sale
- Arrangements for access for EPC/HCR inspection
- Ownership of HIP retained but licensed to estate agent on terms
- Period of appointment
- Obtain advice on transitional period
- Require HIP to be kept up to date
- Obtain copy of HIP and summary of contents
- Restrictions on distribution of HIP to qualifying buyers (beware discrimination)
- Require estate agent to record all buyers' details and give paper copies
- Reports during marketing of provision of HIP to potential buyers
- Termination arrangements – notice period, in writing (converts seller to RP)
- Return of HIP on termination subject to payment of any outstanding fees for HIP
- On sale or termination provide log of HIP changes and copies issued
- Retrieval of distributed HIPs on sale or termination
- Instructions for withdrawal from market on receipt of offer/continue marketing and providing copy HIPs
- Instructions to estate agent concerning disclosure of HIPs – consider confidentiality/non-disclosure undertaking
- Instructions to agent against circulation of electronic HIPs – retrieval/dissemination problems
- Check warranty/indemnity from agent for compliance with Part 5
- Check indemnity insurance of estate agent regarding compliance
- Check access to complaints scheme
- Check/query any terms relating to referral agreements, conflicts of interest and cross-selling of products or services
- Examine contract with III if made through estate agent

B. FOR DEALING WITH A PACK PROVIDER

- Check same points above (save that marketing arrangements will not apply)
- Ownership of/copyright in HIP to remain with seller
- Arrangements for payment for HIP
- Warranty/indemnity from pack provider for compliance of HIP with Part 5
- Indemnity insurance of pack provider to meet any claims
- Check membership of any recognised trade association and access to complaints procedure
- Check/query any conflicts of interest, referral arrangements and cross-selling of goods or services
- Check identity of HI and providers of search reports and EPC
- Check details of access for register of HCRs

C.   FOR DEALING WITH A HOME INSPECTOR

- Consider any conflicts of interest of HI acting for lender and buyer
- Consider any conflicts of interest by virtue of introduction to HI by a third party
- Check prescribed form of contract (who is party and who pays?)
- Check indemnity insurance held by HI
- Check licensed membership of approved certification scheme
- Check standing of approved certification scheme
- Consider access to complaints scheme
- Pre-HCR consider separate contract for 'appraisal' and valuation
- Consider remedial works following appraisal or HCR
- Consider the above in relation to stand alone EPC regulations when made

D.   FOR DEALING WITH A BUYER WHERE NO ESTATE AGENT INSTRUCTED

- Obtain information and advice on RP's obligations to make and provide compliant HIP
- Obtain signature of buyer to confidentiality undertaking
- Obtain full financial disclosure of buyer and any 'chain'
- Obtain details of professionals to be instructed and mortgage lender
- Check 'chain' details and continuing authority to check chain
- Fix cost of copies and postage and provide paper copy HIP not electronic
- Retrieve HIPs on sale
- Consider withdrawal of property from market on acceptance of offer or continue marketing and providing copy HIPs to potential buyers
- Provide full set of HIP and other information provided to lawyers prior to submission of contract
- Obtain legal advice as to pack documents missing or unavailable and how to deal with buyers' enquiries

Appendix K
BUYER'S CHECKLIST

FOR DEALING WITH THE RESPONSIBLE PERSON/ESTATE AGENT

- Check terms of any 'confidentiality' undertaking
- Check/query any disclosure relating to conflicts of interest/referral arrangements/personal interest
- Check HIP is compliant and is current version and complete and arrange for future updates
- Ask to be kept informed of number of HIPs in circulation and of any changes and other offers
- Upon acceptance of offer, request withdrawal of property from market and lock out agreement
- Take legal advice at early stage and information concerning HIP and other relevant information and seller's chain and instruct legal adviser of intentions
- Consider age of documents in pack
- Obtain 'in principle' finance from lender

Appendix L
SOLICITOR'S CHECKLISTS

A. ADVISING A SELLER

The following matters need to be drawn to the attention of the seller client in addition to those required under the SPR:

- Advice on need for a pack, contents and timing and cost
- Advice on transitional period and summary of pack contents
- Advice on role of Responsible Person and any indemnity requested by the estate agent from the seller
- Advise on procedures for terminating the estate agent's retainer so as to bring to an end the Responsible Person obligations and obtain possession of the original HIP and free from claims of copyright
- Advise on obligation to inform anyone who requests a HIP as to who can supply this
- Advice on withdrawal (or not) of property from the market on acceptance of offer; or generally for up to 28 days
- Advice on procedures to protect a seller from becoming Responsible Person
- Advice on liability for agency fees
- Consider client's timing needs for transaction and consider pre-HCR inspection
- Remedial work – separate contract
- Preparation of pack – by whom, for marketing when?
- Set out obligations of RP
- Ownership/copyright in pack
- Terms of new contractual relationships e.g. HI
- Ancillary contracts with HI and payment terms
- Specific instructions to marketing estate agent regarding suitable potential buyers
- Specific instructions to marketing estate agent regarding confidentiality of pack
- Specific instructions to marketing estate agent regarding reports on distribution of packs and pack inspections
- Specific instructions to marketing estate agent regarding return of pack from buyers who are not proceeding with a purchase
- Withdrawal (or not) of property from the market on acceptance of offer
- Complaints, redress, claims
- Advise as to content that is appropriate to seller's needs
- Identify 'missing information'
- Need for updates on changes in information and personal circumstances
- Change of estate agent and 'taking off' the market
- Review and update index

B. FOR DEALING WITH AN ESTATE AGENT TO WHOM THE SOLICITOR IS PROVIDING A HIP

- Procedures for recording issue of HIP to buyers
- Procedures for returning HIP for updating, revising etc
- Procedures for passing on queries by buyers on the pack content

- Prohibition on estate agent amending/revising pack and any summary
- Restriction on estate agent answering queries on pack
- Review and update Index

C.   FOR DEALING WITH A PACK PROVIDER

- Check standing of pack provider and whether properly constituted
- Check membership of any association
- Check terms of indemnity insurance
- Check complaints/redress procedures
- Check terms of provision of pack for payment
- Check terms for ownership and copyright of pack
- Check for cross-selling of other products and services
- Check responsibility to update/revise
- Check responsibility to answer questions on pack
- Check responsibility to advise sellers on content of pack
- Review and update Index and Sale Statement

D.   FOR DEALING WITH A HOME INSPECTOR/SURVEYOR

- Check HI on register of inspectors and approved surveyor for EPC
- Check indemnity insurance position for amount of cover and excess
- Check terms of contract are compliant with the Regulations and disclosure of interest
- Check for conflicts of interest
- Check for collateral contracts with others involved in sale
- Check terms for payment of charges and registration fees
- Check access to complaints scheme
- Check the above in relation to scheme for EPC

E.   ADVISING A BUYER WHO HAS OBTAINED A HIP FROM SELLER OR SELLER'S ESTATE AGENT

- Check date of HIP and ensure it is latest version
- Check standing of HIP producer
- Check contents and revisions against the Index
- Check dates of searches and HCR/EPC
- Check standing of HI/surveyor producing the HCR/EPC
- Check no conflicts of interest involved for HI
- Check for missing/incomplete documents and updated documents
- Check how many HIPs in circulation and dates of issue
- Advise on lock-out agreement and withdrawal of property from market
- Advise on negotiations

F.   ADVISING THE ESTATE AGENT CLIENT

- Check professional indemnity insurance offers appropriate cover
- Check membership of complaints and redress scheme in place
- Review all documentation including marketing to ensure compliance
- Check staff training regarding provision of copy HIP to buyers and TSOs

- Check procedures for inspection of HIP and charging for paper copy
- Check procedures for copying/downloading HIP
- Check instructions for dealing with potential buyers
- Check instructions for withdrawal of property from market upon offer being accepted or property sold or termination of instructions
- Issue instructions for answering questions on HIP by buyers
- Check procedures for updating/revising HIP and Index
- Check procedures for complaints handling
- Check archive and retrieval procedures for HIPs
- Check overall compliance with statutory requirements and age of documents at FPM
- Check procedures for payment and money handling and client account

BIBLIOGRAPHY

Books

RICS (2004) *RICS Manual of Estate Agency Law and Practice* (2nd edition), RICS Books (Looseleaf)

Silverman, F. (2006) *Conveyancing Handbook* (13th edition) Law Society Publishing

Stanton, K., Skidmore, P., Harris, M. and Wright, J. (2003) *Statutory Torts*, Sweet & Maxwell

Murdoch, J. (2003) *Law of Estate Agency* (4th Edition) Estates Gazette

Government papers

DCLG *English House Condition Survey*, August 2005 (produced by ONS and Miller Mitchell Burley Lane on behalf of DCLG)

DCLG *Home Information Pack Regulations 2006: Procedural Guidance*, June 2006

DCLG *Report on the Number of Home Inspectors Required from Introduction of Home Information Packs*, May 2006

DETR *Key Research on Easier Home Buying and Selling*, January 1998

DETR *The Key to Easier Home Buying and Selling: A Consultation Paper*, December 1998

DTI *Government Response to the Office of Fair Trading Report on Estate Agents*, July 2004

DTI *Government Response to the OFT Property Searches Market Study*, December 2005

OFT *Estate Agency Market in England and Wales*, March 2004

OFT *Property Searches: A Market Study*, September 2005

ODPM *Contents of the Home Information Pack: A Consultation Paper* (Appendix P), March 2003

ODPM working group minutes, April 2005

ODPM *Home Information Packs – Dry Run: Observations and Next Steps*, June 2005 (produced by Parnell Kerr Forster)

ODPM *Evaluation of Pilot Seller's Information Pack: The Bristol Scheme*, 2000

ODPM *Home Buying and Selling in Denmark and New South Wales*, 1999

Research

Council of Mortgage Lenders, *Mortgage Lenders, HIPs and the Future of Valuations* with Octavia Research and Consultancy (11 July 2006)

Council of Mortgage Lenders, *UK Mortgage Underwriting Report by Onera Consulting Limited* (27 April 2006)

GMAC-RFC, *The Impact of Home Information Packs* by Oxford Economic Forecasting (27 June 2006)

USEFUL WEBSITES

Association of Home Information Pack Providers	www.hipassociation.co.uk
Awarding Body for the Built Environment	www.abbeqa.co.uk
British and Irish Legal Information Index (Law reports)	www.bailii.org
Building Regulations (DCLG)	www.dclg.gov.uk
Building Research Establishment	www.bre.co.uk
Council for Mortgage Lenders	www.cml.org.uk
Council of Property Search Organisations	www.copso.org.uk
Council of Licensed Conveyancers	www.conveyancer.org.uk
Department of Communities and Local Government	www.communities.gov.uk
Department for Constitutional Affairs	www.dca.gov.uk
Department for Environment Food and Rural Affairs	www.defra.gov.uk
Department for Trade and Industry	www.dti.gov.uk
Elmhurst Energy Systems Limited	www.elmhurstenergy.co.uk
Energy Performance of Buildings Directorate	www.energy2000.co.uk
Estate Agents Ombudsman Scheme	www.oea.co.uk
Gary Webber Property Law	www.garywebber.co.uk
GMAC	www.gmacrfc.co.uk
Habitus Surveyors	www.habitus.co.uk
Hansard	www.parliament.uk
HIPAG	www.hipag.co.uk
The HIP Report	www.thehipreport.co.uk
HM Revenue and Customs	www.hmrc.gov.uk
Home Information Packs (Government website)	www.homeinformationpacks.gov.uk
Institute of Legal Executives	www.ilex.org.uk
Land Registry	www.landreg.gov.uk

Law Society	www.lawsociety.org.uk
Law Society Property Section	www.propertysection.org.uk
Local Authorities Coordinators of Regulatory Services	www.lacors.gov.uk
National Association of Estate Agents	www.naea.co.uk
National House Builders Council	www.nhbcbuilder.co.uk
National Statistics	www.statistics.gov.uk
Office of Fair Trading	www.oft.gov.uk
Office of Public Service Information	www.opsi.gov.uk
Oxford Economic Forecasting	www.oef.com
Parliament	www.parliament.gov.uk
Perpro	www.perpro.org
Property Industry Research Limited	www.pirltd.org.uk
Royal Institute of Chartered Surveyors	www.rics.org
SAVA	www.sava.org.uk
Sector Skills Council	www.assetskills.org
SPLINTA	www.splintacampaign.co.uk
Spring Move	www.springmove.com

INDEX